The Science of Numbers

Dr. Gérard Encausse (Papus)

On Numbers

Louis-Claude de Saint-Martin

Translated by
Piers A. Vaughan

March 2020

This book is dedicated with gratitude to my friend Serge Caillet.

I know of no man living who has a greater knowledge and understanding of Pasqually and Saint-Martin's use of numbers, and who has spent decades tirelessly disseminating his wisdom through books, insightful prefaces to classic works in Martinism, and through his courses and conferences organized under the auspices of the Institut Eléazar.

© Piers A. Vaughan 2020
All rights reserved. No part of this publication may be reproduced, distributed, or transmitted in any form or by any means, including photocopying, recording, or other electronic or mechanical methods, without the prior written permission of the publisher, except in the case of brief quotations embodied in critical reviews and certain other noncommercial uses permitted by copyright law. For permission requests, write to the publisher at the address below.

ISBN 978-1-947907-06-5

Rose Circle Publications
P.O. Box 854
Bayonne, NJ 07002, U.S.A.
www.rosecirclebooks.com

PAPUS
Dr ENCAUSSE
(1865-1916)

I would like to acknowledge the invaluable help and assistance of the following friends in putting together this book:

Serge Caillet, Joseph Wäges, Arturo de Hoyos, Stewart Clelland, and Mathieu Ravignat.

So much can be accomplished when we all cooperate and share our information and sources, which is the very spirit of Saint-Martin, and Willermoz. In my turn I offer these translations for the benefit of anglophone students and scholars, that they may continue the cycle of goodness.

Contents

Contents 5
Preface 9
Notes to the Texts 13

THE SCIENCE OF NUMBERS by PAPUS (Dr. GÉRARD ENCAUSSE)

INTRODUCTION 23
THEORY 25
   Chapter 1 25
  PRELIMINARY ELEMENTS 25
   Chapter 2 30
  THE FIRST TEN NUMBERS 30
   Chapter 3 35
  ANALYSIS OF THE DECADE 35
   Chapter 4 61
  THE CONSTITUTION OF NUMBERS 61
   Chapter 5 88
  THE THEORY OF NUMBERS 88
   Chapter 6 93
  FIGURES 93

PRACTICE 103
   Chapter 7 103
  NUMBERS AND THE KABBALAH 103
   Chapter 8 126
  NUMBERS AND LUCK 126
   Chapter 9 128
  NUMBERS AND DATES 128
   Chapter 10 131
  NUMBERS AND HISTORY 131
   Chapter 11 145
  NUMBERS AND NATIONS 145

Chapter 12 .... *183*
NUMBERS AND MUSIC 183
THE TEXTS **191**
Chapter 13 .... *191*
NUMBERS AND THE OCCULT 191
    ECKARTSHAUSEN *192*
    HOËNÉ WRONSKI *210*
    H. DE BALZAC *216*
    A. DESBARROLLES *219*
    E. LEDOS *230*
    LOUIS-MICHEL de FIGANIÈRES *233*
Chapter 14 .... *235*
THE POWER OF NUMBERS 235
Chapter 15 .... *249*
THE SECRET SECTION ON THE STUDY OF NUMBERS 249
Chapter 16 .... *268*
BIBLIOGRAPHY 268

ON NUMBERS by LOUIS-CLAUDE DE SAINT-MARTIN

Foreword **285**

Preface by Matter **289**

S-M, Mme de Bœcklin, Two Salzmanns, Goethe **297**
    FIRST ARTICLE *297*
    SECOND ARTICLE *304*

Preface by Sédir **309**

ON NUMBERS **317**
    I. GENERAL CONSIDERATIONS 317
    II. CONCERNING THE NATURAL QUANTITY OF NUMBERS 338
    III. ON THE ROOT OF TWO 339
    IV. THE ESSENCE OF NUMBERS 1, 2 AND 3 339
    V. THE HISTORICAL ORDER OF THE ELEMENTAL COURSE OF NATURE 342

VI. THE COURSE OF ELEMENTAL THINGS CONSIDERED IN LIGHT OF THE GENERATIVE 343
POWER OF WOMEN 343
VII. CONCERNING CREATION 344
VIII. ELEMENTS OF THE MESSIAH, WITHOUT THE BINARY 345
IX. THE SPIRITUAL AND CIRCULAR PROGRESSION OF THE QUATERNARY IN THE UNIVERSAL CIRCLE 347
X. FROM WHENCE NUMBERS DRAW THEIR QUALITY 348
XI. NUMERICAL FORMULAE 349
XII. MULTIPLICATION AND ADDITION 352
XIII. NUMBER OF ELEMENTS, THEIR CONNECTIONS WITH THE PERVERSE BEINGS AND THOSE OF DIVINE AND SPIRITUAL POWERS WITH THE UNIVERSAL CIRCLE 359
XIV. PROPERTIES OF THE OCTENARY (8^{RY}) 361
XV. INTRINSIC VALUE OF GEOMETRIC MEASUREMENTS 364
XVI. NUMBER SIX 368
XVII. DIFFERENCE BETWEEN THE MIND AND THE BODY 372
XVIII. PROGRESSION OF THE ACTIVE AGES OF THE REPAIRER 374
XIX. COMPLEMENT OF THE QUATERNARY 375
XX. OPERATION OF THE NUMBER 3 IN THE THREE WORLDS 376
XXI. UNITY OF THE DECADE 376
XXII. PHASES OF THE MOON 377
XXIII. THE CONTENT LARGER THAN THE CONTAINER 377
XXIV. PROGRESSION OF NUMBERS AND THE RESULTING FIGURE 378
XXV. THE SEPTENARY 378
XXVI. NUMBER 9 379
XXVII. CONCERNING THE NUMBER ONE 380
XXVIII. DOUBLE NUMBERS 382
XXIX. THE MANNER IN WHICH THE MIND SHOULD BE EXAMINED 383
XXX. WHY IS THE CIRCUMFERENCE PHYSICALLY THREE TIMES ITS DIAMETER – ABOUT 13 384
XXXI. THE UNIVERSALITY OF QUATERNARY POINTS 385
XXXII. SEPTENARY POWER OF THE SOUL 387
XXXIII. QUATERNARY OF SPEECH 387
XXXIV. WORK OF THE TRIPLE OCTENARY 388

XXXV. Receptacle 390
XXXVI. Descending Progression of Powers 390
XXXVII. Increasing Law of the Repairer 391
XXXVIII. Correspondence Between 4 and 1, and the Inverse of Those from 1 to 4 392
XXXIX. Concerning the Number 21 393
XL. Complement of the Great Name 394
XLI. On the Septenary Power of Man 395
XLII. Proportions 395
XLIII. Time 396
XLIV. On the Nature of Number 397
XLV. Synoptic Table of Numbers 398
XLVI. Plan of Things by the Number and Order of Their Principles 400
XLVII. Progression of Divine Laws Concerning the Various Prevaricators 405
XLVIII. The Cube 405
XLIX. Proportional Mean 406
L. Concerning the Number Eleven in Two Respects 407
LI. The Calculation of Probabilities 407
LII. Demonstration of Our Ignorance of the Principles and Essence of Beings 409
LIII. Difference Between Quantity and Quality in Numbers 409
LIV. Miscellanea 410
   I. Progression of Knowledge 410
   II. Feast of the 15th Day of the 7th Months 411
   III. On the Names of the Elements 411
   IV. Epochs Across the Ages 411
   V. Universal Triangle 412
   VI. Operation of Restoration 412
   VII. The Line of Two Wheels 412
   VIII. Age of the Origin of the World 414
   IX. First Image of God 414
   X. Double Sign of the Cross 415
   XI. Venomous Serpents; Innocuous Serpents 415

Preface

It is two hundred forty-two years since Louis-Claude de Saint-Martin, while spending time in Lyon, France, composed his first book at the young age of thirty-two in 1775.

Concerned by what he saw as the creeping insinuation of atheist forces under the guise of those writing the first Encyclopedia, whom he suspected of using the articles to push their agendas to undermine the Church, he decided to write a book based upon the teachings of his Master, Martinez de Pasqually, to establish a covertly Christian manifesto. The rest, as they say, is history. However, Saint-Martin continued to write throughout his life, regardless of the straitened circumstances in which he was forced to live following the French Revolution. Following his death, a number of manuscripts were discovered, one of them being the treatise in this book, which brought together a number of his thoughts on Numbers into one document, probably intended as study material for his students.

Just over a century later, Dr. Gérard Encausse (more often referred to by his *nomen mysticum* Papus) took up Saint-Martin's mantle and formed an Order based upon his teachings and those of his mentor Martinez de Pasqually, called the *Ordre Martiniste*. Interestingly, although the first incarnation in the 18th Century collapsed due to the permanent absence of its founder and the French Revolution, the second incarnation endured through two World Wars fought on its doorstep and has since grown to take root in many countries around the world. While never a large Order, it has the virtue of being *persistent*.

Unfortunately, while the French speaking members have always had access to an immeasurable library of old and contemporary texts on the subject, the English-speaking world has had to make do with the few crumbs which have made it into English, some collections of generic esoteric teachings, and an admittedly exhaustive supply of good books of the Kabbalah (and I will use this spelling throughout, though I am aware that purists use three of four different spellings depending on the origin of source materials). Finally, what little work that has been done in English to increase our understanding of this philosophic-theosophical path has generally been hoarded away like the Parable of the Talents, or used as a cynical recruitment tool (join us and we will give you the secrets of the Universe) instead of sharing this Christian Path more freely with those who seek it.

More recently, along with some other authors and translators, I have attempted to make more of the source materials available. My efforts have been constrained in that I can usually only provide translations of works out of copyright, for contemporary and near-contemporary authors, their descendants and successors appear reluctant to allow these works to come before an English audience. And herein lies the third barrier to a full participation in the teachings of Martinism by anglophone esotericists and academics.

Many books do indeed exist in English and on the internet, which cover the esoteric and symbolic meaning of numbers, theories as to their origins and how they were initially represented by letters of the alphabet or by hieroglyphs, which then took on a hieratic value. Certain numbers – or the letters representing them – took on very specific and coded meanings, as may be seen in the use of numbers in the Holy Scriptures. Correspondences between words or ideas and the relationships between apparently unconnected things, such as perfumes, angels and precious stones, could be uncovered through the use of techniques of manipulating numbers or the value of words made up of letters which each had their own numerical value. And underpinning all this – at least in the West – was the line in Wisdom 11:21 – "Thou hast ordered all things in measure, and number, and weight"; and the syllabus taught in all universities for over a thousand years, the Quadrivium, which equated arithmetic, geometry, music and astronomy with number, number in space, number in time, and number in time and space: all indicating a Divine Architect who created the Universe and all it contains by the use of a sublime order of numbers, of which our earthly numbers are but a very inferior representation.

What becomes interesting is the fact that, while most of the various esoteric systems of numbers agree in general, the French approach launched itself in a rather different direction towards the end of the 1700s. Pasqually developed, and Saint-Martin expanded, a somewhat elaborate development of the original view that numbers had a significance in the Bible, and saw them as divine tools with their own roles to play in the creation, maintenance and ultimate destruction of the Universe.

While this is not the place to go into detail about those theosophical principles, which can be found in Saint-Martin's books and Pasqually *Treatise on the Reintegration of Being into their Primitive Estate*, it is high time the French contribution to the language and philosophy of numbers be added to the list of sources available to the English speaker.

This book makes two of the most important works in this field, Saint-Martin's posthumous treatise *On Numbers* published in 1861 by Louis Schauer, and Papus' posthumous work the Science of Numbers, collated and published in 1934 by Paul Chacornac, a major publisher and devotee of esoteric works, available in English for the first time. Unfortunately, while both books have been reprinted in French numerous times, the quality is always less than perfect (one suspects they were created through the use of scanning and optical character recognition, since many errors can be found), requiring one to go back to the original books to verify words and images.

Neither book gives up its secrets easily. Saint-Martin is characteristically obtuse, and often hides behind the veil of 'I can say nothing further on this subject'. Papus, in his turn, appears to have written the first several chapters, and then turns to quoting contemporary co-writers for his various magazines at length, in some cases lifting entire chapters from their books and dumping them into his. Perhaps he was using them as placeholders, intending to draw key ideas to reflect in his own clear style at a later date which never came. The unfortunate result of this is a book of very variable quality, moving from rational and well-argued points (usually Papus himself), to distinctly fringe – sometimes verging on the ludicrous – theories, which on occasion are almost untranslatable into English.

Reading some recent French reviews of modern editions of these books, I regularly find the words "impossible to follow" and "difficult" used. However, I draw some solace from the fact that even Baron von Gleichen, one of Saint-Martin's personal pupils, in his memoir on his book *Of Errors & Truth*, said: "Three-quarters of this work are unintelligible…" So, we should not feel too stupid if we cannot follow every argument: there is still more than enough to astound, educate and amaze.

The original publication of Saint-Martin's *Les Nombres* included a long essay called *Shedding Light on Human Association*, which was a follow-up to his *Letter to a Friend or Political, Philosophical and Religious Considerations on the French Revolution*. These are not included in this volume as having nothing relevant to say about numbers. Indeed, they were only included in the original publication to demonstrate that the author also wrote about social circumstances as well as strange theosophical theories. However, the original Foreword and Prefaces have been retained since they are by Schauer and Matter, and although they refer occasionally to the *Human Association*, they focus more fully on the book *On Numbers*.

Finally, as before, I have added a large number of footnotes to try to help point the reader in the right direction. Again, any errors in translation are mine, and again I have tried to render the French in a manner which is easier for an English reader to follow, rather to provide an exact transliteration. The subject matter moves into areas of deep calculus and advanced mathematics on occasion which is far outside my area of expertise. Here I could only do my best to translate those ideas (though I hasten to add that these flights of numerical fancy are normally part of the 'out there' sections which the reader can ignore without losing anything important or relevant to the esoteric theory of numbers).

I hope those who persevere will find a new avenue of research and insight to add to those avenues already provided by the many English books on the subject.

Piers A. Vaughan
Spring 2020

Notes to the Texts

This book is intended to make available for the first time in English two important French books on the esoteric meaning of Numbers.

The first is by Dr. Gérard Encausse, or Papus, entitled *The Science of Numbers*. Although this postdates Saint-Martin's book by over a century it is put first because parts of it are easier to understand, and it also sets the scene for Saint-Martin's.

The second is a work by Saint-Martin, also published posthumously, but apparently discovered in the 1860s in a relatively complete format, entitled *On Numbers*.

These Notes are intended to provide some context to these books, both as an aid to understanding and also as an explanation of the conventions used. I apologize in advance if the Notes appear unusually long: it was my intention to introduce the subject matter and to bring to the reader's attention some basic techniques and definitions which will hopefully make the reading of the books themselves a more rewarding experience.

I realize that not everyone who opens this book will have a deep understanding of the times, the country, of Freemasonry, the work of Martinez de Pasqually, or the key characters who affect this story. I therefore provide the following comments to help the less-familiar reader to navigate these two books.

In an attempt to make a distinction between 'dead' figures and 'living' numbers, Saint-Martin and Pasqually – and to a lesser extend Papus and some of his contemporaries – gave numbers a unique series of names. So, we will find the figures in the first decade (1 – 10) referred to as follows:

One – Unity
Two – Binary
Three – Ternary
Four – Quaternary
Five – Quinary
Six – Senary
Seven – Septenary
Eight – Octenary
Nine – Nonary
Ten – Denary

Papus believed that numbers – at least on the higher planes – are living entities, and that they affect the behavior of numbers on lower planes. Pasqually and Saint-Martin don't appear to hold such a drastic view (indeed Saint-Martin stressed the fact that numbers are *not* living entities), but they nevertheless saw them as crucial tools in the Creator's process of the act of creation. To them, God created everything by number, and all living creations – be they angels of the various Orders or man – possess two numbers, one for their existence and one for their action. However, we must guard against thinking that this is simply a passive system of nomenclature: they had no interest in human classifications of beings and behavior; rather, God used numbers to create beings and imbue them with their appointed actions, and man could but observe what God had created and set in motion.

Both Pasqually and his student Saint-Martin attributed specific characteristics to each number from 1 to 10. This is not the place to go into those, but they can be found expressed both in Pasqually's *Treatise*, in Saint-Martin's books *Of Errors & Truth* and *Natural Table*, and in the treatise *Of Numbers* included here. Similarly, this is not the time to go into the philosophy behind the various philosophical calculations, since that is the purpose of both books (although Pasqually's description of numbers may be found on page 115 of this book). However, we will go through a few of what are termed *Theosophical Calculations* below, in order to ready the reader for what is to come.

What brought about this approach to numbers, which seems to fly in the face of everything we learned in mathematics and geometry at school? Before figures were created to represent numbers, early alphabets represented numbers by letters. These letters meant that words could be summed to give a total value. For example, if in the English language A=1, B=2, C=3 and so forth, the word 'cat' would sum to 3 + 1 + 20 = 24. Further, the ancients believed in the power of the first decade as being more powerful than higher numbers, which were essentially repetitions of the first ten in a denary system. Thus 1, 2, 3, 4, 5, 6, 7, 8, 9 and 10 were accorded more 'weight' and were seen to be closer to perfection. Thus, numbers could be reduced to produce one of these fundamental numbers. In our example above, the value of 'cat' being 24, this could be further reduced to 2 + 4 = 6. This was called *Theosophical Reduction*.

A similar method is *Theosophical Addition*, which consists of adding all the numbers from one (or unity) to the number in question. For example, the number 5 would yield 1 + 2 + 3 + 4 + 5 = 15, which again through *Theosophical Reduction* sums to 1 + 5 = 6. Remember that we are not using numbers as mere arithmetical figures, but rather as entities with their own significance, and we are using these techniques to understand philosophical statements based on the signification or meaning of these numbers.

It should be noted that, while *Theosophical Addition* gives us an indication of all the powers inherent within a number, it can rapidly take us beyond 10 and therefore into ever weakening numbers, in the sense that the further numbers move from the first decade, the weaker is their effect. This is why *Theosophical Reduction* must be applied to understand the base from which the number came, and to bring it back to the first decade.

We should also be aware that the term *root* is used in a Theosophical sense quite differently to traditional mathematics. According to Saint-Martin, there are three kinds of root: the essential root, the square root and the cube root. We will see later he explains this as follows: "through the essential root a being has life or existence, through the square root it has progress, and through the cube root it has end or completion." The essential root is the soul of a number and is found through *Theosophical Addition*. As an example, the essential root of 4 is 10, since 1 + 2 + 3 + 4 = 10. This is the true number of the being. We determine the being's actions through the square (which behaves in a similar manner to arithmetic squares: for example, 2 x 2 or $2^2 = 4$) since, according to Saint-Martin, this is "the means by which that root rises and produces its fruit." Finally, through the cube was see the product or the outcome. So, in the three roots, the see the potential of a being, its actions and the result or product of those actions.

Therefore, it is unsurprising that the number 3 (or the cube) is in this instance a number connected with matter, since the product of a being's act of creation can only be seen in the physical world.

This clearly reflects Saint-Martin's adage of Thought leading to Will, which results in Action. In Papus' book we will see these processes used to extract both the Soul (or what he terms the Spirit) and the Body from a number in order to find the Astral part; number being tripartite like so much else in spiritual philosophy.

Having given some specific techniques that the reader will encounter in the two books, let us now turn our attention to a brief history of the mystical interpretation of numbers, and how they have been associated with Divine action from the earliest times.

The first ten figures have been studied exhaustively through the ages, particularly by Western mystics and philosophers. Pythagoras noted the properties of the number '4' and its ability to contain the first ten number in his image of the tetractys, which was a sacred symbol in his school. Tetra- is the Greek root for 'four', and as the Greeks, like the Hebrews, used letters as numbers, the fourth letter of the Greek alphabet was Delta (Δ), considered sacred by Pythagoras, and which is used even now as a symbol for God.

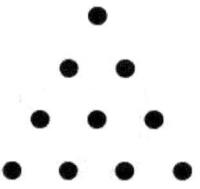

The Tetractys was a four-sided equilateral triangle consisting of 10 dots in descending lines of 1, 2, 3 and 4. In a manner of speaking it was a Greek harbinger of the Kabbalistic Tree of Life, in that the Tree of Life depicts creation through ten successive emanations from God; while the Tetractys similarly depicts the Creator (single point at top) initiating duality, from which comes the birth of the world from the union of the two points above, founded upon the four elements, or the four liberal arts and sciences. Again, the first represented the point, the second the line, the third the triangle or two dimensions, and the fourth the tetrahedron or three dimensions. Indeed, in the books which follow, mention is made of his musical application as well, with the interval 1:2 being an octave, 3:2 a perfect fifth; and 4:3 a perfect fourth.

Later, alchemists were to use this image to depict the hierarchal stages of the process of obtaining the Philosopher's Stone. For example, Philalethes' *An Open Entrance to the Shut Palace of the King* shows a clear symbolic use of the tetractys in rising up from the four ancient elements to form various combinations creating the Principles of Salt, Sulfur and Mercury, which in turn combine to create Philosophical Silver and Philosophical Gold, and the conjunction of which forms the Chrysoprase.

The importance of the numbers 1 to 10 extended far beyond the fact that even early philosophers saw something mystical in the fact that $1 + 2 + 3 + 4 = 10$, and that all the remaining numbers of the first decade (5 – 10) could be derived from the first four figures; that 10 being reduced by $1 + 0$ to 1 showed that it was of the same order as '1', or 'unity', but at a higher octave; and that through what we now know as *Theosophic Reduction* (described above) all numbers could be reduced to a single figures from the first decade 1 through 9. Indeed, the Philosophers took the theosophical 'fact' that 10 was a form of 1 to greater heights: if 1, in representing the Source, as well as the eternal and immobile point of the First Dimension, which was the simplest dimension and therefore the Creator, then the Creator could be represented as a 'point'; and if 0 was a figurative circle, then 10 could be seen as the point within the circle, well-known to Masons, and therefore the continual act of Creation with the Generative Power emanating everything about Him.

Perhaps we sometimes forget in these scientific times that, most subjects studied in earlier times had their spiritual or esoteric counterparts. While we are familiar with astronomy being the study of the heavens and astrology their interpretation according to fixed laws, and chemistry and alchemy having a similar relationship, we sometimes forget that this was reflected in other areas, too. For example, music, while being a discipline in its own right, gave rise to the notion of the harmony of the spheres and the vibration of the different planes, while Pythagoras saw the magic of music in its adherence to the rules of the tetractys, and even popes were not above using music to translate the minds of those at church with the use of plainchant. Similarly, for geometry there is sacred geometry, and even mathematics, the most prosaic subject of the Quadrivium, has its counterpart in numerology and the divine use of "measure, number and weight."

Three thousand years after man saw meaning in the conflation of letter and number, and devised elaborate systems to understand the mystical in the prosaic, hiding symbolic codes in the sacred texts their scribes committed to papyrus, paper, clay tablets or stone, in the 17th through the 19th Centuries we find some of the greatest minds still at work, seeking meaning and the Divine in numbers. Consider Sir Isaac Newton, who we now know spent as much time on alchemy as he did on gravity and the laws of physics, delving into the meaning behind the Books of Chronicles to see God's purpose in the figured design of King Solomon's Temple.

Since then, a number of well-known esoteric authors have written on the importance of numbers. Indeed, Paul Chacornac added a comprehensive bibliography to Papus' book, which is reproduced here. Other noteworthy authors of that time include Eliphas Lévi, who in *La Clef des Grands Mystères* devoted an entire section to the esoteric importance of numbers one through nineteen; while William Wynn Westcott, in *Numbers – Their Occult Power and Mystic Virtues*, wrote a detailed series of correspondences for the numbers one through thirteen, and in less detail many higher numbers (some of which found its way into the lecture on Numbers in the Zelator Grade of the Societas Rosicruciana in Anglia). Both books are indeed listed in Chacornac's bibliography. Later, in 1913 Sephariel (Walter Goren-Old) wrote *The Kabala of Numbers*; in 1928 A. S. Raleigh wrote *Occult Geometry* and *Hermetic Science of Motion and Number* in the 1920s; and Dr. Winslow Plummer of the Societas Rosicruciana in America referred to the esoteric importance of numbers in a number of pamphlets, including *Esoteric Masonry* and his writings of the *Symbolism of the Cross*.

Conventions used in the books

Firstly, it is important to note that certain words have specific meanings in the context of these books. To give a couple of examples, the French word 'opérer' can mean 'to work' or 'to operate' in the sense of operating a magical act. Therefore, the word is usually translated as 'to operate', in order to preserve both meanings which were crucial to Pasqually and Saint-Martin and their theurgical operations. Another word frequently used is 'unity'. While this is generally an alternative for 'one' in the work of Papus and his colleagues, it is used whenever Papus is indicating a number (a concept or an entity) as opposed to a figure (that is, the drawn image such as '1'). For Saint-Martin it takes on an even more sublime role, since in his theosophy it refers to God, and therefore it will be spelled with a capital 'U' when in that context.

Another more general problem comes in translating certain words which have more than one meaning in English. Two examples are 'Science', which can mean 'science' or 'knowledge': again, context will usually reveal which is better suited. Another is the use of 'esprit' and 'âme', normally translated as 'spirit' and 'soul' respectively, but which can offer far richer meaning, and indeed can be interchangeable on occasion. Also, while 'être' generally refers to a being, unless the use is clear (such as when referring to numbers as beings), it commonly refers to man.

All footnotes in Papus' book providing references included a description of the size of the book, which was common in those days (for example, Octavo, or 8vo). These have been omitted as this is not common practice now. Also, all footnotes are from the original book, unless they end with '– PV', which means it was added by the current author-translator; and if the author-translator adds to an existing footnote, it will be denoted by [.... – PV].

Finally, I have tried to include cleaned-up versions of the original images in the first editions. Where this was not possible, I have recreated them as closely as I could.

The Science of Numbers

by Dr. Gérard Encausse (Papus)

1934

INTRODUCTION

A number is a being from the spiritual plane. It has its own specific laws of construction and evolution, and its study is one of the most important that the occultist can pursue.

But, before we begin that study, we need to make some important distinctions.

The first is to distinguish the *quantitative* study of numbers such as is pursued by modern mathematicians, from the *qualitative study* which was followed in the ancient centers of initiation.

This observation is common to everything which involves the occult. The contemporary man grins at the thought that the number 4 could act as a living being in the plane of "idea-powers"[1] or that, in the world of laws, it represents a key which can open many doors which are still closed.

The second distinction we need to make is to avoid confusing *Numbers* which are beings, with *Figures* which are their *clothing*. A man, whether he is dressed in green, yellow or black is still himself. A number, whether represented by a Chinese, Sanskrit or Roman character, or a modern typograph, is still itself. Nevertheless, the issue of figure has often been confused with the issue of number.

Finally, the last distinction to make is that the study of numbers includes many topics. It truly is an intellectual subject. Many authors have devoted every waking hour to this study.

The ancient Kabbalistic book *The Sepher Yetzirah*[2] is concerned with numbers and their analogical relationships. All schools descended from the Pythagoreans and Neo-Platonists follow the same path.

In *Occult Philosophy*, Cornelius Agrippa[3] devotes almost an entire volume to numbers studied both qualitatively and according

---

[1] In French: idées-forces – PV.

[2] *The Sepher Yetzirah*, cf. The Kabbalah, by Papus, pub. Antwerp.

[3] H. Cornelius Agrippa, *Occult Philosophy or Magic.*, Paris, pub. Chacornac, 1910-11, 2 vol.

to their correspondences. Nearer to our times, L.-C. de Saint-Martin[4] and Eckartshausen[5] have also left profound studies on this subject. Eliphas Lévi[6] and Stanislas de Guaita[7], as well as myself with regard to the Tarot, have also addressed this issue.[8]

We will try to put some order into this study of numbers. Our intention is to provide an introduction to reading these authors.

A little clarity in the darkness: this is our sole aim.

As we are trying to bring clarity, we will proceed in steps. The study of numbers is, indeed, so complex, that if we attempt to cover philosophy, computation and analogical extensions at the same time, everything will become confused and difficult to follow.

So we will need to return to the same subjects several times, each time in more detail, and this way we will be able to cover in succession the various correspondences we need to know.

---

[4] L.-C. de Saint-Martin, *Treatise on Numbers*. Paris, Chacornac, 1913 (and in this book in English) – PV..

[5] Eckartshausen, *The Magic of Numbers*, 1st French translation *(in preparation)*.

[6] Eliphas Levi, *Letters to Baron Spedalieri*, Paris, pub. Chacornac, 1932-1933, 1 and 2 (of 10). These letters in manuscript are in the possession of Dr Papus.

[7] Stanislas de Guaita, *On the Threshold of the Mystery*, Paris, pub. Chamuel, 1891, (see note on pp. 112-113).

[8] Papus, *The Tarot of Bohemians*, Paris.

THEORY

Chapter 1

Preliminary Elements

We mustn't confuse *Numbers*, which are idea-powers, Intermediaries between the visible and invisible Planes, and *Figures*, which are how numbers are clothed.

Scale and Progression – All numbers come from the number One. The origin of that emanation is in the Spiritual Light. The more a number moves away from the number One the more it becomes buried in matter; and the more it draws closer to the number One the more it returns towards Spirit and Light.

The first Ten numbers belong to the realm of the Spirit. These are the least materialized.

We will write down this double progression to become familiar with it:

From Spirit to Matter From Light to Darkness	From Matter to Spirit From Darkness to Light
1 2 3 4 5 6 7 8 9 Read from top to bottom ↓	1 2 3 4 5 6 7 8 9 Read from bottom to top ↑

The figures themselves are of no importance: it's the direction of the progression alone which should be considered.

The Sex of Numbers – Numbers are masculine and active, which are Odd; or feminine and passive, which are Even numbers. The active numbers in the series of the ten first numbers are 1, 3, 5, 7, 9. The feminine or passive numbers are 2, 4, 6, 8, 10.

The Life of Numbers – The relationship of numbers between themselves and their reciprocal reactions is shown through *calculation*.

Calculation is composed of two principal operations:

A. – The descent of the Spirit towards matter includes the following as operations: *addition*, or slow descent, and *multiplication* or rapid descent; the square of the number, or descent in the astral plane; and the cube of the number, or descent in the material plane.

B. – The return of matter towards the Spirit includes the following as operations: *subtraction* or slow and progressive ascent, of which the ascending progression: 9-8-7-6-5-4-3-2-1 is the first example. Nine minus one equals eight, eight minus one equals seven, etc.

Division or a more rapid return with the elimination of unnecessary numbers.

Extraction of the square root or direct ascent of the astral in a higher plane.

Extraction of the cube root or ascent of the material plane in a higher plane.

These last two operations are also accelerated forms of division.

The Planes – According to esoteric teachings, there are three principal planes in all creation:

  1. A higher or inner plane usually called the divine or spiritual plane.

2. An intermediate plane usually called the vital or astral plane.

3. An inferior or external plane usually called the corporeal or material plane.

Simple and indivisible numbers relate to the spiritual plane or what belongs to it.

Numbers raised to their square relate to the astral plane.

Numbers raised to their cube relate to the material plane.

Each plane is represented in all the others, as blood (vital plane) and lymph (material plane) circulate in the brain (physical spiritual plane). Thus, the series of spiritual numbers: 1-2-3-4-5-6-7-8-9-10 contains the square of 2, or 4, and the cube of 2, or 8.

The Egyptians determined these relationships in their famous work on the triangle.

Spiritual or Essential Root – To the square and cube roots L.-C. de Saint-Martin added the *essential root* which is obtained by adding all the numbers from unity to the number under consideration. Thus, the root of 4 is 1 plus 2 plus 3 plus 4 which is 10. The root of number 6 is $1+2+3+4+5+6 = 21$.

Numbers with More than One Figure – Numbers with multiple figures need a special comment. First of all, they can be reduced to one figure by the addition of their constitutive elements. This is the *theosophical reduction* of L.-C. de Saint-Martin, which has been known from earliest times.

Consider the number 427. It is formed by three figures, 4, 2 and 7. By adding 4 plus 2 plus 7 we get 13. By adding 1 plus 3, we get 4. This gives us the *theosophical reduction* of 427. Put another way, 427 mystically equals 4.

In this case addition serves to return a material number to the spiritual plane.

Leaders – In all numbers with more than one figure, it's the first figure to the left which denotes the character and the spiritual family of the complete number.

So, with 427, it's the 4 which is the familial key of the number, while in the number 724, which is the same number reversed, it's the 7 which is the leader, and which indicates the family.

Symmetrical Numbers – All numbers containing several figures possess a symmetrical number, obtained by reversing the figures.

So, the symmetrical number of 41 is 14; the first being odd and the second even. The symmetrical number of 32 is 23, the first being even and the second odd.

Numbers composed of two or more identical figures are only symmetrical within themselves.

Thus, 22-33-44-333-555, etc.

We can gain a particular insight from adding two symmetrical numbers.

41 and 14 make 55: 32 and 23 also make 55.

Ascending and Descending Progressions – By writing down all the figures from unity to the figure preceding the one being considered, by adding the numbers on the same line in the two ascending and descending progressions together, we get the number we are considering.

For the figure 4 we write   1   3   Total 4
                                     2   2   *ditto*
                                     3   1   *ditto*

For the number 7; we write the series of the 6 first figures:

```
1  7 ⎫
2  6 ⎪
3  5 ⎪
4  4 ⎬  Total 7 for the whole series
5  3 ⎪
6  2 ⎪
7  1 ⎭
```

Of course, it's the same for any number.[9]

---

[9] Note the example given is clearly incorrect! If we were considering 7, the numbers should go 1, 2, 3, 4, 5, 6 and 6, 5, 4, 3, 2, 1 which would then correctly add up to 7 on each line. But this was how it was presented in the original book – PV].

Chapter 2

The First Ten Numbers

§ 1

General Description of the First Ten Numbers

Before beginning a quick review of each number, it is important to take a look at the first ten numbers together. They all belong to the spiritual plane, but we should know that this plane includes three centers, stages or progressions – however one may wish to call them.

Spiritual, Pure	1	
Spiritual in Spiritual	6 2	3 5 7
Astral of Spiritual *(squares)*	4 9	
Material in Spiritual *(cubes)*	8	
New Series	10	

The Pure Spiritual includes one number only: Unity.
This is the direct way to union with the Divine Power.
Below Unity and in the same Spiritual Plane (Spiritual in Spiritual), we find:
       A. – On the odd side……. 3, 5, 7.
       B. – On the even side……2 and 6.
In the plane below this (Astral of Spiritual), we find 4, the square of 2, and 9, the square of 3. We know that the Astral is the plane of squares.
Finally, in the plane below that (Material in Spiritual), we find 8, the cube of 2. This is a first classification of the first ten numbers.

However, let's not forget the mistrust that the number 2, its squares and cubes inspired in L.-C. de Saint-Martin, as well as the number 5. We'll return to this subject later on.

We can compare the first table to the following diagram taken from Wronski:

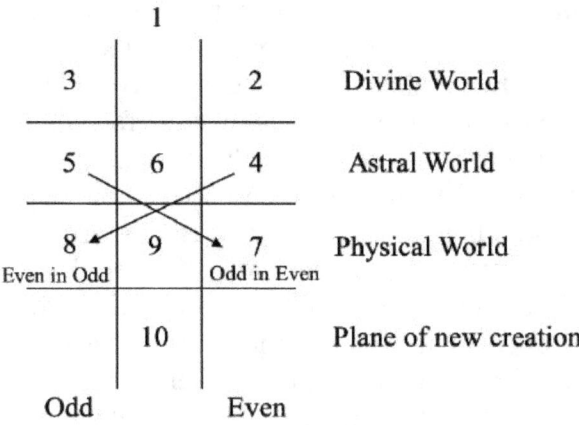

Figure 1.

This should be compared to the ten Sephiroth of the Kabbalah.[10]

1. Supreme Power.
2. Absolute Wisdom.
3. Infinite Understanding.
4. Benevolence.
5. Justice or Severity.
6. Beauty.
7. Victory.
8. Eternity.
9. Fecundity.
10. Reality.

---

[10] Eliphas Lévi, *Elements of the Kabbalah* in ten lessons, cf. *The Book of Splendors*, Paris, pub. Chamuel, 1894, p. 235.

These are the first ideas which L.-C. de Saint-Martin developed in the following passages:

"There is a division of the Universal Table which is recognized by all observers in the class of true philosophy: that is where the divine realm, the spiritual realm and the natural realm are distinguished from one another. It is also recognized that there is a relationship between the divine realm and the spiritual and natural realms, and that as a result the numbers of the divine order must have their representations and images in those two realms. But those who do not have the key to numbers open themselves up to serious misunderstanding when they attempt to determine or consider those relationships.

"The main reason for their error is that they approach such speculation through their knowledge of regular arithmetic, where numbers are recognized by means of their multiples or their similarities, and not by means of their properties; for arithmetic recognizes no properties in those numbers other than the generally accepted ones which man has attributed to them.

"The second error is wanting to contain the three realms mentioned above in three consecutive decades, so that after thirty we would no longer need any other numbers.

"Finally, the third error is wanting to find the same set of principles attributed to the first decade in the second and third decades too, because one sees the same order in the numbers, and the same arithmetic alignment in them as well."[11]

§ 2

The First Ten Numbers and Their Powers

First power: Unity.
Second power: 4-7-8-10.
Third power: 3-6-9.

(Remember the evil numbers 2 and 5).

---

[11] L.-C. de Saint-Martin, *Treatise on Numbers*, Paris, pub. Chacornac, 1913, p. 20 [and in English in this book – PV].

"The second powers have a realm to traverse because they are directly connected to the center. The third powers are connected only indirectly and have no other purpose other than that of producing forms. They are therefore more tightly restricted than the second powers. They do not have the *creative law* that belongs only to Unity; nor do they do have the *administrative law* that is entrusted to the second powers.

"They have only the *executing and operating power* which, as it is always the same (since the result of their work never changes), only transmits itself from one being to another through necessary generation. So, all their actions are equal."[12]

Finally, to conclude these preliminary observations, we have reproduced below our diagram of the arithmetical generation of the first 9 numbers, and a synthetic figure by Bro. Ch. Barlet on the relationships between the first ten numbers.

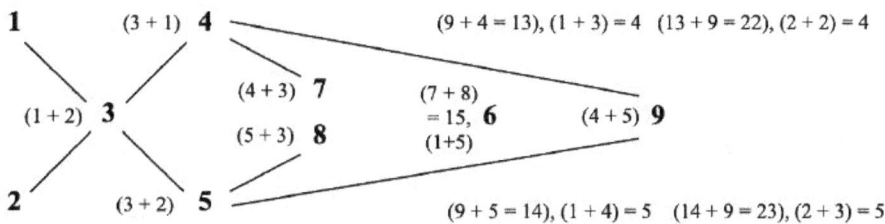

Figure 2. Arithmetical Generation of the First Nine Numbers.

---

[12] Cf. L.-C. de Saint-Martin, op. cit., p. 78.

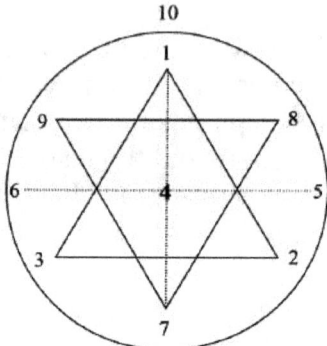

Figure 3: Key to the Relationships between the First Ten Numbers.

Chapter 3
Analysis of the Decade

Having taken a quick look at the various approaches to the qualitative study of numbers, and having considered all the numbers in the first Denary from a number of angles, we will now begin to analyze each of the numbers which constitute this first Denary.

Faithful to our approach, here we will be very careful to avoid covering the metaphysical and mystical problems associated with each number.

We will also set aside for now any information relating to the magical practice of Numbers, those famous "Powers" which fascinate young students of the occult, which we are not permitted to write about without circumspection.

In a special section devoted to this, we will list the texts the seeker should endeavor to interpret following personal work. The purpose of our essay is simply to offer an *Introduction* to the study of numbers: it does not dispense with the need to read the classical works on this subject.

Now let us perform an analysis of each of the first ten numbers.

UNITY

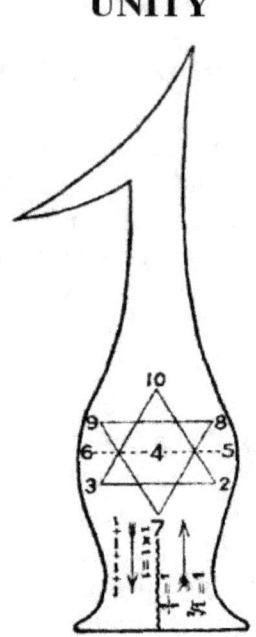

Figure 4.

Sex	Odd, Active, Self-creator.
Origin	Hidden from human beings.
Divisible or Indivisible	Indivisible.
Its Square	The number itself.
Its Cube	Itself.
Its Essential Root	Itself.
Its Name	Unity
Sephirotic meaning	Supreme Power.
Esoteric numerical Significance	Source of all Numbers.
Geometric correspondence	The point as known in a spiritual sense.

Various applications

Tarot............................	First card: The Magician, composition of the game.
Astrology........................	The Creative Principle; the Sun ☉, the Pivot of the World.
Kabbalah.......................	The Mother Letter: Aleph א.

Unity in the Three Planes

"Those who have penetrated the course of numbers can admire the luminous wisdom with which Providence spreads her treasures before us and shows us how she brings her powers to the several realms. They will recognize that numbers are themselves fixed and complete in their fundamental abilities, though they are infinite in the play of their power and in the innumerable emanations that can arise and will arise forever from these fundamental abilities. They will recognize that Unity is the only number that not only doesn't leave the divine decade by its square or cube, but also that it never departs from its own secret or its own center, and which focuses all its operations in itself. They will recognize that when this being called *One* is transported either to the divine, the spiritual or the natural realm, it is transported there by its own fundamental abilities and through their corresponding emanations; but that the plans and properties which it manifests by this are superior to any material notions of arithmetic, and have nothing to do with its coarse and monotonous meaning. They will recognize that through these fundamental abilities and the corresponding emanations, this being called *One* brings its life and spirit into all three realms, and that, therefore, they can spiritually see those three realms as being a great tree whose root is always hidden in the Divine realm as if in its maternal earth, whose trunk or body is manifested in the Spiritual realm by the square, and whose branches, flowers and fruits are manifested in the Natural realm by the operations of the cube. By this they will recognize the communication and active union which must exist between these three realms or between these three worlds because they have a common root, and because there are Spiritual squares that extend into the Natural realm, and Natural cubes which are completed in the Spiritual realm, while the Divine Unity, like the sap which produces everything and fills everything, operates at the same time and in concert with the Spiritual and Natural realms, because it constantly influences it invisibly by its own root, its own square and its own cube, in order to vivify the cubes, squares and roots of all the others depending upon their properties and *virtues*.

"They will recognize that although the being called *One* doesn't transport itself into all those realms, nevertheless it is through the influence of its root, its square and its cube that all its works and all its spiritual and natural creations appear completed and clothed in that expressive character of Unity, which everywhere shows us our God, and everywhere the harmonic cooperation of all His abilities and powers."[13]

"Unity", said Eckartshausen, "is its own root, its own number considered as unity. No calculation can be performed with it: only in the manifestation of its powers is the first quaternary created through its triune power."[14]

....

"Unity, from which everything is born, which is the source of all things, from which everything comes, which preserves everything, which reveals itself in all things visible to the senses without itself being physical, which never changes, which fills everything, which is present everywhere, and manifests itself in a ternary power."[15]

Unity[16] contains all numbers.

---

[13] Cf. L.-C. de Saint-Martin, op. cit., pp. 23 – 25 [and in English in this book – PV].
[14] Von Eckhartshausen, *Zahlenlehre der Natur*, Leipzig, 1794, p. 233.
[15] Id., p. 231.
[16] For the purposes of Papus' Treatise, Unity will be translated as purely the number, although it implies Deity. Therefore 'it' will be used throughout. However, in Saint-Martin's treatise on Numbers, since Unity is specifically the Creative Deity, it will be referred to as 'He' throughout.

Unity emanates its powers only by addition of itself, the only source of creation of all numbers.

Unity is itself its own square, cubic and essential roots, itself: Unity. Unity distributes its influence across all the planes.

NUMBER TWO

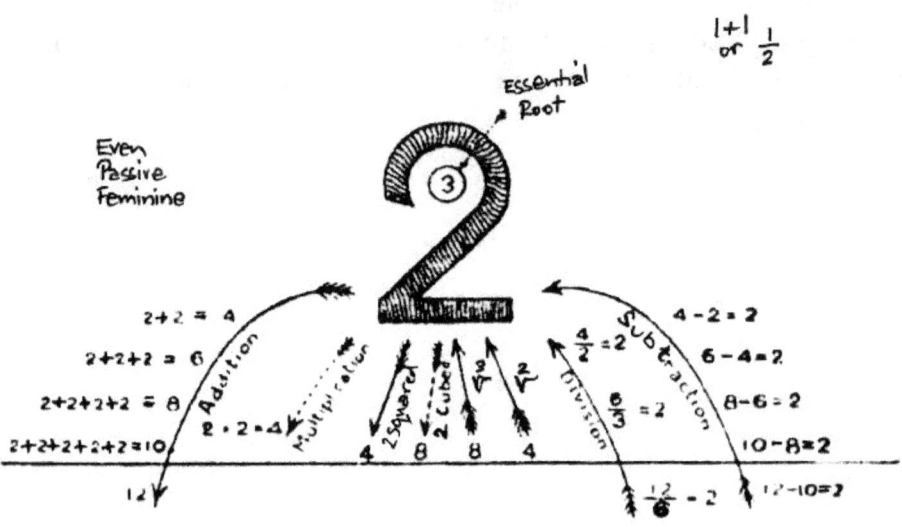

Figure 5.

Sex.................................... Even, Feminine, Passive.
Origin................................. Unity repeated twice (General Rule), Unity becoming a fraction ½ (L.-C. de Saint-Martin)

Divisible or Indivisible..... Divisible into two halves 1 - 1.

Its Square......................... 4 (Even).
Its Cube............................ 8 (Even).
Its Essential Root............. 3 (1 plus 2).
Its Name............................ The Binary, and also the Dual.

Sephirotic meaning........... Wisdom.
Esoteric numerical Significance......................... Passive reflection of Unity. Source of human mental errors.

Geometric correspondence................. Two points . .
Two lines =
An angle L

Various applications

Tarot............................	Second card: The Gate of the Sanctuary.
Astrology.........................	The Moon ☽.
Kabbalah.........................	The letter Beth ב.

NUMBER THREE

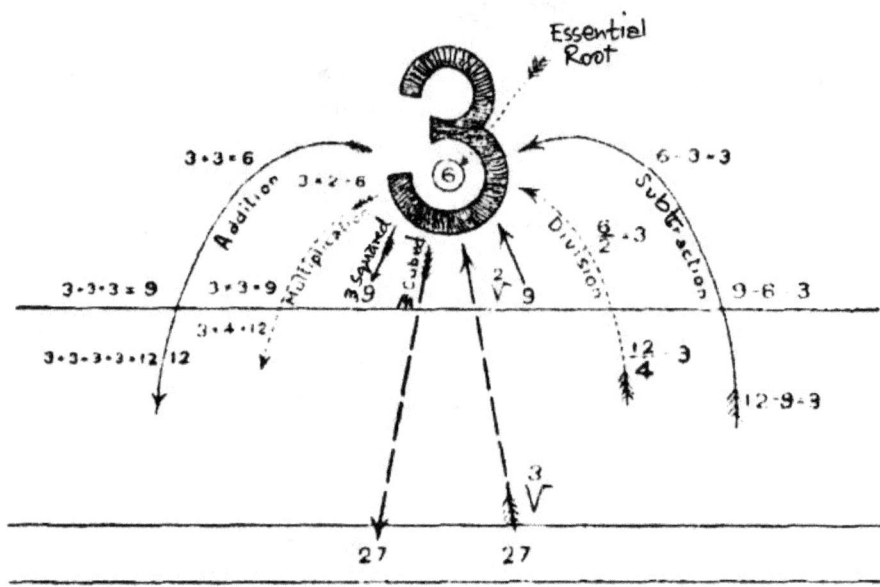

Figure 6.

Sex	Odd, Masculine, Active.
Origin	Unity repeated three times ∴ 2 + 1.
Divisible or Indivisible	Indivisible without a remainder.
Its Square	9 (Odd).
Its Cube	27 (Odd).
Its Essential Root	6 (1 + 2 + 3).
Its Name	The Ternary.
Sephirotic meaning	Infinite Understanding.
Esoteric numerical Significance	First term of all creation (A – S – Th).[17]

---

[17] This is the term used in the original. Now, 'S' is often rendered as a 'Z' in English, so it is probably referring to Azoth, which according to Kabbalistic doctrine represented *Ain Soph*, source of Creation - PV.

Geometric correspondence.............	Three points ∴ 1 + 1 + 1 The Triangle △

Various applications

Tarot...........................	Third card: Nature – Isis – Urania.
Astrology......................	The Three Great Planets (Sun, Moon, Earth). The Central Pivot. The Zodiac. The Heaven of the Word.
Kabbalah......................	The letter Gimel ג. Nature. The Three Mothers (א מ ש).

THE TERNARY: 3 – 7 – 12.

Seven parts are formed by two ternaries, in the middle of which is Unity.

The duodenary is constituted by the (ternary) opposing parts: three friends and three enemies, three living beings which bring to life and three which kill, and God the Faithful King ruling over all on the threshold of His Sanctity.

Unity rules over the ternary, the ternary rules over the septenary, the septenary rules over the duodenary.[18]

"Number 3 is the return to unity, which seemed to be broken by the number 2. It is by uniting the Son with the Father that the Holy Spirit comes into being; and that is why it may be considered as the efflorescence of unity. It emanates from it directly, participates in its virtue, and expresses peace and beatitude. In one aspect, the number 3 contains the entire being, and can be considered as the first development of the idea of being, who was one in his principle. This

---

[18] Cf. Papus, *La Cabbale*, Anvers, Ed. Lumen, 1929 p. 191, Trad. du *Sepher Jesirah*. [Also translated into English as *The Qabalah*, pub. Samuel Weiser, 2000. In fact, this citation only takes the reader to Chapter 5 of Papus' translation of the *Sepher Yetzirah* and is not the source of this text! The numbers 3 – 7 – 12 refer to the division of the Hebrew Alphabet into 3 Mother Letters, 7 Double Letters and 12 Single Letters, the significance of which may be found in many books, and articles on the internet – PV].

number has many reflections in creation, in fluids, in colors and in forms."[19]

---

[19] Lacuria (P.F.G.), *Les Harmonies de l'Être exprimées par les Nombres* (The Harmonies of Being expressed by Numbers), Pairs, Chacornac, 1899, Vol. II, p. 300.

NUMBER FOUR

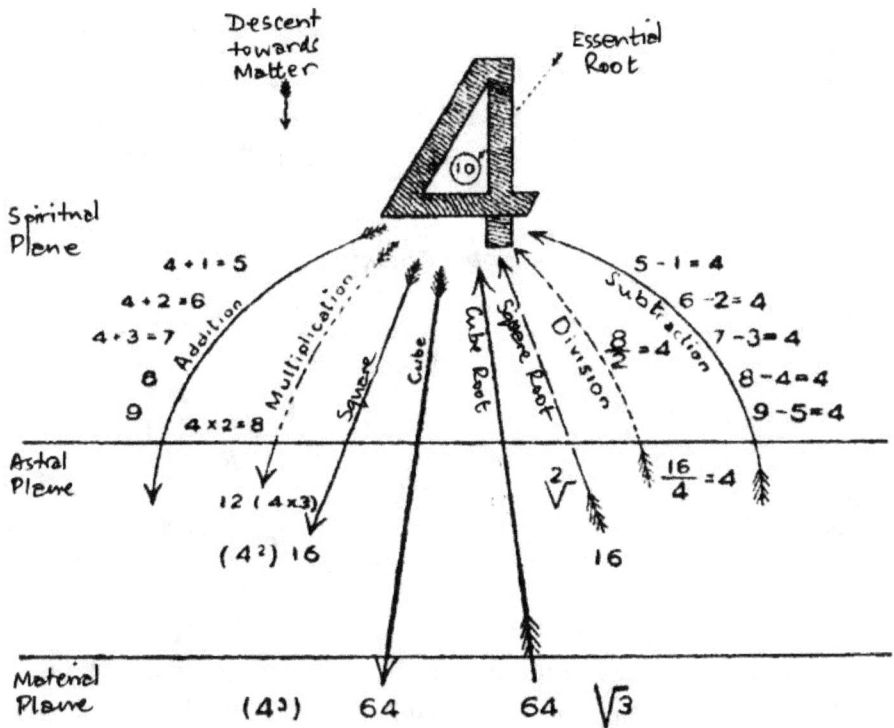

Figure 7.

Sex.....................	Even, Feminine, Passive.
Origin.....................	Unity repeated four times. 2×2; $3 + 1$.
Divisible or Indivisible.....	Divisible by 2.
Its Square.....................	16 (Even).
Its Cube.....................	54 (Even).
Its Essential Root...........	10 $(1 + 2 + 3 + 4)$.
Its Name.....................	The Quaternary.
Sephirotic meaning..........	Benevolence.

Esoteric numerical Significance............……...	First octave of Unity. First creation containing its seed, source of a subsequent creation.
Geometric correspondence............…...	Four points .:. $1 + 1 + 1 + 1$ Two times two lines = $\parallel$, a pointed Triangle, a Square □, The Cross +.

Various applications

Tarot.............................	Fourth card: The Emperor (Jupiter ♃).
Astrology.....................…...	The Astrological Cross (Equinoxes and Solstices). The four celestial forms of the Sphinx.
Kabbalah..................…..…	The letter Daleth ד. Authority.

"The multiplication of the number 4", said Eckartshausen, "the extraction of its root, its multiplication by itself, and the consideration of the proportions of all the root numbers to their root numbers is the greatest secret of the doctrine of numbers. It's what we find in all the secret writings under the expression: the knowledge of the great quaternary."[20]

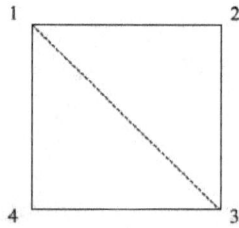

Figure 8: The Quaternary According to the Law of Progression (4 = 10).

---

[20] Op. cit., p. 232.

NUMBER FIVE

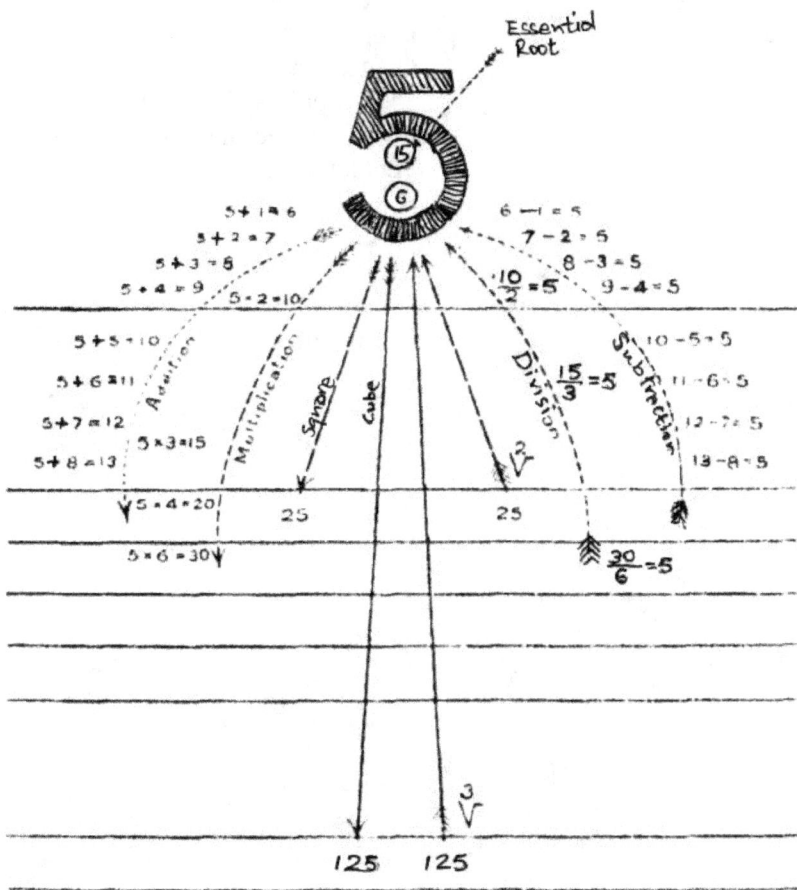

Figure 9.

Sex..................................	Odd, Masculine.
Origin...............................	Unity repeated five times. 2 + 3; 4 + 1. (Number of Evil to L.-C. de Saint-Martin).
Divisible or Indivisible.....	Indivisible without a remainder.
Its Square.........................	25 (Odd).
Its Cube............................	125 (Odd).
Its Essential Root.............	15 = 6.
Its Name...........................	The Quinary.

Sephirotic meaning………..	Justice or Severity.
Esoteric numerical Significance…………....…..	Pentagram, image of Man after the Fall. Binary of the Quaternary.
Geometric correspondence………..….	Five points. Triangle and two lines. Pointed square. Pentagram (5-pointed Star) ★.

Various applications

Tarot……………………….	Fifth card: The Pope (Religion).
Astrology………………....	Mars ♂.
Kabbalah……………....…	The letter Heh ה. Life (Religion).

NUMBER SIX

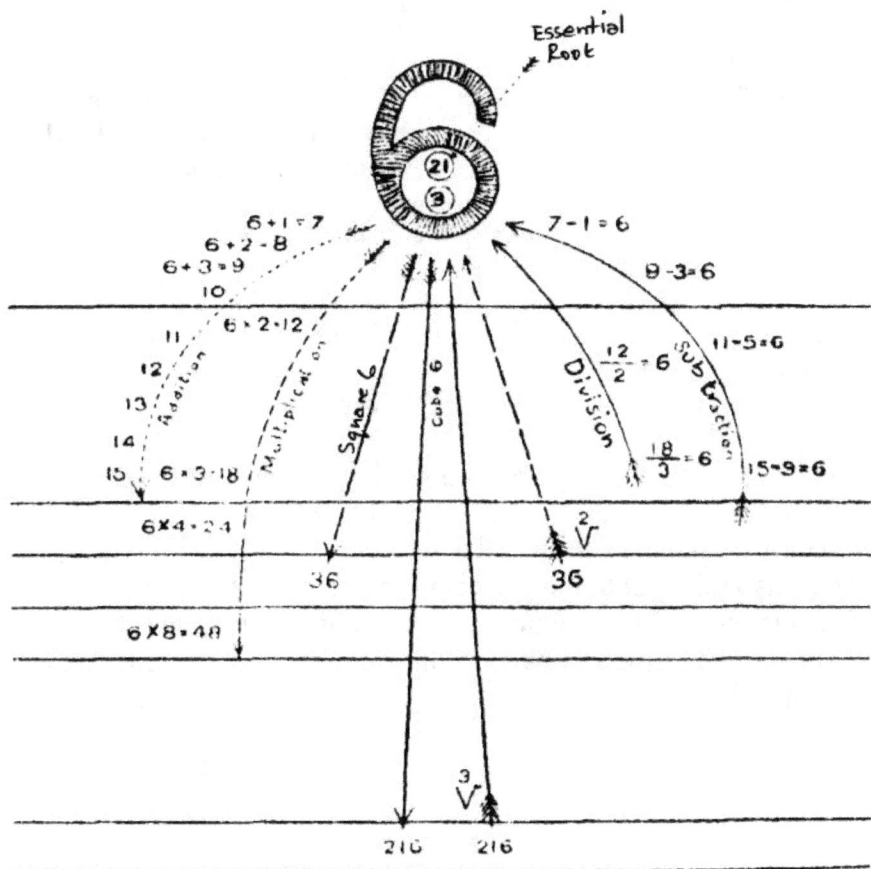

Figure 10.

Sex.....................	Even, Feminine, Passive.
Origin.....................	Unity repeated six times. 3 x 2; 2 x 3; 4 + 2; 5 + 1.
Divisible or Indivisible.....	Divisible by 2 and by 3.
Its Square.....................	36 (Even).
Its Cube.....................	216 (Even).
Its Essential Root...........	21 = 3.
Its Name.....................	The Senary.
Sephirotic meaning..........	Beauty.

Esoteric numerical Significance............…..…...	The Two symmetrical ternaries, the Hexagram.
Geometric correspondence.............…...	Six points ⁝⁝ Two interlaced Triangles ✡. Square and two lines. Pointed Pentagram. Hexagon.

Various applications

Tarot...........................….	Sixth card: The Lovers.
Astrology......................…...	Six periods of Creation.
Kabbalah.....................…..…	The letter Vav ו (the Universal Chain).

For Initiates, the Senary was the *perfect number* par excellence. They attributed it to Nature, and they represented it more commonly by the Hexagram.

They also said that 6, the perfect number, was a *circular number* and this is correct, since extending the radii on the circumference six times gives the Hexagon and allows you to build the Hexagram.[21]

---

[21] 6, the number of the days of Creation, a Divine work, is also the number of days of the week, a human work, 6 x 6 = 36, number of the word *separation* (distinction between light and darkness). BDL = 36, root of the name of the *precious stone* and the *felicitous tree* of terrestrial paradise, *Bdellium*. [Note: this shorthand refers to the fact that the Hebrew word for separation, Bedel or בדל, adds up to 36 (ב = 2, ד = 4, ל = 30, and is the basis of the word Bdellium which is used to denote both an aromatic tree and one of the jewels in the breastplate of the High Priest, Incidentally, this reference to the hexagon within the circle which allows you to build the hexagram is a key part of the design of the Martinist pantacle – PV]). This tree is watered by the four rivers in the Eastward part of Eden, or 36 x 4 = 144, the *original proposition, oriental proposition* and the *first revelation*. If one multiplies 36 or the tree of the precious stone, by 6, that is by a new human work, as opposed to the benediction of providence indicated by the number of 4 rivers, one obtains 216 or the cube of 6, the number of the lion Ari [Note: Ari or ארי is Hebrew for Lion – PV], which signifies personal possession, and spiritually love of one's own excellence. Cf. Thomas (Edme), *Histoire de l'antique cité d'Autun* (History of the Ancient City of Autun), Paris, 1846, p. XXVII. This note is by Abbé Devoucoux (Editor).

"The number 6 descends genealogically from Unity through the intermediation of 3. It is the pair of 3 which is doubled, and the harmony of 2 which is tripled.

"Always in equilibrium in all its groups. It is the perfect number of the Pythagoreans, the type of proportion and natural beauty."[22]

---

[22] Lacuria (P.F.G.), op.cit., p. 300.

NUMBER SEVEN

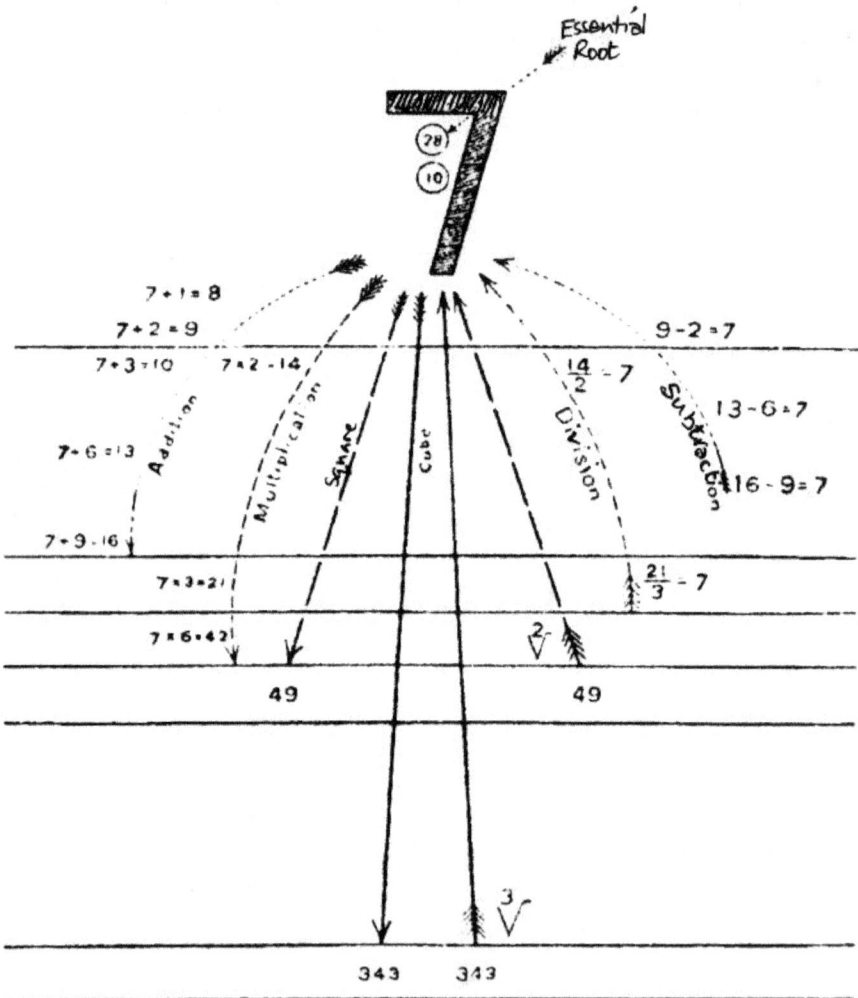

Figure 11.

Sex.................................... Odd, Masculine.
Origin............................... Unity repeated seven times. 6 = 1; 5 + 2; 4 + 3.
Divisible or Indivisible..... Indivisible without a remainder.

Its Square.....................	49 (4ᵗʰ odd decade). Symmetrical number of the square 94.
Its Cube.........................	343 (34ᵗʰ odd decade). Symmetrical number of the cube 343.
Its Essential Root............	28 = 10 = 1.
Its Name.........................	The Septenary.
Sephirotic meaning..........	Victory.
Esoteric numerical Significance........................	Two Ternaries in the middle of which is Unity. Unity at the second octave.
Geometric correspondence................	Seven-pointed star. Pointed hexagram. Square surmounted by a triangle △.

Various applications

Tarot.............................	Seventh card: The Chariot (Victory).
Astrology.......................	The Seven Moving Planets. The week (quarter of the *Lunar Month*).
Kabbalah.......................	Zayin ז. Property. The Seven Double Letters.

There are three types of septenary systems:

The physical septenary system.
The astral septenary system.
The psychic septenary system.

The physical septenary system is written as 6 + 1 and is depicted by two interlaced triangles with the point of unity at their center. It is the seal of Solomon giving the key to the circulation of the Divine Forces in Nature. It is also the caduceus of Hermes formed of two snakes each making three turns around the sacred wand.

Finally, it is the seven-pointed star giving the key to the world of orbs.

The astral septenary system is written as 5 + 2. It relates particularly to man on the terrestrial plane. It is the pentagram with its dual colors of black and white, depicting positive and negative polarization. It is the human hand and its dual polarization, right and left; it is the positive star dominating the negative crescent.

The psychic system is written as 4 + 3. It depicts the final victory of Spirit over matter. It is the triangle above the square (the origin of the Pyramids); It is the triangle above the Egyptian Tau; finally, it is the triangle which joins its summit with the end of the vertical line and its base with the horizontal line of the redemptive cross.

Therefore, when one applies the septenary to any particular order of knowledge, one should first know what kind of septenary is being considered, and if it is the type 6 + 1, 5 + 2 or 4 + 3 that will be used. One should also know if one is going to go up the spiral of evolution, in which case the higher number is always placed first (as in the examples above), or if, on the contrary, one is descending down the spiral of involution, in which case the series becomes 1 + 6, 2 + 5 and 3 + 4.[23]

Observations. – The Septenary is always a derivative, and it remains unclear if one doesn't determine the two constituent ternaries and the synthesizing unity.

The Septenary systems are often produced by three Ternaries whose two elements unite into a single one:

High in High
Middle in High   } 1st Ternary of High
Low in High

High in Middle
Middle in Middle   } 2nd Ternary Middle analyzed
Low in Middle

---

[23] Lacuria (P.F.G.), op. cit., p. 301.

> High in Low
> Middle in Low   } 3rd Ternary analyzed
> Low in Low

Middle in High and High in Middle merge; as do Low in Middle and Middle in Low.[24]

The three Ternaries therefore reduce to a Septenary.

This is the key to the Constitution of the Seven Principles of Men according to the Chinese and the Hindus.

---

[24] This doesn't make a lot of sense. Surely it would be more logical to say that Low in High and High in Middle, and Low in Middle and High in Low blend together to make seven? – PV.

NUMBER EIGHT

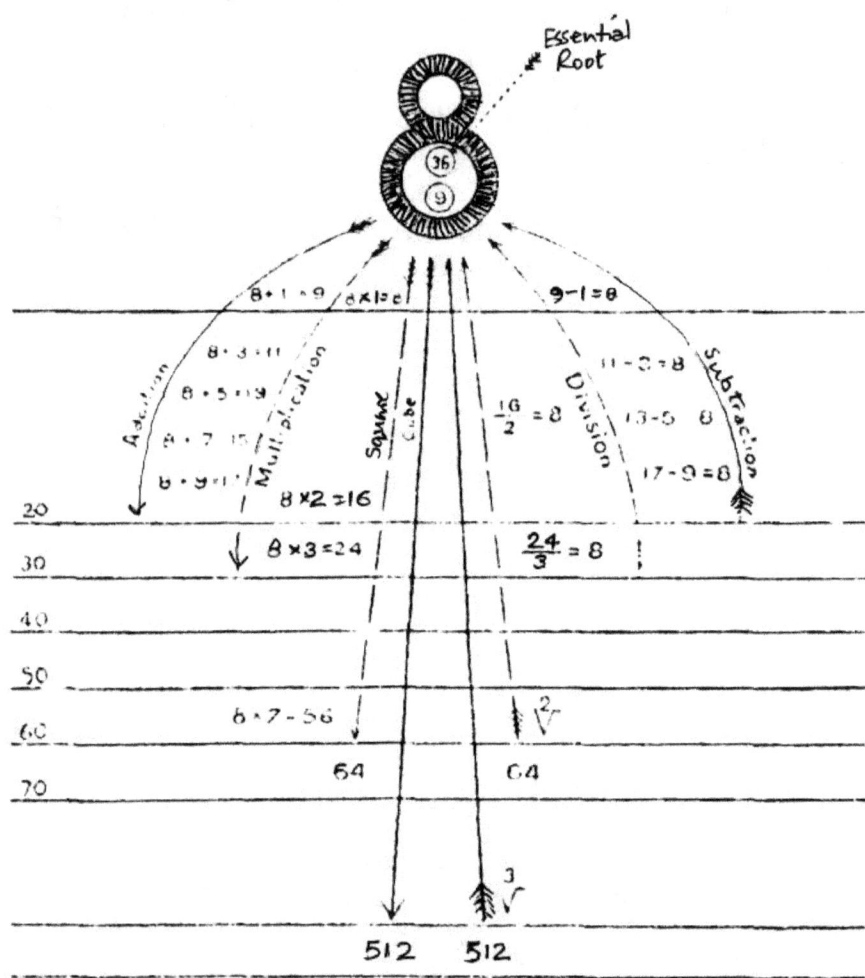

Figure 12.

Sex..............................	Even, Feminine, Passive.
Origin...........................	Unity repeated eight times. 2 + 6; 3 + 5; 4 + 4.
Divisible or Indivisible.....	Divisible by 2 and by 4.
Its Square.......................	64 (Even).
Its Cube.........................	512 (Even).
Its Essential Root.............	36 = 9.
Its Name........................	The Octenary.

Sephirotic meaning………..... Eternity.
Esoteric numerical Significance…………...…….. Binary of the 3rd octave.
Perfection of Form.

Geometric correspondence………..…. Two squares.
The double cross.

Various applications

Tarot……………………….. Eighth card: Justice.
Astrology………………...... The eight centers of the World (Sepher Yetzirah).
Kabbalah……………....…. The letter Heth ח.

NUMBER NINE

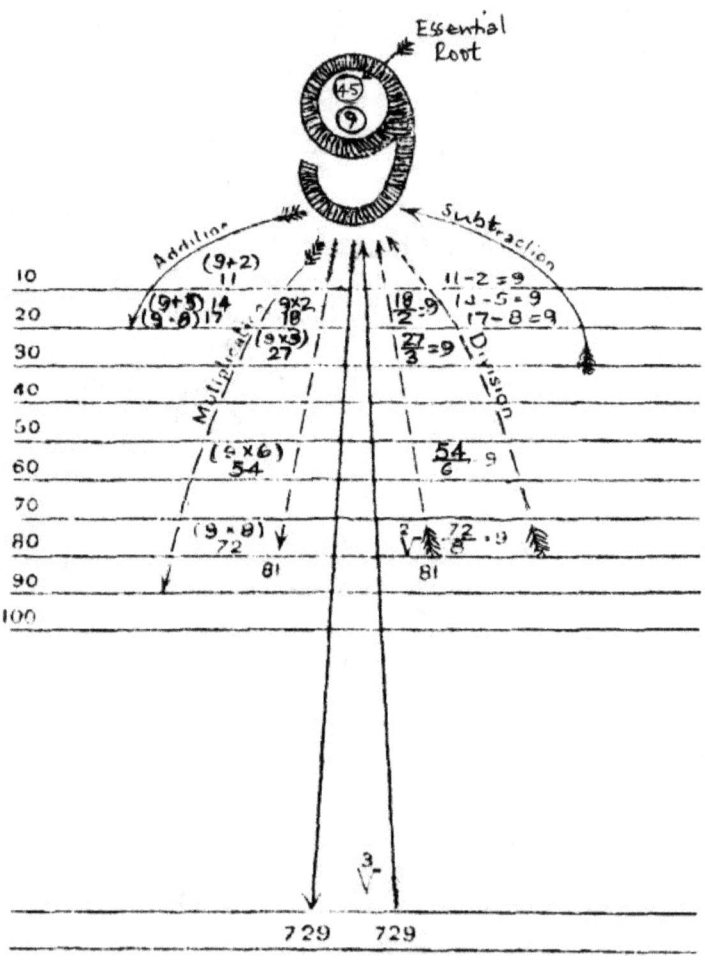

Figure 13.

Sex..............................	Odd, Masculine.
Origin............................	Unity repeated nine times. 8 + 1; 2 + 7; 3 + 6; 4 + 5.
Divisible or Indivisible.....	Divisible by 3.
Its Square......................	81 (Odd).
Its Cube........................	729 (Odd).
Its Essential Root............	45 = 9.
Its Name.......................	The Novenary.
Sephirotic meaning..........	Fruitfulness.

Esoteric numerical Significance..................	Number of Matter. The Ternary (3rd octave). Three triangles.
Geometric correspondence............	Two pointed squares. The circle without a central point O.

Various applications

Tarot.........................	Ninth card: The Hermit.
Astrology....................	Jupiter ♃.
Kabbalah....................	The letter Teth ט.

"The number 9 returns to unity by means of the 3. It is the 3 developed and multiplied by itself, and, as the 3 was already being led to unity by love, this amounted to 1 x 1 which forever remains the original unity. This number of love and beatitude has no reflection save in heaven in the nine choirs of angels."[25]

"The *Nonary* is the number of generation, mystery and initiation, because initiation is a spiritual generation or regeneration, and any generation, material or spiritual, is accomplished in mystery. We can also say that initiation consists of the conscious penetration of that which is veiled to the profane.

"There are nine degrees in initiation which are, so to speak, the nine levels where man halts in order to contemplate the path travelled, and to prepare himself to climb the next level."[26]

---

[25] Lacuria, op. cit., p. 301.
[26] J. Tabris, *La Qabbalah Initiatique* (The Initiatory Kabbalah), Paris, *L'Initiation*, No. 10, July 1897, p.46.

NUMBER TEN[27]

Sex	Even, Feminine, Passive.
Origin	Unity repeated ten times. 8 + 2; 7 + 3; 6 + 4; 5 + 5.
Divisible or Indivisible	Divisible by 2 and by 5.
Its Square	100.
Its Cube	1,000.
Its Essential Root	55 = 10.
Its Name	The Denary.
Sephirotic meaning	Reality.
Esoteric numerical Significance	Unity acting as an even number (R. Schwaller). Beginning of a completely new series (Tarot).
Geometric correspondence	The circle with a point ⊙.

Various applications

Tarot	The Sphinx.
Astrology	Mercury ☿.
Kabbalah	The letter Yod ׳.

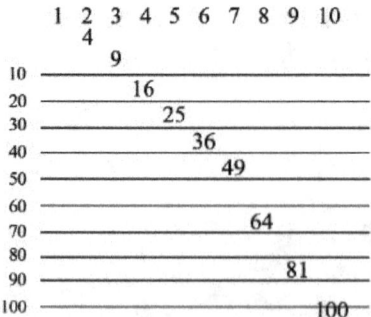

Figure 14: The Squares of the Ten First Numbers.

---

[27] "The 10 summarizes the entire external work of God, of which Jesus Christ is the summit." Lacuria, op. cit., p. 304.

Chapter 4

The Constitution of Numbers

Just as the Universe and Man are formed by Three Principles, Numbers similarly possess a triple sense, with differing applications on different planes. From the point of view of their constitution, Numbers have: 1. a structure, corresponding to Anatomy; 2. an organization, corresponding to Physiology and 3. a philosophy, corresponding to Psychology. We will therefore consider each of these three aspects. Here is the first.

§ 1

Anatomy

The anatomy of a number shows us how it is built, what its constituent organs are and what its place is in its series, because to personal anatomy is added comparative anatomy, which determines its family and race.

A connoisseur of numbers[28], Mr. Boos of Rome made an interesting comment. If for any number, one removes its numeric value by subtraction, the remainder is always 9 or a multiple of 9.

Take the number 127. By adding the three numbers which constitute this number, $1 + 2 + 7$, we get the number 10. If we subtract 10 from 127, we get 117, which gives 9 by the addition of the three digits, $1 + 1 + 7$.

This method can lead to an understanding of the three principles constituting a number.

The spirit of the number is obtained by the addition of its constituent figures: thus, 127 has as its spirit 10, the product of the addition of: $1 + 2 + 7$.

The body of this number is 9: since 3, 6, or 9 are figures connected with matter and in whatever manner we may try to combine, them we will always find them again; so it is that matter

---

[28] In passing it is interesting to note that the French for 'amateur', which is a homonym (*amateur*), also means a lover, devotee or even connoisseur in French! – PV.

may change in appearance, but it will always be found in living bodies identical to itself.

It is easy to find the astral of the number that interests us. This is what remains when we have removed the spirit 10 and the body 9, or 127 minus 19 or 108.

To summarize: the spirit of a number is given by the addition of the constituent numbers. For 127 the spirit is 10.

The body of a number is given by the addition of the number which remains when we have removed the spirit of the number.

For 127, if we remove 10, 117 remains, which the addition of the figures gives 9.

The astral of the number is what remains when we remove the spirit and the physical or material body. For 127, it is that number minus the spirit 10 and the matter 9, or 108. Note that the astral is always greater numerically than the other two constituent elements.

For the number 127 we have:

Spirit of the number.......10
Astral of the number.....108
Material or body of the number 9
Total..........................127

Let's take any number with three figures, for example, 823.
We will make a study of its anatomy, and dissect it.
For this we will first sum the numbers: $8 + 2 + 3 = 13$.
13 is the spirit of the number.
Then we subtract 13 from 823. That gives 810.
By adding up the figures of this last number, we get $8 + 1 + 0 = 9$.
We then subtract 9 from 810 and we get 801.
We can now establish the constitution of our number 823.
This number is made up of:
13, as spirit.
801, as astral.
9, as body.

Special note

All numbers, without exception, after we have extracted the sum of their figures, leave as a remainder a number whose sum of the digits makes 9; the number of matter and the last term in the series 3-6-9.

The number that we consider the astral of the number also makes 9 by the addition of its figures. As this question seems new to us, and has been the subject of personal studies, we will give a few examples:

The first 10 numbers are Spirit. They have neither a Physical body, nor an Astral one. From 10 to 19, the numbers have only a Spirit and a Body; not an Astral one.

	Spirit	Body
10	1	9
11	2	9
12	3	9
13	4	9
14	5	9
15	6	9
16	7	9
17	8	9
18	9	9
19	10	9

Above 20, the Number have a Spirit, a Body and an Astral. Here are some examples:

	Spirit	Body	Astral
20	2	9	9
21	3	9	9
22	4	9	9
23	5	9	9
24	6	9	9
30	3	9	18
31	4	9	18

40	4	9	27
50	5	9	36
51	6	9	36
60	6	9	45
61	7	9	45
70	7	9	54
71	8	9	54
100	1	18	81
1000	1	27	972

§ 2

Physiology

Numerical *physiology* consists of studying the interplay of the agents[29] entering into the constitution of a number, and then this same action on the other numbers and agents constituting these other numbers.

The law which governs this second aspect of the constitution of Numbers is the *Ternary Law*, which is a universal law.[30]

The three terms that constitute the ternary are:

1. An active term;
2. A passive term;
3. A neutral term resulting from the action of the first two upon one another.

As this law must apply everywhere, we will look for those numbers which, by acting on one another, produce 3.

These numbers are 1 and 2, because $1 + 2 = 3$.

At the same time, we can understand the sense of these first three numbers.

Number 1 represents the Active.

---

[29] Papus uses the word 'organe' which can mean 'organ' in the usual sense, which fits better with the image of physiology. However, it also means 'agent', and this is a more accurate term to use here. PV.

[30] Papus, *Traité élémentaire de Science Occulte* (*Elementary Treatise on Occult Knowledge*). Paris, Ollendorff, 1903, pp. 41 – 52.

Number 2 represents the Passive.
Number 3 represents the Reaction of the Active on the Passive.

According to analogical methodology, we can replace the word 'Active' by the figure 1, which represents all the ideas governed by that principle, that is to say Man, the Divine Father, Light, Heat, etc., depending on what we are considering in one or other of the 3 worlds.

	1
Material World:	Light; a gaseous state.
Moral or Natural World:	Man.
Metaphysical or Archetypal World:	God the Father.

The same is true of the words 'Passive', which one can replace by 2, and 'Neuter' replaced by 3.

You see that the calculations applied to figures were also applied mathematically to ideas in the science of the ancients, which makes its methods very general in application, and because of that quite different from modern methods.

Here we have just given the basics of the explanation of the *Rota*[31] by Guillaume Postel.

Now we should demonstrate that what we have said up to now concerning numbers was actually done in antiquity and is not a total fiction of our imagination.

Firstly, we find these applications in a Hebrew book whose antiquity Mr. Franck himself does not contest[32], the *Sepher Yetzirah*, of which we made the first French translation[33]. But as this book is specifically Kabbalistic, we prefer to quote the ancient philosophers:

---

[31] For an explanation of this term see the works of Postel, Christian, and above all Eliphas Lévi. [Note: there is a large number of articles on the internet on this topic, for example: Rota/Taro (no author cited) at http://cartedatrionfi.tripod.com/RotaTaro.html (as of December 20, 2019) – PV].

[32] Franck, *La Kabbale* [*The Kabbalah*]. Paris, pub. Hachette, 1863.

[33] Papus, *Traite Methodique de Science Occulte* [*Methological Treatise on Occult Knowledge*], New edition. Paris 1928 (original date of pub. not given), 2 vols.

"The divine essence being inaccessible to the senses, in order to characterize it let us not use the language of the senses, but rather that of the spirit; let us ascribe to the intelligence or active principle of the Universe the name of monad or unity, because it is always the same; to matter or the passive principle that of dyad or of multiplicity; and finally, because it is subject to all kinds of changes, let us attribute the triad to the world, because it is the result of intelligence and matter."[34]

"Suffice it to say that, as Pythagoras designated God by 1 and matter by 2, he expressed the Universe by 12, which is the result of the union of the other two."[35]

We know that the doctrine of Pythagoras summarizes that of Egyptians, his masters; those of the Hebrews and the Indians and as a result, those of Antiquity as a whole; that is why we quote this philosopher from preference every time we need to clarify a point of ancient knowledge.

We know the meaning that the ancients gave to the numbers 1, 2, and 3. Now let us look at some of the other numbers.

The Quaternary restores the terms 1, 2 and 3 we have just discussed to unity.

Here is an example:

Father, Mother and Child are three terms in which the Father is active and corresponds to the number 1, and the Mother is passive and corresponds to the number 2. The Child has no sex, is neutral, and corresponds to 1 plus 2, that is to say, the number 3.

What is the Unity which contains these three terms within it?

It's the Family:

$$\left. \begin{array}{l} \text{Father} \\ \text{Mother} \\ \text{Child} \end{array} \right\} \text{Family}$$

---

[34] *Doctrine des Pythagoriciens. Voyage d'Anarchasis*, vol. III, p.181 1809 edition). [Note: Anarchasis was a renowned Scythian philosopher of the cynics school who voyaged from the Black Sea to Athens in the 6th Century BCE and impressed the cultured scholar with his outspokenness. For example, Plutarch remarked that he "expressed his wonder at the fact that in Greece wise men spoke and fools decided." Although a foreigner, he was granted the rare privilege of becoming an Athenian citizen. – PV].

[35] Fabré d'Olivet, *les vers dorés de Pythagore* [*The Golden Verses of Pythagoras*], New edition. Paris, 1928 (original pub. date not given).

This is the composition of the Quaternary – a Ternary and the Unity which contains it.

When we say a Family, we express in a single word the three terms of which it is composed, that is why the Family restores the 3 to 1, or to speak the language of occult science, the Ternary to Unity.

We believe the explanation that we have just given is easy to follow. However, there are few people who, prior to this example being given, would have been able to understand the following sentence taken from an old Hermetic book: *...in order to reduce the Ternary by means of the Quaternary to the simplicity of the Unity.*[36]

If you understand the foregoing, you will see that 4 is a repetition of unity, and that it must act as unity does.

So, in the creation of 3 by 1 plus 2, how is the 2 formed?

Through unity in opposition to itself, thus: $\frac{1}{1} = 2$.

So, in the progression 1, 2, 3, 4, we see:

First unity 1.

Then an opposition $\frac{1}{1} = 2$.

Then the action of this opposition upon unity: $1 + 2 = 3$

Then the return to a unity of a different order, of another octave, and if we dare to express it thus:

$$\underbrace{\overbrace{1.2.3.}}_{4}$$

What we propose seems understandable to us; however, as knowledge of this progression is one of the most obscure points in occult science, we are going to repeat the example of the family.

The first principle that appears in the family is the Father, the active unity...1

The second principle is the Mother, who represents the passive unity...2

---

[36] R. P. Esprit Sabathier, *L'Ombre idéale de la sagesse universelle* [*The Perfect Obscurity of Universal Wisdom*]. Paris, 1679. New edition, Paris pub. Chamuel, 1897.

The reciprocal action, opposition produces the third term, the Child..3

Finally, everything returns to an active unity in a higher order, the Family...4

This family is going to act as a father, an active principle upon another family: not to give birth to a child, but to give birth to the caste from which is formed a tribe, a unity of a higher order.

Thus, the genesis of numbers may be reduced to these four conditions, and since, using the method of analogy, numbers express ideas exactly, this law is also applicable to ideas.

Here are these four terms:

Unity or return to unity	Opposition Antagonism	Act of opposition upon unity
1	2	3
4	5	6
7	8	9
10	11	12
(1)	(2)	(3)

We have separated the first series from the others to show that it is complete in four terms, and that all of the following terms only repeat the same law in another octave.

Since in this law we will discover one of the greatest keys to unlocking the ancient mysteries, we will explain further by applying it to any particular case of man's social development. For example:

Unity or return to unity	Opposition Antagonism	Action of opposition upon unity
1. The first social molecule – Man.	2. Opposition to this molecule – Woman.	3. Result – Child.
4. Unity in a higher order – the Family, summarizing the three preceding terms.	5. Opposition between families – rivalries between families.	6. Distinction between families. – Castes.

| 7. Unity in a higher order – the Tribe summarizing the three preceding terms | 8. Opposition between Tribes. | 9. Distinction between tribes. – Nationalities. |

This law which we have given in figures – that is to say as a general formula – can be applied to many individual cases.

But did we notice something unusual in those figures? What did the signs placed at the end of our first example mean?

$$\frac{10\ 11\ 12}{(1)\ (2)\ (3)}$$

To understand them, we must say a few words about the operations used by the ancients upon figures.

Two of these operations are vital to know:
1. Theosophical Reduction;
2. Theosophical Addition.

1. **Theosophical Reduction** consists of reducing any numbers formed from two or more digits to numbers with a single figure, which is done by adding the numbers which make up the number until only one remains.

For example: $10 = 1 + 0 = 1 \quad 11 = 1 + 1 = 2 \quad 12 = 1 + 2 = 3$

And for larger compound numbers such as, for example, $3,221 = 3 + 2 + 2 + 1 = 8$, or $666 = 6 + 6 + 6 = 18$ and as $18 = 1 + 8 = 9$, the number 666 equal 9.

From this follows a very important point, which is that all numbers, whatever they may be, are but representations of the first nine digits.

Since the first nine figures, as we saw in the earlier example, are but representations of the first four, all numbers are therefore represented by the first four.

Yet these first four figures are only of various states of unity. All numbers, whatever they may be, are simply various manifestations of unity.

2. **Theosophical Addition** consists of arithmetically summing all the figures from unity up to a particular number, in order to discover the theosophical value of that number.

Thus, in theosophical addition, the figure 4 equals $1 + 2 + 3 + 4 = 10$.

The figure 7 equals $1 + 2 + 3 + 4 + 5 + 6 + 7 = 28$.

28 is reduced immediately by $2 + 8 = 10$.

If you wish to amaze an algebraist, show him the following theosophical operation:

$$4 = 10$$
$$7 = 10$$
$$\text{Therefore } 4 = 7$$

These two operations, theosophical reduction and addition, are not difficult to learn. They are essential to understanding the Hermetic writings and, according to the greatest Masters, represent the path which Nature follows the in her creations.

Let us verify mathematically the sentence we quoted earlier: *Reduce the ternary by the means of the quaternary to the simplicity of unity.*

Ternary = 3   Quaternary = 4

$3 + 4 = 7$

by theosophical reduction. Next,

$7 = 1 + 2 + 3 + 4 + 5 + 6 + 7 = 28. \quad 2 + 8 = 10$

by theosophical addition, and reduction of the total;

Finally: $10 = 1 + 0 = 1$

The operation is written thus:

$$4 + 3 = 7 = 28 = 10 = 1$$
$$4 + 3 = 1$$

Now consider the example of the figures given in the first instance:

1	2	3
4	5	5
7	8	9
(1)	(2)	(3)

and make a few comments on it using theosophical calculations.

We note first that unity is restored, that is to say that the cycle begins again after three progressions $\frac{10}{1}\frac{11}{2}$; 10, 11, 12, etc., reduced theosophically gives rise once more to 1, 2, 3, etc...[37]

These three progressions represent **the three worlds** in which everything is contained.

We note then that the first vertical line 1, 4, 7, 10, which we have considered as representing Unity in various Octaves, does indeed represent this, because:

$1 = 1$
$4 = 1 + 2 + 3 + 4 = 10 = 1$
$7 = 1 + 2 + 3 + 4 + 5 + 6 + 7^{38} = 28 = 10 = 1$
$10 = 1$
$13 = 4 = 10 = 1$
$16 = 7 = 28 = 10 = 1$

We can therefore continue this progression up to infinity and verify those famous mathematical laws, which some will no doubt treat as mysterious because of their lack of understanding of their importance.

We advise those who believe that these are just nebulous daydreams to read the books on Physics and Chemistry by Louis

---

[37] For the application of this law in Moses, see Fabre D'Olivet, *la Langue hébraïque restituée* [*The Hebrew Language Restored*]. Paris, 1928, 2 vols.

[38] The original book contained the typo 7=1+1+2+3+4+5+6+7=28=10+1 (an extra '1'). Interestingly this error has been carried forward into most if not all modern reprints! – PV.

Lucas[39] where they will find the previous law included under the section on 'series' and applied to experimental demonstrations of Chemistry and Biology.

We also suggest to them, if Chemistry and Physics don't appear to be sufficiently indicative to them, to read the mathematical works of Wronski[40] on which the Institute has issued a very favorable report; a book whose principles are entirely derived from ancient knowledge or Occult Science. Here is a table of the generation of numbers which can perfectly explain Wronski's system:

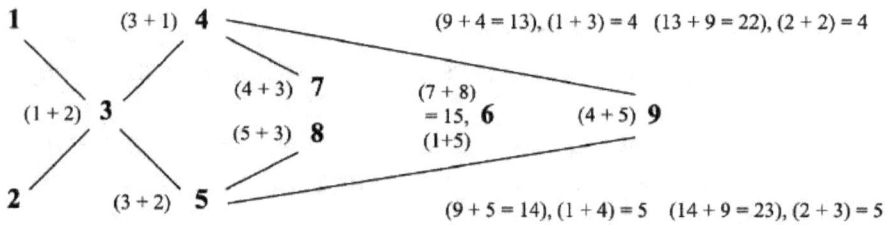

Figure 15.

We see in this table the application of the law of calculation, 1, 2, 3, 4, etc., which we have already discussed at length.

1 and 2 give birth to 3 and from these three numbers come all the others up to 9 according to the same principles. After 9, all numbers whatever they may be, reduce by theosophical reduction to numbers of a single digit.

The remaining numbers are laid out in columns of which there are three main and two secondary ones, indicated by figures of different sizes.

---

[39] Louis Lucas, *La Chimie Nouvelle* [The New Chemistry]. Paris, 1854; *La Médecine Nouvelle* [The New Medicine]. Paris, (undated), 4 vol.
[40] Hoëné, Wronski, *Œuvres mathématiques* [Mathematical Works]. New edition. Paris (undated) 4 vol.

Principal column **1** -- **4** -- (13) **4** -- (22) **4** -- (31) **4**
+
  Secondary column **7** (16) = **7** (25) = **7** (34) = **7**

Principal column **3**----------**6**----------**9**
∞
  Secondary column **8** (17) = **8** (26) = **8** (35) = **8**
Principal column **2** -- **5** -- (14) = **5** -- (23) = **5** -- (32) = **5**[41]

Continuing and extending considerably the study that we have outlined here, F. Ch. Barlet was able to establish the following table, which can be considered as a *definitive key* to the numerical system.

Figure 16: Key to the Numerical System.

---

[41] Curiously, the progressions extend beyond the figures in Wronski's diagram, and this is the case in the original books as well. For example, the top principal column in the diagram only goes as far as **1** – **4** – (13) – **4** – (22) – **4**, yet Papus includes – (31) **4**. This is no doubt to cover all the possibilities of theosophical addition for 4, which are 1+3, 2+2 and 3+1 – PV.

One point of view concerning the *physiology* of numbers is the action of a Number-Being on another Number-Being; an action contained in the calculation of all the degrees and especially in the four major operations: going from unity to multiplicity by a line – or addition; going from the square (of Pythagoras) – or simple multiplication, going from the cube – or cubic multiplication; it is by that route that the Number-Being passes from one plane to another.

3 belongs to the plane of Spirits; 3 x 3 or 3^2 belongs to the plane of Astral Forces; 3 x 3 x 3 or 3^3 belongs to the plane of Matter.

For the first works on the line, the second (3^2) on the plane and the third (3^3) on the solid.

The return from multiplicity to unity is accomplished by subtraction, by division, or by the square or cube root, depending on the planes.

This, then, is the actual and vivid portrayal of that famous evolution and that mysterious involution.

After this first classification of numbers by their component figures, we come to see the representation of the polarities or the sexes. This representation is effected by the existence of even or feminine numbers, and odd or masculine numbers.[42]

Examples of masculine numbers: 1-3-5-7-9.

Examples of feminine numbers: 2-4-6-8-10.

Next, let us note a property of the figure 0, which is to make a figure even when appearing in numbers which are essentially odd: thus 3 is odd or masculine, while 30 becomes even and feminine.

The quality of even numbers doesn't change with the appearance of the 0: thus 4, an even number, remains even when it becomes 40.

Two even numbers joined together result in an even number: 2 and 2 give 22, 6 and 6 give 66; and all these numbers are even.

---

[42] According to Lacuria, masculine and feminine are synonyms of positive and negative. The positive is the first, and negative only occurs as a complement; when the feminine appears, they are two and the being is complete (*Les Harmonies de l'Être*) [The Harmonies of Being], vol. II~ p. 302).

Two odd numbers joined together also give rise to an odd number: 3, an odd number, and 7, also an odd number, give 37 or 73, both odd numbers.

The union (in juxtaposition and not in addition) of an even number with an odd number is determined by the last digit. Thus 3 (odd) and 2 (even) give the even number 32 when the 2 ends, and the odd number 23 when it is the 3 which takes last place.

Another application concerns the numbers called sympathetic or, to speak in images, Soul-Sisters in numbers.

To obtain the sympathetic number of any number of two figures, you simply have to reverse the order of those figures.

Thus, the odd number 13 has the number 31 as its sympathetic number, which is also odd, obtained by reversing the two figures 1 and 3.

Similarly, the even number 24 has the even number 42 as its sympathetic number, obtained in the same way.

However, some numbers which are formed from two identical figures are only seen under a single aspect: these are called selfish numbers, and they are the ones which represent neuter in the numerical hierarchy.

Examples of selfish odd and even numbers include 11, 22, 33, 44, 55, etc.

Numbers are more charged with enlightening power if they are closer to unity and have less light if they are more distant from unity; in other words, the smaller a number is in numeric value the greater it is in actual value, the number one being the most powerful of all.

The geometric or figurative representation of a number can itself give us the key to the "fields of forces" brought to bear, and their system of equilibrium for each number.

As an example, consider the number 3, which has a written representation as '3' and a geometric representation as a triangle. Now, the figure is always identical and one 3 doesn't differ at all from another 3 when written; while the triangle can be either equilateral or rectangular, and indeed shows us by this the different functions in the lines of force generated by the same number.

We now turn to the third aspect of the constitution of Numbers.

§ 3
Psychology

The *psychology* of Numbers reveals to us their action in the Universe, and the character and origin of that action; knowledge which can lead its possessor to effectively manipulate the little-known Power contained in numbers. This is the essence of the *Shemhamphorash* and the truly practical key to the Kabbalah, and this is a truth which must remain forever closed to the profane and to profanators. One can, if one knows the number of each human faculty, act upon that faculty to the level that one acts on the corresponding Number-Being. The Tarot and the subject of Astrology are true applications of this knowledge.

For a study of this subject, we can do no better than to reproduce a masterly work by F. Ch. Barlet, which deals with this question from the ontological and purely initiatory point of view. This study is entitled : *Les Nombres*.[43]

Number is a language, specific to what philosophy calls Ontology, or the Science of Being.

Its alphabet is the series of the first nine Numbers, supplemented by the zero. To understand this definition and this alphabet, we must go back to the idea of Being which Number should explain.

Being, in itself, has neither form nor limit, it is *Infinity*.

To conceive our real world, that infinity is dual: it is as infinitely large as the celestial space which extends around us; it is as infinitely small as the mathematical point which we realize by our perfect points, that is to say by the intersection of three concurrent planes.

Therefore, we can represent it materially and in reality, in its dual conception, as a mathematical point in infinite space. That is the image given to it by Pythagoras, and which Pascal repeated in his famous formula.

---

[43] Taken from *La Revue Mysteria*, December 12, 1913, pp. 215 – 229.

But we should add that this mathematical point isn't *Nothingness*; we should represent it as the extreme condensation of the whole Universe and containing within itself all the energy belonging to it, of whatever nature that might be. It is total Potentiality, the Almighty in action.

Nor is space *Nothingness*. Nothingness truly is a reality, perhaps even the most certain and the most undeniable for us: it is the All-Incapacity to create; it is emptiness, Being reduced to the single ability to contain, to receive. It is the *Power to Be*.

Point and space are inseparable: so, the point must be somewhere, since it must exist.

It is true that, on the contrary, we can conceive as an equally possible reality the Almighty expanding throughout infinite space and therefore rendered void by the latter. The roles are then reversed: the Almighty has become All-Impotent with the single ability of being condensed, and Space has become the Almighty to condense, reduce, cancel the All that it contains to return to Emptiness, to *annihilate* the manifestation of Power: in a phrase, the *All Resistance*.

But regardless of which of the two approaches[44] one adopts, it always defines the Absolute Being as the duality of the Infinitely Small immersed in the Infinitely Large. It is the only possible image for us since we are enclosed in the *real world* where everything is dual; and here each of the two infinites appears dual: infinite in Power if it is nothing in space, and vice versa (or the reverse if the Power fills space).

And isn't the Absolute what we call Being? The Absolute is only conceivable to us through its two poles, we know nothing more about it; what we ordinarily call *a Being* is the combination of those two poles: *zero* and *Infinity*.

---

[44] Not only what are possible designs: but it is very likely that these are realities that succeed one another by alternating periods, as all traditions affirm (*pralaya*, end of the world, etc…)

Everybody knows the mathematical demonstration summarized in the formula $0 \times \infty = 1$. Any number, any reality, any individual is the product of zero multiplied by Infinity.[45]

Extending this concept up to these extreme limits, we call *Being* above all the maximum of this individual, and *Non-Being* his minimum; that is to say, the two values of the actual quantity which come into contact with the poles of the Absolute.

The expression Non-Being doesn't mean Nothingness, or impossibility, but on the contrary, that which, not yet being, is in power of Being. As to Nothingness itself, it is for us a design as impossible as that of the Absolute, if not even more impossible.

There are, therefore, *three essential Numbers* above everything: the *Infinite*, *Zero* and *One*, their product.

We will set aside the first two, for only the last one should concern us. In it we will find the source of all the *Numbers*, or individual beings.

ONE

We call *One* any real being examined in itself, in its essence, in what distinguishes it from all other beings, in what makes it an *individuality*, something which the mind cannot dissect further, even if that something is clothed in a multiple form, which is usual.

One can have an infinite number of varieties which, as we have just said, approach one or the other pole of the Absolute to a greater or lesser extent, up to making contact with one of those poles.

One therefore sees three kinds of *One*: the two extremes, and all the values in between, which are infinite in number.

---

[45] The problem is, this doesn't mean anything mathematically since it is a fallacy to introduce a concept into a numerical equation, and ∞ is a concept, not a number. So, it can only really stand as a philosophical argument (although Measure Theory seems to suggest that the result of multiplying 0 by infinity can result in any value you like, which is what this passage is saying). But then, here we are dealing with theosophical arithmetic, of course, where '1' represents Unity or the source of everything. Thus, the Almighty is the product of the impossibly small and the infinitely large – PV.

The two extremes are: on the one hand, that which, without ceasing to be real, can fill the whole range, the entirety of all the differences between the two poles; and on the other hand, that which, on the contrary, is small enough to leave the entire interval between the poles empty; in other words, they are the *All* and the *Nothing*.

They are also called – which is really an abuse of language, but which is not so much of an issue once the definition is given – *Being* and *Nothingness* (or Non-Being). In fact, they differ from the poles of the Absolute which were given the same names earlier, in that these extreme forms of *One* can give rise to reality and belong to it. For us they are like the place of those poles, whose reverse is on the side of the Absolute.

They are also more properly called *Absolute One*, and *Absolute Zero* (i.e., what reaches the limits of the real).

Pythagoras carefully distinguished this *Absolute One* from the *Real One*, or the essence of any individual. By the definition itself it has two poles: one Infinite, the other nothing.

The Almighty pole of the Absolute One is the Being that we call *God*.

The non-being pole of the Absolute One is what we call *Nothing*, or often, *Nothingness*.

Every finished being is a combination of these two poles of the Absolute One, and as Nothing is essentially incapable of giving rise to being, it is the latter, Nothing, which *receives* the Absolute One in order to form the individual One.

It is therefore true that *God* has created all things from nothing, as the Bible says; it couldn't give any other definition for man's birth without falling into the conflicting systems of Emanation, Pantheism or Naturalism.

In any completed being, the element of infinite nature which animates it is, in our case, what we call *Spirit*. In relation to God, we call it the *Word*, because it is the particular thought which God brings about through creation; its form is *expression*, the externalization of that thought.

Thus, all beings are made by the Word, and without it, everything which has been made would not be (St. John's Gospel, Ch. I).

The first act of creation is the extension of the pole of *Being* to the Pole of *Non-Being*, in order to combine with it: that is the manifestation of the Absolute One. We call this joining together the Celestial *Virgin* like the Tradition throughout all times: the Virgin is a Creature[46] and the first of Creatures.

The Word which animates it is the total Divine Thought since it fills the entire interval between the two poles. This spirit of the Virgin we call *Wisdom*: she is that Absolute Wisdom which witnessed the whole creative formation from the dawn of the first day. She rules as the Virgin in her function as informant, nurturer and protector of secondary beings, a function in which role we call her *Nature*.

TWO

"No One Without Two" is a well-known saying. In effect the individual One, of whatever kind, is the product of the Infinite through zero, and is different from both of them; it only fills a portion of the interval between them; its existence therefore presupposes a surplus of that quantity; and that surplus is its *Two*. In other words, an individual exists only on the condition of differentiating itself from everything which it isn't.

Now normally we have a different concept of the Number Two: we understand it as the being composed by the addition of a Unity to another Unity to make a new All.

In fact, this concept is still that of the One, that is to say, the partial extension of one of the two poles towards one another; only the movement is decomposed into equal parts, which are like so many distinct steps. The result is always a One (it could be formulated as $1 = 0 \times \infty + 0 \times \infty$). The concept obtained by this

---

[46] Or 'Human and the first of Humans'. The word *'créature'* can mean 'creature', but when used in comparison to God it normally translates as 'man'. Note also that the word 'creature' is descended from the root notion of 'creation' – PV.

distinction is rather one of complexity and succession; in other words, that of *Measure* and *Time*; it falls under the domain of Arithmetic whereas we are in the realm of the *Science of Numbers*[47].

This remark applies to all numbers other than Unity and is the principle of all additive operations (addition, multiplication, power, etc.).

However, this arithmetical consideration of Two assumes and includes another Arithmological definition of this number:

To see two or more parts in a complex number, we must begin by decomposing it: that is what we do in the *arithmetic operation* of subtraction and its derivatives (subtraction, division, root, etc.). However, this separation is done by means of the power of the *negative number* (that terror of the beginner algebraist), and with that Number we return to Arithmology: a negative Number is what, by its nature, has a subtractive property. For example, a quantity of ice added to hot water is a negative quantity, since it cools the water again.

We can state this more clearly: a negative number is one which, when added to a Unity, makes the *Two* appear, or increases the *Arithmological Two* we just defined.

We must conclude that *Negative Unity* is a Two, and an inverse Two to that defined above (we can write $1 = \infty \times 0$, instead of $1 = 0 \times \infty$), because it tends toward the zero instead to tending toward ∞.

It is the principle of dissection, decomposition, negation; it is also the number of opposition through separation, and as a result, the number of Evil and discord.

When it is opposed to a Positive One, it becomes the model of the impossible (whose mathematical expression is $\sqrt{-n^2}$). Then it is called the Devil (διαβολοσ), the divider, the letter D and its analogues (t, tz, z…) being signs of division.

On the other hand, the Positive Two can have two forms, depending on whether it is counted from one or the other pole. We call it male if it touches the positive pole; feminine, if it relates to

---

[47] Also known as 'arithmology' – PV.

the negative one. For example, an Angel, a minister of God is, in relation to Him a masculine Two; Nature in relation to Virgin Wisdom is feminine; but that distinction is less profound than the previous one.

To summarize we can define Two as the *relative complement* of *One*; and that this One can either be an Absolute One or an individual One.

THREE

"No One Without Two" is not the complete saying; we must add *"No Two without Three"*. And stated thus, this saying is the very definition of Three

The One and the Two have only been separated in Divine Thought, as they are in the two poles of the Absolute, in order to give rise to Love, through that agreement and assent which joins them together once again in the new unadorned Unity, where each becomes the life of the other. It is this what Christianity is expressing, when it tells us that God created the World so that it might participate in His own Blessedness, on condition that He accepts it and to the extent that He accepts it.

The three is the *spark of Union which restores Unity between the One and the complementary Two, by bringing them together in itself and by penetrating both with its essence, which is insurmountable indivisibility.*

It differs from the One and the Two in that it has no complement, no possible contrast; it escapes any measure, any variation, any formal externalization: it is pure Spirit; it is the very essence of *Being*. Only the individual, a completed One may accept or refuse it in its varying proportions; its perception is a variable subjectivity to man, otherwise that love would become tyranny.

There is the source of evil, alongside that of Freedom; revolt against the *Holy Spirit* (which is the three) is the only one that, by definition, God *can* forgive, since it is the free refusal of His love.[48]

In penetrating the One and the Two in order to unite them, He identifies with each of them in a way, in order to gather them into Himself. Pythagoras calls it a *Hermaphroditic Unity*.

For the Absolute One and Two, the union so formed is a *Tri-unity*. Such is the Christian Father, Son and Holy Spirit, which expresses the notion that the Word, in His creative and multiplicative descent, is inseparable from the Father.

As the One and Two are susceptible to *quantity*, their tri-unitary union is too, but in their absolute quality, this partial union is always one; it corresponds to the current state of the eternal and progressive Union of the two extreme poles; it is always harmonious: such is the generation of the celestial powers (theogony, generation of the gods, the angels, etc.) and the creations of Nature.

But when it comes to creatures endowed with will and initiative or primordial beings, which are only partly accessible to the Spirit of Unity, these beings can produce nothing whole without borrowing Unity from Nature by decomposing prior individuals (either their own or others foreign to themselves), and their more or less inharmonious creations are subject to Death. Then their union is expressed by a special Trinity, that *generative* power perfectly characterized by the popular Trinity of India: *Brahma*, the creator; *Shiva* the destroyer, agent of division, and of the decomposition necessary for new creation, as well as for the reduction of its imperfections; and *Vishnu* who maintains harmony. We also see it in our Trinity: *Father, Mother, Child*. It is never a Tri-Unity.

---

[48] For the law of free will is sovereign, and if God were to force man to accept anything – even His love – he would by definition deny free will and man would become His slave – PV.

Transition to Other Numbers

Not only is the Three triple in order to accomplish its unifying function, as has just been said, but it also realizes a ternary arrangement in the other two Numbers. It must, in effect:

1. cause One to unite with Two through a kind of polarization towards it;
2. take it into its essential unity, as an intermediate term;
3. cause it to penetrate the Two along with the One, in order to create the complete union. It also entails the same series of provisions within the Two, and it is through this that the union is accomplished by reciprocal penetration.

Thus, for the creative union of the Absolute One with Two, of the Creator with the Celestial Virgin, the Spirit of Unity, of Love, the original source of all creation, first makes One a *Cause* of realization: first comes His thought, His Word within him; next it creates a *Means*, a *Possibility*, the plan of creation itself to manifest His thought; and third, the source of effectiveness of the *End*, the *Power* over the inertia of Non-Being. These are so many stages in the Word's descent in His sacrifice of love.

On the other side, in the heart of Nature, He dispenses *Intelligence*, capable of receiving the Divine Thought; He gives the *Idea* of the form that can respond to the plan of the Word; and the *Energy* which will fulfill and maintain the resulting form.

That is why St. John also said in his Epistle: "There are three which bear record in heaven: the *Father*, the *Son* and the *Holy Spirit*;...and three which bear witness on Earth, the *Spirit* (Intelligence), the *Water* (Idea of form), and the *Blood* (Energy)." It is also what is symbolized by the *Seal of Solomon*.

Out of this arise several consequences:

Firstly, there will be three phases in creation, and therefore three classes of creatures: the Divine Plane or Divine Realm of Thought, that of the *One*; the Middle Plane, that of transition, or the Middle Realm, that which is *Intelligible*, and that of the law; and the Plane of *Execution*, of the possibility of becoming real – that is to say, tri-unitary, the Realm of Forms.[49]

Secondly, the existence or rather the operation of the Three immediately leads to the existence and operation of the Six: they are concurrent because of the original polarization and its purpose, so in a way we can say: "Not One without Two, not Two without Three, not Three without Six."

Finally, not only does the existence of the Spirit of Unity involve that of Six, but the creative purpose which is its reason for existence and the reason for creation involves a third Trinity. It is not enough, in fact, that the Two has been enabled in order to bring about the final realization or union: in its own turn, it must execute it through its own efforts. To each of the faculties just described, as being received by the Two of the Spirit of Unity, is added its own active ability, which is awakened.

To Intelligence is added Love, Attraction and *Desire*, the source of all evolution.

To the Idea is added *Will*, the decision to produce the appropriate form to that sentiment.

To Energy is added *Movement*, the product of Desire and Will, the actual occupation of space by *extent*.

There are therefore Three trinities necessary for Creation and not only Two.

Thus, the sole existence of One which leads to that of Two also necessitates that of Nine Numbers in total. That is why Pythagoras and the Ancients said there is *only one Number*, which is written: 0, 1, 2, 3, 4, 5, 6, 7, 8, 9. Any other is not truly a number, but a compound made of *The Number* repeated more or less: this series alone is *The Number*.

Only two division were distinguished by them:

1. The Trinity, the fundamental element of this series; and
2. The six numbers which follow, *duplicata* of the Trinity.

The first included the Numbers called *Ideal* (1, 2, 3), and the second series (4, 5, 6, 7, 8, 9) was that of the *Mathematical*

---

[49] Compare this to Saint-Martin's fascination with Thought, Will and Action – PV.

Numbers; as for all the other possible numbers, they were collected under the term *Complex Numbers*. The ten which summarized them in expressing the Union accomplished by the two poles was the *Perfect Number*.

That is the reason for the decimal system of numbering.

That is the great thunderbolt of Creation symbolized by the Tree of the Sephiroth.

The Numbers other than the One, the 2, the 3, the 6 and the 9, are distributed in the three trinities to play the role corresponding to their rank, by analogy to the original trinity, according to the table:

$$\begin{array}{ccc} 1 & 2 & 3 \\ 4 & 5 & 6 \\ 7 & 8 & 9 \end{array}$$

That is the key to their respective meanings.

Those in the first column, having the function of One or of *Being*, are called *Divine*; those of the third column, having the function of Two born of *Non-Being*, are called *Natural*; as for the others, they are called *Voluntary* or Psychic, because it is to them that belongs pronouncement on the acceptance or refusal of the Union of love and, consequently, of the Holy Spirit. It is in them that is the root of Evil; it has already been seen in Two; it is much more in *Five*, the middle of the table above.[50]

It will suffice to quickly review these arithmetic Numbers to give an idea.

The *Four*, leader of the Second Trinity, the second One is the Second Hypostasis of the Word: *Deus de Deo, Lumen de Lumine, Deus verus de Deo Vero, ex Patre natus, ante omnia secula*[51], the revealer of the Divine Thought.

The *Five*, Word of this Trinity, is the Source of all Real Power, free and accountable: Elohim, Adam Kadmon.

---

[50] Again, note the similarity of treatment of these two numbers 2 and 5 to that of Saint-Martin and Pasqually, even if the arguments cited are slightly different – PV.

[51] Part of the Latin Credo: "God of God, Light of Light, Very God of Very God ... begotten of the Father before all worlds" – PV.

The *Six*, Spirit of Unity in this Second Trinity, is above all the *Nature Naturante*, the Beauty of Form.

The *Seven* is the leader of the Third Trinity, that of the first realization. It is the vivifying Spiritual Power, the Council of God (according to Saint-Yves), the pagan Olympus individualized into seven guiding Principles.

The *Eight* (the third Two) is the number which rules Will, the Number of the law, and therefore of Destiny and Death.

Finally, the *Nine*, the harmony of that Trinity, is the Power of Virtue, the Blessing of the harmonic forms.

These are, however, only very summarized directions, for each Number requires a study which as more profound as it is detailed, because each has far more different meanings than unities.

In a few pages, this presentation by F. Ch. Barlet gives us a penetrating summary of the traditional doctrine of Numbers and shows us what profound philosophy they reflected – and still reflect – in the eyes of Initiates. Next we will see profane mathematics make their contribution to the study we are undertaking.

Chapter 5

The Theory of Numbers

We know that a subtle, yet real link joins the *Science of Numbers* to official mathematics. This section on the results of writing the natural sequence of numbers in three columns will allow us to follow the chain[52].

Occult education teaches us that all numbers are reduced to the first three. The 4, which brings the ternary back to unity, renews the 1; the new ternary, 4, 5, 6, renews the first one – 1, 2, 3 – and so on, so that the indefinite series of numbers can be written as:

$$\begin{array}{ccc} 1 & 2 & 3 \\ 4 & 5 & 6 \\ 7 & 8 & 9 \\ 10 & 11 & 12\ldots \end{array}$$

All the numbers in the first column lead back to 1; those in the second to 2; and those in the third to 3. These are the *types* of numbers. And in this series of ternaries, of trinities, all the numbers in the first column play the role of the first term, those in the last of the third term, and those in the second of the median term.

The operations by which a number however large, is taken back to its type, are Theosophical Reduction and Theosophical Addition. Thus, 4 gives:

$1 + 2 + 3 + 4 = 10$ by theosophical addition....

And: $10 = 1$ by theosophical reduction...

And the same for all the others.

---

[52] This note by Mr. X***, S.I. is taken from the review *l'Initiation*, No. 9, June 1898, pp. 212 – 217. [Note: S.I. means Supérieur Inconnu, or Unknown Superior, title of the Third Grade in Martinism – PV.]

*
* *

However, in making calculations of this kind, we have been struck by an irregularity in the numbers of the second type.

Take 5, for example. We find:

$$1 + 2 + 3 + 4 + 5 = 15$$

and 15 is a number of the third type, leading to column 3 and not to 2.

It can be seen that by Theosophical Addition 5 changes class. It is the same for 2, 8, etc.

By contrast, Theosophical Reduction still leaves a number in its class.

Thus:

$$14 = 1 + 4 = 5$$

As we reflect on this apparent anomaly, we had the idea of trying out raising the number to its square, and obtained the following results:

$$2 \times 2 = 4$$
$$5 \times 5 = 25 = 2 + 5 = 7$$

It can therefore be seen that raising a number to its square moves a number of the second type to the first type. Here is the set of operations on a single number. We have taken 11 as being the smallest number of type 2 which has more than one digit (in order to show Theosophical Reduction at the same time).

Theos. Addition: $1 + 2 + 3 \ldots + 10 + 11 = 66 = 12 = 3$
Theos. Reduction: $1 + 1 = 2$
Square: $11 \times 11 = 121 = 4 = 1$

It therefore appears that number 11, while shown to be equivalent to 2 by its place in the columns and by Theosophical

Reduction, is polarized in the other two operations, passing to the first type by the elevation to the square and the third type by Theosophical Addition.

*
* *

We will recall that Theosophical Addition serves the precise purpose of finding the *essential root* of a number. It is like an ascent of the number towards the spirit; whereas the formation of the square is a descent into matter.

But we must leave to men more educated than us the task of discovering the rationale behind a fact which has struck us in passing. We note only that there seems to be new evidence that in any trinity the second term is of a double essence, and can, in splitting, stretch at the same time toward the two extremes it unites. We felt that we should report this fact, probably already known, but on which we have found no mention anywhere.

*
* *

To avoid people having to perform long calculations in order to validate the point we have just made, we will give the mathematical verification.

It is known that in high arithmetic, the sum of a certain quantity of numbers departing from unity forms what is called a triangular number.

The diagram above is both the sum of the first five numbers, and a triangle with sides of 5.

We have placed it next to the diagram of a square.

THEORY

Now, the formula of triangular numbers is:
$$\frac{n \times (n+1)}{2}$$

That of square numbers: $n \times n$

n being the side of either the triangle or the square.[53] On the other hand, the numbers of the three series have the general forms:

$3m + 1$ for the first type
$3m - 1$ for the second type
$3m \times 1$ for the third type

That is to say, a multiple of 3 increased by a unit, a multiple of 3 decreased by a unit, and a multiple of 3.[54]

One only has to see what happens with these three types of formulas above.

Triangular number
1ˢᵗ type

$$\frac{(3m+2) \times (3m+2)}{2} = \frac{9m^2 + 9m + 2}{2} = \text{mult. of } 3 + 1$$

2ⁿᵈ type

$$\frac{(3m+1) \times 3m}{2} = \text{mult. of } 3$$

3ʳᵈ type

$$\frac{3m \times (3+1)}{2} = \text{mult. of } 3$$

Square Number

---

[53] Therefore in this example with a triangle of side 5: $5 \times (5+1)/2 = 15$, the number of dots in the triangle; while $5 \times 5 = 25$, the number of dots in the square – PV.

[54] This works for types 2 and 3 but type 1 seems to end up in the following row! For example, if we take row 1: $3 \times 1 + 1 = 4$, $3 \times 1 - 1 = 2$, $3 \times 1 \times 1 = 3$. And for row 2: $3 \times 2 + 1 = 7$, $3 \times 2 - 1 = 5$, $3 \times 2 \times 1 = 6$. So, in each case the value in the second or third column works, but the value of the first column is the figure in the following row – PV.

1st type

$$(3m + 1) \times (3m + 1) = 9m^2 + 6m + 1 = \text{mult. of } 3 + 1$$

2nd type

$$(3m - 1) \times (3m - 1) = 9m^2 - 6m + 1 = \text{mult. of } 3 + 1$$

3rd type

$$3m \times 3m = 9m^2 = \text{mult. of } 3$$

In conclusion, we note that another operation, raising to the cube, leaves the numbers in the second column intact – that is, they remain in their type:

$$2 \times 2 \times 2 = 8$$
$$5 \times 5 \times 5 = 125 = 8$$

And algebraically:

$$(3m - 1)^3 = (3m)^3 - 3(3m)^2 + 3 \times 3m - 1$$
$$= \text{mult. of } 3 - 1.$$

We can say that this ends the theoretical part of our study. We have examined the constitution of the primordial numbers, their physiology, their connection with the three planes of the Universe, their philosophy and their symbolism. We are therefore now in a position to address the practical part of the science, and to do this we must first consider the material representation of numbers; that is, figures.

Chapter 6
Figures

We have seen that Number is a real being; but its body, its material vestment, "the figure" can threaten to overwhelm us and, because of this, we must stop to focus on it for a moment.

Here is an excerpt from the *Grande Encyclopédie* which will very adequately educate our readers on this subject:

"Arab figures are the technical designation of the ten characters 1, 2, 3, 4, 5, 6, 7, 8, 9 and 0, as opposed to the numerical symbols called Roman figures. It would be preferable to say modern figures, since in the proper sense Arabic numerals are those used by Arabs, whose form differs significantly from ours. Moreover, the representation of figures, as they have been adopted nowadays by all civilized European Nations, has only been universally fixed since the invention of the printing press. In Western manuscripts of the Middle Ages, depending upon the period and the country, we find many variations which haven't yet been adequately determined and classified, and of which there is still a trace visible in the secondary form of the written 5.[55]

Figure 17: From a 12th Century manuscript by Thott.

---

[55] Although not in the original book, I have included an image of medieval counting to give a sense of how there were two versions of 5 in those days – a second form more familiar to us and a first form which looks more like a 'y'. Even now, many European countries write a '1' with a long serif to the left which can sometimes extend to the base, and lead to it being confused with a '7', which is why a crossbar is normally put through the 7. Also, we have two common variations for the number '4', either closing the top by writing it in one stroke (as in Fig. 17 above) or leaving the top open by writing an 'L' shape and then a downward stroke through the base of the 'L' – PV.

"The exact time that digits were introduced into the West isn't known: the most ancient manuscripts in which they are found don't seem to go back beyond the 11th Century. In all cases, the more archaic form is known by the term: the 'Apices of Boethius'[56], because it is found in the Geometry attributed to that author, but which is in fact the work of a forger whose age is also unknown, and which cannot be written earlier than the 9th Century. According to this writer's story, the nine significant figures would be a Pythagorean invention, linked to that of the abacus. And Pseudo-Boethius doesn't provide the rules of calculation. Those are found in the works of Gerbert (*Liber abaci* by his student Bernelinus)[57], but it has not been established that Gerbert ever used the figures described by Boethius; instead, he appears to have used tokens exclusively marked with Roman figures. The true origin of the abacus used in the Middle Ages is also unknown, since it was quite different to those used in antiquity, and nobody has discovered anything similar to it in earlier history. The written numbering system we are discussing was only introduced into the West as a result of the translation into Latin (probably by Adelard of Bath, around 1120) of the *Treatise on Calculation* by Mohamed ibn Musa al-Khwarizmi, whose name (Algorithmi[58], algorithm) passed into the school of the new method of calculation which it explained. It was therefore only in the 12th Century that the zero

---

[56] Page 14 of *A History of Elementary Mathematics With Hints on Methods of Teaching* by Florian Cajori, pub. The MacMillan company, New York, 1905 gives an interesting window into theory on the origins of figures by an American contemporary of Papus. It explains how Boethius, a 6th Century CE writer, attributing the abacus to the Pythagoreans (which used stones to count), instead employed 'apices' (plural of the word 'apex'), or small cones, each bearing one of the 9 digits upon it. However, Cajori is quoting this story anecdotally, and continues to explain how these early theories had been superseded in the meantime by such writers as Woepcke, also mentioned in the *Grande Encyclopédie* quoted by Papus. Indeed, the Encyclopedic quotation is so close to Cajori's book, one might be tempted to wonder if one document 'borrowed' from the other! – PV.
[57] Gerbert was a Frenchman born in the 10th Century, who went on to become Pope Sylvester II. A remarkable man, his knowledge of mathematics was legendary, and he improved on the abacus by creating the version which uses beads for counting, with which we are familiar today. A decent short biography can be found in the work of Cajori (op. cit.) – PV.
[58] The Latinized miswriting of his name in early times – PV.

actually became known in Europe under the name of figure[59] (sifr, etc., a transcription of its Arabic designation which means empty): This word has since been wrongly extended to other numerical signs. Whatever has been said about Pseudo-Boethius, it is very likely that those signs, already known for one or two Centuries and used by abacists, had been borrowed from the Western Arabs, including the figures called 'gobar'[60], and indeed they have a physical similarity to the apices, whereas those of Eastern Arabs are significantly different. The Greeks remained faithful to the ancient traditions far longer than the Latins; their system of alphabetical counting was in any case infinitely superior to that of the Romans. However, figures similar to those of the Eastern Arabs were already appearing in Greek mathematical manuscripts by the 12th Century. But the true role of the zero is not yet known. According to a marginal note by Neophytos the monk, each figure should be surmounted by a number of small circles equal to the exponent of the power of 10 which multiplies it. This system is found actually used by elementary Arab authors to facilitate their teaching, and it was even thought for a long time that it was a form of special enumeration, which used 'gobar' figures. Woepcke has demonstrated that this opinion is incorrect.

"The Latins imported their figures to Constantinople in the 13th Century, and they continued alongside the Arabic or Persian forms (adopted by Maxime Planude in his *Treatise on Hindu Calculation*, written around 1300). This latter title indicates the true origin of figures, also unanimously recognized by all the Eastern authors. After first creating an alphabetical system in imitation of that of the Greeks, which was long continued for astronomical calculations, the Arabs learned the Hindu method of counting around the second half of the 8th Century. At the beginning of the 9th Century al-Khwarizmi marks the period of its final adoption. In the present state of study, it is difficult to investigate the origin of figures in more detail, as in India there are

---

[59] This comment works better in French, where the word 'figure' is 'chiffre', which is rather closer to 'sifr' or 'cipher' – PV.
[60] For an explanation of 'Gobar' versus 'Devanagari (Hindu) numerals, see Cajori p. 14 (op. cit.) Incidentally, later editions published by MacMillan – in 1908, for example – considerably expanded on the historical section – PV.

now a dozen variations which all differ in varying degrees from the forms adopted by the Arabs of the East or West. But if it can be said that by the end of the 5th Century the Hindu mathematician Aryabhata already knew the numeration of position we do not know the forms commonly used at that time and the date of their invention. And so, conjecture used to deduce the original forms of our initial figures, being Sanskrit words, therefore lacks any true foundation. On the other hand, epigraphic research has so far only provided documents which are not decisive, when bringing us up to around the 12th Century CE. Many scholars (Woepcke, Th.-H. Martin, M. Cantor) have supported the truth of the story of the Geometria of Boethius and tried to reconcile it, through various hypotheses, with other facts relating to the transmission of figures. They would indeed have been known to the Neo-Pythagoreans (without the zero for calculation on the abacus): either that they had been invented by borrowing in part the numerical signs of hieratic Egyptian writing, and that, from Alexandria, those figures had passed into India by means of trade; or, on the contrary, that the Neo-Pythagoreans had directly adopted signs already in use in India. The abacus and figures passed on to Rome as well as to Roman Africa, where Arabs would have found them during their conquests. From that the apices of Boethius on the one hand, and the figures of 'gobar' on the other would have come to them; while the Eastern Arabs found similar symbols in India, but this time with the zero, which in any case would be a Hindu invention... As attractive as these assumptions are in various respects, and although, as our knowledge currently stands, they aren't an absolute impossibility, they are based on far too much uncertainty to be accepted as valid.

"As to the origin of the curious names which accompanied the apices in the manuscripts, this has given rise to numerous dissertations. One (Vincent) notably attempted to discover Greek words in them, and thus support the thesis of a Neo-Pythagorean origin. Although several of the proposed etymologies are unacceptable, it is certain that thanks to the rich mystical synonymy of Pythagoreans for the numbers in the decade, this is still the easiest way to explain all these names in totality, although two of them at least – 4 and 8 – directly represent the Semitic roots of the names of these numbers.[61] But such research is illusory, as are all etymological attempts when they don't have sufficient elements of proof; in this instance, it would be essential to begin by discovering the names in the form from which they had been transcribed. That form is certainly Semitic; it may either be Arabic or Hebrew, because it is quite likely that the Jews had been more or less active agents in the transmission of figures. It is also very possible that the names in question were only attributed to figures in an accidental manner. They might simply represent the conventional designations of a secret jargon used by merchants, or perhaps by astrologers. We will add two crucial remarks: the relationship between various types of figures can often be hidden by inexplicable anomalies; it is certain, however, that each Nation has modified theirs by bringing them more in line with the characters in their writing. This fact is very visible among the Eastern Arabs, as well as among the Byzantine Greeks, and the apices of Boethius have certainly suffered from influences of this kind. The invention of the first nine figures is scientifically a secondary fact relative to that of zero. However, if indeed the application of this latter symbol to the system of numeration appears to be thanks to the Hindus, we must not be forget that, at the beginning of the 2nd Century BCE, following their adoption of a sexagesimal numbering system for the division of the circle, the Greeks (according to Hypsicles) employed the zero in their manuscripts to replace missing orders. Sexagesimal division goes back to the Babylonians, and although very ancient monuments (the Tablet of Senkerch) have proved this to us, no trace of the zero appears, so it seems unlikely that they had ever received it from them."

---

[61] The Greek for the contemporary numbers 4 and 8 are tessera (τεσσερα) and octo (οκτω) respectively. Since early Hebrew used letters to denote numbers, 4 and 8 are daleth (ד) and cheth (ח), and since we know that the early Greeks also used letters to denote numbers, we may remark that the 4th and 8th letter of the Greek alphabet are delta (Δ) and theta (θ), which are much closer in sound to the Hebrew – PV.

On the other hand, if we adopt the opinion of the scholar and profound occultist, Marius Decrespe:

"The forms of those figures that we know are neither Hindu nor Arab figures are derived from prototypes. By what mechanism, as a result of what ethnic revolution did this take place? That, we are unable to say. In the collection of Hindu figures, the 2, the 3, the 6 and the 9 alone reflect our current forms; the 9 seems to have been turned around; the 4 has the shape of our 8; the 7 looks like our 6; the 5 and the 8 bear no relation to our figures; finally the 1 could be taken for the image of a phallus pointing downwards, and only the presence of *testes* in the Hindu figure prevents us from equating it with our 1."[62]

Add to this opinion the following table of figures, the "Chinese apparel" of numbers.

1 一 *y.*
2 二 *eulr.*
3 三 *sen.*
4 四 *se.*
5 五 *ou.*
6 六 *lou.*
7 七 *tsi.*
8 八 *pa.*
9 九 *kieou.*
10 十 *che.*

The Chinese in particular make a great distinction between odd and even numbers.

One, an odd number, denotes the one divine power, creator of everything. It also denotes *P'an-Ku* as the first man who was upon the earth according to the writings of *Lo-Pi* in his *Lu-tze.*

---

[62] M. Decrespe, *Symbolisme des chiffres dits Arabes (Symbolism of the So-Called Arab Figures),* Paris, *l'Initiation,* N°. 1, October 1895, p. 34.

By this, we see that *one* is both the Divine Tetragram and the human tetragram.

Two denotes the elements which can give birth: father-mother, active-passive, spirit-matter, etc. This is the principle called binary.

Three, a venerable number which represents the Trinity. The Supreme Being in three persons.

It also represents Tien-Hoang[63], who rules over the heaven, the earth and man.

Tien-Hoang represents:

$$\left.\begin{array}{l} \text{TIEN} \\ \text{TIE} \\ \text{GIEN} \end{array}\right\} \text{HOANG}$$

who presides, accompanied by ten great agents or Ten Divine Members, or:

$$11 = \text{GIEN - HOANG} + 10 \text{ members}$$
$$12 = \text{TIE - HOANG} + 10 \text{ members}$$
$$13 = \text{TIEN - HOANG} + 10 \text{ members}$$

from which it follows that:

Tie-Hoang represents the entire universe.

Tien-Hoang, with 12 members, brothers all with the same rights, is therefore the Zodiac with its 12 constellations, the year with its 12 months, the day with its 12 hours.

Gien-Hoang, with 10 members, brothers with the same rights, are the ten divine *Ki*, the ten heads of heroic dynasties.[64]

---

[63] Normally rendered as Cheng-Huang in English. However, only the most general information can be found in this character, and since Papus doesn't cite any source for the rest of this passage, the names have been left in the original French versions and Papus allowed to speak without possibility of validation – PV.

[64] Note there seem to be little connection between the numbers cited here, and in the diagram above, but that is how it appears in the original book. Indeed, under the

Four, we have found no comment concerning this number, and so we do not know its meaning.

Five, an odd number, considered as the middle term between the divine numbers. It is the symbol of the earth.

Thus, it represents the five canonical books:

$$5^2 = 5 \times 5 = 25 \text{ (man)}$$

Six, the double of three, is composed of *Tien-Hoang* and the universal product:

$$\begin{aligned} &\text{TIEN} + \text{spirit} \\ &\text{TIE} + \text{matter} \\ &\text{GIEN} + \text{universe} \end{aligned}$$

We also find among the people of the Celestial Empire a theoretical tetragram.

Seven, an august number, serves as an amulet against diseases. It is the septenary, it represents the Tree of Knowledge. The model Emperor, *Huangdi* of the Antediluvian or Heroic Era, is the seventh head of the dynasty. For the Chinese, *seven* is the number which has most value.

Eight and *Nine*. Their meaning isn't known.[65]

Let's now turn to Roman numerals, whose numbering system has no zero.

I					
II					
III					
IV	XIV	XXIV	XXXIV	XLIV	LIX
V	XV	XXV	XXXV	XLV	LV

---

description of the number 6, it would appear a better analysis would place GIEN-HOANG as representing the Universe, TIEN-HOANG representing the zodiac as having a value of 12, and therefore TIE-HOANG, representing matter belonging to the mortal dynasties – PV.

[65] I.T. Ulic, *Y-King, Tao-see, Tao-Te-King et la numération* (I-Ching, Tao-Tze, Tao-Tze-Ching and Numbers). Paris. *l'Initiation*, No. 3, December 1897. Pp. 2, 11-273.

VI	XVI	XXVI	XXXVI	XLVI	LVI	
VII	XVII	XXVII	XXXVII	XLVII	LVII	
VIII	XVIII	XXVIII	XXXVIII	XLVIII	LVIII	
IX	XIX	XXIX	XXXIX	XLIX	LVIX	
X	XX	XXX	XL	L	LX	LXX
XI	XXI	XXXI	XLI	LI	LXI	LXXI
XII	XXII	XXXII	XLII	LII	LXII	LXXII
XIII	XXIII	XXXIII	XLIII	LIII	LXIII	LXXIII

The Roman Numerals

The ancients, as we can read in Boethius, saw in the 9 digits of the decimal numbering system 9 unities which we responsible for the generation of a perfect and happy existence:

1 is *Igin* – mother.
2 is *Andras* – father.
3 is *Ormis* – sympathy
4 is *Arbas* – union.
5 is *Quimas* – fertility.
6 is *Cellis* – perfection, beauty.
7 is *Zebis* – wealth.
8 is *Temenias* – happiness.
9 is *Celentis* – power.
10 is *Sipos* – wheel, circle, crown.

The Fathers of the Church[66] saw in the first 10 figures:

1. The unity of God.
2. The incarnation.
3. The trinity.
4. The revelation, the cross.
5. Fruitful suffering.
6. Creation, the work.
7. Justice, rest as the fruit of labor.
8. Perfect happiness.
9. Celestial harmonies.
10. Divine law.

---

[66] We have taken the most recognized opinion in St. Eucherius, *Form. Spirit.* Ch. XI. [This list is a little confusing, since in St. Eucherius of Lyon's *Formulae*, in which Chapter 10 is devoted to numbers, these only match up to some extent. Numbers 1, 3, 6 and 7 appear to correlate. However, St. Eucherius equates 2 with the two cherubim; 4 with the four Evangelists; 5 with the five books of Moses; 8 with the Day of Resurrection; 9 with the ninth hour when Jesus cried out with a loud voice on the cross and gave up the spirit; 10 with the ten-stringed lute of the Psalms. Given the vague reference to the 'Fathers of the Church' being the overall source, there is no reference material to check – PV.]

Our intention here is not to create a work of scholarship. We will not expand further on the history of figures, and the foregoing are largely sufficient to provide the student with the documentary concepts he may need. We now look forward to addressing the truly initiatory part of the *Science of Numbers*, which is one of the principal areas of knowledge associated with the Kabbalistic tradition.

PRACTICE

Chapter 7
Numbers and the Kabbalah

The Kabbalah, the esoteric tradition of the Hebrews, whose doctrine is the real basis of Western initiation, has a large place in the Science of Numbers. We can even say that given the very close links which exist in this tradition between numbers and letters, the Science of Numbers is, in reality, the very foundation of the Literal Kabbalah and the Practical Kabbalah. We know, in fact, that each letter of the Hebrew alphabet corresponds to a spiritual or cosmogonic power, which itself is expressed by a number and relates to a Divine Name. This is the basis of all theurgy, and all the magic of the Hebrews. We shall soon see how it's also linked to Astrology. The formation of the alphabet and the creation of numbers are compared to the creation of the world. By virtue of the law of analogy and of the correspondence existing between the various planes of the Universe, the Kabbalists were led to consider the form, number and value of letters, no longer as allegories, but as actual forces. This is completely valid, and comes from a generally widespread concept:

"You have already observed everything that the ancient sages recognized concerning power and mystery in the science of numbers", Josse Clichtoue wrote in the 16th Century in his book *On the Mystical Significance of Numbers*.[67] "Pythagoras in particular, that philosopher so famous among his contemporaries and throughout posterity, has appeared to you, aided by the science of numbers, expounding with amazing insight on the things of

---

[67] Josse Clichtoue, born in Nieuport (Flanders), a doctor at the Sorbonne, who ended his years as a lecturer in divinity of Chartres in 1543. Cf. *De Mystica numerum significatione opusculum*. Paris. Henr. Stephanus, 1513.

Nature, and even on the *mores* of men and on supernatural powers. It has not escaped you that he calls even numbers the numbers of justice, because of the equal division of their parts up to unity. Now, it is in equality that right and the extension of all justice is to be found. He indicated that the decade was the limit, the boundary, the sum of all the numbers. It was thought that numbers greater than ten were only a repetition of the first ten, and for that reason he attributed great dignity to the ten. He said that odd numbers are analogous to forms of natural things, and even numbers to matter, from which he concluded that even numbers lead to an understanding of physical substances and odd numbers to an understanding of spiritual things. I omitted to mention that the *tetragon* was a number of sanctity to Pythagoras, a qualification rightly given by Aristotle to the *square*, because of its admirable properties which help us to know the nature of supercelestial substances.

If, in the philosophical tradition of human schools, numbers show such great power, can we believe that the holy letters of which God is the First Author, these very numbers hold no mysteries and do not contain high truths? Certainly, the more Holy Scripture prevails in dignity over the human sciences, the more the mystical significance of numbers which are found there is more august and more eminent."

The author goes on to cite Boethius and St. Augustine, also quoted by Cornelius Agrippa[68], of which this is the passage:

"All that has been ordered by the primary nature of things, Boethius said, appears to have been due to the power of numbers. That power is the principal type that the Creator intended. From that came the multiplicity of elements, the succession of time, the movement of the stars, the rotation of the heavens. *The disposition of all things has as a necessary principle the series of numbers. Thus, numbers contain in their nature the broadest and most*

---

[68] Cornelius Agrippa, *Occult Science or Magic*. Paris. Chacornac, 1910 – 1911, Vol 1, p. 219. [Also available in English in an excellent version edited by Donald Tyson, pub. Llewellyn, 15th printing 2014 – PV.]

sublime virtues. For the philosopher who considers how great and numerous are the wonders hidden in natural things, despite the physical impressions which force us to suspect rather than to see them, it is not surprising that the powers attached to numbers are all the more admirable, all the more effective; that these numbers are more formal, more perfect, more identical to heavenly things, more mixed with distinct substances, more imbued with that character of grandeur and simplicity which approaches divine notions, from which come the very real powers which they possess.

"Everything that exists and everything which is made exists in accordance with certain numbers and derives its power from them. Time is based on number, as is all motion and action, and all things subject to change in position or a succession of moments. The harmony of instruments and voices is accomplished by the numerical harmonies which calculate their proportions and their strength. And the proportions arising from a comparison of numbers translate into lines and points which make characters and figures. Finally, all the forms that exist in the natural and supernatural worlds are joined together by certain numbers.

"Pythagoras, meditating on these things, said that everything exists through number and that number determines the virtues proper to each being. Proclus said that number exists in everything, although different in voice, in physical proportion, in soul and in reason, and then in divine things. Themistius, Boethius and Averroes of Babylon, adopting the perceptions of Plato, raised numbers to such a high level that they were convinced that it was impossible to address philosophical questions without their aid. They were speaking, it is true, of rational and formal numbers and not of the material, physical and vocal numbers of the vulgar calculations of merchants, devoid of any metaphysical meaning, which had no value in the eyes of Pythagoreans, academicians and St. Augustine; but rather they spoke of spiritual connections, the quantities they called natural, formal and rational numbers from which emanated the great mysteries, both in natural matters and in divine and celestial matters, numbers opened the way to a knowledge of everything that can be known, examined and understood. *Through them one comes very close to natural prophecy*; and the amazing forecasts of abbot Joachim should not be attributed to any other cause than the use of formal numbers."[69]

"The most illustrious voices in philosophy therefore agree that there is a hidden virtue in numbers whose efficacy is striking, either for good or for evil. Such was also the belief of the Catholic authors. It will suffice to mention, among others, St. Jerome, St. Augustine, Origen, St. Ambrose, St. Gregory of Nazianzus, St. Athanasius, St. Basil, St. Hilary, Raban Maur and Bede.

"In his Commentary on the Psalms, St. Hilary asserts that the Septuagint prepared the Psalter in accordance with the effective correspondence between numbers and ideas. The Pythagoreans had predicted many things by use of the numerical value of names, and if there was no great mystery in that, St, John would not have said in the Apocalypse: "Let him who has understanding count the number (of the name) of the Beast; for it is the number of a man."[70] This way of counting is held in high esteem among the Hebrews and the Kabbalists. Above all one must know that simpler numbers indicate divine things, tens heavenly things, hundreds earthly things, and thousands indicate things in the century to come."[71]

The foregoing clearly shows that the importance given to number by the Kabbalah is echoed in all the authors of the Western tradition. After this digression – in which we only appeared to stray from the immediate object of this chapter – let's return to the Hebrew alphabet.

There are two series of numeric correspondences in the Hebrew alphabet. In the first, each of the 22 letters[72] corresponds to the number which indicates its rank in the alphabet. In the second, the

---

[69] Papus provides no closing quotation marks, but it can be seen from Book II Chapter 2 of Agrippa's work that this passage ends here, so it may be assumed that the following paragraph beings the quotation from Edme Thomas – PV.

[70] Revelation 13:18. Note also the original Bible passage doesn't include the words 'of the name', since this is assumed – PV.

[71] Edme Thomas, *Histoire de l'antique cite d'Autun* [*History of the Ancient City of Autun*]. Aytun-Paris, 1846. Extract from the Introduction by Abbot Devoucoux, pp. 13 – 16.

[72] The number 22 which is that of beauty, gives by its multiplication by its simple number 6, the number 132, indicating the Kabbalistic Tradition.

letters correspond to the number which denotes their rank up to the tenth inclusive (Yod).

Examples: Heh is the 5th letter and its numerical value is **5**,
Yod is the 10th letter and its numerical value is **10**.

From the 10th letter to the 19th inclusive, in order to form the numeric value of the letter, the two digits of the number representing the rank of the letter in the alphabet are added together, and the product is considered to represent *tens*.

Example: Lamed is the 12th letter of the alphabet; its numeric value is therefore: $1 + 2 = 3$ tens or **30.**

From the 19th to the 22nd and last letter, we add the two digits of the number representing the rank of the letter in the alphabet, and the product of the addition is considered to represent *hundreds*.

Example: Shin is the 21st letter; its numeric value is therefore: $2 + 1 = 3$ hundreds or **300.**

Finally, five letters change their form and numeric value at the end of words. These are:

		Finals	Numeric Value
כ	Caph	ך	500
מ	Mem	ם	600
נ	Nun	ן	700
פ	Pe	ף	800
צ	Tzaddi	ץ	900

This correspondence of letters and numbers constitutes the essential instrument of the process of *Gematria* with the aid of which the Kabbalist initiate is able to discover the mysteries of the Hebrew text of the Torah[73], and its knowledge is indispensable to the construction and decryption of magic squares.

---

[73] Papus, *La Cabbale* (also available in English - PV).

It is impossible for us, in this book devoted specifically to the Science of Numbers, to expand upon the mysteries of the Kabbalah. However, we believe it essential to give the correspondences of the first 22 numbers with the letters of the Hebrew alphabet, the Divine Names and their symbolic meaning in Kabbalah.

The First 22 Numbers[74]

1   – א – *Aleph*

Corresponds to the first name of God, Eheieh אהיה which is interpreted as Divine Essence.

The Kabbalists call it that which the eye cannot see because of its exaltation.

It is seated in the world called Ain Soph which signifies the Infinite, its attribute is called Kether כתר, interpreted as a crown or diadem: it reigns over the angels the Hebrews call Chayoth-ha-Kodesh חיות הקדש, i.e. the animals of holiness. It forms the first choirs of angels, called the Seraphim.

2   – ב – *Beth*

2nd Divine Name corresponding to this letter: Bachur בהור (clarity, youth), designating angels of the 2nd Order, the Ophanim. *Forms or wheels*.

---

[74] This section is inconsistent and difficult to read in the original (particularly the Hebrew). A more recent transcription published in France was also consulted, but this omitted all the Hebrew and made a number of errors. Hebrew and names of God, archangels and angels have been standardized according to Golden Dawn usage. Where there were inconsistent omissions of Hebrew words these have been added. As a final point the similarity between this text, Papus' *La Cabale* and A.E. Waite's *The Occult Sciences* (pub. 1891), pp. 19 – 21, at least for the first ten letters, are astonishing. Either both were drawing from an identical source, or one read the other's work and some of it found its way into their manuscript. This book and Waite's were published a year apart, and it is not the intention of this translator to suggest anything other than the reader refer to both and make up their own mind – PV.

The Cherubim (by their ministry, God brings order from chaos).
Numeration: Chokmah חכמה, wisdom.

$$3 \quad -\, \gimel\, - Gimel$$

Name: Gadol גדול (magnus), indicating the angels Aralim אראלים, i.e. *great* and *strong*, thrones (through them, God Tetragrammaton Elohim maintains *the form of matter*).
Numeration: Binah בנאה, providence and intelligence.

$$4 \quad -\, ד\, - Daleth$$

Name: Dagul דגול (insignis), angels Chashmalim חשמלים – *Dominations*.
It is through them that God El אל *represents* the images of bodies and all the various forms of matter.
Attribute: Chesed חסד, clemency and goodness.

$$5 \quad -\, ה\, - Heh$$

Name: Hadom הדום (formosus majestuosus), Seraphim שרפים, Powers (through their ministry God Elohim Lycbir produces the Elements).
Numeration פחד (pachad), fear and Judgment, *left of the Stone*.
Attribute: Geburah גבורה, strength and power.

$$6 \quad -\, ו\, - Vav$$

Has formed Vezio וזיו (cum splendore), 6th Order of angels, Melekim מלכים, Choir of Virtues (through their ministry God Eloah *produces* the metals and everything that exists in the mineral kingdom).
Attribute: Tiphereth תפארת, Sun, splendor.

$$7 \quad -\, ז\, - Zayin$$

Has formed Zakaï זכי (purus mundus), 7th Order of angels, Principalities, Children of Elohim (through their ministry God

Tetragrammaton Sabaoth produces plants and all *that exists in the vegetable kingdom).*

Attribute: Netzach נצח, triumph, justice.

$$8 \quad - ח - \text{Cheth}$$

Designates Chased חסיד (misericors), Angels of 8th Order, Beni Elohim בני אלהים, Sons of the Gods (*choir of archangels*) (*Mercury*); through their ministry God Elohim Sabaoth produces animals and the animal kingdom.

Attribute: Hod הוד, praise.

$$9 \quad - ט - \text{Teth}$$

Corresponds to the name Tehor טור (mundus purus), Angels of the 9th Order which preside over the birth of men (through their ministry Shaddaï and Elohim send the guardian angels to men).

Attribute: Yesod יסוד, foundation.

$$10 \quad - י - \text{Yod}$$

From where comes Yah יה (Deus).

Attribute: Malkuth (מלכות), kingdom, empire and the Temple of God or influence by heroes. It is by his ministry that men receive intelligence, industry and knowledge of divine things.

Here ends the Angelic world.

$$11 \quad - כ - \text{Caph}$$

Name Kabir[75] כביר (potens). Designates First Heaven, Primum Mobile, corresponding to the name of God, expressed by a single letter, that is to say the First Cause, which puts all of that is mobile into movement. The first sovereign intelligence which governs the

---

[75] The name is missing from the original. Note also that the name in brackets after each Hebrew and English transliteration is the Latin form of the name – PV.

Primum Mobile, that is to say the First Heaven of the astrological world assigned to the Second Person of the Trinity, is called Metatron מטטרון.

His attribute means Prince of Faces: his mission is to introduce all those who should appear before the face of the Great God; he has Prince Orifiel under him along with an infinity of subordinate intelligences; the Kabbalists say that it is through the ministry of Metatron that God spoke to Moses; it is also through him that all the inferior powers of the physical world receive the virtues of God.

Caph, final letter figured thus ך, corresponds to the two Great Names of God, each composed of two Hebrew letters, El אל, Yah יה; they rule over the intelligences of the Second Order which govern the heaven of the fixed stars, including the twelve signs of the Zodiac which the Hebrews call Galgol hamnazeloth; the intelligence of the Second Heaven is named Raziel. His attribute signifies vision of God and smile of God.

12 – ל – Lamed

From which comes Lumined למד (doctus), corresponds to the name Shaddaï, the Name of God in five letters, named the emblem of the Delta[76], and rules over the Third Heaven and over the intelligences of the Third Order which govern the sphere of Saturn.

13 – מ – Mem

Meborake מברו (benedictus), corresponding to the Fourth Heaven and the Fourth Name of Jehovah rules over the sphere of Jupiter. The intelligence that governs Jupiter is called Tzadkiel.

Tzadkiel צדקיאל receives the influences of God through Sabbatïel to transmit them to the intelligences of the Fifth Order.

Mem final letter ם corresponds to the Fifth Heaven and the Fifth Name of God. It is the Fifth Name of Prince in Hebrew. Rules over

---

[76] This appears to be an error. It would make more sense, since Shaddaï is a word of three letters (שׁדי), and a Delta is composed of 3 sides, it would make more sense to say 'the Name of God is three letters, named the emblem of the Delta" – PV.

the *Sphere of Mars*. Intelligence which governs March: Samaël. Samaël, receives the influences of God by the intervention of Tzadkiel and transmits them to the intelligences of the Sixth Order.

14   – נ – Nun

Name: Nora נורא (formidabilis), also corresponds to the name Emmanuel (nobiscum Deus), Sixth Name of God; dominates the Sixth Heaven, the *Sun*: First Intelligence of the sun, Raphaël רפאל.

Final form thus depicted ן relates to the Seventh Name of God Ararita, composed of 7 letters (Immutable God). Governs the Seventh Heaven and *Venus*. Intelligence of Venus: Haniel האניאל, the love of God, justice and grace of God.

15   – ס – Samekh

Name: Samekh סומך (fulciens, firmans), Eighth Name of God; the planet Mercury; First Intelligence of Mercury, Mikaël (מוכאל).

16   – ע – Ayin

Name: Hazaz הזאז (fortis), corresponds to Jehovah-Sabaoth. Governs the Ninth Heaven; the Moon. Intelligence of the Moon, Gabriel (גבריאל).

Here ends the Archangelic world.

---

17   – פ – Peh

Eighteenth Name corresponding to Him: Phode פודה (redemptory), *intellectual* soul (Kircher, II, p. 227).

This letter indicates *Fire*, the Element where the Salamanders live. Intelligence of Fire: Seraphim שרפים and several Sub-Orders. Governs in summer *over the South or Midi*.

The final letter ף as drawn designates *Air*, where the Sylphs live. Intelligence of Air, Seraphim and several Sub-Orders. The intelligences of Air govern in the Spring over the *Orient or the Occident*.

18   – צ – Tzaddi

Universal matter (K)[77]. Name: Tzedek צדק (Justus). Designates *Water* where the nymphs live. Intelligence: Tharsis. Governs in the Fall over *the West or the Occident*.

Final form ץ designates the elements (Air, Water, Earth, Fire) (K).

19   – ק – Qoph

Derived name Kodesh קדש (sanctus). *Earth* where the gnomes live. Intelligence of the Earth, Ariel. In Winter to the North. *Minerals*, inanimate (Kircher).

20   – ר – Resh

Name: Rodeh רדה (imperans), plants (Kircher), attributed to the First Principle of God which is applied to the Animal Kingdom and gives life to all animals.

21   – ש – Shin

Name: Shaddaï שדי (omnipotens), which means God Almighty, attributed to the Second Principle of God (animals), that which has life (Kircher), which gives the seed to all vegetal substances.

22   – ת – Tav

Name: Thekinah תהנה (gratiosus), Microcosm (Kircher), Third Principle of God, which gives the seed to everything that exists in the Mineral Kingdom.

---

[77] The (K) is assumed to mean: attributed to Kircher – PV.

This letter is the symbol of man because it indicates the end of all that exists, just as man is the end and the perfection of all creatures.[78]

There is also a correspondence between the first 10 numbers and the 10 *Sephiroth* (whose name correctly signifies *numeration*) which are ten Divine attributes, ten cosmogonic forces acting in the Universe and in Man. These ten *Sephiroth* are already listed in the explanation of the 22 letters above, but it is important to meditate upon the passage of the Sepher Yetzirah relating to them. This is what the old Kabbalistic text says.

"The first of the Sephiroth, One, is the Spirit of the living God, it is the blessed and doubly blessed name and of the ever-living God. Voice, Spirit and Word, this is the Holy Spirit.

"Two is the breath of the Spirit, and with it are engraved and carved the twenty-two letters: The three mothers, the seven doubles, and the twelve singles, and each of them is spirit.

"Three is the Water which comes from the breath, and with it He carved and engraved the first matter, which was inanimate and void. He established TOHU, the line which meanders around the world, and BOHU, the occult stones buried in the abyss and which the Waters pour forth.

"Four is the Fire that comes from the Water, and with them He carved the throne of honor, the Ophanim (celestial wheels), the Seraphim, the Holy Animals and the Serving Angels, and He made their dominion His domain, as the text says; It is He who made His ministering angels and spirits by agitating the fire.

"Five is the seal with which He sealed the height when He contemplated it above him. He sealed it with the name IEV (יהו).

"Six is the seal with which He sealed the depth when He contemplated it beneath him. He sealed it with the name IVE (יוה).

"Seven is the seal with which He sealed the East when He contemplated it before him. He sealed it with the name EIV (היו).

"Eight is the seal with which He sealed the West when He contemplated it behind him. He sealed it with the name VEI (והי).

---

[78] Papus. *La Cabbale*, op. cit. pp. 77 – 81.

"Nine is the seal with which He sealed the South when He contemplated it to His right. He sealed it with the name VIE (ויה).

"Ten is the seal with which He sealed the North when He contemplated it to His left. He sealed it with the name EVI (הוי).

"Such are the ten ineffable Spirits of the living God: Spirit, Breath or Air, Water, Fire, Height, Depth, East, West, North and South."[79]

We said earlier that the Science of Numbers, such as it exists in the Kabbalah, is also associated with Astrology. Indeed, of the 22 letters of the Hebrew alphabet, 3 – the three "mothers" – alone relate to the domain of Principles; 7 – the seven "doubles" – relate to the seven astrological planets (they are called "double", and this is understandable, since the planetary influences act both in good and evil ways); finally 12 letters – the twelve "singles" – correspond to the signs of the Zodiac. We have seen that each letter is a number in a certain plane; it is therefore evident that numbers themselves participate of the correspondences which exist between letters and stars. That is what leads to the table below.

To study in detail this aspect of the Science of Numbers, we still need to have recourse to the *Sepher Yetzirah* which gives us the astrological correspondences, as well as those permitted by the Kabbalah between the letters (and consequently the numbers) and the parts of the human body.

---

[79] Papus, *La Cabbale*, op. cit., pp. 184-185.

N°	Numeric Value	Hebrew Letter	English Equivalent	According to the Sepher Yetzirah correspondences			According to the Archeometer correspondences		
				Mother letters	Planetary letters	Zodiacal letters	Mother letters	Planetary letters	Zodiacal letters
1	1	א aleph	A	I			I		
2	2	ב beth	B		♄			☽	
3	3	ג gimel	G		♃			☿	
4	4	ד daleth	D		♂			♃	
5	5	ה heh	H			♌			♌
6	6	ו vav	V			♉			♉
7	7	ז zayin	Z			♊			♊
8	8	ח cheth	Ch			♋			♋
9	9	ט teth	T			♌			♌
10	10	י yod	I			♍			♍
11	20	כ caph	K		☉			♂	
12	30	ל lamed	L			♎			♎
13	40	מ mem	M	II					♏
14	50	נ nun	N			♏		☉	
15	60	ס samekh	S			♐	II		
16	70	ע ayin	Aa			♑			♐
17	80	פ peh	P, Ph		♀				♑
18	90	צ tzaddi	Tz			♒		♀	
19	100	ק qoph	Q			♓			♒
20	200	ר resh	R		☿				♓
21	300	ש shin	Sh	III				♄	
22	400	ת tav	T, Th		☽		III		

The Seven Doubles

Seven Doubles $\begin{cases} \text{T R P K D G B} \\ \text{ט ר פ כ ד ג ב} \end{cases}$

These constitute the syllables: Life, Peace, Knowledge, Wealth, Grace, Fertility, Domination.

They are double because they are reduced to their opposites through permutation; in place of Life is Death; of Peace, War; of Knowledge, Ignorance; of Wealth, Poverty; of Grace, Abomination; of Fertility, Barrenness; and of Domination, Slavery.

The seven doubles are opposed in the seven terms: East, West; Height, Depth; North, South, and the Holy Palace fixed in the center which supports all.

These seven doubles – He sculpted them, engraved them, combined them and created with them the Planets in the Universe; the Days in the Year and the Doors in Man, and with them He sculpted Seven Heavens, Seven Elements, Seven Animalities empty since the work. And that is why He chose the septenary under the heavens.

1. Seven double letters, *b, g, d, k, p, r, t;* He has traced, carved, mixed, equilibrated and permuted them; with them He has created the planets, the days and the doors.

2. He made *Beth* to reign and He gave it a crown, and combined them one with the other, and with it He created Saturn in the Universe, the Sabbath in the year, and the mouth in man.

3. He made *Gimel* to reign, He gave it a crown and combined them one with the other; with it He created Jupiter in the Universe, Sunday in the year, and the right eye in man.

4. He made *Daleth* to reign, He gave it a crown and combined them one with the other, and with it He created Mars in the Universe, Monday in the year, and the left eye in man.

5. He made *Caph* to reign, He gave it a crown and combined them one with the other, and with it He created the Sun in the Universe, Tuesday in the year, and the right nostril in the person.

6. He made *Peh* to reign, He gave it a crown and combined them one with the other, and with it He created Venus in the Universe, Wednesday in the year, and the left nostril in man.

7. He made *Resh* to reign, He gave it a crown and combined them one with the other, and with it He created Mercury in the Universe, Thursday in the year, and he right ear in man.

8. He made *Tav* to reign, He gave it a crown and combined them one with the other, and with it He created the Moon in the Universe, Friday, in the year, and the left ear in man.

9. He separated the witnesses and set each apart, the Universe apart, the year apart and man apart.

Two letters build two houses, three build six; four build twenty-four; five, one hundred twenty; six, seven hundred twenty; and from there the number progresses towards the ineffable and unknowable. The Planets in the Universe are: the Sun, Venus, Mercury, the Moon, Saturn, Jupiter and Mars. The days of the year are the seven days of creation, and the seven doors of man are: two eyes, two ears, two nostrils and a mouth.

The Twelve Singles[80]

Twelve Singles { Q Tz Aa S N L Y T Ch Z V H
ה ו ז ט י ל נ ס ע צ ק

Their foundation is the following: Sight, Hearing, Smell, Speech, Nutrition, Coitus, Action, Movement, Anger, Laughter, Meditation, Sleep.

Their measure is established by the twelve terms of the world – the Northeast, the Southeast, the East-height, the East-depth; the Northwest, the Southwest, the West-height, the West-depth; the South-height, the South-depth; the North-height, the North-depth.

The boundaries grow and advance across the centuries and these are the arms of the Universe.

These twelve singles – He sculpted them, engraved them, gathered them together, weighed them and transmuted them, and with them He created the twelve signs in the Universe, namely: Aries, Taurus, etc.; twelve months in the year.

And these letters are the twelve directions of man, as follows: the left hand and the right hand, the two feet, the two kidneys, the liver, the gall, the spleen, the colon, the bladder, the arteries.

He made *Heh* to reign, He gave it a crown and combined them one with the other, and with it He created Aries in the Universe, *Nisan* (March) in the year, and the liver in man.

He made Vav to reign, He gave it a crown and combined them one with the other, and with it He created Taurus in the Universe, *Iyyar* (April) in the year, and bile in man.

He made *Zayin* to reign, He gave it a crown and combined them one with the other, and with it He created Gemini in the Universe, *Sivan* (May) in the year, and the spleen in man.

He made *Cheth* to reign, He gave it a crown and combined them one with the other, and with it He created Cancer in the Universe, *Tammuz* (June, in the year, and the stomach in man.

---

[80] The diagram of the twelve singles in the original book has a number of errors: these have been corrected here – PV.

He made *Teth* to reign, He gave it a crown and combined them one with the other, and with it He created Leo in the Universe, *Ab* (July) in the year, and the right kidney in man.[81]

From the few documents which precede, one may realize that the Science of Numbers is part of the very essence of the Kabbalah, and that its applications are virtually endless. From the Kabbalah, the Science of Numbers has passed into Freemasonry, and it is with good reason that Bro∴ Clavel, in his colorful history of Freemasonry, puts in the mouth of the Venerable Master the following words: "There is in Freemasonry a point of similarity with the doctrines of the initiations of antiquity: that is the use of mystical numbers."[82] Martinism in particular has retained a large part of the tradition on this point, as on many others; the "catechisms" of the Elus Cohens contain transparent references to the mysticism of Numbers.[83] Martinez de Pasqually, whose knowledge in the field of Jewish esoterism was so extensive, developed an entire arithmosophy in his *Treatise on the Reintegration of Beings*[84] which, according to him, was only made known by men through divine revelation: "The Creator Himself instructed, by way of his spiritual envoy Héli, the fortunate man Seth in the Science of Numbers."

Here, according to the work of Martinez of Pasqually, is the esoteric meaning of the first twelve numbers.

"*Unity*, First Principle of all being, both spiritual and temporal belonging to the Divine Creator.

"*Two* is the number of confusion, belonging to woman... Number two is given to confusion where one finds the perverse spirits and men who unite with the minds of evil spirits.

---

[81] Papus, *La Cabbale*, op. cit. pp. 191 – 194. [It is noteworthy that he only lists 5 of the twelve figures, both here and in the original book The Kabbalah. This is probably an oversight or misprint which has been perpetuated through later editions and finally into this book – PV.]

[82] *Histoire Pittoresque de la Franc-Maçonnerie*, F.-T. Bègue-Clavel, 1844, p.88 – PV.

[83] Papus, *Martines de Pasqually*. Paris, pub. Chacornac, 1902.

[84] Martines de Pasqually, *Traité de la Réintégration des Êtres*. Paris, pub. Chacornac, 1899.

"*Three* is the number belonging to the earth and to man... The number 3 denotes the three spirituous essences which constitute all forms; it further denotes by the origin of these same essences the direct action of those inferior and ternary spirits, since they have emanated from them: *mercury, sulfur and salt* for the structure of the Universe... We divide the whole body of the human form into three parts, namely: the trunk, the head and the bones of the Isles.[85] We cannot disagree that these three parts are different in their shapes and in their proportions; they are very distinct from one another and one can easily distinguish them without the need to break them apart, nor fracture the cartilaginous ligaments which unite the three together; so that these three things make one by means of this intimate connection. However, they each have different properties and abilities, and these different abilities are a perfect allusion to the three Kingdoms that we know in Nature: the Animal, Vegetable, and the Mineral. These 3 Kingdoms are contained in the terrestrial body, just as the three parts of the human body to which I have referred are contained in the envelope which surrounds the whole body... The corporeal shape of man is capable of containing 3 kinds of different lives, which I am going to explain. The first is the life of matter, which we call instinct or passive life, and which is innate both in the form of the rational animal as well as in that of the irrational one. The second is the demonic spiritual life which can incorporate itself into the passive life. The third is the divine spiritual life which governs the first two.

"*Four* is the number of the quatriple Divine essence... it is the Divine spiritual number which the Creator employs for the spiritual emanation of all living spiritual beings... The quaternary number is the one that contributes to the perfection of forms taken from indifferent matter, because it gives movement and action to the corporeal form, and because it governs all created beings as the principal number from which everything originates. Thus, we call it the number which has become powerful through the Creator, as containing within it all species of number of Divine, spiritual and

---

[85] That is, the iliac bones, which are the bones which protrude from the hip (Editor's note).

terrestrial creation. Finally, the quaternary number is the one which the Creator used for the emanation and the emancipation of Man or the Spiritual Minor... You will find in yourself the repetition of this quaternary number which makes you correspond with your Creator, and both of you bear the quaternary number, namely: 1. *the central axis*; 2. *the body of the Inferior Spirits;* 3, *the body of the Major Spirits*; 4. *the Major Spirits, body of the Divinity*, just as you, O Israel, have 1. your body; 2. the body of your soul; 3. your soul the body of the major spirit; 4. and the Major Spirit, body of the Divinity... The quaternary number is the number from which all temporal things and all spiritual actions originate.

"*Five* is the number of the demonic spirit... The perverse spirits joined an arbitrary unity to the quaternary number of their origin, by means of their private authority and by their will alone, which denatured their spiritual power and transformed it into a power which was limited and purely material, led by a leader taken from among them. That is why the quaternary number no longer belongs to them and why the quinary number is the number of demons.

"*Six* is the number of daily operations... The Senary number is that by which the Creator brought forth from His thought all kinds of images, manifest corporeal forms which exist in the Universal Circle. Doesn't Genesis teach us that God created everything in six days? We should not believe from this that Genesis wished to set bounds to the power of Divinity by limiting Him to a single time, either 6 days, or 6 years. The Creator is a Pure Spirit superior to time and successive duration, but He may have operated six divine thoughts of Universal Creation, and this number 6 effectively belongs to the creation of any visible form of matter. By this same number, the Creator made his creature sense both spiritually and temporally the duration of time that Universal Creation should endure. This, then, is the virtue of the senary number and the use that that the Creator has made of it.

"*Seven* is the number of the Holy Spirit, belonging to Septenary Spirits... The septenary number is the more than perfect number that the Creator used for the emancipation of all Spirits out of His Divine Immensity. The Class of Septenary Spirits must serve as the First Agent and the Certain Cause; to contribute to the operation of any kind of movement in the forms created in the Universal Circle... The sages established the septenary number among their disciples, following the example of the second and septenary posterity of their father Noah, in the number by which they were themselves composed; they also fixed this septenary number because the Almighty had operated six divine thoughts for Universal Creation and because, on the seventh day, He gave 7 Spiritual Gifts and assigned 7 Principal Spirits to all His creation to sustain it in all its temporal operations, according to the septenary duration that He had fixed for it. The first 7 sages of the posterity of Noah took this example to direct their conduct, in order to perpetuate among men to follow the knowledge and correspondence of these 7 Principal Spirits which the Creator had assigned in His Universe to teach His will to the inferior and minor creature, and to raise him, by this means and by that of the spiritual mind, to a perfect knowledge of the Divine works. Scripture further teaches us this by the 7 Angels, 7 Archangels, 7 Seraphim, 7 Cherubim, the 7 Spiritual Places, the 7 Thrones, 7 Dominations, 7 Powers, the 7 Judges of Israel, the 7 Principal Chiefs who were under Moses or Aaron, the 70 years of Captivity of Israel, the 7 weeks of Daniel, the 7 days of the temporal week, the 7 gifts that Christ gave to his Disciples (from which came the first 7 principal Fathers of the Christian Church who have exercised the 7 Spiritual Orders among their Disciples), the 7-Branched Candlestick which was placed in the Temple of Solomon and which is still represented in St. Peter's Church in Rome. The septenary number is calculated philosophically as 7,000 years with respect to the temporal and to duration, but when Scripture says that on the seventh day God dedicated His own work by blessing Universal Creation, one should understand by this blessing the coming together of the seven Major Divine Spirits that the Creator united with any creature included or contained in His Universal Creation.

This coming together of the 7 Principal Spirits is shown to us by the operation of the 7 planets which operate to modify, temper and support the action of the Universe. Finally, since the Universe was designed in its full perfection by the septenary number, it will also be reintegrated by that same number into the imagination of the One who had conceived it.

"*Eight,* is the number of the doubly strong Spirit belonging to Christ... the number of Divine double spiritual power that had been entrusted to the first minor for him to manifest the glory and justice of the Eternal One against the prevaricating spirits. It was that Divine power which your Fathers knew under the name of Abraham, Isaac and Jacob. But Adam, having lost this dual power because of his crime, had been reduced to the simple power of a minor. His descendants became wandering and tenebrous like him; and man can no longer obtain this dual power from the Creator without infinite work and incurring suffering of the body, mind and spirit. Finally, this number is the one which the Creator intends for the Spiritual Elect who He wishes to favor and prepare for the manifestation of His glory.

"*Nine* is the demonic number belonging to matter... Add the quinary number to the quaternary, and you have the number of the subdivision of the spirituous essences of matter and those of the Divine spiritual essences; and this arises from the joining of the quinary number, imperfect and corruptible, with the quaternary number, perfect and incorruptible. It is through this joining together that man degrades his spiritually divine power by making it spiritually demonic; and that was how Adam's crime was operated, a crime that has caused an inconceivable revolution among all the spiritual beings.

"*Ten* is the Divine number... This is the very denary number that gives rise to all major, inferior and minor spiritual beings, as well as all laws of action, either spiritual or spirituous. The addition of the four numbers included in the quaternary gives 10 in this manner: $1 + 2 + 3 + 4 = 10$, and it is by the various comings together of these different numbers that you will conceive how all things are originated... There are 10 Patriarchs, there are 10 Spiritual Names which operate the worship of Divinity through His own Denary Name.

"The number *eleven* is opposed[86] to any kind of complete corporeal body, analogous to the terrestrial body and everything that comes from it.

"Twelve is the principle of the division of time."

Such, from the arithmosophical viewpoint, was the doctrine of the man who was the first initiator of our Venerable Master Louis-Claude de Saint-Martin.

As we have already said above, Martinist initiation uses the symbolic language of numbers, and its study has an important place in it: and so, to the initiate of the First Grade, the luminaries and their disposition teach the esoteric doctrine of Unity, the Ternary Law and its correspondences. To the initiate of the Second Grade, the profound symbolism of the two columns gives the key of oppositions in the whole of Nature: these columns, of different colors though of identical essence, opposed to one another in appearance, come to be harmonized in the unity of the intermediate ternary, the Altar of initiation illuminated by its shining triple ternary. It is the only initiation which allows one to discover, through knowledge of the laws of balance, the common term which reconnects all the opposites. Finally, to the initiate of the Third Grade the distinctive signature of the order S∴I∴ indicates to him or her alone all the lessons of the symbolic ritual. The points arranged in two opposing triangles symbolize the disposition of the luminaries and their placement symbolizing ∴, the ternary in the three worlds.

The opposition of the two letters S and I, and the opposition of the two triangles indicate to any perceptive eye the *two columns* in

---

[86] The text of the Treatise on the Reintegration of Beings clearly says "opposed" (opposé), but it is probable that this was a misprint and that it should read "apposed" (apposé) (Editor's Note).

their active (letter) and passive (points) position, a vertical opposition and a horizontal opposition.

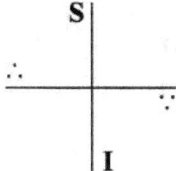

This is the key to the quaternary, the key to the symbolism of the Cross.

Chapter 8

Numbers and Luck

The study of numbers plays a considerable role in mystical works and we are going to deal with one of the two interesting problems posed by this study.

The first problem we shall look at is that concerning Luck, a magic word which stirs even the most skeptical minds.

There are people who do not believe in God or the Devil but who believe firmly in Luck, in good luck, and also in bad luck and being unlucky.

Now, Luck absolutely exists, and we can even identify it if it flees, call it if it goes away and verify it when it is present.

But how?

There are three factors that preside over the establishing or return of Luck: the Human Will, Providence and Fate. Luck is therefore a real problem, able to be of interest to any soul eager for mysterious things like any positive spirit and wishing to take account of the origin of terrestrial powers.

Every human being possesses a characteristic number which gives the key to his formula of Luck, or the reasons for certain Misfortunes. A number of people have noticed that a certain number has always accompanied the most important moments of their lives, and that number is the one which exactly characterizes those people. But there are others, enemies on principle of all superstition or those who, on the other hand, are too busy and haven't noticed this kind of thing.

In the latter case, how do you find your characteristic number?

That is what we will attempt to show.

First of all, the date of birth, and especially the date in the month should be carefully noted. Thus, in many cases, a person born on the 'thirteenth' will have this number as a sign of Luck in his life.

Then, the really important events in his life should be noted and the dates compared with the date of birth.

Finally, if these means don't produce clear results, it would be sufficient to take the alphabet with its numerical correspondences and replace each letter of the family name and all of the first names with its figure, and then add them to give a total and divide the total obtained by 9.

The remaining digit represents the Kabbalistic number.

On the other hand, the days of the week ruling over births are a rather useful guide for the determination of the dominant planet.

By remembering the day that ruled over your birth, you will have valuable suggestions for identifying the number of Luck.[87]

---

[87] With regard to lotteries, we refer the reader to Chapter IV of *Traité méthodique de Magie pratique* [*Methodical Treatise on Practical Magic*] by Papus, and the Chapter entitled: '*The Magic of numbers and lotteries.*'

Chapter 9

Numbers and Dates

The second problem consists of another, more interesting, calculation.

When finding the sum of a number representing a date of birth or a historical fact, one gets a new number which can shed light in a curious way on both personal or historical events, depending upon the case.

But it is necessary to establish some distinctions, without which one can get lost in such inquiries. The following comments are dedicated to examining the different parts of the problem.

As an example, let's take a date from history, say, the final Constitution of the German Empire in 1871.

You can consult the numbers in three ways.

1. **By adding all the figures in the number**. This 1871 gives $1 + 8 + 7 + 1 = 17$.

$$\begin{array}{r} 1871 \\ \underline{17} \\ 1888 \end{array}$$

We continue in the same manner:

$$\begin{array}{r} 1888 = 25 \\ \underline{25} \\ 1913 \\ \underline{14} \\ 1927 \end{array}$$

2. Instead of adding up all the figures of the numbers we can simply **add together the last two**. This gives us a new series:

$$1871 \quad 7 \text{ and } 1 = 8$$

$$\frac{8}{1879}$$
$$\frac{16}{1895}$$
$$\frac{14}{1909}$$
$$\frac{9}{1918}$$

3. We can also **add the last number or digit of each year**. This gives a third source of studies.

1871	1892	1914
1	2	4
1872	1894	1918
2	4	8
1874	1898	1926
4	8	6
1878	1906	1932
8	6	2
1886	1912	1934
6	2	
1892	1914	

4. Up to this point everything is mathematical. We can make an appeal to the imagination by mixing the various methods without rules. Total figures followed by the addition of a figure to return to that of the previous two. We only quote this process from memory because it gives too much weight to the arbitrary and to the imagination.

The dates we have just studied are those of the foundation of the Empire of Germany and its derivatives.

According to these methods, let us now look at the life of Emperor Wilhelm II.

Wilhelm II was born in 1859. The major dates of his life are:

1859 equals 23 being 23 years:

```
  + 23
 1882 then 19 years later, making 41 years (23 +19)
    19
 1901 then 11 years later, making 52 years
    11
 1912 then 13 years later, making 65 years
    13
 1925 then 17 years later, making 82 years
    17
 1942
```

The addition of the last two numbers of each date gives us:

```
 1859
   14
 1873 then: 1883-1894-1907-1914-1919-1929-1940
```

The addition of the last number of each year only gives us:

1859-1868-1876-1882-1884-1888-1896-1902-1904-1908-1916-1922-1924-1928-1936-1942.

What is interesting to study are the figures which return the same numbers or at least very close together in different series.

New studies would allow us to know how to determine which of these years are favorable and which are unfavorable. Even or odd numbers and astrology would play a large role here, but such a study would go beyond the framework of this book. Let everyone get to work use numbers to erect their personal horoscope. We are going to give an example by taking our own date of birth, being 1865.

Zodiacal revolution of the horoscope: using only last digit.

1865-1870-1877-1884-1888-1896-1902-1908-**1916**-1922-1924. (Note: 1916 was the year in which Papus died).

Chapter 10
Numbers and History

The language of Numbers is almost unknown to the researchers of our times. We are just beginning to stammer through the alphabet. Yet this mysterious language is an active key to prophecies concerning individuals, families and States. A good deal of research has been done on this topic. We will draw attention to the wisdom of our readers just two important works:

The first of these two works is entitled: *Recherches sur les fonctions providentielles des Dates et des noms dans les annals de touse les Peuples.* Published anonymously, this remarkable work was written by François Jean-Baptiste Mouesan, Count of Villirouet.[88] The subject outlined in this remarkable treatise is completely new, like its method, which is expressed very clearly and with a perfect simplicity. The book became rare as soon as it appeared. This was because it openly unveiled the providential meaning of the Science of Numbers; and because it wasn't a purely theoretical study, but rather a wonderful scientific system unencumbered by the thousands of facts supplied by universal history.

Here are the main excerpts as well as a part of the conclusion.

---

[88] *Research on the Providential Functions of Dates and Names in the Annals of all Nations.* Paris, ed. Dumoulin, 1852. The author was born in Lamballe on June 24, 1789. We would inform erudite readers that there were a series of papers under the title of: *King Jesus Universal Monarch and Divine-Sun* (sic.) *of Humanity, or History Considered From a New Point of View.* Rennes, 1873. De La Villirouet is also the author of *Figures for the Reign of Napoleon, or History of Yesterday and Today.* Rennes. 1879. (Editor's Note).

FIRST CLASS OF PHENOMENA[89]

Numerical relationship between the extreme[90] dates and the total number of Sovereigns of a State or Dynasty

1. *There is a constant relationship between the actual number of heads of any State, or the princes of a dynasty,* **and the sum of the figures** *of either the first or the last date, or of these two dates combined.*

1. FRANCE

A. Merovingians... 13.

1. Accession of the 1st Merovingian CLODION[91], in **427**, the year in which the three digits, 4, 2, 7, added together, are .... **Thirteen.**
2. Accession of CLOVIS, the true founder of the monarchy, **481** ; sum of digits 4, 8, 1, as above… **Thirteen.**
3. Accession of CHILDÉRIC II, last of the active Kings, year **670**[92]; Still… **Thirteen.**
4. Accession of CHILDÉRIC III, last of all the Merovingians both figureheads and active, in 742; again… **Thirteen.**

Sums:

1. CLODION	**427**	13
2. MÉROVÉE	448	16

---

[89] Op. cit. pp. 1 – 2.
[90] Note that here 'extrême' or 'extreme' applied to dates refers to the start and end years of a reign or of a dynasty – PV.
[91] We omitted Pharamon, whose existence is disputed.
[92] After Childéric II, assassinated in 673, began the reign of the Mayors of the palace. [Later in the Merovingian rule the kinds became more figureheads while true power was wielded by the mayors of the palace. Curiously, a 'roi fainéant' is a 'do-nothing' king while a 'roi non fainéant' means an active king. So, the fully phrase used here: 'Mérovingiens fainéants et non fainéants' translates to 'figurehead and active kings' – PV].

3.	CHILDÉRIC I	458	17
4.	CLOVIS	**481**	**13**
5.	CHILDEBERT	511	7
6.	CLOTAIRE I	558	18
7.	CARIBERT	561	12
8.	CHILPÉRIC I	567	18
9.	CLOTAIRE II	584	17
10.	DAGOBERT I	628	16
11.	CLOVIS II	638	17
12.	CLOTAIRE III	655	16
13.	CHILDÉRIC II	**670**	6 + 7 = **13**

Thirteen kings.

OBSERVATION: To apply the proposed rule, just one of the extreme dates would be enough; and yet here we have three and even *four*, including the year 742 of Childéric II[93], which precisely reproduces the number **Thirteen**: a quadruple result which is all the more striking as each of the ten intermediate epochs[94] gives a different sum.

SECOND CLASS OF PHENOMENA[95]

Combined Relationships between Letters, Names and Figures of the years to the number of Sovereigns

The alphabetic elements of the names of the first and last Prince of an Empire or a Dynasty counted separately, or combined with the sum of the figures of the rulers at the extreme ends of the reigns,

---

[93] The original text incorrectly says 'Childéric III – PV.
[94] In fact this should read either 11 if counting from Clodion, or 8 if counting from Clovis – PV.
[95] Op.cit., pp. 69 – 70.

always correspond to the complete succession of Sovereigns of that Empire, and that Dynasty.

Here are multiple proofs of this new relationship:

1. FRANCE

A. MEROVINGIANS... 13, 14, 22.

Until the 'do-nothing' kings, there were 13 or even 14 if we include Pharamond; but CLODION generally passes for the first king, and it is his son MÉROVÉE who gave the dynasty its name.

```
a) Clodion ............................................. 7 Letters
   Mérovée.............................................. 7    "       Kings
                                                       14           14

b) Clodion (first king)........................ 7    "
   Clovis, founder.................................. 6    "
                                                       13           13

c) Clodion............................................ 7    "
   Clovis............................................... 6    "       Kings
   Childéric III, last Merovingian............ 9
                                                       23           22
```

(22 Kings, including the figurehead ones).

THIRD CLASS OF PHENOMENA[96]
Homonymic relationships between the extreme terms of Empires and Races

Having solidly proved the continuous connection between the number of reigns and of the sum of the years, and next the

---

[96] Op. cit. pp. 84 – 85.

concordance between the number kings and the dates and names combined[97], we are going to study a specific aspect of the latter, which is the harmonic repetition and the almost infallible return of the same family name, as the origin and extinction of both families and societies. Ancient and modern history proves the reality of this new phenomenon with numerous pieces of data.

1. ANCIENT HISTORY

Homonymy in extreme names

A. HOLY HISTORY

1. *THE PATRIARCHS.* -- JUDAH.... JUDAS.

Judah, one of the twelve sons of Jacob, sold his brother Joseph, a name that signifies Savior.

Judas, one of the twelve spiritual sons, or disciples of the true Jacob, sold his brother and his master Jesus, whose name has the same meaning as that of Joseph.

2. JACOB, JOSEPH. – JACOB ... JOSEPH.

In the genealogical order, as Joseph succeeded his father Jacob, so Jacob, the forebear of Our Lord, is followed (by Mary and) by Joseph.

3. JOSHUA ... JESUS.

Joshua (an anagram of Jesu[98]) or Jesus, who put the Hebrews in possession of Canaan, corresponds to Jesus, introducer of the chosen people of the elect, into the True Promised Land.

4. HIGH PRIESTS. – ELEAZAR... ELEAZAR.

---

[97] Not strictly speaking true, since no account of dates was made in the Second Class of Phenomena – PV.
[98] But only in French, and even then, only tenuously. In French, Joshua is Josué, and the short form of Jesus being Jésu, we still have to drop the 'o' to make the anagram work...
– PV.

Founder – Aaron. To the first High Priest who succeeded him, called Eleazar, we add the pontiff Eleazar who, at the time of Jesus Christ, exercised the sovereign sacrificer[99].

FOURTH CLASS OF PHENOMENA[100]
Prophetic Order of Figures

The numeric signs of an extreme age, taken according to their absolute value and in their respective order of position, each have a prophetic sense of their own.

In other words, each figure is specifically a true echo, a faithful monitor of the future, which identifies the most important reigns, as well as the most characteristic events of a Nation or a sovereign family.

This fourth law again provides clear proof of a universal and powerful verification. In order not to tire one's attention, we shall only give a few examples, which will be sufficient to put those readers who would like to examine this in more detail on the right track.

1. WESTERN ROMAN EMPIRE

The precise date of the first apportioning which divided the Roman provinces in two separate empires is the year **364**, when the West ceded to Valentinian I.[101] We say that each of the three numerals of that date, 3, 6 and 4, being studied in the rank it occupies, seems to us to expressly indicate a time, a reign or a fact of special importance.

---

[99] It is hard to find any reference of this name in the New Testament other than as an ancestor of Jesus. Turning to Flavius Josephus, the only mention appears to be of the leader of the Sicarii who died at Masada, but that was 73 CE, a good 40 years after the crucifixion. Another possibility is that Eleazar is also another spelling of Lazarus, though why one would imagine only the High Priest could be termed the 'sovereign sacrificer', and that in Jesus' time would have been Annas, and later Caiaphas – PV.

[100] Op. cit., pp. 100 – 103.

[101] When Valentinian I, or Valentinian the Great became Emperor (in fact, he was the fifth choice!), he made his brother, Valens, Co-Emperor, assigning him the Eastern provinces, while he ruled the Western ones – PV.

To make this clearer, let us outline the nominal succession of the Western Emperors.

1. Valentinian 1, 26 February **364**
2. Valentinian II (strangled in 392) 375
3. And Gratian, his brother 375

Interregnum.

4. Theodosius the Great 394
5. Honorius, 17 January 395

Died in 423. Under him Rome was besieged three times by Alaric.

Interregnum.

6. Valentinian III, 25 October 425

Died March 26, 455. After him, Maxime, who is not counted, reigned three months.

7. Avitus reigned for fourteen months 455

Interregnum.

8. Majorian, 1 April 457
    Worthy prince, assassinated in 461.
9. Severus III, 19 November 461
    Died 15 August 465.
10. Interregnum.
11. Anthemius (assassinated in 472) 467
12. Olybrius (reigned seven months) 472
13. Interregnum.
14. Glycerius, 5 March 433
15. Julius Nepos, 24 June 474
16. Dethroned 24 August 475.
17. Augustulus, 31 October 475
18. Deposed in 476.

In all there were 14 emperors; and really only 13, not counting Gratian, who reigned jointly with his brother Valentinian II.

ANALYSIS OF THE DATE 364

Three... The first digit, 3, indicates that one must count three emperors to arrive at a culminating epoch, the reign of Theodosius the Great.

Six... The second digit, 6, tells us that: 1. we must count forward six emperors from Theodosius: which led to a reverse epoch, being the reign of the despicable Olybrius[102], whose appearance for a few months, followed by a final interregnum, was the harbinger of the final collapse; 2. the sixth of those included is Valentinian III, whose reign of 30 years[103] and the exploits of the famous Aetius cast a last ray upon the agony of the Roman Empire.

Four... Tells us: 1. to pass to the fourth successor to Olybrius inclusive, that is to say, to Romulus Augustulus[104], who was the last of the Caesars of the West; 2. to the fourth successor of the first of the Valentinians, to the Emperor Honorius, who reigned for 28 years, and under whom Rome was taken and sacked twice by Alaric. In effect, after Theodosius, Valentinian III and Honorius are the only heads of the Empire whose reign has any interest for history; just as Olybrius and Augustulus accomplished the humiliating end of the destiny of the Eternal City.

FIFTH CLASS OF PHENOMENA[105]
Relationship of the addition to a date and the sum of its figures

The chronological harmonies are so inexhaustible, and they abound in combinations so varied that they participate visibly in the very infinity of numbers. Some partial indications of the formula that we are going to review have already appeared in a

---

[102] Apparently, the author means six Emperors *between* Theodosius and Olybrius; that is, seven Emperors – PV.

[103] In the original text this says 20 years. However, as the table above correctly states, he ruled from 425 to 455, and presided over the collapse of the Roman Empire – PV.

[104] Though according to the table above, he was the *third* successor (unless this time the author is including both Olybrius *and* Augustulus in his count) – PV.

[105] Op. cit., pp.120 – 122.

few fleeting outputs of the press. Stories of this nature cannot fail to excite attention, due to our attraction to any peculiarities which are in any way provocative. But, as long as they appear as isolated instances, as exceptional coincidences, it must be admitted that they prove nothing, and that their value is reduced to momentary surprise or a distraction for idle minds. But this isn't the case when we see that a common principle links them together, and when their hidden intricacy is openly revealed. Then these phenomena acquire serious meaning, and their prophetic importance becomes all the more clear.

To demonstrate this particular system of relationships which highlight the addition to a distant date either of the total or partial sum of its elements, or of the sum of the figures which comprise the total itself, it is not necessary to examine the chronicles of a large number of people; and the study can be brought down to a circle of verification which is much narrower. Limited to a specific history – for example to the chronology of the kings of France – the test may still be conclusive; even if, instead of forcing ourselves to verify the principle by applying it to every reign from Clovis to Louis XVI, we only look at the most important ones.

Let us begin by clearly stating this fifth harmonic rule:

The connections are revealed by the addition to the radical years of the total and, if necessary, the subtotal of their figures; and this total or subtotal, added to each new result, successively reveals all the important periods of any reign.

Here, **radical** years are those of the birth or the accession (of each king).

I. CLOVIS

Radical Years

Birth 465   Accession 481
Sum of 465 15
Sum of 15 6

Coincidences

1.	Birth..	465	
	Sum of the number..............................	15	
	You have the first year of his reign........	480	81
2.	Add the subtotal......................................	6	
		486	
	Victory of Clovis at Soissons................	486	
	Accession..	481	
	Radical sum...	15	
3.	Victory of Tolbian, conversion..............	496	
	Radical sum...	15	
4.	Death of Clovis..	511	
		481	
	Subtotal of $15 \times 2^{106} = 6 \times 2 \ldots 12$ ...	12	
5.	Marriage of Clovis..................................	493	
	Radical sum...	15	
6.	Victory at Vouillé....................................	508	507

SIXTH CLASS OF PHENOMENA[107]
Anagram or reversal of dates

There is an clear and enduring relationship between the founding date and the duration of an empire, a society or a family; and this relationship is revealed by swapping the figures around, that is to say, by taking the anagram of the whole or a part of the radical year, and, in the case of the latter, the anagram of the last date.

We will therefore try to demonstrate this by looking at the annals of all Nations:

---

[106] Remember that theosophical reduction is being used, so $15 = 12 + 5 = 6 \times 2 = 12$ years – PV.
[107] Op. cit., pp.143 – 145.

Let the regular inversion of chronological signs reproduce either the duration of the Empire or Dynasty, or the specific time of its fall, or a great change or political crisis, or finally, some other event of the first order.

1. ANCIENT HISTORY

It is particularly in studying the mysterious correspondences and Divine Accords hidden within the timeline beneath transparent veils, that the uncertainties of this science become more seriously handicapped and of almost insurmountable difficulty. However, we will try to verify the existence of this sixth class in the ages prior to the Christian era; and in order to accomplish our goal, which is to find a reliable number of relationships – if not rigorous, at least approximate – we will base our calculations not on the much contested number of years of the world since Creation, but rather those counted before Jesus Christ. Since this latter basis offers historians much less variation than the former, we will find more reliable data there to establish the actual date of each event.

1. THE JEWS

A. DURATION OF THE JEWISH CONSTITUTION

From the exodus from Egypt up to the destruction of the kingdom of Judah.

Departure from Egypt, B.C.[108] .... 1,491 years
Judah destroyed, B. C.. 588
Duration of independence .... 903 years

---

[108] For all our calculations, we follow the former the chronological system, that is to say, that of Usserius, adopted by Bossuet and by all writers of the 18th Century. [It seems odd that, having dismissed the use of the date 4004 B.C. to perform any calculation, the author immediately says all dates are based on those of 'Usserius' – and *Jacobus Usserius Archiepiscopus Armachanus* was indeed...Bishop Ussher! – PV.]

Let us now look at the result of reversing the two extreme years 1491, 588.

```
Anagram of 588 . . . . . . . . . . . . . . . . . . . . . . . . . . . .885
Anagram of 1,491(last 2 figures) . . . . . . . . . . . . . . 19
Product of the double inversion . . . . . . . . . . . . . . . .904
Period of Existence  . . . . . . . . . . . . . . . . . . . . . . . . .903
```

SEVENTH CLASS OF PHENOMENA[109]
Extraordinary Function of the Number of Letters of the First Name

When an entire succession of sovereigns of a State or leaders of some society show a considerable variation in names which exceed normal bounds, in order to determine the true figure, one must in the first instance take the name of the founder, or otherwise the final name, and count all the letters. Then, beginning with the radical year, one should add between them as many dates as there are alphabetical letters in the original name. This complex operation will precisely reproduce the exact number of leaders that have come and gone from the beginning till the end.

This new combination of proper names with years is a most unexpected fact: but before deriving any proofs from this, we should first observe that, in order to obtain a credible outcome, it is essential for the succession to be known precisely. However, such positive certainty is something we look for in vain in records prior to the Christian era, and it doesn't even exist in most of the lists in modern history. We will also say that the rule doesn't apply when the chronological succession is small, for we should understand that the sum of the dates would, in such cases, result in too high a number. Thirdly, we should recall that the spelling of proper names is a troubling problem, since it would be best if each name were written in its own language. It follows that this last law

---

[109] Op. cit., pp. 198 – 200.

would only govern a quite limited series of numbers but, on the other hand, as it is more complicated than the previous laws, the more the links in the chain are multiplied, the greater the precision of the results should astound us, leading to unprecedented accuracy, as we will find in the comparisons which follow.

1. HIGH PRIESTS OF THE JEWS

Let us attempt a first application to the 81 High Priests whose names are recorded in the Jewish records. We must therefore take the name of the first of all, who is **Aaron**, composed of **five letters**, to count the **first five dates** or years of the **first five** Hebrew Pontiffs, and check whether the sum of these dates will produce 81. But, here, we find ourselves stopped completely by an insurmountable difficulty. The years of the fourth and fifth Pontiffs, Abishua and Bukki, who operated under the Judges, are completely unknown. The absence of these necessary elements therefore requires us to work on the other far end of the succession, ending with Phannias or Phanasus, 81st and Last High Priest, whose two names each contain eight letters:

PHANNIAS	PHANNASUS
8	8

The above rule therefore requires that we count eight dates, beginning with that of Phannias, to return up to the eighth.

		Years of Accession	Totals
81st	1. Phannias (year of J.C.)	69 (70)	15
80th	2. Mathias	64 (65)	10
79th	3. Jesus, son of Gamaliel	64	10
78th	4 Jesus, son of Ananus	64	10
77th	5. Ananus	63	9
76th	6. Joseph	63	9
75th	7. Ismaël	63	9
74th	8. Ananias	63	9
	Total of the eight dates		81
	Equal number of High Priests		81

If all the letters of a name, if all the numeric signs of an era, are invisibly penetrated by a principle of life, that is to say, a seed and a thought for the future; if their meaning and their own value possesses a prophetic element, then all the more reason that the facts themselves and the people who are related to those names and dates must participate in the same character. For it is the figurative power, the spirit of divination which, assimilated and incorporated into things and into historical characters by a most intimate union, must extend into the basic signs of those things and those people, rather than the signs coming first, in order to communicate the facts they express and on which they depend. Such is the natural and necessary order of that generation. However, if it were truly thus, the whole of history would be a continued reflection of the future in the past, a figurative mirror of future times, a universal system of types and predictions, a harmonious ensemble of allusions and relationships which its infinite radiation would gravitate mainly to certain times which would dominate all others. That is the place to which the threads of induction and the rules of analogy lead . Such is also the general and definitive result of our study on the functions of numbers.[110]

---

[110] Op. cit. pp. 282 – 283.

Chapter 11
Numbers and Nations

The second book from which we will publish a long passage has as its author the renowned Robert Bruck and is entitled: *Manifeste du Magnétisme du Globe et de l'Humanité*.[111]

Robert Bruck was an unrecognized genius of his generation, and is quite forgotten nowadays; however, his work is there[112] to show the almost perfect accuracy of the historical and physical law proposed by him. Here is an account of it:

He demonstrates in a positive and incontrovertible way that the earth is traversed by magnetic currents following the approximate direction of the meridians. Meteorological and astronomical influences alter the speed of these currents, which as a result differ at all points of the surface of the globe. As a result, there exists a magnetic meridian where the speed is at a maximum. This maximum current moves from East to West while undergoing weekly, monthly, four-year, sixteen-year, five hundred-year[113], etc. fluctuations.

These currents have a very marked action on the intensity of vegetative, animal and intelligent life; this influence is made evident by an almost infinite number of observations, *and history shows that where the speed of the magnetic current reaches its maximum, civilization and the power of Nations whose land it affects also reach their greatest progress.*

---

[111] *Manifesto on the Magnetism of the Globe and Humanity*; or *A succinct summary of terrestrial magnetism and of its influence on human destiny*. Brussels. Pub. Guyot, 1866. pp. 141 – 180.

[112] Robert Bruck, Major in Belgian Engineering, was born in Dirkirch (Luxembourg), and died in Ixelles on February 21, 1870. He is the author of: *Electricity or Magnetism of the Terrestrial Globe*, Brussels, pub. Delevingue & Callewart; *The Origin of Shooting Stars*, Brussels, pub. Guyot, 1868; *Study on the Physics of the Globe*, Brussels, pub. Macquardt, 1869; *Humanity: its Development, its Duration*, Brussels, 1864. (Note by the Ed.)

[113] Meaning every five hundred sixteen years (or less precisely 520, as we see on the following page) – PV.

Every 520 years, approximately, domination moves around the white races from one Nation to another, following the laws of replacement through which the entire human race has passed.

A Nation which runs the complete cycle of its destiny takes 520 years to reach its period of highest elevation and 520 years to gradually descend once again.

Each period of 520 years is made up of 32 periods of 16 years, plus 2 periods of 4 years which begin and end the cycle.

These periods of 16 years also correspond to changes in the distribution of those dominating white humanity, and as a result to the deadly battles of greater or lesser intensity between them.

But let's not get ahead of ourselves, and allow Major Bruck to speak for himself:

Electricity circulates in the superficial layers of the globe with the magneto-electric speed of magnets. Its accumulations make it freer; the influence of the environments where it is concentrated, and especially the influence of the conductors which lead to those regions, have a strong influence on its freedom of action and expansion, and significantly alter its character and movement.

I have shown the conditions under which electricity becomes Galvano-, magneto- and neuro-electricity. It is in this last quality as vital fluid, that is, as the primary, principal and physiological cause acting on the ethical, religio-philosophical and political world, that it plays its main role. The study of this role constitutes *Humanity*.

Strictly speaking, man's body is only a machine, or an instrument maintained by the circulation of blood and nervous fluid. What propels the blood and the nervous circulation? This impulse, called *Magnetism*, must be independent of man's will, since man certainly continues to live when he sleeps.

Physiology says that the heart, acting as an aspiring and pushing pump, is what propels the blood. I would like to believe that, but it seems to me firstly that this small aspiring and pushing pump possesses a power to inject which is so powerful, it would be difficult not to suspect something *vital*. Then, accepting the pump, I ask myself where is the pump-maker? Breathing, you say, makes the pump work; then what controls breathing? The pump! It's a vicious circle. If the pump makes us breathe, respiration doesn't pump. There is a reciprocal action, a coming and going, an oscillation or movement of the pendulum. There must be a motor agent or propeller to maintain the movement.

It is the nervous system which operates the human machine, and terrestrial magnetism is the propeller. That is what scientifically establishes the *Magnetism of the Globe* and what will historically prove *Humanity*.

This historical proof will establish, through evidence, that humanity develops through five hundred-year periods, and that these periods exactly follow those of the revolution of the five hundred-year[114] magnetic system.

THE FIVE HUNDRED YEAR HISTORICAL HUMAN PERIOD

From historical times, there has always been a Nation at the first tier of Humanity, an Initiating or Civilizing People who exercised a preponderant and dominant action which was both physical and ethical, for a period of approximately five centuries over all its neighbors.

This Nation and its neighbors form the core of Humanity; its capital is the center of all the principal activity of the civilization of that period.

The Nations which have successively occupied the first place as conductors or leaders were: 1. the Babylonians; 2. the Egyptians; 3. the Jews-Phoenicians, 4. the Greeks; 5. the Romans; 6. the Franks; 7. the Monarchal Catholics[115]; 8. the French or Gallicans.

These Nations began around -2284 and ended their eight periods in 1830. Divide 2284 + 1830 by eight, and you will get *five*

---

[114] The French word 'séculaire' means 'happening once a century, century-old, ancient and time-honored' (it also means 'secular'). The author uses the word in many paragraphs, and it became apparent that he was actually using the phrase for the unique purpose of identifying his five hundred-year cycles. Therefore, in Bruck's extract, the word 'séculaire' will be substituted by 'five hundred-year' – PV.

[115] The Papacy.

hundred and fifteen years as the duration of each period of civilization, that is to say, a period close to the duration of the five hundred-year magnetic period of 516 years.[116]

Since the year 2284 is not historically certain, take -750 as the foundation of Rome and add to it 1830, the end of the French period; divide 750 + 1830 = 2580 by five, and this time you will have precisely the half-millennium magnetic period of *five hundred and sixteen years*.

Examine history carefully, and you will see that this period has had the same duration for all leading Nations. And so it should be!

I will give you all the necessary clarification concerning this if you will follow me for a moment.

APOGEES OF THE HUMAN PERIODS

Each period of civilization has an apogee which is perfectly shown by history. These apogees are so similar in nature that a description of one of them can be applied to all of them. They signify physical and ethical power, grandeur and splendor!

The apogees of the periods of known civilization all took place at the same five hundred-year magnetic period, that of the five hundred-year passage of the pole over the capital, or rather, over the center of the possessions of the leader Nation; and they lasted as long as that passage.

That is, I believe, a remarkable and conclusive fact, which will perhaps establish the political period of a civilization more certainly and unimpeachably than has previously been achieved. Below is a historical table[117] in support of what I am saying. A

---

[116] Remember that, although it was said earlier that a Nation rises over 520 years and falls over 520 years, during the first half that Nation will be rising while another one is still dominant, and in its decline it will still hold sway until being crushed towards the latter half of its rule. Therefore, the apogee of a Nation's dominance will tend to be 520 years, even if its total existence will be 1040 years – PV.

[117] In studying this table, we note first that the center of civilization moves by following the path of the Sun in relation to the Earth, that is to say from the East to the West; next, that the apogee of a Nation's civilization and power coincides with the arrival of the

represents the leader Nations; B, the capitals; C, the political leaders at their apogees; D, the true dates of the middle of the apogees; E, the differences between two successive apogees or the duration of the period of the civilization; F, the periodic date of the five-hundred year corresponding to the center of the reign; G, the date of the five hundred-year passage of the magnetic pole over the capital.

	A	B	C	D	E	F	G
1.	Babylonians	Babylon	Semiramis	2012		1600	1598
2.	Egyptians	Thebes	Sesostris	1474	538	1622	1613
3.	Jews	Jerusalem	Solomon	981	493	1599	1611
4.	Greeks	Athens	Pericles	436	545	1628	1624
5.	Romans	Rome	Vespasian, Trajan	93	529	1641	1631
6.	Franks	Metz	Clotaire II	613	520	1645	1646
7.	Catholicism	Rome	Pascal II, Honorius II	1115	502	1631	1631
8.	Francs	Paris	Louis XIII, Richelieu	1628	512	1627	1631
9.	Francs	Paris	Louis XIV, Colbert	"	"	1663	1663
			Mean.............		529	1628	1628

The first French period was the participation of France in the European apogee, or the Gallican-European apogee; and the second period was that of the purely French apogee.

The middle of the reign of Solomon twelve years early with regard to the passage of the pole over Jerusalem corresponds with the passage of the pole over the center of the Jewish possessions which included the Western boundary, rather than only to its passage over their center of action.

The powerful Roman Apogee, more Western than Eastern, in being extended, arrives a little late.

The enormously and abnormally lengthened reign of Louis XIV (72 years), exceeds by 32 years the regular duration of apogees which is 40 years.

---

magnetic pole over its capital. In studying this Table, which is based on the period of 520 years, we see that the next great change in the capital of civilization will come approximately around the year 2140 or 2147.

Louis XIV began precisely at the time of the apogee in 1643, but this period only continued up to 1683, the year of the revocation of the Edict of Nantes.[118]

Those are the only insignificant irregularities which show the parallels between the apogees of civilization and the passages of the poles, irregularities which the above comments satisfactorily explain.

The average duration of 520 years which separates the apogees includes the period of 516 years, plus the displacement of the center of action from one period to the next.

The middle of the kingdoms' apogee corresponds exactly to the middle of the magnetic pole's passage over the centers of civilization.

We have demonstrated this for political apogees.

Now, here is how the philosophical apogees are seen:

Assuming that A represents the middle of the reign or the middle of the life of the principal philosopher of that period, B, the corresponding date, and C, the passage of the ancient magnetic pole, one can create the following table:

	A	B	C
Solomon	931	1599	1611
Socrates	433	1631	1624
St. John	83	1631	1631
St. Gregory the Great	597	1629	1631
St. Bernard	1111	1627	1631
Pierre de Cluny	1123	1629	1631
Abeilard	1111	1627	1631
Descartes	1623	1623	1631

Here are the main historians :

Thucydides 433   1634   1624

---

[118] From a practical sense, we can see that the center of his reign was 1663, so 40 years would extend from 1643 to 1683. In passing, it is interesting that the author sees the revocation of tolerance towards Protestants (Huguenots) in France and their enforced expulsion as a an 'end' to this civilization, which is why the author completely discounts the final 32 years of the Sun King's reign from 1683 to 1715! – PV.

Tacitus	97	1645	1631
Gregory of Tours	570	1602	1631
Suger	1119	1635	1631
Bossuet	1665	1665	1663

Christ was *thirty years* old *the exact year*, 30 (1578), of the passage of the pole over the axis of the Euro-Asian valley where he preached.

Thucydides and Socrates were each *thirty years* old in -441 (1623), the central year of the passage of the pole over Athens.

Tacitus was *thirty years* old in 83 (1631) *the central year* of the passage of the pole over Rome.

Suger was *thirty years* old in 1115, *the central year* of the Monacal Catholic apogee.

Bossuet was *thirty years* old in 1657, the year of the passage of the pole over Paris, setting aside the displacement by sixteen-year periods.[119]

Four of the five main historians of the last five human periods were thirty years old in the year of the passage of the pole over the center of the civilization they represented. The fifth belongs to the disrupted or abnormal period of the Franks, which is itself an exception, that is to say a *Teutonic* civilization misplaced in the center of Celtic civilizations, as we will see later.

If this is due to chance, we must agree that randomness is sometimes most strange.

The years cited above, their correspondence with the apogees, and their coinciding with the passages of the magnetic pole, irrefutably establish an intimate connection and dependence between magnetic movements and human movements.

Humanity explains and details this connection and draws conclusions from it. It institutes all the periods and all the influential ages of those ancient periods, with their temperaments and the consequences of those temperaments: the souls, the characters, the aptitudes, the patterns and trends which are reproduced identically and consistently from period to period.

---

[119] Being 8 years either side of 1665 – PV.

The terrestrial regions located beneath the five hundred-year passage of the magnetic pole are temporarily under the influence of the most energetic magnetic flow; that is to say, the flow which is both the densest and the most active. It is therefore the energy or the magnetic power which provides Nations and humanity with that energy, physical and moral power.

This is a first indisputable fact.

A second fact, also uncontestable, is the length of each period of civilization.

Thirdly, a leading Nation only governs and leads humanity during a five hundred-year period of civilization. When that period is ended, the initiatory role of that leader Nation ceases and it must give place to another, no matter what it does, because no human power can oppose the forces and the physical laws, any more than they can the powers and the moral laws of the world.

The connection between the magnetic movements which dominate all the physical forces of the earth, and the moral, historical, political and religio-philosophical movements, proves from the evidence that the physical forces are at the disposal of the world spirit.

THE PERIOD OF THE REFORMATION AND ORGANIZATION, THE GREAT HUMANITARIAN AGE

The humanitarian apogees are preceded, a century earlier, by an era which is also magnetically noteworthy and perhaps even more remarkable than the apogees; this is the arrival of the five-hundred year system in its initial or fundamental Colombo-Asiatic position; this is the arrival of the pole and the principal meridian at 98°30' longitude East, coinciding with the principal Colombo-Asiatic meridian or with *the backbone of the globe*.

With the five hundred-year magnetic system occupying this position, the circulation universally realizes the greatest activity, and this increase in activity which lasted thirty-two years, from 1509 to 1541, provided humanity and the Nations with the greatest physical and ethical activity.

The period of the greatest physical and ethical activity, the initial period, was that of all the reformations and organizations. It was fundamentally religious, enthusiastic, ascetic, powerfully intelligent, revealing, and creative. It lasted for two sixteen-year periods.

Humanity owes it all its ideas, as it should to all its works during the apogee.

The phase (1541-1610) which separated these two powerful eras of both activity and intelligence, propagated the ideas of the Reformation, to which the apogee should be dedicated. This is the great human phase framed between the two historical, religio-philosophical and political eras, the most strongly accentuated of the five hundred-year period, coinciding with the principal magnetic phase between the two principal events and movements of the five hundred-year system. Studying this phase proves *that magnetic activation predisposes towards physical and ethical activity, and that physical energy predisposes towards energy, and physical and ethical power.*

HUMAN PERIODS AND PHASES, SIXTEEN- AND FOUR-YEAR PERIODS

The coincidence of clearly determined ethical and political states of affairs with important magnetic positions, whose two principles I have just explained, are continued throughout all periods of civilization, in which there are also other epochs which are clearly identifiable outside of those of renewal and apogee... These modifications are every *sixteen* and every *four years*.

Ethical and political situations are ruled so well by the sixteen-year cycle of magnetic movement, that that it usually sees political leaders such as reigning emperors, popes, kings or princes disappearing or being replaced.

As the truth sometimes seems unlikely, and as the foregoing may seem extraordinary or paradoxical, I will explain this very clearly.

The latest sixteen-year magnetic movements of **1831**, **1847** and **1863** are the best known to us by facts and will be the first clearly recognized.

Starting from the middle, **1847**, and going toward the future and back to the past we can establish the following general sixteen-year pattern as follows:

1847; 1863; 1895; (1379)[120]; 1395; 1411; 1427; 1443; 1459; 1475; 1491; **1507**; 1523.

1847; 1831; 1815; 1799; 1783; 1767; 1751; 1735; 1719; 1703; 1687; 1671; 1655; 1639; 1623; 1607; 1591; 1575; 1559; 1543; 1527; 1511; 1495.

In counting up and down with sixteen-year intervals from **1847** to the initial position, we come to **1507** and 1511, because the five hundred-year period of 516 years contains thirty-two sixteen-year periods, plus a quadrennial or four-year period which must be lost. It is lost prior to the initial position of **1491** to **1495**, or from 1507 to 1511. For this reason, these two periods, the quadrennial at the opening of the five hundred-year period, and from the beginning of the Reformation and into the major phase of human activity, are strongly disturbed.

That being so, here is the political movement of the last Gallican human period, directed and indicated by the reigns of the kings of the leading Nation or in this case France:

A represents the true beginning of the reign; B, the five hundred-year correspondence[121]; C, the four-, eight-, or sixteen-yearly magnetic movements, underlined by one, two or three traits.

	A	B	C
Louis X............................	1314	1830	1830

---

[120] There is absolutely no explanation given in the text why the author jumps from 1895 to 1379, instead of continuing the forward series as he had said he was going to do. The only apparent reason is that the difference between 1379 and 1895 is 516 years, which is the period of his magnetic Great Cycle, or period in which a civilization reaches its apogee, and then fades away into oblivion, particularly as the book was written in 1866, so he cannot claim that 1895 would be the highest point in French civilization as it was still 29 years off – PV.

[121] In other words, column B is the date in column A plus 516 years. As the book was written in 1966, the author clearly saw no benefit in extending this series beyond 1880 – PV.

Jean I	.1316	1832	1831
Philippe V	.1316	1832	1832
Philippe VI	.1328	1844	1843
Jean II	.1350	1866	1867
Charles V	.1364	1880	1879
Charles VI	.1380	-----	1379
Charles VII	.1422	-----	1423
Louis XI	.1461	-----	1459
Charles VIII	.1483	-----	1483
Louis XII	.1498	-----	1499
François I.................	.1515	-----	1515
Henri I....................	.1547	-----	1547
François I.................	.1559	-----	1559
Charles IX	.1560	-----	1559
Henri IV	.1589	-----	1591
Louis XIII	.1610	-----	1611
Louis XIV	.1643	-----	1643
Louis XV	.1715	-----	1715
Louis XVI	.1774	-----	1775
Napoleon I (Consul)	.1799	-----	1799
Id. (The Emperor)	.1804	-----	1803
Louis XVIII	.1815	-----	1815
Charles X	.1824	-----	1823
Louis-Philippe	.1830	-----	1831
Louis-Napoleon (President)	.1848	-----	1848
Ditto. (The Emperor)	.1852	-----	1852

In this Table, the coinciding of political movements with magnetic movements is irrefutable and obvious.

The dates 1421, 1525, 1631 and 1660 are fundamentally magnetic, as are 1267 (1783) and 1315 (1831).

The fundamental magnetic dates are central to the principle reigns, as was the case for the last period of civilization, for the reigns of François I, Louis XIII–Richelieu and Louis XIV–Colbert.

The dates which open and complete these reigns are fundamental, like their centers, although the three reigns above of the last great human phase, those of François I, Louis XIII and Louis XIV, are all delayed by four years or a quadrennial period in addition to the general sixteen-year movement.

To cut short any objections of sophistry and empiricism, let us remove all the fundamental start dates for the principle reigns and, therefore, the clearest evidence of the coincidence of political movement with magnetic movement, only retaining the general sixteen-year coincidences. Ten changes of reign remain in the previous Table coinciding with the general sixteen-year magnetic movement. Since a sixteen-year movement often includes *three* years as years of action which end the previous period and which begins the next period, the probable number of times a change of kingdom coincides with these triennial movements is 3/16, or *four* times during the 22 reigns in the previous Table.

Thus, in reality and outside the fundamental magnetic and principle dates, the triennial movement of the magnetic sixteen-year period leads in the last period to ten changes of reigns instead of the expected four changes.

It is simply chance which produces these coincidences, says sophistry and empiricism!

A singular coincidence, in truth, which *is reproduced as clearly and in the same proportions in all the periods, whether Catholic, Frank, etc., as also for all the thrones, both those of the German Emperors and the pontifical cathedra, and for the thrones of every hereditary or elected sovereign of all historical times and all European regions.*

If the reader still isn't convinced, read the following table:

Treaty	Real Date	Magnetic Date
Treaty of Madrid	1526	1527
Treaty of Crépy.......................	1542	1543
Treaty of Cateau-Cambrésis.........	1559	1559
Treaty of Monçon....................	1626	1627
Treaty of Berwald....................	1631	1631
Treaty of Prague......................	1635	1635
Treaty of the Pyrenees...............	1659	1659
Treaty of Aix-la-Chapelle...........	1668	1667
Treaty of Westminster...............	1674	1675
Treaty of Nimègue...................	1678	1679
Treaty of Ryswyck...................	1697	1695
Treaty of Utrecht.....................	1713	
Treaty of Bade........................	1714	1715
Treaty of Barrières...................	1715	
Treaty of la Haye.....................	1717	
Treaty of Vienna.....................	1738	1739
Treaty of Belgrade...................	1739	
Shameful Peace of Paris	1764	1763
Treaty of Paris	1783	1783[122]

This Table contains all the Peace Treaties of the last period from the middle of the Reformation up to the *Transformation*. However, there can be no doubt that the Peace Treaties exercised an influence on the political direction of Nations, and that in general these are usually acts which result in the beginning or ending of a period of action.

Six Treaties among the *sixteen* changed the political direction of the predominant Nation of the last period during the *general sixteen-year* magnetic movements, while the 3/16 of probabilities only require three coincidences. The connection between actual

---

[122] Continuing the list of these dates data by the period of 16 years, we get: 1783-1799-1815-1831-1847-1863-1879-1895-1911-1927-1943. Each of these periods of 16 years being composed of four periods of 4 years, starting from 1863 we will obtain the following dates: 1863-1867-**1871**-1875-1879-1883-1887-1891-1895-1899-19031907-1911-**1915**-1919-1923-1927-1931-1935-1939. The major changes in the equilibrium of the Nations which constitute the white race occur in one of these time periods.

and probable coincidences is as strong for Peace Treaties as for changes in reigns.

Three of the *sixteen* treaties above belong to three *absolutely fundamental* dates: 1525, 1631 and 1783. *The Treaty of Troyes* in 1420 complements the coincidence of the *four fundamental or initial dates*, as follows:

Troyes	in 1420	1421
Madrid	in 1526	1525
Bernwald	in 1631	1631
Paris	in 1783	1783

That is, the four fundamental political and magnetic dates of the last period strictly coincide; these are those of the powerful double passages of the principal magnetic meridian at the zenith of the Colombo-Asiatic and Euro-Polynesian meridians; these are the dates of the arrival of the magnetic five-hundred year system in their fundamental and initial positions.

History's highlighting of the physiological, religio-philosophical and political influence of terrestrial magnetism and its movements proves first that, whoever we may be, Pope, Emperor, King, Prince, Philosopher, Moralist, Historian or Legislator, we are powerless to cause or to stop a magnetic movement in the general physics of the globe. Man can do nothing in such a situation: he finds the situations already established and can only hasten or delay their progress, facilitate or impede their resolutions, and make them more or less complete.

Humanities is a study of temperament, of mind, the trends and aptitudes of all ages and all the phases of the five hundred-year period from which it draws all the ethical and political situations.

By highlighting the physiological, religio-philosophical and political implications of magnetic movements, history gives such importance to the analysis of these movements, that is to say the Magnetism of the globe and to Mankind, that their study must be given the highest priority. It even gives history a scientific value by providing a new viewpoint on the facts it reports, and on the events whose cause it seeks to find or whose effects is seeks to judge.

Placing it outside of the challenges which history raises about the physiological consequences of magnetic movements, would corroborate and clarify what I said about the origin of epidemics.

Plagues are constant accompaniments of great magnetic and political movements, and they have for inseparable companions famines, wars, political convulsions and physical disturbances, earthquakes, volcanic eruptions, etc. The most powerful and splendid eras are those of the greatest convulsions and the greatest disturbances; these are the apogees. No apogee proves this better than the last one, that of 1631.

Still, the Greek, Roman, Frank and Catholic apogees were not during a volcanic event any less remarkable that the last French apogee. It began in 1610 with a *colossal* eruption of Etna, continuing without interruption for ten years. Its central year, 1631, was indicated by the principal European volcanic fact, the five-hundred year reopening of Vesuvius which had remained mute during the entire Catholic period and which took up its activity again in the same year as the arrival of the pole in the initial meridional position in Europe, of which Vesuvius and Etna are part, *after five centuries of silence and six months of violent tremors.*

Etna, which had begun the European apogee in 1610, ended it in 1643, having signaled the middle passage by a quadrennial eruption in 1634. These eruptions of Mount Etna were all reported as being *colossal*.

In 1138 (1654), the sixteen-year movement of closure of the Catholic apogee was signaled by an eruption of Vesuvius which was also reported as *colossal*.

In the year 1631, already quoted, the leading Nation and the temporary Northern leader of humanity came together at Bernwald to accomplish the *mission of the period*, the definitive emancipation of the Christian idea in the first, second and third degree, the *supremacy of Gallicanism*, the *independence of Anglicanism* and *tolerance of the German way of life*, three conquests which had been extorted by arms by *Catholicism*, which received a mortal blow and fell back five centuries at the same time that the German Empire, the second Teutonic term which was to end with the period, was killed. This mission was accomplished in the same central year in the fateful plains of Saxony in Leipzig, by the one who was then the moral and military leader of Europe, Gustavus II Adolphus, in the middle of the most appalling European plague that history has recorded.[123]

It is around this same year that Descartes debuted *The World, or Treatise on the Light, 1633*, and Galilee produced his capital work: *Four Dialogs on the World Systems of Ptolemy and Copernicus.*

Catholic and Frankish highlights are less known to us: However, it is likely that we would find similar facts if we went through the annals around 1115 and 599.

With respect to obligatory accompaniments to the apogees in the Greek and Roman periods, we find them among the key facts recorded by history, and which are:

The destruction of Herculaneum and Pompeii and the death of Pliny, one of the two moral leaders of the Roman apogee[124] began with Titus and the central quadrennial period 79-83 (1627-1631) of this apogee, in the midst of a terrifying plague.

The plague which claimed Pericles in -429 (1635) closed the central quadrennial period of 425-429 (1631 to 1635), the second year of the Peloponnesian War in the midst of the moral splendors and Greek power.

---

[123] The unusual alliance forged in the Treaty of Bernwald (or Bärwalde) between Louis XIII of France (head of the author's the 'leading Nation') and Gustav II Adolphus, king of Sweden (the 'temporary Northern leader') joined together a Catholic and a Protestant king to fight other Catholics. This was the Thirty Years' War, the bloody battle which raged across Europe and set Protestants against Catholics, led by the Holy Roman Emperor. France was concerned about being surrounded by Nations committed to the Catholic cause, and fearing they may be overrun, threw their support behind the Swedish king and his Northern Germany supporters. Overall the war, with the attendant starvation and bubonic plague, were devastating, resulting in over 8 million deaths. It took the Holy Roman Empire 60 years to recover. Interested readers can consult texts on the Thirty Years' War – PV.

[124] The two Roman moral leaders outside of the Christian movement were Pliny and Tacitus.

Thus:

Herculaneum-Pompeii and the plague of Rome in . . 79 1627
The principal known eruption of Vesuvius and the
European plague in 1631
The plague of Athens in . . . . -429 1635

Note the quadrennial movement of the passage of the magnetic pole on the axis of the Central European Meridian Ridge and the European apogees for twenty-five centuries, from Greek times up to our days.

GENERAL STATE OF HUMANITY AND ITS CONSEQUENCES

The general state of humankind, the relative position of the Nations that compose it, rational principles of history, religio-philosophy and politics, that is, the positive rules of conduct for these Nations, derive directly from the rise and fall of Nations destined to succeed one another as initiators, civilizers and dominators at the head of Mankind.

The progress of these Nations takes place in two five hundred-year periods, the first of which I call the *first term*, and their slow but constant and continuous decline which lasts the same length of time. I call this the *second term*, and history has given it the name of *Late Empire*.

Rome had its two full terms: the first in Rome and the second in Byzantium.

The Teutons also had their two full terms: the first, Frankish, at *Metz* and the second, German, at *Nuremberg*.

Catholic Rome is beginning its fourth and final period.

France began its third period, or began its second term, in 1848.

England is between its second and its principal period, that of initiation and leadership of humanity.

Prussia is entering into its first period.[125]

Such is the general situation of Europe today. It specifies the rule of conduct of each.

The first period of pagan Rome, -750 (1830) up to the battle of Zama in -202 (1862), was that of its preparatory development. Its second period from -202 (1862) to 330 (1878) was that of its universal government.

In its third period (its first as Empire of the East) the Greco-Roman Empire of the East fought successfully against destruction by dissolution.

In its fourth and final period, the destruction by dissolution of the Greco-Roman Empire of the East progressed rapidly.

In each of the five hundred-year human periods, four types of Nations are seen: numbers *One*, *Two*, *Three* and *Four* in the *First*, *Second*, *third* and *Fourth* periods. These Nations constitute the essential core of humanity during the period. Everything which happens outside of this core is only of secondary importance.

Number *One*, fearless and aggressive, seeks movement and action, and dreams only of upheavals.

Number *Two*, quiet and strong, powerful and proud, selfish and imperious, sees everything in relation to itself, only sees itself, rules and imposes its rule far and wide by force if it meets resistance; its role as initiator requires it to do so.

Number *Three*, though calmer, shares domination and its initiatory mission with the new Number *Two*, over which it remains superior in many ways especially in the development of material interests, at least during the first half of the period. The superiority of Number *Two* only clearly manifests itself through the great humanitarian phase and only becomes evident at the apogee.

Number *Four*, provocateur like number one, only dreams of war and carnage, is the recipient of all the attacks and departs the stage

---

[125] It can be seen that, in 1866, Bruck was able to claim some victories for Prussia. [The Austro-Prussian War or Seven Weeks' War took place in 1866, the year the book was written, and the comment clearly indicates which side the author was on. Ultimately the war ended with Prussia being the main power in a united Germany, with Austria now excluded as a separate country, and Germany now taking its place as one of the most influential European powers. – PV.]

mutilated by all the fights during this period, at the end of which it disappears.

It is Number *Two which is now ruling* and which kills off Number *Four*. It is assisted in this by Numbers *One* and *Three*.

A new Number *One* is preparing itself during this period, in order to be ready to take the place of Number *Four* at the time of the departure of the latter from the universal political movement.

Nations *One* and *Two win* in the first term , and *Three* and *Four* in the second term necessarily *lose* in all the political comotions (*sic*) or in the hand-to-hand struggles. These struggles develop and strengthen the *One* and *Two* Nations in the first term; they deplete and destroy the *Three* and *Four* Nations in the second term.

Young and vigorous Nations seek quarrels with the old because of their temperament. They have a sense of their destinies; this feeling gives them great confidence in the future. They seem to anticipate that the final results will be favorable.

To moderate the need for action of Number *One* and the pride of Number *Two*; to maintain intact for as long as possible the physical forces and morals of Number *Three*; and to soften the fall of Number *Four*, by ameliorating the effects of that fall: *such are the essential principles of rational politics*.

The four Nations which have successively formed the nucleus of humanity are[126]:

---

[126] The Russian people will be called to enter and occupy the place listed under Number One in the table of evolutions.
This will occur when the papacy is on the point of disappearing, when England is defeated by Germany, allied to either France, or rather to Russia.
The crash of England will mark the entry of Russia into full activity.
We should therefore add the following two lines in the above table in the period:

	1	2	3	4
Prussian	Russia	Prussia	England	France
Russia	France & Latin Union	Russia	Prussia	England

According to the prophecies, indeed France, unified by the Latin Union, should enter once more into a new and very brilliant cycle. Cf. Papus: *Le conflit Russo-Japonais et les nombres magnétiques [The Russo-Japanese conflict and Magnetic Numbers]*, 1904.

	1	2	3	4
Greek	Rome	Greece	Jews	Egyptians
Roman	Franks	Rome	Greece	Jews
Franks	Catholics	Franks	Rome	Greece
Catholic	France	Catholics	Germans	Greco-Roman
				Germans
French	England	France	Catholics	(Austrian)
England	Prussia	England	France	Catholics
			(1848)	

Greece effaced the last vestiges of the Egyptians.
Rome scattered the latest remains of the Jews.
The Franks began the destruction of pagan Hellenized Rome.
Catholicism destroyed the Eastern Empire.
France destroyed the second Teutonic German period.
England will destroy Catholic politics.[127]
These are the key actions in history.

Regular progress in humanity requires the agreement of Numbers *Two* and *Three*, that is, of its principal physical and ethical powers.

The whole Universe couldn't do anything against Nations denoted as *Two*. It can therefore do nothing, for all more reason, against *Two* and *Three* in league together.

PERIODS OF ACTION

The conflicts of Numbers *Two* or *Three* produce the most terrible outcomes and the most troubled and violent times. These eras are seen with the same periodicity as reformations and apogees; they extend from 1543 to 1610 and the corresponding earlier dates. Their central years, 1575 or 1578, times of major humanitarian periods, are among the most disturbed years, both physically and physiologically, of the period.

The great Jewish period was that of David; its center was the date of the plague of -1005 (1575).

The Greek period was that of Miltiades, Themistocles, etc., or the struggle of the Greeks against the Persians.

---

[127] An interesting comment viewed in hindsight... – PV.

The Roman period was that of Tiberius, Caligula, Claudius, Nero; of Agrippina and Messalina, and the persecution of Christians.

The Frankish period ended with the struggle between Fredegund and Brunhilda.

The Catholic period was ended by Pope Gregory VII, King Henry IV of Germany, Countess Mathilda, the Guelphs and the Ghibellines.

In its last period, the fight between Gallicanism and Catholicism was even more pronounced than the previous one between Catholicism and the Germans.

With Charles IX, Henry III and Henry IV on one side, and Philippe II, Medici, Mary Tudor, the Guises and the Duke of Alba on the other, these were active leaders who didn't shrink from the use of force.

This was a period of action, but violent action, preparing for the power, grandeur and splendor of the apogee.

The humanitarian period was in the ascendant until the apogee but descended from the apogee until its end. The ascending half-period was spiritual; its spirituality grew with its intelligence and developed its physical forces as well as its moral ones up to the apogee.

THE PERIODS OF MORAL REACTION

The downward half-period of the century was materialistic and sensualist. Materialism and sensuality, with all their consequences, reached its zenith toward the middle of the downward half-period.

The time of that zenith was the counterpart of the apogee; it was one of moral subversion and dissolution, of licentiousness and debauchery, of cruelty and crime; it was an encyclopedic, empirical, verbose and ignorant time, a destroyer of physical and moral strength. It began on the date corresponding to 1703, reached its center in 1745 and ended in 1783.

It had as representatives and produced, in the Jewish period:

– Ahab, Jezebel, Jehoram, -876 (1704); Jehoram, Athaliah and Joash -831 (1749). – *Baalism*.

In the Greek period: – the Macedonian yoke, Lamian War, etc. around 318 (1746) – *Epicureanism*.

In the Roman period: – Commodius, 180 (1728); Severus, 293 (1741); Caracalla, 211 (1759); Heliogabalus, 218 (1766). Principal persecution by Severus: *Gnosticism*; *subversive Alexandrian philosophies (Marcion, Montanus, etc.)*.

In the Frankish period: – The *figurehead* kings, monastic debauchery, dark shadows of superstition, legendary verbosity, Justinian, Leontius, Absimare, – Tiberius, Philip Bardanus and Anastasius II, 713 (1745). – *Iconoclasm*.

In the Catholic period: – The Albigensians, the Stedingers, the Dominicans; superstition, crime and cruelty; the debauchery of the Templars, a further increase in general monastic debauchery; courtly behavior; the courts of love; the White Queen and the Count of Champagne; the revolt of Coucy against Louis IX. The periodic return of Manicheism, Albigensian Baalism and the Satanism of the Stedingers, 1229 (1745).[128]

In the French period: – Louis XV, Pompadour, Dubarry, Terray, Maupeou, Law. – Anti-intelligence, irresponsibility, verbosity; anti-philosophical and irreligious spirit; incapacity. General dissolution through licentiousness and debauchery. Shameful defeats of the best armies due to the incompetence of generals appointed by favorites. – Public flaunting of all vices in public and private. – Moral demolition by Voltaire and Rousseau. – Philosophical outrage of Condillac and Helvetius over all that the empiricism, scepticism and cynicism of the earlier periods had produced. – Materialism and universal sensuality in all their fullness, and with all their consequences (1745).

---

[128] In 1229 Pope Gregory IX issued an instrument of 49 Articles by the Council of Toulouse, thus establishing the Inquisition. As an example of the wretchedness of these heinous activities, the Stedingers were simple peasants who resisted the Bishop of Bremen's attempts to obtain tithes from them by force, and as a result they were accused of being Satanists and murdered in one of the most despicable acts in the history of the Catholic Church. It is to be hoped that the author is not perpetuating these slanders in this passage... – PV.

You may ask whether, aside from all theoretical ideas, and taking into account only the human and historical periods which have been clearly identified and established by the apogees of the different periods of civilization, it might simply be chance that is responsible for the strong correlation of all the virtues and human grandeurs from age to age and year to year?

Is it chance which accumulates in an identical phase of three sixteen-year periods 1719 – 1735, 1735 – 1753 and 1753 – 1767, all vices, all weaknesses, all cowardly actions, all crimes, all cruelties and all abominations, as well as all aberrations and subversions: materialism and sensuality, licentiousness and its sister debauchery?

Finally, is it chance, which has produced all the correspondences in the following table (A, Apogee; B, phase of dissolution and subversion):

A		B	
Solomon	1611	Baalism	1734
Socrates	1628	Epicurianism, skepticism and	
St. John	1631	cynicism	1753
Titu	1631	Gnosticism and	
St. Bernard	1631	Manichaeism	1745
Pierre de Cluny	1631		
Abelard	1631	Albigensians and Stedingers;	
Suger	1631	Ballism and Manichaeism	1745
Descartes	1623	Libertinage, debauchery and	
Bossuet	1665	irreligious, skeptical and	
		cynical encyclopedism	1745

Is it still by chance that Lamoignon belongs to 1647 and Maupeou to 1743, that Rocroi, Fribourg, Condé and Turenne belong to 1643 and Soubise and Rossbach to 1757; that Colbert belongs to 1642 and Terray to 1747?

Is it chance which led Luther, L'Hospital, Copernicus, and Michelangelo in 1525; Bacon, Kepler, Galileo, Descartes, Richelieu, Molé, Poussin, Lesueur, Rubens, Velasquez, etc., in 1631?

Do not believe that, dear Reader. These very men, or at least their spirits, have appeared in each precisely corresponding time in prior human eras: they will reappear at all future corresponding times to create, develop and proclaim the principles, ideas and all the creations of successive civilizations. These men, twenty-two centuries earlier, were called Pythagoras, -539 (1525), Socrates, Thucydides, Zeuxis, Phidias, etc., in -433 (1631).

These same men were always followed by a century of distance, by demolishers and destroyers, necessary to complete the current period and to bring about their disappearance and replacement. Indeed, it is in the phase of dissolution that the retrograde movement of the four active Nations is prepared: that Number *Four* receives the death blow[129]; that Number *Three* moves backwards[130]; that the organization of Number *Two* is destroyed and prepared by the second term, and that Number *One* is strengthened and definitively prepared for its mission, like Number *Two*.

At the same time that Number *Four* receives the death blow, the future Number emerges. In the final period, the future Number *One* was prepared in the Seven Years War, which happened at the expense of Number *Four*.

The retrograde movement of the last period of civilization is as simple as it is complete.

All systems and political bodies dissolved in the phase of demolition are transformed, and the retrograde movement is effected, immediately after the phase, by the time of *transformation* of 1767, 1783, 1799 and by the general upheavals of the Earth, both political and martial, which followed this time and which occupied the sixteen-year period from 1799 to 1815.

I repeat, the foregoing is independent of any theory and comes from a careful study of history; but it is certain that real political situations being known by their causes, the central dates and stringent duration of eras and phases and the spirit of those being both scientifically established and *a priori*, convictions acquire

---

[129] War of Succession of Austria (1741 – 1748) and of seven years length.
[130] Quadruple alliance against Spain and the destruction of the Jesuits.

more force and precision, and ideas more scope and acuity. Certain parts of human history can only be clarified by the intervention of magnetism and terrestrial geo-magnetism.

Chance doesn't and has never existed any more in the ethical, religio-philosophical and political world than it does in the physical world.

The skepticism of the last dissolution which, under the pretext of destroying superstition, suppressed any kind of moral law, is no more appropriate than empiricism which, for fear of theoretical aberration, has banned the idea of knowledge, claiming everything must be applied to its laws, and rejecting *a priori* the means to discover them.

It is recognized that physical, atmospheric and terrestrial disturbance are regulated by laws, and we might indeed wish that chance alone directs the political convulsions and moral crises of the Nations!

But that isn't logical.

TIMES AND PHASES OF THE HUMANITARIAN PERIOD

The main phases and ages of the human period are:

The time of constitution[131] .... 1830 – 1848 – 1865
---------- of preorganization[132] .... 1405 – 1421 – 1437
-------- of organization[133] .... 1509 – 1525 – 1541
-------- of apogee[134] .... 1610 – 1631 – 1651
-------- of transformation[135] .... 1767 – 1783 – 1799

---

[131] Passage of the principal five hundred-year meridian over the Euro-Asiatic valley by 57°30' longitude East. The historical facts clearly establish the phases and eras. The considerable number of events that humankind exhibits concerning this subject cannot be condensed enough to be included here.

[132] Passage of the secondary five hundred-year pole over the peak central European meridian.

[133] Initial positions, or arrival of the pole at the initial position in Asia.

[134] Passage of the pole over the European peak.

[135] Arrival of the pole in the initial Columbian position.

These eras are separated by phases, of which the principal ones are:

The phase of action of. . . . . .1541 to 1610
The phase of reaction or subversion. . . . . .1707 to 1767

How is it that when an age arrives, it invariably brings with it its own political leader endowed with all the qualities required to accomplish its mission?

Why is this validated in all age and in all regions?

How is it that in hereditary monarchies the political leader was quietly born near to the throne?

How is it that this leader was born to have the required age at the beginning of the age, and that he lives exactly as long as that age? This was the case for François I ($1515 + 32 = 1547$) and Louis XIII ($1611 + 32 = 1643$), who occupied precisely the two sixteen-year periods that lasted the entire periods of reformation and apogee, that is to say, the two major ages of the last hundred-year period.

How is it that, when the political leader is elected, it *seems to be more difficult* than when the position is hereditary; that the election is tentative and that in general men in quite difficult situations only succeed after several elections made amidst political convulsions and disturbances which, removing the first ones elected, only stop when the right men are elected? This is so true that the elections of leaders and the political circumstances without which these elections are made, better indicate times of great physical and physiological disturbance than observations of the immediate phenomena which result from them.

The spirit or soul of the world has provided mankind:

As constituents: – Lactance, Scot Erigene, Occam, Constantine and Napoleon III.

As preorganizers: – St. Ambroise, St. Augustine, d'Ailly, Theodosius and Charles VII.

As organizers: – Samuel, Daniel, Pythagoras, St. Benedict, Gerbert, Luther, Clovis and Theodoric.

As leaders of the apogees: – Moses, Solomon, Socrates, St. John, St. Gregory the Great, Pierre de Cluny, St. Bernard, Descartes, Bossuet, Ramses, Pericles, Titus-Trajan, Godefroy de Bouillon, Gustave-Adolphe and Richelieu.

As dissolvers and destroyers: – Athaliah, Commodius, Severus, Heliogabalus, Apsimar-Tiberius, the Dominicans, Pompadour, du Barry, etc.

As the last great fanfare: – Valerian, Charlemagne, Boniface VIII and Napoleon I.

So, the spirit of the world regularly changes all the simple, double and triple sixteen-year periods, overthrows ideas, removes and sweeps away men and their systems!

Given this, who could accept that this spirit is alien to human affairs, development and the transformation of society?

Cyclically, mankind reaches its highest ethical spirituality with examples such as Socrates, St. John and Descartes at times of its greatest physical energy; a century after this time it cyclically plunges back into the depths, into the mire of materialism, sensuality and degrades itself in its greatest physical and moral weakness.

Materialism and sensuality and all their vicious consequences, products of selfishness and exaggerated individualism are the dissolving infirmities of humanity, as rigorously cyclical as the virtues of moral, spiritual, Socratic and Cartesian heights.

The Reader will find this complete and definitive demonstration in *Humanity*, where he is able to disentangle it from any theoretical ideas and judge it solely through historical facts.

Mankind should rely on the principles and facts of its major human, moral and spiritual period which correspond to 1510 – 1647, and most especially on those of the apogees which, corresponding from 1610 to 1652, close this period. It should repudiate all creations of the period of moral reaction and not accept the inheritance of transformation except under the benefit of careful evaluation.

This is one of its principal rules of positive conduct in religio-philosophy and politics.

PURPOSE AND ACTION OF THE GREAT HUMANITARIAN PHASE OF THE LAST PERIOD

The *first year* 1510 of the last great human period began with reform. If its beginnings took place at an opportune time, they also showed themselves on well-chosen ground. These are the moral leaders of the leader Nation, the *Gallican* or *French clergy*, gathered in Council in Tours and Lyon, who began the reform by resuming the work of the councils of Constance and Basel and suspending the Pope.

During the *religious* time of organization and renovation, 1510, 1525, 1543 and 1547, *the whole of Europe was animated by feelings favorable to reform.*[136]

The clergy of Germany acclaimed the resolutions of the Councils of Tours and Lyon.

During the religious time of the Reformation, monastic Catholicism didn't breath a word. It knew instinctively that circumstances were not favorable to it; it also objected to the meeting of the Councils *up to the last year of the period*, indicated by the deaths of François I, Henry VIII and Luther in 1546 – 1547. It was in that same year that the Council of Trent initiated the mission of the Jesuits: its activity began, it grew quickly, and soon its consequences were felt. The sixteen-year period, 1543 – 1559, which followed the Reformation prepared the struggle which burst forth in the sixteen-year period 1559 – 1575. Recatholicization reacted with fury as soon as this sixteen-year period had ended, and during the whole of the following period (1575 – 1591), which became a fight to the death. Western recatholicization ended with that period at the battles of *Arques* and *Ivry*.[137]

It is the central sixteen-year period (1567 – 1583), formed of the two halves 1567 – 1575 and 1575 – 1583, which is the most

---

[136] Except for Spain and Italy, which are the old Catholic regions.
[137] Henry IV, a Protestant, battled against the Duc de Mayenne at both locations when many French cities would not accept him as king, and soundly defeated him. However, the irony is that, having failed in his subsequent siege of Paris, in 1594 he converted to Roman Catholicism since the people of Paris – along with many of the French in general – would not accept a Protestant king. In this instance, politics trumped belief. – PV.

disturbed, the most violent and bloody: that period included the St. Bartholomew's Day Massacre and the sack of Antwerp.

The definitive fight was resumed, but this time under the fundamental meridian of central Europe, on the meridian plateau and not under the meridian of current civilization; it resumed at the beginning of the apogee, at the time where the five hundred-year magnetic meridian, arriving over the initial fundamental European position, animated the central meridian plateau to an extraordinary level: this comprised Italy, Switzerland, Swabia or the Rhine Valley with its tributaries from Basel to Mainz, the Weser Valley, Thuringia, Hesse, Brunswick, Hanover, Denmark and Scandinavia.

The principal action was apparent in the Northern Danish and Scandinavian regions of the plateau (the closest to the pole) and during the central sixteen-year period of 1623 – 1639. Danish at the beginning under Christian IV, it became French and Swedish through the greater ethical activity united to the greater ethical and physical energy of the moment, and it took as its leaders Gustave-Adolphe, the hero, and Godefroy de Bouillon of the French centennial period.

The age of the Reformation had provided the ideas and showed the purpose; the phase of action broke down all the obstacles; the apogee attained its goal, dedicated its ideas and overcame the progress of the period. In the *last year* of the restricted European apogee (1631 + 16 = 1647), the universal European goal of the last period of French civilization was achieved, and settled by the Peace Treaty of Westphalia, the first monument to European public law.[138]

What was the purpose?

To understand this, study the Nations who were present which were:

---

[138] While part of the Treaty dealt with a readjustment of territories, by far the most important outcome was the right of leaders of countries in future to determine the religion of that country, be it Catholicism, Protestantism or Calvinism. This naturally horrified the pope, who lost no time in petulantly issuing a papal Bull declaring it invalid, but which was largely ignored and only added to the dwindling support of papal infallibility. - PV

1. England; 2. France; 3. Catholicism or the Papacy, and 4. The Second Teutonic or German term.[139]

Number *Four*, the empire of Germany, is broken and its dissolution is prepared.

Number *Three* is beaten, supplanted by Number *Two* which takes its most beautiful possessions and its most recent conquests; it undergoes a first amputation, after serious failures.

Number *Two* wins completely and takes on the supremacy; its quality as leader Nation becomes obvious.

Number *One* undertakes a definitive organization on its own account.

The advent of the future Number *One*, Prussia, is prepared.

Such was the political movement; nevertheless, it is accomplished, or at least prepared. It will end with a slow decomposition over a little more than a century, and during that time tremors will unsettle the old leadership and identify and facilitate the movement which must take place in the transformation of 1767 – 1799 and in the sixteen-year period 1799 – 1815 of the great universal concussion which will resolve the final accounts.

THE SPIRIT AND THE ETHICAL AND MATERIAL PROGRESS OF HUMANITY

The great humanitarian phase was, before all, strongly ethical. It was formed by the two main ages of the five hundred-year period, the religious and revelatory age of the Reformation[140] and the more philosophical, thoughtful, deductive and inductive age of the apogee[141], joined together by the religio-philosophical phase of action.[142]

---

[139] The author has excluded Sweden, Switzerland, Spain, Holland and others for some reason; also, England was not involved: it was in the throes of the Civil War, and December saw the arrest of King Charles I. This may be what the author is cryptically referring to later in his comment about 'Number *One*' – PV.

[140] Zwingle, Luther, Melanchthon, Calvin, Knox.

[141] Descartes, Bacon, Kepler, Galileo.

[142] Bèze and Montaigne.

The concept behind the work of the period is therefore religious: the actions are religio-political and religio-warlike and it is accomplished religio-politically.

The apogee of the leader Nations was powerful because it was virtuous and ethical. Ethical power gives rise to physical power.

The growth of humanity was above all ethical; material development was simply a consequence driven by ethical progress.

All movements which are *humanitarian* politico-warlike have a moral *religio-philosophical* goal; often this goal is hard to see; where there really no such goals the activities we see don't have much importance associated with them.

WHAT IS A CONQUEST?

Before saying a few words about the moral religio-philosophical goal of warlike activities, I will try to explain what a conquest or a territorial extension is.

Human races, sub-races and the least natural subdivisions of populations are located in regions limited by geo-magnetic lines, and these lines which are well-defined and scientific, as well as historical, usually bear little resemble to those created by the imagination and by national interest.

Races occupy fractions of large geographical subdivisions, and they are separated by meridian and latitudinal crests.

Sub-races are established in river valleys and have as bounds the hills which divide the sharing of the waters of these rivers. The smallest subdivisions of races and sub-races occupy the valleys of rivulets and streams. The crests or ridges sharing the waters separate the races, the sub-races and the smallest subdivisions of the populations, *whether these ridges are or aren't pronounced, and whether they are or aren't difficult to cross*. These latter considerations are of very low importance: the question of races is geo-magnetic, it is a question of equal vitality. Often, even equal vital action is not curtailed by the apparent winding ridge or distortions of the first geological upheavals, it's the direct magnetic expansion underground in the form of an arc of a great circle of the globe which is the producer of the ridge in the latest upheavals forming the boundary.

The crests meet and form *nodal regions* which play a role as important as interesting in the lives of Nations and humanity. We find some indications concerning these regions in *Humanity*; but their full explanation belongs to *Geo-Magnetism*, which probably follows *Humanity* quite closely.

It is in these nodal regions that hegemonies were born.

The main nodal regions in Europe are:

1. The Sabino-roman region of Gransasso or Abruzzo[143];

2. Franconia with the Fechtel mountains (Coburg-Nuremberg);

3. Swabian Germany or of the Raahe-Alp (of Hohenstaufen and Hohenzollern);

4. The Swiss regions of Mont-Blanc (Savoy), Gotthard (the Four Cantons) and Bernina (Lombardy);

5. The Saxon region of Harz (Brunswick, Hesse, Anhalt)

6. The other Saxon region of Brunswick-Luneburg and Holstein (Eutin and Gottorp).

The main ridge which separates the human races is a latitudinal crest which extends, without a break in continuity other than the Dardanelles, from the Atlantic Ocean to the Pacific Ocean. Today it is called – at least a part of it – the Indo-European shelf.

This shelf enters Europe by way of Constantinople, follows the Balkans, the Illyrian Alps, the Great Alps, the Jura up to the Ballons d'Alsace[144]; from these Ballons up to Boulogne it separates the Belgian waters from the Scheldt, the Meuse and the Moselle, of those of the French rivers the Seine and the Rhone. Beyond Boulogne, the Indo-European shelf runs along the South of England as far as Land's End.

Part of this shelf that extends from Constantinople to Land's End divides Europe into two: the Northern Teutonic part, and the Southern or Celtic part; the European part of the Indo-European shelf is therefore Celto-Teutonic. It is strongly in relief in the East

---

[143] Cavallo (Neapolitan), Corsica and Sardinia.

[144] The Ballons d'Alsace and the Ballons de Vosges refer to the rounded mountains found in those regions (ballon = balloon) – PV.

and weakly so in the West, because the last upheaval was associated with the meridian of the Colombo-Asiatic ridge, and lessened as it got further away from that ridge.

The two European races are subdivided into Eastern, Central and Western.

The Celts are Pelasgians from the Pindus mountains and the Iberia in the East, to the Iberian ridge in the West.

The Teutons are Slavonic to the East of the extended Pindus range, that is to say in the valleys of the Theiss and the Vistula; they are Bretons in the West of the ridge of Moorlands, the extension of the Iberian ridge, with which it forms the Western meridional Ibero-Breton ridge. This latter runs along the coast of France and separates Brittany from the Celtic or French Plateau. Brittany is Breton-Celtic.

What changes have the numerous warlike expansions, the Celtic overflows and the Teutonic counter-overflows produced in the territorial possessions of the two races?

What have they won since Caesar crossed the Celto-Teutonic shelf for the first time at Soissons nearly two thousand years ago, at the foot of his Southern setbacks, and definitively at the edge of the Sambre following the Teutonic reversals, where he met the energetic resistance of the Merovingians?

What did the Celts conquer following Soissons in -57, until they were finally driven back to the boundaries of their last expansion through war, and the last Celtic overflow in Waterloo, in 1815; after three centennial Celtic periods (Roman, Catholic and French) and a Teutonic period (Frankish)?

The Celtic race occupied the plateau-sill to the West, covered with fields of battle where the whole formed a vast field of blood, which they conquered by hand-to-hand combat through their apogee and maximum period of expansion, which was both physical and ethical, political and warlike. It is the result of the expansion which had just ended, and which was one of the greatest expansions across the Celtic plateau.

In addition to the part of the Celto-Teutonic plateau-shelf to the West, France had two Belgian Teutonic dependencies in the Celto-Teutonic center of the balloons: Lorraine and Alsace.

The Teutons occupied roughly the same position in the East as the Celts did to the West.

The field of blood, the North-West boundary of the Celts and Teutons, or the plateau-shelf won inch by inch in the last centennial period by the Celts over the Teutons through their temporarily superior power of expansion, was limited in the North by the fields of Gravelines, Cassel, Bouvines, Lens and Denain. Its axis is delineated by Agincourt, Saint-Quentin, Rocroi, Wattignies and Valmy, and its Southern bounds include the fields of Crécy, Soissons, Arcis-sur-Aube and Fère-Champenoise.

A field of blood, a band of mixed terrain, a plateau of separation fifteen to twenty miles in width and fifty leagues in length where the races touched, and which belonged to one or the other depending upon which one prevailed at the time; such was how territorial extension or conquest was the ultimate result of twenty centuries of struggle and many bloody battles, undertaken particularly in the latest human centennial period, that of the maximum expansive strength from the Celtic plateau, and consequently of maximum action exercised over the lower Western part of the Celto-Teutonic shelf across the past five centuries.

Outside of any historic, philosophical or political concerns, *Magnetism of the Globe* established: that the magnetic circulation reached its *greatest annual energy on June 18* and continued until *June 22*, the day where the discharge began. However, it was on *June 18*, the day where the greatest physical and moral energy of the year was attained that the battle of Waterloo took place, and it was on *June 22*, the last of the five days of the greatest physical and moral energy of the year, that everything was consumed by the abdication. That is certainly singular!

Magnetism of the Globe also fixed (p. 401, Table LIV in Vol. 2) *November 9* to be the day of the transformation of the magnetic circulation of November, just as *June 22* was the day of transformation of June; or, in other words, *November 9* was the day of the *lesser magnetic circulation,* and the *lesser physical and moral energy* of the year, as *June 22* was the one of *greater energetic circulation.* Now, *November 9* or *18th Brumaire* was the beginning of the First Consul, and *June 22* was the date which marked the end of the Empire. If it is by chance, chance is also the reason that *18th Brumaire* belonged to the *sixteenth year* 1799[145], and that *June 22*, belonged to *the sixteenth year* 1815[146]; that is to say that the *18th Brumaire* was the *same day* which saw the end of the time of transformation and the beginning of the sixteen-year *period* of the last great refulgence (of the last French centennial period) and that *June 22* was the *same day* of the closure of this sixteen-year period, the next to last of the French centennial period. Thus, the political leader and warrior of the last great French refulgence took the reins in a convulsive movement on the *first day* of the sixteen-year period which fell to him, and ended by abdicating on the *last day* of that period: he imposed himself on the day of *lesser physical and moral energy,* and fell on the day of the *greatest physical and moral energy* of the two ends of the sixteen-year period, 1799 and 1815 respectively, which governed the sixteen-year period of the last and greatest moral, material, political and warlike expansion of the five hundred-year French human period.

One may perhaps find these coincidences too remarkable to assign them exclusively to chance, all the more so because leaders of final great refulgences are quite rare, and because the last centennial period being the greatest and the most providential, it should be better as a rule for time and place than any of its antecedents.

After November 9, 1799 and June 22, 1815, it would perhaps be hard to find more remarkable *fortuitous* chance encounters. History, however, offers if not a better, at least as good an example. The time of the Reformation (1525) was one of asceticism, religious enthusiasm, reforms, revelations, inspirations, conversions and everything arising from religious

---

[145] The date Napoleon Bonaparte became First Consul of France following a coup – PV.
[146] The date on which Napoleon abdicated. Indeed it is also interesting to note that, when Napoleon retired from the battlefield at Waterloo and returned to Paris, hoping to retain his position as Emperor and to continue the war, and instead was asked to abdicate, he considered a *coup d'état* along the lines of the 18th of Brumaire (when Napoleon became First Consul as seen in the previous footnote), but he decided against it – PV.

movements and moral activity; however, the central year 1525 is not the most remarkable time of this epoch. The sixteen-year periods 1527 and 1528 compete for first place, since these are the most religio-political years of the five hundred-year period. Please tell me, dear reader, if you believe it was chance that situated in 536 (1528) and 496 (1528) the two *principal religio-political facts of history*: the conversion of Cyrus to *Judaism*, and the subsequent introduction of Judaism into all the ancient civilizations of his Asian possessions [to prepare the ground for Christ *five hundred years before His coming*]; and the conversion of Clovis, which introduced Christianity into the European possessions of future civilizations *a five-hundred year period after the arrival of the Christ*?[147] Also, do you think that the third historical fact of the same nature and of nearly the same importance, the conversion of Constantine, fell by chance on 312 (1860), the precise central year of the age of Roman reconstitution and the founding of Catholicism?

If you believe that, you have a strong dose of Neo-Aryanism in you![148]

Be that as it may, *the current respective territorial situations of the Celts and Germans after twenty centuries of bloody battles, proves that from an exclusively territorial point of view the terrible game of war is a game which is so very absurd, so very unjust and so very cruel, which doesn't lead to any absolute final result of any importance, or any lasting result at all.* It proves that the spirit of conquest is a mania when it does not come from an excess of physical and moral energy, expended with the intention of

---

[147] Here the author is again referring to one of his five hundred-year periods, since he refers to the 'conversion' of Cyrus as being in 536 BCE, Christ on earth around year 0 and the conversion of Clovis in 496 CE – PV.

[148] This is an interesting phrase, since Madame Blavatsky didn't establish the Theosophical Society until 1875, and the Thule Society didn't begin to popularize the concept of Aryansim until the mid-1910s. However, as far back as the 1860s the concept of Aryanism as an 'ideal' race had been put forward, and some had even begun to speculate a German origin, putting forward anthropological theories, and even suggesting that the Aryan race had begun in Germany, before migrating East into Asia. Thus, the author's cynical comment was probably a prevailing one at the time: that those who proposed this theory were little more than gullible dreamers – PV.

producing an ethically humanitarian result. It proves that annexation is simply a dangerous disease.

An impartial glance cast upon history, outside of any theoretical concerns, proves that Nations live and age like men.

It shows that the Nation which has completed its first five hundred-year term has reached its apogee in every way; it has completed its five hundred-year period as a leader of humanity; and now it commences its second term, during which no Nation have ever made any territorial conquest. A Nation which ends its first term is also usually great enough, powerful enough and glorious enough to no longer dream either of enlargement (which would be a danger for it), or power (which would not be worth more than it already possessed), or glory (with which it is saturated).

The Nation which begins its second term has indeed something to do other than to focus on the external; it must mitigate within itself the deleterious moral effects of its final phase of dissolution, effects that up to now none of them have managed to destroy completely. It must prevent the Rhetorist and the Sophist from multiplying to excess and destroying the moral background which the last period of corruption allowed to exist.

No power lasts forever. A Nation, when its mission is completed, like the man who has completed his, give up its place. The Nation which places itself outside of the natural flow of events and offends against moral laws is punished, as is the man who transgresses those same laws. The Nation is punished, even if it is the most powerful on earth; even if it had millions of soldiers and its soldiers were the most experienced in the world; even if those soldiers no longer had any rivals in tactical and strategic organization; even if their prior victories had doubled their strength by the confidence they have in themselves and in their leaders; even if their prestige alone discouraged the strongest of their adversaries, the field is still open! If it is called *Marathon, Capua, Morgarten, Sempach, Granson, Morat, Bouvines, Orleans, Denain, Valmy, Leipzig, Quatre-Bras* or *Waterloo*, it will calm the nerves and increase the bravery of the weak and debilitate and paralyze the strong. It will give the victory to the one to humiliates the pride of the other and punishes its iniquity. The type of punishment is related to that of the crime. God punishes the strong along with the weak: He has the physical means and He uses them at the chosen time and place. Chance means nothing in the moral world, any more than in physical floods; in both, the reaction responds to the action: an action, a reward. Obedience to the Divine Law, the Christian Law, the Law of Brotherhood – universal or local, the hour and the *field of battle*!

If you consider that this was written around forty years ago[149], these last words will appear as truly prophetic. Indeed, we only harvest the seeds we sow with high interest. If we sow a bad seed, we cannot blame the heavens when the seed multiplies in its fruits and infects the field of good grain.

---

[149] This final paragraph was written by Papus as a summary to Bruck's except – PV.

Chapter 12
Numbers and Music

Numbers have a close relationship with music, Plato demonstrated this harmonically in the accord of the four elements which compose the soul[150], and in the cause of that reciprocal symphony between natures which are so dissimilar.

A more modern author, the chevalier Eckartshausen wrote in his books on *Numbers* some pages which are really characteristic on the subject. Here are two passages:

Music is the most beautiful image of the laws of the progression of Nature.

The perfect chord gives us the image of that unity from which all comes, which vivifies all, which preserves all in accordance with the eternal laws, in the most beautiful uninterrupted order.

All the tones of the perfect chord played together give the most splendid image of Divine unity, in which all the tones are equally harmonic, – the source of all harmony.

The permutation of several tones, from which are born several chords, is shown by the permutations of several numbers, which have different results, yet always following the laws of unity.

The perfect chord always remains invariable, like unity in numbers, although they go to infinity.

That chord is the most perfect; it contains every harmonic, as unity contains every number.

The first 3 tones in the manifestation of the perfect chord are the image of the 3rd power. They are separated by two intervals of different thirds, which although different are still linked.

The third is followed by the fourth, which has its fullness in the octave.

This octave is the division of the principal tone.

We see that the fourth is the actor in the chord. It is located between two thirds, to administer, so to speak, the action and the reaction.

---

[150] Though Plato is better known for his division of the soul into three parts: rational (logos - head), appetitive (eros - stomach) and spirited (thymos - chest) – PV.

With a word, the thinker finds that the harmony of tones is regulated by the Law of Progression as is everything else. It is the sublime image which opens up to the thinker an immense space in the depths of the secrets of Eternity.[151]

....

The body of harmony is the tone, the soul of the tone is harmony, immortal, spiritual and enduring. Harmony veiled in the tone and acting on the ear is music, harmony acting on the eye is beauty; therefore, harmony is for all the senses, 5 sensory expressions. Harmony is therefore the foundation of everything that is pleasant and beautiful, a model of the eternal order, alone enduring, resolving all the dissonances in the octave, a symbol of the proportions of order, where the small is as important as the great, the rest as necessary as pressing on a note. Different notes from the lowest to the highest tone, all defined according to laws, all important, with a noble freedom but obeying the laws of harmonics, with a noble equality but according to different points of view, each note, necessary notation, but one higher than the other, each assigned to its place from which it cannot move without destroying the harmony, that image of morality and the fundamental constitution of States.[152]

More recently J. Ed. Groehaerts, Director of Music at Antwerp, has also studied the same concept. We have extracted the following passages from his work:

Among the movements which our senses register and whose speed we evaluate by means of numbers, the least rapid are *apparent* movements, those that we can follow with the eye; the

---

[151] Von Eckartshausen, *Zahlenlehre der Natur* [*The Mathematics of Nature*]. Leipzig, 1794, pp. 237- Extract unpublished.

[152] Von Eckartshausen, *Ausschlüsse zur Magic* [*Addendum on Music*], Vol. IV. Munich, 1792. The Magic Numeral, extract (cf. Initiation, 20th year, No. 11, August 1906, p. 175.

more rapid ones are those which our eye perceives in the form of light.[153]

Between these two extreme terms we perceive two mean terms: acoustic vibrations, and *caloric* vibrations.

The movements we can follow with the eye are necessarily those which come and go at the same place, for if a body animated by a certain speed doesn't return to its initial position, it would leave the field of our visual observation and would disappear from view. This is the to-and-fro motion which is called "*oscillation* or *vibration*."

To obtain it in a body, two contrary conditions are required: 1. the body must be free to go where the movement leads it; 2. it is maintained at the same place so that it has to return to its initial position. This dual condition is met by pendulums and by vibrating rods.

When we move the untethered end of a pendulum or the free end of an elastic rod in one direction, a to-and-fro movement is established in two opposite directions by the effect of gravity or of elasticity. Vibrations are therefore dual in nature. Each complete vibration consists of four separate movements, two outward and two returning. To determine the speed of the vibratory movements we associate them naturally with the vibratory movements of our being – that is, to our pulse – whose average duration equals almost that of the *modern second* (1/75 of the present-day minute).[154]

The extreme limit of the speed of apparent movement is theoretically fixed by the most low-pitched sound of the musical range which we can hear. That sound results from 16 complete vibrations per second.[155] Indeed, the distinction between sounds

---

[153] J. Ed. Groegaerts, *Traité complet de la tonalite (Harmonie et contrepoint), basé sur des données positives* [*Comprehensive Treatise on the Tone (Harmony and Counterpoint), Based on Positive Data*]. Antwerp, J. Mées, 1884.

[154] Meaning that the resting human pulse, being around 75 beats a minute, is not far off that of a second, there being 60 in a minute – PV.

[155] "The human ear has receptors that can detect sound frequencies ranging from 15 vibrations to 20,000 vibrations per second". S. Haskel and D. Sygoda: *Biology, A Contemporary Approach*. New York, pub. Amsco, 1996 – PV.

begins as soon as the origin of the numerical relationships entering into the constitution of the whole system is complete.

These relationships are seven in number; the *octave* 1:2, the *fifth* 2:3, the *fourth* 3:4, the *major third* 4:5, the *minor third* 5:6, the *second* 8:9 or 9:10 and the altered unison (increased or decreased) 24:25, 15:15, 24:27 or 25:27.

The first five are chosen from among the original elements of the genetic system of relationships provided by numbers in their natural succession:

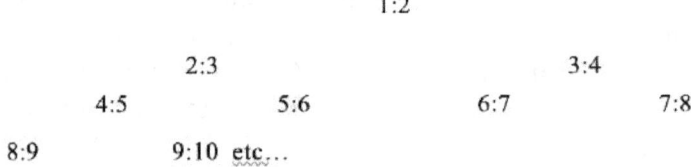

The octave represents the original identity of the elements of this system. The fifth and the fourth represent their original diversity.

The octave, the fifth and the major third are the elements subject to identical conditions of existence, and they reproduce the character of the underlying element in the various degrees of its evolution. For this reason, we call them *teleological relationships*, observing that they enter only as *organic* elements necessary in the construction of the tonal system.

The fourth and the minor third also reproduce the character of the underlying element, but in different forms. They still belong to the category of necessary teleological relationships, although already they enter only as *functional* elements in the construction of the system.

Seconds (relationships of 8:9 and 9:10 since they result either from the difference between the 5th and the 4th, or from the difference between the 4th and Major 3rd) still belong to the category of teleological relationships. They are necessary to the construction of the system, the first as an *organic* element, the second as a *functional* element.

The altered unison (relationships 15:16, 24:25, 24:27, or 25:28 seeing that it represents the difference in the major 3rd to the 4th, the minor 3rd to the major 3rd, the *organic* 2nd to the minor 3rd or of the *functional* 2nd to the minor 3rd), doesn't belong to the category of teleological relationships. It only enters into the construction of the system as a *contingent* element.

The genesis of the seven relationships we have just considered is complete above the 3rd degree of evolution.

		Vibrations perceptible to the eye			Vibrations perceptible to the ear
		1st Degree	2nd Degree	3rd Degree	4th Degree
Necessary Relationships	Octave 1:2	2:4	4:8	8:16	16:32
	Fifth......	2:3	4:6	8:12	16:24
	Fourth	3:4	6:8	12:16	24:32
	Major or organic 3rd	4:5		8:10	16:20
	Minor or funct^{al} 3rd.	5:6		10:12	20:24
	Organic 2nd......			8:9	16:18
	Functional 2nd.....			9:10	18:20
Contingent Relationship: altered unison				15:16	30:32 / 24:25 (24:27, 25:27)

Number 16 is therefore the first value of the series of numerical relationships perceptible to the ear. It is the foundation of the *tonal organization of sounds.*

Number 24 is the first perceptible value of numerical relationships entering into the constitution of the tonal system called contingent.

It is the foundation of the *tonal functioning of sounds.*

The secret of the organization and tonal functioning of sounds lies in the power of numbers.

The power of numbers is manifested in the genesis of their natural relationships; to each new degree of evolution from this genesis the power of the number 2 – the resulting term of the first of the relationships generated – attains a higher degree.

$$2^1 = 2;\quad 2^2 = 4 \text{ (square)};\quad 2^3 = 8 \text{ (cube)}, \text{ etc...}$$

However, we know that in any creative evolution the first two degrees form a natural step. The first three powers of any number therefore also form a natural step in the indefinite extension of the power of that number.

The numbers 16, 256 (16^2) and 4,096 (16^3) are therefore the terms of the organizational power of music in numbers.

The numbers 24, 576 (24^2) and 13,824 (24^3) are the terms of the functional power of music in numbers.

The first series are neutral numbers. They can be returned to unity by means of theosophical addition and reduction. From an absolute point of view, they represent a unique term: the unity DO. The second series are numbers related to DO[156]. They can be reduced to 3 or 9 (by theosophical reduction and addition: 24 = 6 = 3, 576 = 18 = 9, 13,824 = 18 = 9). From the purist point of view the latter two differ from the first but they do not differ from one another. To be able to distinguish between them clearly, we must consider the relationships in which each of them finds itself with regard to the others.

Now, the numbers we are concerned with are among those in relationships where we find the musical values DO, RE, SOL, LA.

The number 576[157] reduced to 9, is to the number 24 reduced to 3 as RE is to SOL, that is, in relationship to the descending fifth (if account is not taken of the difference in the octave): *direct relationship*. It is to 1... as RE is to DO – in relationship to the descending major second (if account is not taken of the difference in the octave): *direct relationship*.

The number 13,824 reduced to 9, is to the number 24 reduced to 3 as RE is to SOL – relationship of descending fifth: *immediate relationship*. It is to 1... as LA is to DO – relationship of the major sixth (minor 3rd reversed): *mediate relationship*, obtained from the *mean* of the reversal.

---

[156] This word in the text ('utraux', singular presumably 'utral') appears to be invented. The best guess I can make is that the author has made an adjective out the French equivalent of 'Do' (as in Do-Re-Mi), as the French is 'Ut-Re-Mi'. Therefore, 'utral' would mean 'related to Do' in English. The words at the end of the passage – *autothetic* and *autogenetic* – similarly do not seem to exist in English or French – PV.

[157] In the original book this is rendered as 567, which is clearly a misprint – PV.

The number 576 therefore relates *immediately* to numbers reduced to 3 and to 1, while the number 13,824 only relates immediately to the single number 24.

Now these distinctions have been made, we can clearly recognize the constituent elements of the original type of reality in the four numbers in question. The note DO is the *neutral* teleological element of the tone; RE is the teleological element related to DO; SOL, the autothetic element; TI, the autogenetic element.

From these four elements flow, as from their sources, all the determinations of creative musical reason. These are the *four Rivers of Paradise* of musical science.

It can be seen that the Science of Numbers is intimately related[158] – and this goes without saying – to music which, like the science of rhythm, acts on the physical and psychic rhythms of man and can place him in conditions proper for him to be able to penetrate the hidden side of Nature. Such was the profound role of music among the ancients. That is why Plato considered this science as indissolubly linked to the constitution of the Republic; it is that which explains the symbolic and real wonders of the lyre of Orpheus[159]; it is that which gives the reason for the magical effects of the sound of the flute and the singing of the Korybantes.[160]

---

[158] As in the previous chapter, Papus adds a paragraph of his own at the end of the long quotation from the work by Croegaerts – PV.

[159] Interestingly, this allusion made it into Martinist ritual as an allusion to the concept of duality linked by a third term, in this case the two sides of the lyre resting upon its elegant base – PV.

[160] However, the Korybantes, offspring of Apollo and the Muse Thalia, were male dancers who were armed, and worshipped the goddess Cybele with drumming and dancing.

THE TEXTS

Chapter 13

Numbers and the Occult

We believe we have provided the studious researcher with all the elements necessary for an understanding of the Science of Numbers. It remains for us to provide some documentation, cautioning that he should exercise wisdom in his understanding of them.

To this end, we will firstly provide him with the principal passages devoted to the subject we have been studying, written by some of the masters of the occult science: the profound mystic Eckartshausen; Wronski, that prodigious scholar who was Eliphas Lévi's master; the great occult thinker that was Balzac; the palmist Desbarrolles; the astrologer Eugène Ledos;[161] and the seer Louis-Michel de Figanières.

An understanding of these powerful pages will require long hours of study, and it is with the purpose of making our students work by themselves that we have thought it good to provide these themes for study.

---

[161] It is E. Ledos who Huysmans put in a scene in his novel on magic, *Là-Bas,* with the name of Gevingey.

I

ECKARTSHAUSEN[162]

The number of the Quaternary[163]

The number of force, 4, or the number of the quaternary, is the most necessary for an understanding of numbers; it shows the progression of force in the physical world, which is to say:

- each force is 1.
- this power has an effect: force and effect = 2.
- each effect has a result: force, effect and a result = 3.
- the result has a realization: force, effect, and a result in its realization = 4.

Everything being realized in the universe, 4 is called the number of force, which constitutes the great quaternary of all things.

From this number was born 10, or the number of the Universe; because 10 is contained in 4. I can explain this with an example:

---

[162] Eckartshausen was born in 1752, and Saint-Martin wrote *Of Errors & Truth* in 1775, when Eckartshausen was 23 years old, and Saint-Martin 9 years older. The excerpt quoted by Papus here dates from 1794 and bears a striking similarity to Saint-Martin's comments about the number 4, the quaternary, unity (point) and 10 (circle), and thought, desire (or will), action, which the author himself states expresses later on. But then, in his Preface to Saint-Martin's book On Numbers, Matter expressly calls Eckartshausen "...a learned pupil of the Martinist school." – PV.

[163] Eckartshausen, *Zahlenlehre der Natur* [*The Mathematics of Nature*]. Leipzig, 1794, pp. 221 to 225. These pages are in their first French translation.

```
force . . . . . . . . . . . . . . . . . . . . . . . . . . . . . . . . . . . . . . . . .1
effect and force . . . . . . . . . . . . . . . . . . . . . . . . . . . . . . . . .2
result, effect and force . . . . . . . . . . . . . . . . . . . . . . . . . . .3
realization of the result, effect and force . . . . . . . . . .4
```
$$\frac{1\ 2\ 3\ 4}{10}$$

10, when viewed as an image, is the proportion of force at the periphery 1 to 0 – from the point to the circular line – and is called 10 or *numeris universalis*, because everything that exists is in proportion of energy to its expansion.

9 is called the number of the circular line or of expansion, and is caused because the force, by expansion, forms the natural circle.[164]

To have a clearer understanding, one mustn't confuse it with an ordinary circle: the mechanical or geometric circle is quite different from the circle of Nature.

The circle of Nature is formed by the movement of a force toward its expansion.

There, where the energy of the force ends, the circumference begins:

I will explain with an example.

If I throw an object into water, a circle is formed; it is proportional to the force of the throw and the size of the stone; both of them – the force of the throw and the size of the stone – together give the point of the fall and the energy of the expansion. Straight lines then emanate from the point according to the amount of the energy[165]; where it stops the beginning of the circular line is found.

---

[164] While not precisely theosophical arithmetic, he is reflecting Papus' idea of reduction to some extent, by taking the number 10 and deducting the number of the point – 1 – to give 9 as the number of the circle, which is the limit of the force in all directions around the point – PV.

[165] Note that a circle is formed by an infinite number of straight lines of equal length emanating outward form the source of the energy (the point, in this instance the stone): the boundary formed by the infinite number of lines of equal length form the circle – PV.

The circle of Nature gives us the image of the manifestation of the first forces; action and the birth of reaction.

Everything about the expansion is ruled by the law of the circle.

The movement of all things is a result of the expansion of the force and its going back into itself.

The force of expansion is the first in Nature; that force returning into itself is called the force of attraction; if it expands again, it is the force of repulsion.

There is therefore a single force, of which all the others are modifications.

Regarding the number 4, one should also note that it is the number of the body and the senses.

Geometry reduces everything that is measurable to this number, for all triangles are considered to be parts of the square, or what forms the base of the quaternary.

In Geometry, we cannot find the area of a plane without having first divided it into squares.

We cannot calculate the area of the squares into which it is divided without splitting them into triangles, and by multiplying the diameter with half of the base.

And so, according to Nature I cannot calculate any realization or any physical phenomenon without previously classifying the 3rd force, effect and result, which are contained in their realization as 4.

Therefore, each number which produces a being is the number which forms the measure of that being.

Three progressions produce everything which forms the basis of the sensory; thus, everything which forms the basis of the corporeal is measured or calculated by 3.

Four progressions produce everything that is sensory and corporeal. and therefore, it is necessary for all things sensory and corporeal to be measured and calculated by 4.

From this observation of the laws of progression we can see that there is also an intelligent quaternary, which rules in the same manner over force, effect, result and realization, because it is not necessary for realization to always be physical. For example:

> thought 1
> will 2
> action 3
> fact 4

The fact[166] doesn't manifest physically, but it is the realization of thought, will and action, and therefore has the number of the quaternary for its calculation.

This analysis of numbers is more important for the salvation of men than that of numbers, which are only physical, for by means of them we discover the errors in our judgment.

We observe that thought and will create the fact.

Each fact is a number whose parts are action, will and thought, and so in order to create that fact, the progression must be followed through completely within the fact; and so, for example, the following progression arises from a bad fact:

> to think evil 1
> to want evil 2
> to act evil 3
> to do evil 4

This progression composed must become the number as:

> to think evil. 1
> to think and want evil. 2
> to think, want and act evil 3
> result, an evil fact 4

---

[166] In French the word 'fait' can be interpreted many ways. However, here 'fact' or 'outcome' might be an appropriate choice, since Eckartshausen makes the interesting point that, while thought, will and action, being purely internal processes, lead to a fact or internal result; whereas force, effect and result lead to an external creation. To give a couple of examples: 1. I have the thought to stop smoking; I decide or will this to be so; I act by not smoking; and the result or outcome is not lighting a cigarette. In this case the four stages are internal . 2. However, if I decide to make a chair, I conceive, design and implement my thought internally, but the creation or outcome is a physical, externalized chair, existing separately in the real world – PV.

We have shown in detail that the measure of a thing is also its number, that force and energy are subject to its number, and because of that all objects can be consumed.[167]

The energy of number 4 in Nature is found by multiplying it with itself.

Arithmetic calls the multiplication of a number with itself a squared number.

The square root is the same number which has been multiplied with itself.

As a result of arithmetic each number can be multiplied with itself, therefore each number has its square number, of which it is the square root.

The doctrine of numbers in Nature is distinguished from arithmetic in that it only accepts one true square number, for which there is only one single square root.

As the doctrine of numbers seeks the circle in Nature, it also looks for the square number and its root in Nature.

The only true square number in Nature is 16, the only true root 4; because it forms the square number in 4 progressions, each of which again has 4 numbers.[168]

The other arithmetic numbers which are called squares are only seen in the doctrine of the progression of number in Nature as proportions of numbers with the square number, and the arithmetic root is only organized as a root of numbers relative to the square root: e.g.:

3 x 3 = 9; 9 is an arithmetic square number, of which 3 is its root; the squared number 9 considered with the squared number of Nature 16 gives the proportion of 9 to 16, as the arithmetic square root 3 shows the proportion to the square root of Nature 3, the proportion of 3/4-9/16.

Thus, like a square number, a single number is a single root like a square root in proportion to unity; all other arithmetical numbers and square roots can be regarded according to the law of

---

[167] Ibid., pp. 229 – 231.
[168] That is, 4 x 4 = 16, and 4 + 4 + 4 + 4 = 16 – PV.

progressions as square numbers, because their proportion to unity will never be quadruple.

Each number multiplied with itself gives a proportional mean between unity and the product; therefore, the product of the number multiplied with itself is to the root what the root is to unity: e.g.: $4 \times 4 = 16$, $16 \times 16/4 = 4/1$.

We see well enough that each number multiplied with itself may be called a number-root, but not a number-square, because in Nature there is only a single square number and a single square root.

Number 4 directs everything in each multiplication, because we also have unity in the arithmetical progression; the first factor, the second and the result, or the product which is born out of the joint action of the two factors.

The extraction of the square root gives the image of its producing force.[169]

The number multiplied with itself is the image of the agreement of all the products of the producing numbers with their root number if it is considered in proportion.

Unity is revealed by its trine force in the first quaternary which, multiplied with itself, gives 16 as the number-square, where 4 is the number-root.

These 4 progressions constitute the great Quaternary, which by the laws of progressions provides explanations of the highest things.

Unity is itself its own root, its own number considered as unity; no calculation can happen with respect to it; only in the manifestation of its forces is the first quaternary made by its trine force.

Only in the compound of what is actually in progression do the laws of number work, because they are precisely what constitutes progression or composition.

---

[169] Ibid., pp. 233 – 235.

I will therefore draw the quaternary according to the law of progression and add the explanation that remains to be given.

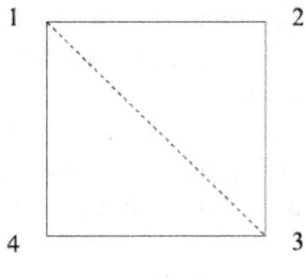

Figure 18

The first line of the square considered as an image successively represents the base, the foundation and the root of the other numbers.

It is the unity from which everything is born, which is the source of all things, from which all comes, which preserves all; which reveals itself in all physical things without being physical itself, which never changes, which fills everything, which is present everywhere, and which manifests itself in a 3rd force.

The second line of the square considered as an image successively represents that second active and expressive cause of all things.

Through this second active and expressive cause arose everything in the realm of spirits as did that in the physical world.

Its cause is the Word of God, which is the foundation and strength of all things.

But I do not want to explain this spiritual image of the second line of the square more fully, because men who think little about the importance of religious things would find the idea ridiculous.

The third side of the square considered as an image represents all results, both sensory and corporeal.

The first is the force, the second is the effect, and the third has the result as its purpose, because everything that forms the basis of the sensory and the physical has the 3rd number as its foundation, as we have already said more circumspectly when explaining numbers.

> 1 gives the point,
> 2 the line,
> 3 the area, where finally 4 arises.

The numbers constituting the number 4 will be named according to the state of things, the principles or originating beginnings of each thing.

....

With regard to man, considered as a realized being, I calculate 4. His number is therefore 4; a being composed of body and spirit. The spirit unites with the soul giving 2, the soul unites with the body giving 2, therefore 4 is his number – 22/4.[170]

It may be considered as follows[171]:

$$13 - 4$$
$$22 - 4$$
$$31 - 4$$

22 is his material composition; 13 forms the base, $\frac{13}{22}$ which means: the spirit has the law of unity, which is manifest in 3 – force $\frac{\frac{1}{2}}{3}$.

---

[170] Ibid., pp. 238 – 242. [Note this last figure 22/4 means 2 and 2 come to 4. It is not a division being portrayed! – PV.]

[171] This is actually explained more clearly towards the bottom of page 199 and the top of page 200. Bear in mind again that these are not numbers but collections of symbols. Thus, 13 means force and its manifestation by will from the initial premise of 1 = force/thought, 2 = effect/will, 3 = result/action and 4 = realization/fact – PV.

His body $\frac{2^3}{5}$, the proportion of matter – 4, which is again united to a unity which is above him, and that is manifested by the 3rd force $\frac{22^{13}}{35}$.

He has a double possession, the spiritual in thinking, wanting and acting 3|5; the sensory by the use of his five senses:

```
        1         3
              X
        2         2
        5------------------3
              3  |  5
```

Unity in its progression gives him the type of its 3rd force; this 3rd force in the realization in the body: the five senses.

Above him, there is no law, below him his destiny.

$$13 - 4 \text{ force } 1$$
$$22 - 4 \text{ effect } 2$$
$$31 - 4 \text{ result } 3$$

The law shows his relationships with unity; his $\frac{1}{\text{thought}}$, $\frac{2}{\text{will}}$, $\frac{3}{\text{action}}$ must become one according to the law of unity, which constitutes his first spiritual essence $\frac{13}{4} = 4$

The number below him shows him his destiny $\frac{31^{22}}{5/3}$.

The senses give him experience, the strength of his soul commands him to think, to compose, to judge.

We will apply the same progression to another object, for example – 4.

Every realization is 4, as we have already said, therefore each realization is considered according to the same laws.

If, therefore, I set down fact – 4, I again have the same proportions of 4 as:

$$13 - 4$$
$$22 - 4$$
$$31 - 4$$

or fact considered as realized, or as $4 - \frac{22}{4}$.

The parts of the fact consisting of this, the interior gives us 13.

The interior must have a simple being as its object; it is necessary for this simple being to think, to will and to act $\frac{\begin{smallmatrix}13\\22\end{smallmatrix}}{3/5}$.

The simple being constitutes force or thought, will and action, 3; to think, to will and to act is only brought to expression by 5, or the senses.

This results in an outcome of $\frac{\begin{smallmatrix}22\\32\end{smallmatrix}}{5/3}$ or the sensory result with 5 as its object; but the proportion of this result again relates to 3, or to force, will and action. For example, if I play billiards, the shot which has actually taken place and which determined the outcome for the ball is 4; before the shot, there was force, will, and action or:

1

The force to make a shot

2

The will to make the shot

3

The actual shot.

Then the shot follows as the realization, 4.

This shot is proportional to the force, will and action; they determine the shot that is taken in this way and no other, and are its law.

After the shot the ball which is hit receives its determination in accordance with the first will and action, and adjusts itself anew by the 3 forces which only the expansion of the first; therefore, the proportion in Nature is:

13 force and manifestation,
22 realization,
31 effect according to the manifestation of the first force.

13 therefore gives me a representative image which is firstly 1 or force, and then 3 or the manifestation of force by will, action, fact, which therefore gives 13.

Number 22 shows me that in realization, force and effect, action and fact are always divided as 2 by 2; force and effect constitute the interior, action and outcome the exterior; and these together therefore give 22.

Now the doctrine of progressions provides me with the number 31, or the representative image of effect, which follows force which is manifested in the interior by 3; it is by having force take a shot, by wishing to take a shot, and by actually taking the shot, but in the exterior by 1 or the shot which took place. Everything is ruled in this way.

Action ⎰ Force – force of the shot
⎨ Effect – proportion of will, effect of skill
⎱ Result – take a shot

Fact ⎰ Shot which took place, force – force of the
⎱ billard ball, force or shot

Reaction ⎰ Effect – effect of skill
⎱ Result – result, determination of the whole

We see that according to the law of progressions in Nature, the imagination is one of the most magnificent powers of the human spirit.[172]

It creates the simple from the multiple and gives it the ability to learn and to reason.

---

[172] Ibid., pp. 268 – 272.

It is called the power of imagination, the power to draw ONE from many images. It assimilates, unites. If the imagination is suited to the order of things, it is the inventor of the highest truths, but if it is suited to disorder, so that it isn't based on a proper foundation, it is the source of all errors and daydreams.

A soul which is in order has an imagination which is in order, a soul in disorder has an imagination in disorder, and that is the source of true and false, good and evil.

So, we see clearly that the false and the evil that is in the world must come from a disorder in the influence of the spirits; this disorder results from order being diverted, where evil in the world is the outcome.

The soul is a simple being, it cannot amass a multitude of images; it needs a force which brings the many to unity. This force is the imagination: the ability to make numerous images ONE. Only the point depicts the point, as the simple depicts the simple.

This is how the imagination represents things to the soul; it brings everything together. This union works if images are delivered to it according to the order of Nature or truth, – and number and measure, or experience and progress, are the sure basis for correct knowledge.

The imagination has been considered from various points of view. Man's inner sense is that common sensorium[173] in the body which is imagination in the soul. Everything is linked and goes from multiple to unity. And so, a thousand nerves connect them in the human body; the latter is attached to a main nerve, which is entwined with everything according to the same law of progression.

So long as the human soul is in the body for a long time its effects are progressive. Action on the organs and reaction constitute its effects. But without a body it behaves very differently; its progressive manifestations pass into unity.

Imagination, judgment, intelligence, memory, recollections, the power to think are nothing more than progressions of a single power of the soul which is necessary for the soul when dealing with the human body, because they are controlled by the

---

[173] Sensorium also means 'brain' – PV.

successive laws of time and by the "plurality"[174] of images; there, where time and images cease they return to their source, and intent and knowledge then remain with the spirit. So, too, do the colors of the rainbow disappear and are lost in one single beam of light, from which they were only progressions in the realm of phenomena.

Thus, what in man was the power of thinking, memory, intelligence, judgment, imagination, is in the spirit a single intuition, and constitutes its essence.

In this intuition is its beatitude, because it determines its rank in the world of the spirits depending on the similarity of its essence to God, which determines whether it is closer or further away from Him or separated entirely from His essence.

This is the eternal reward and the eternal punishment of thinking beings.

The different actions we take for good or bad follow us and form us into that unity of the spirit which remains with us forever.

Here in the land of "plurality"[175] we will be explained, removed, added, changed; but time disappears, and when account of our deeds is made eternity will undertake their addition and the result will be a happy or unhappy figure, which will remain for eternity.

We now return to the laws of progression, through which we still wish to consider man.

We see in man an interior and an exterior; an exterior which depends upon the interior, in that it is directed by the interior. Man lives and dies; the change in death is made in the interior; in the exterior, the effect of the power which vivifies man on the inside ceases; the body remains as an inanimate mass.

The power which animates man must be in the interior and cannot be linked with the exterior except in acting upon it...

---

[174] In fact, the word used in inverted commas is 'pluvalité', a word which doesn't appear to exist, but is almost certainly *not* a misprint, since it is repeated three paragraphs later. Here it has been translated here as "plurality", which fits. However, if the word was indeed meant to be 'pluvalité', then perhaps the introduction of the 'v' suggests something more like rain – as in teeming – since *pluvial* means 'rainy' and *pluviosité* mean 'rainfall' – PV.

[175] See note 174 above – PV.

We see in man that he lives, that he has the ability to think. He possesses intelligence, judgement and imagination, and as we no longer see any of these abilities in the dead body, these abilities must be qualities of the interior and not of the exterior, since otherwise they would exist even after death.

This interior is thus essentially distinguished from the exterior as it has qualities which are completely different from it, and these qualities constitute the entirety of a person. What is in the interior must be a power and each power is essentially different from matter, because it has neither sensory divisibility, nor physical extension.

This power of interior life in man is therefore the soul and is essentially different from the body.

....

In olden times, man was the intermediary between the spiritual quaternary and the temporal one, whereas now he is at the end of the quaternary of time.[176]

He therefore had a vast and all-embracing view, whereas now distance and error are his lot.

If one wants to calculate something according to the quaternary, let one first observe if what is to be calculated is an object that is:

- metaphysical;
- or geometric;
- or simply corporeal and physical,

which will indicate the numbers of the quaternary.

If one has looked at that, one can reflect on how many times the thing can be transposed in order to find mutual relationships.

Know how many times the thing can be transposed in and of itself, then with one side of the quaternary to which it belongs, and finally the whole quaternary and the root.

---

[176] Eckartshausen, *Ausschlüsse zur Magic*. Munich, 1792, Vol. IV. Appeared in *l'Initiation*, 72rd Vol., July 1906, No. 10, pp. 52 – 59.

1	2	3	4	10
point,	line,	plane,	depth,	mathematics
1	2	3	4	10
wisdom,	ability,	multiplicity,	movement,	nature
1	2	3	4	10
power of the seed,	natural development,	simple form,	composite form,	creation of Nature
1	2	3	4	10
to be,	to be there,	power and virtue,	action,	metaphysics
1	2	3	4	10
intelligence,	justice,	power,	moderation,	ethics
1	2	3	4	10
warmth,	dryness,	humidity,	cold,	qualities
1	2	3	4	10
Spring,	Summer,	Autumn,	Winter,	Year

THOUGHT[177]

What happens if I think? My soul touches the object or the image which the expression of divine thoughts has left in me. My soul, as it thinks about the thoughts of God, touches as it were the border of God's robe, and each touch of a thought which is more elevated, closer to God, awakens emanated powers which are closer to God, which act on us according to the Laws of the Spirit.

Each thought becomes a power in man which remains in him, and which slumbers as it were and waits for him to develop. I can think a thousand thoughts, millions of thoughts, always of the same object once again without the image extinguishing such a sea of spiritual forces in my soul!

THE FALL OF MAN AND DESTINY

1

Man called to intuition and not to enjoyment of the body, was in Eden.

---

[177] Eckartshausen, *Ausschlüsse zur Magic*. Munich, 1792, Vol. IV. Appeared in *l'Initiation*, 72rd Vol., August 1906, No. 11, pp. 176 – 179.

2

He was not forbidden to gaze on the tree, but to eat of its fruit.

3

The fruit was sensory; in order to eat it, he needed sensory organs; he wanted to eat it, and so he became a possessor of the sensual, and became mortal.

4

Man's destiny is the ascent of man the sensate animal to man-spirit; therefore his fall was a descent from man-spirit to man, the sensate animal.

Sum = 10

AGES OF MAN

1

The first age of man is childhood; he nourishes his body and forgets his years as he ages.

2

After childhood, the second age comes and the man makes use of his memory.

3

Then, the third age comes and Nature gives man the ability to produce children and to be a father.

4

The fourth age, he gives himself over to business, he acts according to his desires, sometimes well, sometimes badly and most often according to his passions.

5

In the fifth age man, after work and fatigue, approaches the gray years and feels the need for repose.

6

In the sixth age, he falls into the weakness and disease, a child of disease and of death.

Sum = 6

YEARS OF MAN-SPIRIT

1

The man-spirit nourishes himself in his first age of good examples, and incitement to virtue, society, books, history.

2

In the second age, seeing the decrepitude of the temporal, he aspires to higher things, he seeks, he examines, he is led by grace and draws near to the eternal laws.

3

In the third age, man submits his soul to the spirit and makes a covenant with virtue and wisdom.

4

In the fourth, he lives according to the rules of that holy covenant and cheers his spirit with divine powers.

5

In the fifth, he enjoys peace and inner repose and lives under the unvarying laws of the Kingdom of God and of Wisdom.

6

In the sixth, he renews himself completely; he begins the life of the spirit and receives the pure form of this image, after which he has been created.

7

In the seventh, he is in possession of the Kingdom of God, and his heart becomes the Temple of Divinity, and just as death is the end of the life of the man-animal, eternal life becomes the end of the age of man-spirit.

Sum = 7

II

HOËNÉ WRONSKI[178]

Architectonic System of Algorithms According to the Law of Creation[179]

A) *Theory* or *Autothesis*; that which is *given* in man's knowledge to establish Algorithms.
  a) Algorithmic *Content* or *Constitution*.
    a2) *Elementary* part = BASIC AGLORITHMS (seven in number).
    a3) Original elements = ORIGINAL ALGORITHMS.
    a4) Fundamental element; neutral generation of numbers = REPRODUCTION (1).
        α) Progressive = MULTIPLICATION.
        β) Regressive = DIVISION.
    b4) *Primordial* Elements.
    a5) *Discontinuous* generation of numbers, implying only the idea of the end = SUMMATION (II).
        α) Progressive = ADDITION.
        β) Regressive = SUBTRACTION.
    b5) *Continuous* generation of numbers, implying the idea of *infinity* = GRADUATION (III).
        α) Progressive = POWERS.

---

[178] The inclusion of this passage in Papus book is something of a mystery. Firstly, the theories were discredited even during the life of Wronski. Secondly, a long dissertation about algorithms, sines, cosines and logarithms goes completely against the tenor of the rest of the book, which utilizes numbers in a theosophical manner, not mathematical (even if the notes are somehow attempting to prove the Creation by numbers). It is quite possible the inclusion was to pay homage to Papus' theory that Eliphas Lévi (when he was still Alphonse Louis Constant) had been initiated – and profoundly influenced – by Wronski. However, more recent scholarship suggests that Wronski's influence on Lévi was both minor and fleeting – PV.

[179] Hoëné Wronski, *Messianisme ou Réforme absolue du Savoir Humaine* [*Messianism or the Total Reform of Human Knowledge*], Vol 1. Réforme des Mathématiques, Paris. 1847. Pp. 65 – 68.

β) Regressive = ROOTS.
- b3) *Derived elements* = ORGANIC ALGORITHMS
  a4) Immediate or distinct derived elements = IMMANENT ALGORITHMS.
  a5) Summation combined with Reproduction. NUMERATION (IV).
  Note: – This specific case forms the NUMERALS.
  b5) Graduation combined with Reproduction = ABILITIES (V).
  Note: – This specific case forms the *factorials*.
  b4) *Mediate* or *transitive* derived elements = TRANSCENDANT ALGORITHMS.
  a5) Transition of numeration to *Abilities*; Summation doing the function of *Graduation* = LOGARITHMS (VI).
  b5) Transition of the Abilities to *Numeration*; Graduation doing the function of *Summation* = SINE and COSINE (VII).

- b2) Systematic part = SYSTEMATIC ALGORITHMS (four in number).
  a3) *Diversity* in the systematic reunion of the primordial elements.
  a4) *Partial* influence.
  a5) Influence of Summation on Graduation in their systematic reunion = CALCULATION OF DIFFERENCES And DIFFERENTIAL (I).
  b5) Influence of Graduation on Summation in their systematic reunion = CALCULATION OF DEGREES AND SUBDEGREES[180] (II).
  Note: – See *'Introduction to the Philosophy of Mathematics'* to understand the direction of this new algorithmic calculation, discovered by the current application of the Law of Creation, as well as several other algorithms that follow which we did not previously suspect.

---

[180] 'Grades et Gradules' in original text – PV.

b4) *Reciprocal* influence of these primordial elements; systematic *harmony* between Summation and Graduation by their teleological coming together for the generation of numbers. = CALCULATION OF CONGRUENCES (III).
Note: – The type of this algorithmic teleology is:
$$x^m = \alpha \quad (Module - M).$$
It was Gauss who first conceived the problem; but this illustrious geometrician was unable to resolve it except for the simple case of quadratic residues, and even this only within very restricted limits.
b3) final identity in the systematic reunion of distinct derived elements or of the immanent algorithms of Numeration and Abilities, by means of the neuter element or the algorithm of Reproduction, which is common to them = CALCULATION OF EQUIVALENCES (IV).
Note: – This is what is called the *Theory of algebraic equations of different degrees.*
(b) Algorithmic *form* or *comparison* .
a2) In the *elemental* part = RELATIONSHIPS.
    α) Relationship dependent on the neuter algorithm of Reproduction = RELATIONSHIP (called) GEOMETRIC.
    β) Relationship dependent on primordial algorithms.
        α2) Of Summation. ARITHMETICAL RELATIONSHIP.
        β2) Of *Graduation*. SALTATION RELATIONSHIP .
b2) in the *systematic* part = EQUATIONS.
    α) Equations dependent on the aforesaid systematic *diversity*
    α2) of *partial diversity*;
    α3) Equations with DIFFERENCES and DIFFERENTIALS.
    β3) Equations with DEGREES and SUBDEGREES.
    β2) of *reciprocal diversity* = EQUATIONS OF CONGRUENCES (Indeterminate equations in general).
    β) Dependent equations of aforesaid systematic *identity* = EQUATIONS OF EQUIVALENCES.

B) *Technique* or *Autogeny*[181]; what it must do to fulfill the Algorithm.
a) In the *content* or in the algorithmic *Constitution*.
a2) In the *elementary* part of that Constitution.
a3) For the measurement of quantities by the *immediate* or *distinct* elements; completion of *immanent algorithms* = TECHNICAL ALGORITHMS OF THE 1st ORDER.
a4) Completion of *Numeration*.
a5) With a preponderance of *Summation*; primordial technical instrument = SERIES.
b5) With a preponderance of *Reproduction*; *secondary* technical instrument = CONTINUOUS FRACTIONS.
b4) Completion of *Abilities*.
a5) With preponderance of *Graduation*; primordial technical instrument = EXPONENTIAL ABILITIES.
b5) With preponderance of *Reproduction*; secondary technical instrument = CONTINUOUS PRODUCTS.
b3) For the determination of quatitites by mediate or transitive elements; completion of transcendat algorithms = TECHNICAL ALGORITHMS OF THE 2nd ORDER.
a4) Completion of *Logarithms* = SUPERIOR ORDERS OF LOGARITHMS.

Note: – These are the logarithms of *ideal* quantities (falsely called *imaginary*) as is, for example, the logarithm by which Johann Bernouilli was able to determine, in a definitive way, the famous relationship π of the circumference with the radius of the circle; a finding which could also be definitively determined thus by the sole *primitive algorithms*, as we have done in finished expression as follows:

$$\pi = \frac{4 \cdot \infty}{\sqrt{-1}} \cdot \left[(1 + \sqrt{-1})^{\frac{1}{\infty}} - (1 - \sqrt{-1})^{\frac{1}{\infty}} \right];$$

---

[181] The first word in French is 'Technie', which doesn't really exist, although an obscure dictionary mentioned that, as a very rare suffix, it could mean 'technique' as in cristallotechnie, mnémotechnie, pharmacotechnie, for example. 'Autogeny' (Autogénie in French) broadly means the creation of life from non-living matter, as in Spontaneous Generation which was so popular in the 17th and 18th Centuries – PV.

an expression which in consequence gives the final solution to the famous problem of Squaring the Circle.

b4) Completion of the *Sine* and *Cosine* = SUPERIOR ORDERS OF SINE AND COSINE.

Note: – To form an idea of these superior orders of Sine and Cosine constituting new periodic functions, which have remained unknown to geometrists, see *"Introduction to the Philosophy of Mathematics"*, at marks (53) to (59), and the Note on page 513 in the second volume of *Philosophy of Algorithmic Technique.*

b2) In the *systematic part* of this Constitution.

a3) For the completion of *preordained harmony* or *original* preformation in the two primordial elements; *sufficient reasons* to determine their quantities by their systematic conditions, that is to say, by the values of their differences or differentials, and by those of their Degrees or Subdegrees = INTERPOLATION.

b3) For the accomplishment of the *original identity* of the two primordial elements; absolutely universality in the generation of quantities = SUPREME LAW OF ALGORITHMS.

Note: – The form of this Supreme Law is:
$$F_x = A_0.\Omega_0 + A_1.\Omega_1 + A_2.\Omega_2 + A_3.\Omega_3 + etc.\ etc.$$
The famous theorem of Taylor, which is its most specific case, was the first attempt at this universal generation of quantities.

b) In *form* or in algorithmic *Comparison*.

a2) In the *elemental* part of this Comparison; completion of algorithmic relationships, in view of the *uniformity* of the generation of quantities; *rule* of this uniform generation = ALGORITHMIC CANON.

Note: – The theory of *generative functions* of Laplace presents us with a specific case.

b2) In the *systematic part* of this Comparison; completion of algorithmic *equations*, in view of the *final identity*, or of the universal generation of quantities. UNIVERSAL PROBLEM OF ALGORITHMS.

Note: – The form of this Universal problem is:

$$0 = FX + x_1.F_1x + x_2.F_2x + x_3.F_3x + \textit{etc. etc...}$$

The famous theorem of Lagrange, which is the most specific instance, was the first attempt at a solution to this universal problem of Mathematics.

III

H. DE BALZAC

Number[182]

"You believe in number as the foundation on which you place the edifice of what you call exact sciences. Without number there would be no more mathematics. So, what mysterious being who has been granted the ability to live forever, could ever finish counting, and in what sufficiently precise language could he state the numbers contained in the infinite number whose existence is demonstrated by your reason? Ask the finest human genius, and he would sit for a thousand years leaning on a table with his head between his hands, and what would he reply to you? You know neither where number begins, where it stops, or where it will end. Now, you call it time; then, you call it space. Nothing exists except through number, but without it everything would be the same substance, because number alone differentiates and modifies. Number is to your mind what it is to matter, an incomprehensible agent. Is it a being? Is this a breath emanated from God to organize the material Universe, in which nothing only receives its shape except through Divisibility which is an effect of number? Aren't the smallest, as well as the most immense creations, distinguished from one another by their quantities, qualities, dimensions and force, which are all attributes arising from number? The infinity of numbers is a proven fact, for which no evidence can materially be given. The mathematician will tell you infinite numbers exist but cannot be demonstrated. God is a Number endowed with movement, Who can be felt but not proved. Like Unity, He begins numbers but has nothing in common with them. The existence of number depends on unity which, without being a number, gives rise to them all. God is a magnificent Unity Who has nothing in common with His creations, but Who nevertheless is their Creator.

---

[182] H. De Balzac, Séraphita. Paris, pub. Calmann-Lévy. Pp. 129 – 133. [It should be noted that this appears to be a slightly edited version of the original text – PV].

Why, if you believe in number, do you deny God? Is Creation not placed between the infinity of unorganized substances and the infinity of the Divine spheres, as unity finds itself between the infinity of fractions which you now call decimals, and the infinity of numbers that you call integers?

"You men alone of all things on earth understand number, that first step onto the forecourt which leads us to God, and there your reason already stumbles. What? You can neither measure the first abstraction that God has given you, nor grasp it, and yet you wish to submit God's purposes to your gauge? What if I were to plunge you into the abyss of Motion, that force which organizes number? What if I were to tell you that movement and number are generated by the Word? That term, the Supreme Reason of the seers and prophets who once heard that voice of God beneath which St. Paul fell down, is a source of mockery to you, you men whose visible works, however, the societies, monuments, activities, passions are called forth out of your own feeble word, and which, without language, would so closely resemble that neighboring species the Negro, or the Orang-utan...[183] So you believe firmly in number and movement, yet you say that force and result are inexplicable, incomprehensible?... Let us proceed. You have found for yourselves a place in the infinity of number, you have fitted it to your size by creating – if indeed you can actually create anything – arithmetic, the foundation upon which everything reposes, even your societies.

"Number, the only thing in which you self-styled atheists believe, organizes physical creation; just as arithmetic, or the use of number, has organized the moral world. This use of numbers should be absolute, as everything that is intrinsically true; but in fact it is purely relative, and has no absolute existence: you can give no proof of its reality. Firstly, even if this arithmetic is good for summing organized substances, which are finite, it is powerless

---

[183] Clearly the views of late 19th Century Europe were not that of modern people, and like a similar reference in Saint-Martin, should be understood to be confined to those times. The reference to an Orang-utan in itself, however, is more interesting: consider the famous case of the Bishop of Polignac who, on seeing an Orang-utan (some say it was a chimpanzee) in the Jardin du Roi in Paris in the 1730, was so overcome by its humanlike gait that he was said to have said to the creature: "Speak, and I shall baptize thee." – PV.

when applied to organizing forces, which are infinite. Man, who can conceive the infinite through his intelligence, cannot handle it in its entirety; for if he could, he would be God. Thus, your arithmetic, applied to finite things and not to the infinite, is true in relation to the details that you perceive, but false in relation to the whole, which you cannot perceive at all... also, you do not encounter two identical objects anywhere in Nature; thus, in the natural order two and two can never make four, because it would have to join two units which were exactly the same, and you know that it is impossible to find two similar leaves on one tree, or two identical specimens in the same species of tree. This axiom of your arithmetic, which is false in visible Nature, is also false in the invisible universe of your abstractions, where the same variations exist in your ideas, which are things of the visible world, but extended by their relations: indeed, differences are even more clear cut there than elsewhere. Everything there varying due to temperament, strength, manners and the habits of individuals who are never alike, the smallest things represent individualized thoughts. Surely, if man has been able to create units, it was by giving equal weight and value to pieces of gold? Well, you can add a poor man's ducat to the ducat of a rich man at the ducat, and say to the Public Treasury that both are equal amounts; but, in the eyes of the thinking man one is certainly morally more substantial than the other: one represents a month's happiness, the other represents the most ephemeral whim. Two and two only make four by a false and monstrous abstraction. Fractions don't exist in Nature, where what you call a fragment is a complete thing in itself... Number, with its infinitely small and its infinite totalities, is therefore a power of which only the smallest part is known to you, and whose breadth escapes you. You have built a little hut in the infinity of numbers, you have adorned it with hieroglyphics cleverly designed and painted, and you have cried: Everything is there."

IV

A. DESBARROLLES

Numbers[184]

The system of numbers taught by Pythagoras, who of course learned it from the Priests of Egypt, was disseminated by his students.

"Since the divine essence", they said, "is inaccessible to the senses, in order to characterize it, let us not use the language of the senses, but rather that of the spirit; let us give to intelligence or the *active* Principle of the Universe the name of Monad or Unity, because He is always the same; and to matter or the *passive* principle that of the dyad or multiplicity, because it is subject to all sorts of changes; finally, to the world that of the triad, because it is the result of intelligence and matter."[185]

Regardless of the way in which the system is presented, it is always Kether, Binah and Chokmah.

It is always the battle between the active principle and the passive principle giving movement, the source of life.

The meaning of the lessons of Pythagoras concerning numbers is that numbers contain the elements of all things and even of all knowledge. Pythagoras applied the system of numbers to the worlds of the spirits and solved problems perfectly unknown to our current arithmetic. Here is what was said by a learned man on this subject more than two centuries ago:

"The great system of the world rest upon certain bases of harmony, of which the being, the form and the action of all things, both individual and general, are a natural consequence. These bases of harmony are called numbers. He who knows them knows the laws by which Nature exists, the comparison of its relationships, the type and extent of their effect, the link between

---

[184] Desbarrolles, *Les Mystères de la main révélés et expliqués [The Mysteries of the hand revealed and explained]*. Paris, Dentu, 1860, pp. 299 – 313.
[185] *Voyage d'Anarchasis*. Paris, 1809, Vol. III, p. 181.

all things and all facts, the physics and the mechanics of the world. Numbers are the invisible vessels of beings, just as their bodies are their visible vessels, that is to say that there is a dual nature to things, one visible and the other invisible. The visible is the visible form, the body; the invisible form is number. And everything that there is, and which manifests itself is the result of an inner energy, and that energy is the outflowing of a force. The greater and lesser forces come from real numbers, and greater and lesser energy from virtual numbers.

"There are clearly invisible envelopes, because every being has a principle and a form: but the principle and the form are two extremes which can never unite without a specific link which joins them together; and that is the function of number. For the laws and qualities of invisible things are written in invisible numbers. Now, since one receives impressions of how a thought feels through our senses, so our mind similarly receives lucid ideas about the invisible position and purpose of things as soon as it can grasp them. Because an idea, like a physical object, has number, measure and weight, but whose location is visible only to the intelligence. Real numbers in the world are infinite, it is true, but their progression is simple and direct because everything is based on the fundamental numbers from one to ten. Their infiniteness is based on the infinite and indeterminate number of beings they contain, in the same way that those same beings have many kinds of qualities.

"There are therefore numbers for the basis and the substance of beings, their effect, their duration and the degrees of their development (progression). All these things are so many stations where the rays of divine light stop and cast backward reflections, sometimes to exhibit their own image, sometimes to take in a new life, a new measure, a new weight in that same backward glance. There are also numbers equipped to express the different relationships and the different positions of beings, their action and their effect. In this manner there are central numbers and numbers of circumference; there are also false numbers and impure numbers. Despite their infiniteness, the idea is very simple, since everything comes from the first basic figure up to ten being the simple numbers; and those are also based again upon the first four basic numbers whose union (through addition) gives 10, from which comes the amazing form of the quaternion, which seems madness to people nowadays because they really cannot understand the concept. Here we see, in a way, why the number 10 was so very sacred to the Pythagoreans, for it was their most revered number, a genuine αρρητον[186]. They swore by the number 4, and an oath on the holy τετραχτοξ[187] was more sacred than could be imagined. It contained all the symphonies and the forces of nature. Ten was the number of the world, or Absolute Pan (παν) . According to Pythagoras, numbers are the basis of the divine spirit, and the unique way in which things manifest themselves; the union of all the numbers in all the worlds, or the basis of agreement between beings and their outcomes, forms the harmony of the great whole. That is why Pythagoras saw astrology and astronomy as closely intertwined branches of one and the same science ."[188]

"Pythagoras also distinguished between numbers, and figures which can be counted; the former are destinations (terminuses, αροι) and consist solely of spiritual dimensions: the latter, on the contrary, are concerned with corporeal things and are the visible expression of the invisible. All spiritual figures, according to Pythagoras, are rays, reflections (emanations) of Unity, just as *one* or *unity* is the beginning of figures which can be counted. One is also the name and character of the Most High, the Grand Principle, the Sole, the Infinite. One is the center of everything, the basis of every being and of all specific unities which are not absolute and inevitable, but which are mediate or immediate rays from the Absolute Unity. Ten numbers form a unit of ten up to a hundred; ten tens are a unit of one hundred, and so on; all larger units contain smaller ones, with the result that the smaller ones are contained within the larger, and so a mutual

---

[186] Unspeakable or unspoken – PV.
[187] Tetractys – PV.
[188] Thionis Smyrnoi, *eorum quae in mathemat. ad Platonis lectionem utilia sunt exposito.* Paris, 1646, book. 1, cap. 1, p. 7.

coming together takes place. And it is the same in Nature. Every superior world contains all the subordinate units of the inferior worlds, and conversely the smallest are part of the worlds, spheres, figures or superior creatures, as the subordinates contained within them. In the hundreds, for example, are contained all the numbers from one up to a hundred, and in the animal kingdom are contained all the animals in creation; and as all the numbers from one to a hundred rise more and more towards one hundred, so even the animals at the lowest place ascend from their grade by rising up and growing continually, until the most distinguished of their members come to join with man, without however being able to achieve his eminence.

"The infinite variety of breeds of animals descending from one another also expresses the relationship between numbers in the sense of unity shining brightly in an infinity of rubbish. This luminous system which comes from the Orient, corresponds to the system according to which the lowest orders arise from the highest, which contain them and penetrate them."[189]

"Not only the most famous philosophers, but even the Catholic doctors, among others: St. Jerome, St. Augustine, Origen, St. Ambrose, St. Gregory of Nazianzus, St. Athanasius, St. Basil, St. Hilary, Rabanus Maurus, the Venerable Bede, and several others, assure us that there is an admirable and efficacious virtue hidden in numbers."[190]

"Severinus Boethius said that all things which Nature first made, seem to have been formed by means of numbers, for that was the principle model in the mind of the Creator; from there came the quantity of elements, the revolutions of time; from there came the movement of the stars, the changes in the heavens and the state of all things subsists by the uniting together of numbers. It is not surprising, since there are such great occult virtues and in such great numbers in natural things, that there should be in numbers all the greater, more occult, more wonderful, more

---

[189] *Geschichte der magic*, von Joseph Ennemoser. Leipzig, 1844, p. 548 (unpublished Translation).
[190] *The Occult Philosophy of Cornelius Agrippa*. The Hague, 1727, book 2, p. 215 (see the edition by the Chacornac Library, 1910, Vol I, 2nd Book, pp. 217 – 219).

efficacious, because they are more formal, more perfect, and they are found in the celestial bodies."[191]

"Everything that is made subsists and draws its virtue from numbers; for time consists of numbers, and all motion and action, and all things are subject to time and motion. Harmony and voices, too, are composed of numbers and proportions and have no power except through them. Finally, all species of things which are in Nature and which are above Nature are joined together by certain numbers, which has led Pythagoras to say that all things are composed by number and that it distributes each virtue to all things."[192]

Agrippa and Saint-Martin were preoccupied with numbers; Saint-Martin in a very special way.

Did Saint-Martin and the Abbé Joachim[193] come to prophecy by means of numbers? That is something we haven't studied.

We will not attempt to give an idea of Saint-Martin's system of numbers here, since it is very mystical and therefore quite obscure, and would require us to go into considerable detail. We will simply quote without comment what he says about the Number One; and we will quote Agrippa after him.

"Unity," said Saint-Martin, "multiplied by itself, only ever makes *one*, because it cannot come out of itself.

"The seed of a plant which has produced its annual fruit in accordance to the number of actions that are included in its powers, no longer produces, and returns to its principle.

"Each thought that comes out of us is the product of an action of power that is relative, and which, by being like the seed, ends

---

[191] Idem, pp. 213 – 214.
[192] Idem, p. 214.
[193] Joachim of Fiore lives from 1135 – 1202) and was known for his prophecies. He put forward the notion of three Ages, that of the Father (Old Testament times), the Son (from the birth of Jesus till 1260), and the Age of the Holy Spirit, predicting a utopian period with the dispensation of universal love, when all would join together in harmony. Despite always being in harmony with the Church during his lifetime, it was his teachings and groups which were later formed in his name which were declared heretical.

with the particular thought it produced when it has fulfilled its course.

"Although Deity is the Infinite, Unique and Eternal Source, of all who have received being, every action of His operating and productive abilities is used for a single work and is retained by it without being repeated, because that action is completed and accomplished. Thus, since each operation is one, and each root of that operation being new, it is probably that that root which acted in its creative function, acts only in its conservative function as soon as it has produced its work, even though the resulting works are permanent and immortal, because roots are only like the organs and channels by which Unity manifest and achieves the expression of His abilities outside of Himself.

"However, in all possible philosophies, only the means are transient, and the end is stable."[194]

This is what Agrippa said:
"Number is nothing but a repetition of unity. Unity most simply penetrates all numbers, and being the common measurement of all numbers, their source and their origin, it contains every number each being uniquely joined to it, while remaining incapable of being a multitude, being forever the same and without change: that being multiplied by itself produces nothing but itself. One is the principle of all things and all go up to one, and beyond it there is nothing, and all things that are desire that one, because everything came from one. For all things to be the same, they must participate in the one; and just as all things have gone to the many from one, so everything that wants to return to one must quit the multitude. One therefore is referred to God Who, being One and beyond number, yet creates innumerable things and the contains them within Himself.

"There is *one* God, *one* world which is God's, *one* sun for *one* world, *one* Phoenix in the world, *one* king among bees, *one* leader among the herds, *one* commander of an army. There is *one* element which surpasses and penetrates everything, which is fire; there

---

[194] *Les Nombres* [*Numbers*], by Saint-Martin, autographed edition. Paris, 1843, pp. 80 – 82. See edition of the Chacornac Library, Paris, pp. 78 – 82.

is one thing created of God which is the subject of all admiration, which is on the Earth and in the heavens, and is actually the vegetable and mineral soul which is found everywhere, that few know, and nobody called by its true name, but which hides itself in numbers, figures and riddles, without which neither Alchemy nor Natural Magic might be successful."[195]

Unity is the principle of everything: but the light of unity cannot be a light without shadow, and the unity of voice cannot be a voice without echo. One is a principle without comparison; number is harmony, and without harmony nothing is possible; unity is necessarily active, and its need to act leads it to repeat itself; it partakes of itself, or rather multiplies itself to produce two. But two is antagonism, a momentary immobility when the forces are equal, but the battle is the principle of motion. Saint-Martin, in calling the number two bad and baneful, proved that he didn't understand one of the greatest arcana of magic. The earth is naturally a place of passage and trials: number two is therefore a necessity, since it represents that life which is action, which is contention, which does not cease to exist except through repose. Two is therefore antagonism[196], but three is existence. With three, life is found. Three is the pendulum which sometimes goes to the right, sometimes to the left, to balance and cause to move.

Thus, three uses the conflict of the binary and draws movement from it, which is life.

"Three," said Balzac in *Louis Lambert,* "is the formula of the created worlds, it is the *spiritual* sign of creation as it is the material sign of the circumference.

"Three: it is God."

---

[195] *The Occult philosophy of Cornelius Agrippa*, Book 2. The Hague, 1727 p. 218. [Note that in those days it was assumed that the large bee which founded hives was in fact male. Also, some translations call the famous *prima materia* so well described here as 'animal, vegetable and mineral, everywhere found', whereas in this excerpt it is clearly called 'the vegetable (or vegetative) and mineral soul. – PV.]

[196] It seems an odd comment by Desbarrolles that Saint-Martin didn't understand the meaning of the number two, since he goes on to describe it exactly as Saint-Martin does! It may be that Desbarrolles didn't understand Saint-Martin... – PV.

We cannot resist the pleasure of quoting a few sentences from *'Les Harmonies de l'être, exprimées par les nombres'*, an eminently deep and remarkable book.

In the Gospel of St. John, the author read three words: *Vita, Verbum, Lux*: Life, Word, Light. There he sees the Trinity, and examines the profundity and the meaning of these three words in several pages, which may be summarized as follows:

"Let us say that the Father is *Life*, and therefore power and strength, and that the special characteristic of this life is expansion.

"What will the Son be? Everybody knows; He is the *Word* or the voice. But what is to be understood by the Word or the voice? All philosophers agree in saying: it is form...

"Therefore, *Light* remains. How will the Holy Spirit be the Light? Let us try to understand...

"Light is neither substance nor intelligence, but it is the result of their union; it is not a compound of the two, it is not half substance, half intelligence, it is something different from either... which doesn't proceed by composition, but is simple in itself and indivisible, which is neither lesser nor greater than substance or intelligence, because light is everywhere, and only where intelligence is joined to life, and if that life and intelligence are infinite, shall the light also be. Therefore, the light which is different to life and intelligence... will be a third person, the Holy Spirit."[197]

"...Wisdom which we have always regarded as the Divine Word, the Son of God, speaks in the Proverbs thus: "When He prepared the heavens, I was there. When He gave the depths a law and a bound; when He established the firmament and distributed with measure the sources of the waters; when He put a restraint upon the sea and placed a law over the waves, so that they might not exceed their limits; when he laid the foundations of the earth: I was with him, arranging all things; I delighted in every day,

---

[197] *Les Harmonies de l'Être* [*The Harmonies of The Being*], by Lacuria. Paris, 1847, Vol. 1; pp. 37 – 38.

playing before Him, and forever playing in the Universe; and my delight will be to be with the children of men.[198]

"Isn't this the variety and distinction of beings?"[199]

You will recall that the Word is form.

"As for the Holy Spirit, when it appears, it is to inform that it is the one who inspires the prophets, who reveals the future and removes the blindfold from the eyes. When God promised the outpouring of His Holy Spirit, these are the effects that He said must follow: "Your sons and your daughters will prophesize, your old men shall dream dreams, and your young people visions. *Et prophetabunt filii vestri and filiæ vestræ, senes vestri somnia somniabunt, and juvenes vestri visiones videbunt* (Joel).[200]

Number Three is the movement which creates balance in passing successively from one point to another; number Four is perfect equilibrium, the square, positivism, realism.

Four, in magic, is the cube; the square. It is the image of the Earth; the Quaternary is the consequence of the Ternary; the Ternary is the spirit of movement and resistance which leads naturally to the Quaternary, which is stability and harmony.

For the ancient Kabbalists, number Four encompassed the four Elements.

"The four astronomical cardinal points are, in relation to us, the 'yes' and the 'no' of light: the East and the West; and the 'yes' and the 'no' of warmth: The South and the North," say the Kabbalists.

Number Four is the Cross.

In numbers, Pythagoras' disciples sought properties whose knowledge could raise them up to understand Nature: properties which, to them, appeared to be found in the phenomena of resonating objects.

"Make a string taut, they said, divide it successively in two, three or four parts, and in each half you will have the octave of the whole string; in three-quarters, the fourth; in two-thirds, the fifth:

---

[198] This passage comes from Proverbs 8: 27 – 31. However, here the passage has been translated directly from the French text, since it differs significantly from the King James Bible version – PV.
[199] Idem, Vol. I; pp. 40 – 41.
[200] Idem, Vol I, p. 41. [Quotation from Joel 2:28 – PV.]

The octave will therefore be 1 to 2; the fourth, 3 to 4, the fifth, 2 to 3. The importance of this observation gives the numbers 1, 2, 3, 4, the name of the sacred Quaternary. According to these discoveries, it was easy to conclude that the laws of harmony are invariable, and that Nature has irrevocably established the values and intervals of tones.[201]

But as all is in all, so that Nature has only one law in the general system of the Universe, as it is all harmony and simplicity, they rightly came to the conclusion that the various laws which govern the Universe could be discovered by seeking their relationship with those of harmony.

"Soon, in the numbers 1, 2, 3 and 4, not only was one of the principles of the musical system discovered, but also those of physics and ethics, since everything becomes proportion; and harmony, time, justice, kindness and intelligence are simply relationships between numbers, and as the numbers that make up the sacred Quaternary, in reuniting (in being added together) produce the number ten, number four was regarded as the most perfect of all because of this very reunion."[202]

We said that number four represents the four elements recognized by the ancient Kabbalists: four is therefore the earth, and form; one is the principle of life, the spirit: therefore, five is four plus one = five. It is therefore the spirit dominating the elements, it is the quintessence. And the Pentagram (the five-pointed star) expresses this domination. Also, the five-pointed Pentagram is the number of Jesus, whose name has five letters, it is the Son of God made man, it is Jehovah incarnate.

It is by using the sign of the pentagram that the Kabbalists claimed to bind the genii of the air, the Salamanders, the Undines and the Gnomes.

The Pentagram is the blazing star of the Gnostic Schools, but according to how it is used it will be more or less pure when directing matter, turning to good or evil, day or night.

---

[201] *Voyage d'Anarcharsis*, Vol. III, p. 183. Paris, 1809.
[202] Aristotelis opera omnia quæ exstant græce et latine. *Metaph.* Parisiis, 1539, Vol. IV, Book 1, Chap. V, p. 268.

Five is therefore the spirit and both its forms.

Black magic draws on the Pentagram by putting two of its points upwards, which signifies the antagonism between good and evil, and therefore immobility and ignorance, since when the Pentagram is placed thus, those two horns rule over the ternary which, representing the influence of the divine spirit, is reversed.

Five thus becomes a baneful number, a number ill-placed under the name of Geburah which is the number of antagonism, autonomy, excessive freedom, and whose antagonism causes severity.

The Pentagram represents the human body, with the upper point forming the head: if the head is downwards, it is the sign of madness.

The hand, which is a microcosm, also provides an explanation of the number five: the thumb represents intelligence which dominates matter represented in turn by the four fingers which, without the thumb, would become all but useless. The positive thumb is opposed to the negative fingers. The thumb is therefore spirit, it is human intelligence, giving worth, usefulness to the four fingers which represent matter.

The four members which comprise man's complete makeup are governed by the head as the fingers are by the thumb, we constantly find spirit and its forms; now the head can give both good and bad directions. We need say nothing more to explain number five.

V

E. LEDOS

The Relationship Between Numbers and the Planets[203]

Unity or Number One belongs to the Sun; this number belongs entirely to this kingly star, which spreads light and life upon our planetary world; and which, as unity, is the principle and the source of numbers.

Number Two is attributed to the Moon, which is the second light illuminating our planet, and whose action joined with that of the Sun produces the tides; which also has a specific and considerable influence on the atmosphere and therefore upon the order of time.

Number Three belongs to Jupiter, which is like this number, being characterized by the veneration of divine and sacred things by reason, moderation, and by love of peace and justice.

Number Four belongs to the sun, which, by its location in the points of the equinoxes and solstices, divides the year into four parts and governs the seasons. This number is also assigned to Mercury because of the four elements on which it very particularly acts by accommodating and adapting itself to their nature and qualities. Number Four is also assigned to the four cardinal points that fix the system of the winds.

Number Five which, composed of the sum of the first even number and the first odd number which join together as both the masculine and the feminine sexes, belongs to Mercury by reason of its androgynous nature. Five expresses intelligence and analysis, qualities of Mercury.

Number Six, symbol of natural beauty and perfection, belongs to Venus, which is the perfect example of form and beauty. Number Six, which is formed by three multiplied by two, shows

---

[203] E. Ledos, *Les types physionomiques associés et les phénomènes psychiques* [*The Physiognomic Forms Associated with Psychic Phemonema*]. Paris, undated. pp. 125 – 129.

two triangles whose meeting is the symbol of the union of the two sexes and the figure of marriage and generation, which naturally relates to Venus.

Number Seven, which ends all, which completes all, and which in all things is the end and the conclusion, which is succeeded by repose, belongs to Saturn, the symbol of time and eternity, and which marks the fatal ending of things and beings. Number Seven is also has relationship with the moon because it regulates the movement and the phases of this planet.

Number Eight belongs to the Earth, which represents the cube in general; it also belongs to Vulcan, image of the Central Fire.

Number Nine belongs to Mars, which represents will and action, strength and physical power, as Venus represents the attractions and seduction of perfect beauty. In addition, Mars is the emblem of power which animates and also destroys.

Number Ten is attributed to the Universe, and also to the stars because of their circular movement.

Geometric figures

The geometric figures which are produced by numbers have, like numbers, their own power, virtue and symbol. Thus, the point and the Circle relates to Unity and the number Ten; because Unity is at once the center and circumference of all things; and number Ten being connected to Unity, returns to Unity as to its principle, being the end and complement of all the numbers.

Thus, the circle is the image of Unity, because like Unity it has neither beginning nor end. That is why circular motion is considered to be infinite, not in respect of time, but in respect of place; it is for this reason that the circle is considered to be the most noble and perfect of all the figures.

The other figures, such as the triangle, the quadrangle, the pentagon, the hexagon, the heptagon, the octagon, and all the other figures which are composed of several different sections, have symbols, virtues and specific meanings, depending on their shape and the numbers to which they relate.

Squared and Cubic Powers of Certain Numbers

Number 121, the square of number 11, shows two unities or principles divided by the number 2 which represents evil.

Number 1331 is the cube of number 11. In this number 1331, the two 3s by uniting form number 6, which is a number of peace, harmony and perfection; which is also the symbol of the return of the sinner to good, and the power which is given to him to raise himself up towards perfection.

Number 100, the square of number 10 expresses complete perfection and it marks the extreme limit of human conception.

Number 1000, the cube of number 10, contains the perfection of a multitude of numbers; it signifies consummated and absolute perfection, the accomplishment of all things, and the consummation of the centuries.

Number 144, the square of number 12, contains many mysterious things concerning the Divine Order and the Spiritual Order.

In the Temporal Order it marks the great changes which come to human societies, to laws, to regimes as well as Empires, and even to cities. The changes signified by the square of 12 are not necessarily bad: they may be good and favorable to men if they govern themselves with wisdom and prudence.

But number 1728, the cube of 12, is fateful and fatal; it always brings disastrous changes, misfortunes and disasters which lead to the ruin of societies and Empires.

VI

LOUIS-MICHEL de FIGANIÈRES

Living and Perfecting Mathematics. Dead Mathematics.[204]

Thus, we designate the omniversal science of life, or the science of God and of human science. As everything is alive, everything falls under the omniversal science of life. It is the science of the laws and the functions of life, including everything that relates to it in the three orders of magnitude, combined by the 4 living rules, the four rules of life which are addition, subtraction, multiplication, and division; living rules which God alone can execute and following His example man, who lives in knowledge of the Divine Law. We call this science and its rules living, because they are exercise themselves actively in the course of life and apply only to living and moving objects. The science of living and functioning mathematics is one with the Divine Law of Analogy, and that is understandable. This mathematics acting in the same way everywhere, in similar situations, always represents Divine Analogy in their effects; and Divine Analogy being the result, the expression of the wishes of Supreme Perfection can only be the repetition of the living and perfecting mathematics of God. It is named as such because it's by virtue of its provisions that the life of everything and everywhere functions, the omniversal life, in the three orders of magnitude, in the order of the infinitely great, of the small or medium, and of the infinitely small.

Dead mathematics on the contrary, is so named in the *Key to life* because it only serves death. Based on the four numeric rules, abstraction, simple abstraction, and the fumes of living mathematics, they only operate for the benefit of a dead science. Instrument of the covetous to calculate his treasury, numeric mathematics serves the administrator to manage a dead world: it

---

[204] Louis-Michel de Figanières, *l'eveil des Peuples* [*The Awakening of the Nations*], Paris. 1864. Chap. X.

serves as the assistant to human science going from death to end in death.

Chapter 14
The Power of Numbers[205]

In the last Chapter we have been reading the authorized teachings of a few initiates. It will not be without interest to meditate next upon the work of a learned profane who, through his intuition alone has no doubt discovered much esoteric data. We are talking about J. B. J. Dessoye. We have extracted the following pages from his rare book: *Embryogénie methodical de l'entendement de l'esprit humain fondée sur la puissance des Nombres*[206]:

I. – SAMPLE PROSPECTUS

A. Pythagoras, Greek philosopher born in Samos around the year 600 B.C., said: "Numbers govern the Universe."

B. Pythagoras was right, which is what we just explained in 1857.

C. We have the integral calculation, the differential calculation, the decimal calculation, the duodecimal calculation and the infinitesimal calculation. But we don't yet have concordance between these 5 calculations, and we get lost in solutions which should easy if only we had a safe, invariable, simple and foolproof method by which these calculations could be reduced to a standard approach. Then we would no longer have to

---

[205] I can find no reference anywhere this this author, save a book entitled 'Practical Guide to the Use of Steel', published in 1863, which appears to be a highly regarded contribution in this field. However, this fact doesn't fill the translator with confidence regarding the following commentary on numbers. Apart from the fact that he appears to be attempting to put forward another 'theory of everything', and it uses a lot of numbers (usually in pretty shapes), there is little to be lost in ignoring this chapter; though I salute anyone who does manage to work out what he is trying to say! – PV.

[206] Property of the author: J. B. J. Dessoye. Registered 7 January, 1857. B. N. Cote: Vp. 24 815. [*Methodical Embryogenesis of Understanding the Human Mind Based on the Power of Numbers* PV.]

deal with infinitely small quantities; and all the quantities obtained would be complete.

D. Logarithms, or the ratio of numbers, teaches us that 0 (zero), is the logarithm of 1. If this is so, we have nine digits and 1 zero:

That is to say there are

$$\frac{0.\ 1.\ 2.\ 3.\ 4.\ 5.\ 6.\ 7.\ 8.\ 9.\ 10.}{1.\ 2.\ 3.\ 4.\ 5.\ 6.\ 7.\ 8.\ 9.\ 10.\ 11.\ 12 \times 12 = 144 = 9.} \quad \text{twelve signs}$$

placed on twelve columns. Pythagoras' Table was crafted on the square of 144, which is the measure of time.

E. But if we take the nine figures and the zero and place them in reverse in the following manner, giving the zero the value of two unities, $2.^0\ 1$; –

$$\begin{cases} 1.\ \ 2.\ \ 3.\ \ 4.\ \ 5 = 15 \\ 0.\ \ 9.\ \ 8.\ \ 7.\ \ 6 = 32 \end{cases} \overline{47}$$

$$\begin{array}{c} 3 \| \ \ 11\ \ 11\ \ 11\ \ 11\ \ 44\ \text{et}\ 3.\ \ 47 \\ 3 \| \ \ \ 2.\ \ \ 2.\ \ \ 2.\ \ \ 2. = \overset{*}{8} = 16.\ 94 \end{array}$$

$$\cdot \times \cdot$$
$$8 = 17 - 9, \quad 7\ \ 13$$
$$2 = 11. - 4.$$

we obtain as the result the square of 143, the product of 13 x 11.

F. This figure appears to show us that the reason for the numbers is based on the formation of double squares or triangles with the number 3 in the construction of which we must represent the zero by two ones: Example:

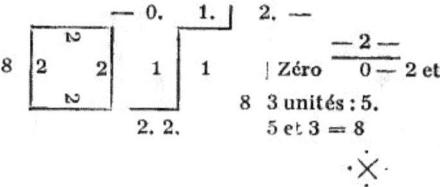

The figure above is the equivalent of a square:

G. The law of squares demonstrates this effectively:

1. That, if one places numbers under square or triangles, and if we give ordinal order to the lines and columns, i.e. transversely and vertically, the addition of a one taken from each side of the zero, unites with the numbers to furnish the proof.

2. That, on the other hand, if the additions are between each two numbers, i.e. in a triangular manner, the numbers so added together are summed up into a single digit, precisely to the number of the transverse line which is used to obtain the proof. The figure that we are going to give as an example, recalls that of Abracadabra. The number is 2868 = 24 = 6.

1. Figure or explanatory table of the property of the numbers when one gives the zero the value of two and a unity in the additions.

2. This same table provides an example of the manner by which one obtains the proof.

						·✕·	7.	5.	7.	·✕·						
							16.	32.	16.							
0.		1.	2.	3.	4.	5.				5.	4.	3.	2.	1.		0.
1.		1.	2.	3.	4.	5.				6.	7.	8.	9.	0.		1.
2.			3.	5.	7.	9.		11.			13.	15.	17.	11.		2.
3.				8.	12.	16.	20.			24.	28.	32.	28.			3.
4.					20.	28.	37.		45.		52.	60.	60.			4.
5.						49.	65.	82.			97.	113.	122.			5.
6.							114.	147.		179.		210.	235.			6.
7.								261.	326.			390.	446.			7.
8.									587.		717.		837.			8.
9.										1304.		1554.				9.
10.											2868.					01..
57.	12.										24.				21..	75.
12.									3.		6.		3.			21.
13.									9.		1.		9.			31.
14.									17.		8.		71.			41.
15.										8.		8.				51.
16.									15.		77.		51.			61.
17.											3.					71. .
132.									6.		0.		6.			231.
										8.		2.		8.		

It will be seen that, in this table, the numbers are verified and checked in the reverse and reciprocal sense. Concordance is established on the geometric progression 11, 22, 44, 88 and 1. 89.

H. The reason for this concordance is based on a simple fact.

    With the Square of   144
The product of 12 multiplied by itself were obtained   ===
by addition of the number   9
But if, instead of this square one takes that of 13 x 11, one gets 143 equaled by   8

So that as a result one gets two   8 $8 = \overline{17}$

The calculations are thus verified twice over. This is the zero logarithm of 1 which is the agent of this verification, from the moment it is used to take two units to make the additions.

II. – FIGURES & REASONING

J. This becomes evident when one divides the nine digits and zero into two parts, in order to transform them into arithmetic proportions, each with three terms and two relationships. We will demonstrate that, in forming these two proportions, one simultaneously obtains a geometric proportion.

The letter o is split into two unities.[207]

K. Therefore, as an example of the five calculated proportions of the application, first through reasoning, then justified by the numbers A, B, C, D, E.

---

[207] The image on the following page is taken directly from the original book. Given its complexity, it was decided to simply reproduce the image rather than translate or attempt to recreate it. Similarly, for the complex diagrams which follows it – PV.

L. The proof of these calculations is based on the relationships that exist between the numerical distances, with the value of 2 being attributed to zero in order to establish, by a kind of rule of false position, the concordance between the decimal and duodecimal calculations and the simultaneous creation of arithmetical and geometric proportions in the opposite and reciprocal direction, without the use of fractions.

A. Mots. Syllabes.	Chiffres et Nombres.	Lettres.	ont d'égales propriétés.	B. Pour exprimer	avec une précision rigoureuse	les calculs	de la pensée et de la raison humaines.
244 — 12 — 34 —	— 82 —	— 32 —	— 84 —	353 — 16 — 42 —	— 110 —	— 38 —	— 146 —

C. Les secrets mystérieux	de la nature et les combinaisons,	du Créateur	seront dévoilés d'une manière certaine.	D. Le jour	où l'on aura	découvert et démontré	(lettre) que 0 zéro = égalent un, deux, trois, quatre.
415 — 40 — 46 —	— 130 —	— 40 —	— 156 —	309 — 24 — 42 —	— 90 —	— 36 —	— 106.

664426 4 2 | 664626   E | Dieu, Vérité, | Unité Réciprocité. | Justice. | Rapports et Balance. | 46644 6 | 1 24 24 2 2 6

Rapports || Balance || 36
           34

7 — 16 — 9 — 211 — 4 ———— 16 —— 28 —— 64 —— 22 —— 80 —— 44 ——— 30.5.— Justice || 22 = 4.

⊙ × 7 = 16 soit 8 :: 8
                    2

$$8 \times 8 \atop 79$$

$8 - 8 \quad 8 = 4 \times$
$16. \ 16 \ldots . . \ 32 \odot$

	A.					B.					C.					D.				
0.	1.	2.	3.	4.	5.	— 6.	7.	8.	9.	10.	— 11.	12.	12.	11. —	10.	9.	8.	7.	6.	— 5.	4.	3.	2.	1.	0.
1.	12.	34.	82.	32.	84.	— 16.	42.	110.	38.	146.	— 16.	28.	64.	22.	80.	— 40.	46.	130.	40.	156.	— 24.	42.	90.	36.	106.	1.
2.	46.	116.	114.	116.		58.	153.	149.	184.		44.	92.	86.	103.		87.	177.	172.	197.		66.	133.	127.	152.		2.
3.	162.	230.	230.			211.	302.	333.			136.	178.	199.			264.	349.	369.			199.	260.	279.			3.
4.	393.	462.				523.	645.				314.	377.				613.	718.				460.	540.				4.
5.	855.					1168.					691.					1331.					1002.					5.
16.	18.					16.					16.					8.					7.					16.
7.	9.					7.					7.					8.					7.					7.

M. All the numbers involved in the creation of the proportions contribute to the creation of the evidence. For this brings them back to the first numbers: 1, 2, 3, 4, 5, 6, 7, 8, 9, in order to summarize them in a single figure. This figure must be the expression of a number with which we can return to the root of the square of 144. The value of the product is 32, from which, with the zero having a value of 2, we obtain 34 x 3 = 102, from which 102 and 2 of zero = 104. 7 = 34, as 104 = 7.

Thus, following this explanation:

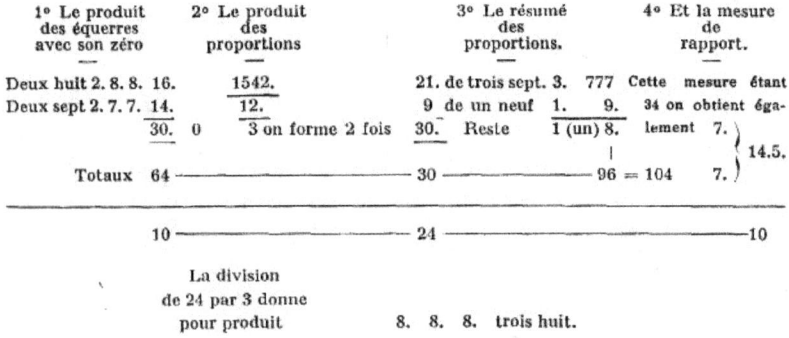

III – SAMPLE PROSPECTUS

N. Number 104 is the product of 13 x 8, but 13 x 2 produces 26, and with number 26 we obtain the number 8. The circle goes up to 26, instead of 24, because the value assigned to the zero remains, which forms 26 with the number 24. This is how we work in the square of 13 x 13 = 169, a number which is reduced to 16 and 7. It follows that the square of 169 is a sort of envelope of the square of 144. The latter is summarized by 9[208], in such a way that, by addition we form 16 once again, in the same way that 13, summarized to 4 forms 13 again; where 16 and 13 = 29 = 11 = 2.

---

[208] Note that many of the calculations use theosophical addition. For example, "13 x 13 =169, a number which is reduced to 16 and 7" means: 1 + 6 + 9 = 16, 1 + 6 = 7. – PV

That is to say $\frac{2}{0}$ and 9 = 11, which brings us back to the geometric progression 22, 44, 89 and 171, with a difference of 82. This final number is the distance of the geometric proportion, as 13 is the arithmetical proportion. These two distances joined together form the number 95 = 14 = 5. The number 95 is barely superior by 1 to the number 94, or 49 in reverse, with which we form 13 x 2 and consequently 26, whose summary is 8 and 1 = 9^{209}. The placing of these two figures 8 and 9 serves as evidence, because we form $\frac{17}{8}$ by addition and 17 x 2 = 34 = 7. 7 + 9 = 16 = 7. It goes without saying that number 94 is obtained by the addition of the numbers of $\frac{1}{0}$ 1 to 13 by giving a value of two to the zero of 10, being $\frac{1}{0}$ 1, 2, 3, 4, 5, 6, 7, 8, 9, $\frac{2}{10}$, 11, 12, 13 = 94 = 13 = 4 and 7 = 11 = 2 x 16 and 0 = 34.

O. The reason for the value assigned to the zero is peremptory. All proportions that exist in Nature are based on numbers concerned with the course of the sun and the operation of the calorific value of light; and therefore, to the measurement of time. Now, time is divided into hours, minutes and seconds. 1 hour is composed of 60 minutes = 61, as 1 minute consists of 60 seconds = 61. So, we have 2|61 which sum to 7 and 7. It follows that 2, the number of 7s there are, must be divided for any calculation. Then we have 1 and 1. It is the manner in which, by omitting nothing, we come to get 2|8..., or 8 and 8. These 2|8s summarize the count of 1 day, 1 night, 1 hour, 60 minutes, 1 minute and 60 seconds, which equals 124 = 7.

P. But to bring these details together in a single rule, it is much simpler form a scale of 1 to 60 as follows; it follows that there will be a double control that will be reciprocally exercised by each of the lines over the other. There will be a delay of 4 between 15 and 19, which means that at 60 we will find the number 64 and at 120

---

[209] Here is another example of theosophical manipulation. The author takes 94, reverses it to 49, noting that 4 + 9 or 9 + 4 both = 13. Therefore, there are 2 x 13 = 26. 2 + 6 = 8 and adding the 1 gives 9 – PV.

the number 124. But also, 60 and 60 equals 124 by giving zero the value of 2. There is no more possibility of error with these precautions. The numbers are taken inversely for the proof.

0.	1. 2. 3. 4. 5. 6. 7. 8. 9. 10. 11. 12. 13. 14. 15.	159 = 15 = 6
1.	1. 3. 5. 7. 9. 12. 13. 14. 15. 16. 17. 18. 19.	6
	10. 11.	
2.	0. 2. 4. 6. 8. 21. 31. 41. 51. 61. 71. 81. 91.	
3.	3. 5. 9. 13. 17. 3. 2. 33. 44. 55. 66. 77. 88. 99. 110.	En
4.	3. 5. 9. 4. 8. 3. 2. 6. 8. 10. 12. 14. 16. 18. 4.	résumé
5.	3. 5. 9. 4. 8. 3. 2. 6. 8. 3. 3. 5. 7. 9. 4.	79
16	————————————————————————————	16 = 7 et 7
		13, 13
		26

We demonstrate by the 2|61. 61, against which we oppose 2|16, 16; and therefore 4|7, 7, 7, 7. Thus, the square of 13 x 13 = 169 serves to check the calculations; because 169 = 16 and 16 = 7 where 7 x 5 = 35 = 8 and 8 = 16 = 7.

Q. If we are challenged that there was a 1/6 doubled, under 15 of 159, we would prove that in not doing so, we would have had 7 + 7 + 6 = 20 = 4 with which we can make $\frac{4}{20}$ 26 = 8, just as 16 is produced by 4 x 4. When we multiply 169 by 4, we get:

$$\left. \begin{array}{l} 676 = 19 = 10 = 3 \\ \underline{576} = 18 = 9 = 9 \\ (1251) \end{array} \right\} 12 = 3$$

and when we multiply the square of 144, the product of 12 x 12 by the number 4, we can only check the duodecimal calculation by a measure of relationship, without which there would be to errors, because the accuracy of the checks results from a outdistanced comparison works using the number of zeros from $\frac{1}{0}$ to 1252.

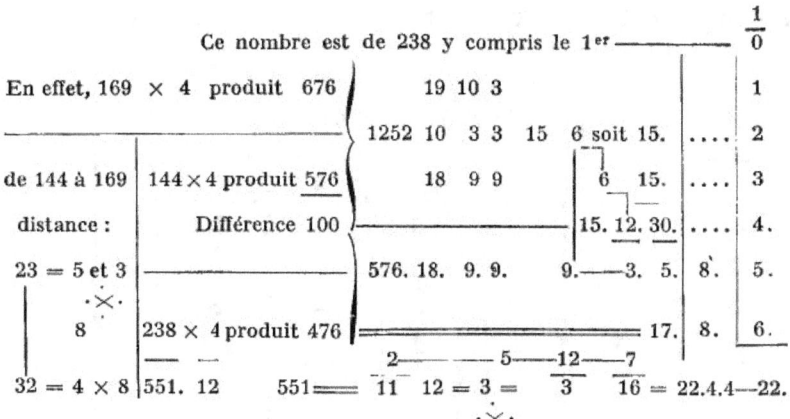

R. It is therefore important to take the zero as 2 in calculations of rigorous precision. There is also a need to make the proportions dual with 3 terms and 2 products, being 10 for 2 proportions. The first term must be lower than the second, the third higher than the second; the first product should be less than the second term. With regard to the second product, its value is unimportant.

IV. – THE REASON FOR EVERYTHING BY MEANS OF SQUARES

S. We conclude this drawing board with two tables. The first concerns the reason for numbers combined with the law of the square the numerical distances. The second is the reason for the alphabet.

U. Explanations.

We give the name of the law for the creation of the two tables presented below.

There is indeed a law, from which we find in the nature of things concerning the coherent cause of effects and consequences, whose dual relationship gives the reason for the problem in an invariable manner, being as follows: 08 numeric signs are placed in the middle of 16 squares formed from 2 x 5 lines, which gives 5 x 5 = 25.

LAW OF THE FORMATION OF SQUARES FROM NUMERICAL DISTANCES

					8								
0	1	2	3	4	5 6 4 4 6 5	4	3	2	1	0
1	8			0 1 2 8 2 1 0			8	1
2	4			1		1		4	2
3	9			2	0 2 3	2		8	3
4	18			8	4 5 6	8		19	4
5	17			2	7 8 9	2		17	5
6	4			1		1		4	6
7	8			0 1 2 8 2 1 0			8	7
8	68			136			68	8
37	14		5	101	5		14	73
10.1			3	3	3			1.01
11			2 6	1	6 2			11
12			3	2	3			
13			4 9		9 4			
14			5	2	5			
15			6	6	6			
67	13		4 8		8 4		31	76

25 sums to 7 and 16, and also summed by 7.

2 3, 4, 5, 6, 7, 8, 9 sums to   44

Zero has a value of   x 2
The product is equal to   88

The zero forms the signs 1 and 1, which with 1, unity, gives 3.

REASON FOR THE ALPHABET

par 222 = 6 du nombre   596.695 = 40 = 6

```
                            4
  0  |  1   2   3   4   22  |  4   3   2   1  |  0
                           ———
  1  |         5   9   6  |  3  |  6   9   5     |  1
  2  |            14  15     12     15  14        |  2
  3  |                29  27     27  29           |  3
  4  |                    56  54  56              |  4
  5  |                       110 110              |  5
  6  |                            2               |  6
  7  |                         2  2  2            |  7
  8  |                            8               |  8
  
  37 |  10.1 ————————— 3     3 ————————— 10.1  |  37
                            6
         596 ═══════════ 20  44  20 ═══════════ 695
                            8
```

The 3 unities give us, with 44 and 44 = 88. 88 and 1 = 89, finally 89 and 2 = 91. The number 91 is worth 10 = 3; let us return now to the geometric progression. 1, 11, 22, 44, 89, 171 from the Table on page 216.

88, 89 and 91 form three numbers with which, by adding them, we obtain by adding 268.

By addition	<u>268</u>
Either	<u>88</u>
Or	<u>16</u>
Summarized by:	7

Now, the number 268 = 16 = 7 is at a distance,
from 169 expressed by 99
and from <u>171</u> expressed by <u>97</u> | |
       340   196   16 = 7

----------------538 = 16 = 7 ------------- 32 14
Making: 7, 5, 5 = 17, 8, 8   5   5

Besides, 169 and the 2 of zero correctly give us the 171 of the geometric progression from 89. Finally, 268 divided by 4 gives us 4|67. 13 x 4 = 52 = 7, which gives us:
25 = 7 in the reverse direction.

Thus 169, square of 13 x 13 and the 2 of the zero 171, are to the integral calculation of the proportions of the nature, what the dimensions that the smelter gives to his molds to compensate for shrinkage in the material.

The two sixty-eight (2|68) which form the numbers shared, to the right and to the left of the square of 25, on which the zero and 8 signs are placed, were obtained by counting the lines of this square one by one, to the extent that the figures were counted to go from one end to the other.

N. B. Those who wish to take our 5 proportions A B C D E as a topic for study will notice that we have not always taken the zero as 2.

Here is what they will find:

A. In summary 856 = 19 = 10 = 3. E. 736 <u>A</u>, <u>B</u>, <u>E</u>, <u>C</u>, <u>D</u>.
= 16 = 7. D. 1004 = 9 from which – 3., 7, 7, 8, 9 = 34 = 7.
Now, with 3|8 = 24 of the proof,
We have 1st 34 and 24 = 58 = 13 = 4.   15 = 6.

2nd 24 and 7 of 34 =   31 = 4.13 and 31 44 = 8.

Chapter 15
The Secret Section on the Study of Numbers

We hope we have done justice to our intention to make every effort to be as clear as we are allowed in this study of Numbers.

It is obvious, however that documents distributed in public cannot provide information which might lead to practical results, personal action on the Invisible Plane and on the secret forces of Nature without being veiled

In Kabbalah, this section is called the Shemhamphorash and it is almost exclusively composed of manuscripts.

In practical Arithmology, it is the key to powers over the forces of the Astral Plane. However, these powers are only given to those who understand them sufficiently in their essence to know almost never to use them. It is the same with regard to certain parts of the Divinatory Sciences.

Nevertheless, on this subject we are authorized to give – but *without any explanatory commentary* – a document which is given to the public for the first time, and which comes from the archives of an association of Hermetists to which J. J. Bourcart (Jacob), the author of *l'Esquissee du tout Universel*, belonged.[210] Let's not say that this group was a part of the Rosicrucians, since this title has been monopolized in such a way that true Rosicrucians don't call themselves by that title, which was in any case only an exoteric name for them.

Those who are assisted by a guide on the other plane will be able to make use of this document, and it is for them alone that we are publishing it.[211]

---

[210] Jacob, *Esquisse Hermétique du Tout Universel* [*Hermetic Outline of the Universal All*], with a Preface by Dr. Papus. Paris, Chacornac, 1902. [It is curious that Papus claims this is being given to the public for the first time, since it had already been published by the publisher of the current book – PV].

[211] We don't believe we are contravening the discretion that Papus believed he had to impose upon himself by giving a few pointers here, without which the published document runs a strong risk of remaining incomprehensible even to students who are qualified but whose studies have never extended to the subject of Geomancy. In fact, the

TABLE OF KNOWLEDGE OF SYMBOLIC NUMBERS OR ASTRAL TEMPERATURES

Planets

♄	Direct	12. Sadness	21. Fecundity	34. Poverty	43. Danger of death.	67. Prison, prevention.
	Retrograde	29. Hate	92. Jealousy	39. Sickness	95. Persecution	76. Death
♃	D	13. Gaiety	31. Acquisition	35. Favor	53. Honor	68. Victory
	R	28. Enjoyment	82. Custom	58. Flourishing	85. Amiable, brilliant	86. Strength
♂	D	14. Anger	41. Fire	36. Injury	63. Poison	69. Sword
	R	27. Quarrel	72. Dispute	57. Decomposition	75. Fermentation	96. Destruction
☉	D	15. Major fortune	51. Success	37. Gain	73. Usefulness	78. Perfection
	R	26. Minor fortune	62. Pleasure	56. Growth	65. Success	87. Certainty
♀	D	16. Beauty	61. Approbation	38. Reconciliation	83. Mixture	79. Divorce
	R	25. Mind	52. Marvel	49. Grudge	94. Weakened	97. Degenerated
☿	D	17. Inconstancy	71. Reunion	39. Mean equation	93. Resemblance	89. Union
	R	24. Lightness	42. Indifference	48. Equilibrium	84. Inertia	98. Diversity
☽	D	18. Speed	81. Growth	45. Prevention	54. Noise	– Destruction
	R	23. Obsolescence	22. Early corruption	47. Corruption	74. High degree of corruption	– End of a Being
☊	D	19. Superfluous	91. Enlargement	46. Hardening	64. Revision	– Obstinacy
	R	44. Sobriety	11. Uniformity	33. Instinct	88. Management	– Consistency
☋	D	55. Poverty	66. Worn out	99. Weak sound	– Usury	– Wear and tear
	R	22. Weakness	77. Loss of senses	– Suffering	– Disappear	– Degradation

In all 81 symbols

11
☿ ♎
Conjunctio
☋

1 Sober life; 2 Win at games; 3. Aid of parents; 4 Gaining ground; 5 Bad news; 6 Dangerous sickness; 7

---

names found in the margin of each number (page 232 onwards), show that it is about the figures used in Geomancy.

*

Each number is given the symbol of a figure when it is placed in each of the 12 Houses used in Geomancy.

*

We would also make the following comments:
1. There are only 16 Geomantic figures (and there can be only 16). The Table on this page gives 18.
2. In Geomancy a "direct" or 'retrograde' planet (even the Sun and Moon) is affected where each figure which, along with ☊ and ☋ (head and tail of the Dragon, ascending and descending nodes of the Moon) makes 2 x 7 + 2 = 16.
In the above Table, the two supplementary figures comes from the fact that ☊ and ☋ are each considered as direct and retrograde, which makes 2 meanings extra (in relation to traditional Geomancy).
Moreover, Geomantic figures are considered from 5 different aspects, which means that each figure is repeated 5 times in the list. We should note that for each of these 5 groups the general meanings have points of similarity (*Editor's Note*).

12 ♄ ♐ *Tristitia* *Senectus* *tarditas*	False friends; 8 Death; 9 Economic science; 10 Embassy; 11 Letters from protectors; 12 Lawsuit.[212] 1 Composure; 2 Poverty; 3 Quarrel with brothers; 4 Disagreements with parents[213]; 5 Annoyance with children; 6 Rheumatism; 7 Quarrels in household or with enemies; 8 Longevity; 9 Theological or theosophical knowledge; 10 Goodwill from prelates or judges; 11 Goodwill from elderly relatives; 12 Despair.
13 ♃ ♉ *Lætitia* *Victor* *in amore* *Gaudium*	1 Gentle and gay character; 2 Gain in livestock; 3 Affection among brothers; 4 Legacy from parents; 5 Many strong children, reciprocated love; 6 Health or convalescence; 7 Fidelity in marriage or triumph over one's enemies; 8 age of eighty years; 9 Jurisdiction; 10 Favor with sovereigns and superiors; 11 Gifts from wealthy people; 12 Dangers overcome.
14 ♂ ♊ *Puer* *Fortitudo* *B Colum* *T Salum*	1 Anger, Cholera, impetuosity; 2 Brigandage and losses; 3 Hatred of brothers or sisters; 4 Hatred of parents; 5 Fertilization, bad children, bad servants; 6 Venereal sores or wounds from fire; 7 Dispute in marriage and course of action, injuries from battles with enemies; 8 Death from injury; 9 Surgery, anatomy, help while bedridden; 10 Disgrace in the service of sovereigns, disgrace among judges or tribunals; 11 Cooling of benefactors; 12 Assassination, violent death.

---

[212] It was mentioned that, along with regular Astrology, Geomancy when applied to the 12 Houses is another way of attributing fortune and prediction to the Houses. The Reader should note, for example, that the 6th House refers to health, while the 9th generally refers to career, for example. For a more comprehensive introduction to Geomancy, the books of John Michael Greer and Stephen Skinner are recommended. This will also provide a more up-to-date and relevant interpretation of the Houses. While it may seem that the prognostications listed for each combination are quite bizarre and old-fashioned, one should remember that at the time of Papus, some 90% of France was agricultural, and one will always find extensive sections on folk magic and farm-oriented material in his books: he wrote for the intelligentsia, but also made sure he aimed his books at the more general readership, too. It is worth looking at a few categories to see the very day-to-day obsessions of people of the times, such as loss of livestock, illnesses, family discord, faithfulness of spouse, honesty of servants, activity of enemies, etc. – PV.

[213] The word for parent can mean 'parent' or relative'; the two terms have been used where they seemed to best fit – PV.

15 ☉ *Fortuna Major Aurum Testum T Salum*	1 Gay temperament; 2 large profit in gold; 3 Respect from relatives on father's side; 4 Underground treasure in gold; 5 Triumph in love, beautiful and healthy children, fertility; 6 Fortunate healing of the sick, women in labor; 7 Peaceful marriage, rest from enemies; 8 Deliverance from dangers of death; 9 Fortune in (al)chemy; 10 Goodwill of the sovereign and tribunals; 11 Support of friends; 12 Deliverance from worries.
16 ♀ ♊ *Puella Pulchritudo I Colum T Salum*	1 Susceptible, excitable, inclined to love; 2 Neither gain nor loss; 3 Love of sisters or female relatives; 4 Love of mother; 5 Benevolence of lover, conception; 6 Venereal disease, leprosy; 7 Infidelity in marriage; 8 Life saved; 9 Eloquent style, charm; 10 Good luck through intervention of women; 11 Benevolence among elderly women; 12 Chagrin.
17 ☿ ♎ *Conjunctio*	1 Lightweight, indecisive, hesitant; 2 Loss through trade; 3 Slander among relatives; 4 Slander by scandalmongering women; 5 Inconstancy in love, disobedience of children; 6 Phlegmatic sicknesses; 7 Tittle-tattle by women, victory by enemies; 8 Death by water; 9 Navigation; 10 Disgrace to the court; 11 Persecution by women; 12 Death.
18 ☽ ☊ *Fortuna Oriens Via*	1 Dry temperament; 2 Beginning of gain; 3 Good counsel from family; 4 Hope of inheritance; 5 Certain conception; 6 Happy cure or happy marriage-bed; 7 Reconciliation with enemies, peaceful marriage; 8 Healing of a sickness; 9 Astronomy; 10 Coming into favor with great people; 11 Beneficence; 12 Deliverance from dangers.
19 ☿ ☋ *Fortuna Occidens*	1 Cold, humid temperament; 2 Inevitable painful loss; 3 Disputes with relatives; 4 Loss of an inheritance trial; 5 Cold love, sterility; 6 Danger of death from illness if alkaline remedies don't work; 7 Disputes in household and with enemies; 8 Short life; 9 Agriculture; 10 Jealousy of the court; 11 Negative response from protectors; 12 Loss by theft.

20		1 Melancholy, sad tone; 2 Loss through infidelity of domestics or usurers; 3 Vicious slander among relatives; 4 Large legacy from former thrifty people; 5 Pregnancy of lover, moral and respectful children; 6 illness of the feet; 7 Infidelities of husband or wife; 8 Age of sixty years; 9 Arithmetic; 10 Success of lawsuit; 11 Favor among former ministers and counsellors; 12 Loss of the senses.
21		
♄ ♐		
Tristitia		
Senectus		
Tarditas		
22		1 Lively temperament; 2 Gain of trade; 3 Prosperity of parents; 4 Prosperity through ancient documents; 5 Pleasant letters; 6 Mercurial healings; 7 Correspondence with enemies; 8 Deliverance (from²¹⁴) danger of death; 9 Uranology; 10 Letters from kings; 11 Letters from protectors; 12 Loss of important documents.
♋ ☿		
♌		
Epistola		
Albus		
23		1 Indifferent, cold; 2 Loss of trade; 3 Injury by female relatives; 4 Injury by domestics; 5 Abortion, disputes in love, fickleness of children; 6 Crisis in a disease; 7 Infidelity in marriage; 8 Long illness, short life; 9 Meteorology; 10 Benevolence of the court; 11 Favor among young women; 12 Deceit.
☽ ♉		
Via		
24		1 Sluggishness, insensitive nerves; 2 Short journey; 3 Wicked jealousy; 4 Slander among parents or superiors; 5 Tricks in love, deception of servants; 6 Ailing health; 7 Thoughts of divorce, fear of one's enemies; 8 Prolongation of life by 7 years; 9 Physiology; 10 Prosecution by superiors; 11 Disaffection; 12 Danger from water.
☿ ♋		
Alatus		
25		1 Airiness, carefree; 2 Loss of money; 3 Hatred of a young woman; 4 Hatred of an old woman; 5 Cooling of love; 6 Poor sleep; 7 Jealousy in marriage, victory of enemies; 8 Short life; 9 Painting; 10 Favor of sovereigns; 11 Gifts from ladies; 12 decreasing good fortune.
♀ ♐		
Amissio		
26		1 Good and happy in business; 2 Gains in silver commerce; 3 Relief of kinship; 4 Legacy in capital; 5
☉ ♋		

---

²¹⁴ Word missing in original text – PV.

Fortuna *Minor* *Argentum*	Lukewarm love; 6 Weakness of the sick; 7 Victory over enemies, peaceful marriage; 8 Long life; 9 Financial studies; 10 Honors; 11 Gift of favors; 12 Deliverance from persecutors.
27 ♂ ♏ *Ruber* *Nocens* *Lædere*	1 Pride, wickedness, hypocrites, false friends; 2 Loss in business; 3 Disaffection of parents; 4 Disobedience with respect to one's superiors; 5 Fickleness in love, conception; 6 Dangerous fevers; 7 Militant marriage, victory of enemies; 8 Wishing for death, life which doesn't last longer than 10 years; 9 Chemistry (Alchemy); 10 Failure in court, loss of a lawsuit,; 11 Reproaches of protectors; 12 Shame.
28 ♃ ♈ *Acquisitio*	1 Debonair, sensitive, beneficent; 2 Profits from real estate; 3 General esteem; 4 Increase in fortune; 5 Fertility in marriage, victory in love, faithful servants; 6 Pustules, rashes, cure by purgatives; 7 Peaceful marriage, victory over enemies; 8 Longevity; 9 Historian, discovery of secrets; 10 Win a lawsuit, succeed in a petition; 11 Support of friends; 12 Good conscience.
29 ♄ ♓ *Carcer* *Impedi-* *mentum*	1 Jealous, sulky, coarse nerves; 2 Gains by lawsuit; 3 Lawsuit against relative; 4 Lawsuit for inheritance; 5 Preference for rival in love, dispute with lover; 6 Cold and long fevers; 7 Dispute in household, enmity of a minister; 8 Age over 60 years; 9 Legislator; 10 Slander in court; 11 Favor of clergy; 12 Prison or broken leg.
30 31 ♃ ♉ *Lætitia* *Victor* *in amore* *Gaudium*	1 Fine nerves, strong tension, agreeable, moral; 2 Gain in livestock; 3 Appreciated by relatives; 4 Appreciated by superiors; 5 Victory in love, faithful friends, strong children, especially the son; 6 Loss of blood, astringent remedies; 7 Reconciliation with enemies, faithful spouse; 8 Life over 70 years; 9 Statesman; 10 Employment and favor at court; 11 Favor with ministers; 12 Deliverance from danger.
32 ☽ ♌ *Via*	1 Weak complexion, inconstant, often changeable; 2 Profit in travel; 3 Deceit of female relatives; 4 Many losses in the house, water damage; 5 Slander concerning one's lover; 6 Swollen feet, dropsy; 7

Reconciliation talks; 8 Dangers of death; 9 Commerce in leather; 10 Administrative travel; 11 Bad slander; 12 Losses by theft.

33 ♀ ♌ *Alatus volatilis*	1 Fickleness, forgetfulness, ingratitude; 2 Deception in commerce; 3 Ambushes by relatives; 4 Denunciation; 5 Theft by domestics, infidelity of lover; 6 Breakouts on the face, refreshing remedies; 7 Snares of the enemies, household restless; 8 20 more years of life; 9 Architecture; 10 Empty promise, hope without foundation; 11 Aid of wise men; 12 Losses.
34 ♄ ♐ *Tristitia*	1 Fearful, sad; 2 Losses in livestock; 3 Debts accumulated; 4 Purchase of houses; 5 Aversion of lover, uncertain domestics; 6 Problems with lungs; 7 Discontent in marriage; 8 Age of more than 50; 9 a retired life, theological studies; 10 Loss in a lawsuit; 11 Help from an old man; 12 Wounds.
35 ♃ ♉ *Lætitia Victor Gaudium*	1 Sanguine temperament, gracious, truthful; 2 Gain by sheep (*sic!* – PV); 3 Gifts from parents; 4 Legacy; 5 Good news in love, joys; 6 Diseased liver; 7 Happiness in marriage, enterprises without obstacles; 8 Age greater than 60 years; 9 Man of State; 10 Hope crowned; 11 Reputation; 12 Happiness.
36 ♂ ♎ *Puer Fortitudo B. Col.*	1 Coarse, nervous, daring, combative; 2 Loss in game; 3 Deception of relatives; 4 Disputes of inheritance; 5 Hurt in love or by domestics; 6 Tumors, wounds; 7 Discontent in marriage, disputes with enemies; 8 Dangers of death; 9 Mathematics and Pyrotechnics; 10 Wrath of kings; 11 Prosecutions; 12 Loss of blood.
37 ☉ *Fortuna major aurum*	1 High courage, cheerful soul, visionary; 2 Profit in and outside the country; 3 Aid of parents; 4 Acquisition of large properties; 5 Pleasure with children, success in love; 6 Asphyxiation, fainting; 7 Happiness from wife, success against enemies; 8 Long and peaceful life; 9 Military science; 10 Luck at the court; 11 Favors; 12 Peaceful death.
38 ♀ ♊	1 Tender, good education, cheerful, lover of good living; 2 Profit through the other sex; 3 Profit through

Pulchritudo *I. Col.*	sisters; 4 Profit through old women; 5 (Profit?) through concubinage; 6 Profit through prostitution; 7 Favor of unforgettable women; 8 Weaknesses by turns up to an advanced age; 9 For women: protection at court, for girls: dressing; 10 Aid through women; 11 Praise of women; 12 Sudden death.
39 ♀ ♎ *Conjunctio*	1 Bad humor, unsettled temperament; 2 Wrongs by merchants; 3 Wrongs by a single relation; 4 Loss or inheritance; 5 Egotistic love, quarrelsome domestics; 6 Pregnancy; 7 Desire for reconciliation with enemies; 8 Healing of serious disease of the chest; 9 Extended travels, geographical knowledge, means of transport; 10 Slander by the jealous among superiors; 11 Loss of honor; 12 Persecution.
40 41 ♀ ♊ *Puer* *Fortitudo* *B.*	1 Choleric temperament with strained nerves, conciliatory to relaxed nerves, angry madman; 2 Loss in agriculture; 3 Backbiters; 4 Losses in housing; 5 Impurity and fickleness in children; 6 Ailments of the bladder, kidneys, hemorrhoids, constipation; 7 Bad news of enemies, antipathy of spouse; 8 Apoplexy; 9 Military; 10 Favor from marshals; 11 Insults from protectors; 12 Poor consciences.
42 ♀ ♎ + ♋ *Conjunctio*	1 Spiteful humor, talkative, changeable, indecisive; 2 loss of economies and by a former servant; 3 Loss by a young relative; 4 Blame and revenge by an old woman; 5 Jealousy in love, mistrust of servant; 6 Sluggishness and colic: 7 Balance between enemies; 8 Bad cure from which one returns; 9 Merchant; 10 Medium favors in court; 11 Great progress among protectors; 12 All kinds of obstacles.
43 ♄ ♐ *Tristitia* *Tarditas* *Senectus*	1 Discreet, thinking a lot, good temperament, spiteful; 2 Loss of reputation; 3 Bad reputation and hate among relatives; 4 Sale of fields; 5 Trouble in love and with domestics; 6 Diseases of the neck and mouth; 7 Deception of women outside the household; 8 More than 50 years; 9 Mechanic; 10 Hatred of a wealthy person; 11 Gifts from bishops; 12 Persecutions by old women.

44	1 Well-proportioned body, good temperament, tolerant; 2 Profit from industry and know how; 3 Friendship among relatives; 4 Legacy from influential people; 5 Bleeding from the head, tepid in love; 6 Healing of hemorrhages; 7 Ruses of enemies or spouse; 8 7 years of life after a great illness; 9 Architecture; 10 Advancement; 11 Reputation and honorific gifts; 12 Sweet death.
☿ ♌ *Alatus volatilis*	
45 ☽ ♒ *Populus garrulitas*	1 Gentle yet active character, quiet; 2 Profit at games and gambling; 3 Small and dangerous gifts from friends (et timeo Danaos dona ferentes[215]); 4 Legacy of old women; 5 Good pregnancy, good compliance of lover; 6 Jaundice, deteriorated tone; 7 Propositions of enemies; 8 Danger of death; 9 Agriculture; 10 Fortune at court; 11 Aid of protectors; 12 Fretful death.
46 ☿ ♌ *Alatus volatilis*	1. Quiet blood, pure soul; 2 Profit in betting; 3 Vexation with brothers; 4 Disputes over legacies; 5 Conception or fertilization, constant and faithful love; 6 Cure of diseases; 7 Quarrel in household; 8 Immediate death; 9 Mineralogy and Alchemy; 10 Slanders by the jealous in court; 11 Slander among protectors; 12 Injuries.
47 ☽ ♉ *Via*	1 Changeable, capricious, talkative, quarrelsome; 2 Gain in money; 3 Friendship among relatives; 4 Discovery of a secret; 5 Good news, cheerful love, favor of lovers; 6 Cure of fantasies when a good planet is in opposition; 7 Proposals of settlement by a woman; 8 Few years of life; 9 Manufacturer; 10 Consideration at court; 11 Great favor, great reputation; 12 Accidental misfortune.
48 ☿ ♋ *Albus Epistola*	1 False, unfaithful, inconstant; 2 Losses in household; 3 Arguments with wife and parents; 4 Arguments with old women; 5 Disputes in love, unpleasant letters; 6 Hypochondria, healing if Jupiter is in opposition; 7 Arguments in marriage; 8 Certain death; 9 Beaux Arts; 10 Harassment by superiors; 11 Regrets of protectors; 12 Great misfortune.

---

[215] From Virgil: 'Beware Greeks bearing gifts' – PV.

49 ♀ ♐ *Amissio*	1 Voluptuous, not knowing how to abstain; 2 Losses in business and the household; 3 Damage by relatives; 4 Disgraces among superiors; 5 Fertility, lechery, thoughtless children; 6 Constipation; 7 Jealousy, reproaches in marriage, contempt; 8 Deliverance form dangers of death; 9 Music and poetry; 10 Reputation at court; 11 Favor among old women; 12 many sorrows, secret sorrows.
50 51 ☉ ♉ *Fortuna major aurum*	1 Noble thoughts, gentle, amiable, discreet; 2 Profit in multiplication of gold; 3 Aid of parents; 4 Great inheritance, gifts from priests; 5 Good luck in love, pleasant letters with money; 6 Healing of weakness and dizziness; 7 Unmistakable victory over enemies, unity in household; 8 Age of 90 years; 9 Knowledge of men; 10 Favor among princes and ministers; 11 Support in enterprises; 12 Deliverance from fears.
52 ♀ ♐ *Amissio*	1 Courteous, pleasant, delightful; 2 Poverty and misery; 3 Criticisms of female relatives; 4 Unpleasant news from superiors; 5 Problems with lovers, anger towards domestics and children; 6 Kidney disease; 7 Disputes in marriage, harm by enemies; 8 Short life; 9 Painter; 10 Prosecutions by the highly placed; 11 Disfavor of friends; 12 Injuries.
53 ♃ ♉ *Lætitia Victor Gaudium*	1 Beautiful and slender, light approach, clear blood; 2 Gain in business; 3 Reputation among relatives; 4 Pleasant letters from noteworthy people; 5 Birth of a son, or rendezvous with lover; 6 Persistent fevers and healing if ☉ is in opposition; 7 Favor of women or finding stolen objects; 8 Age above 50 years; 9 Police; 10 Success of a petition at court or in tribunal; 11 General reputation; 12 Injury by livestock.
54 ☽ ♒ *Populus*	1 Health in youth, capricious, talkative; 2 Profit beginning; 3 Fraternal compassion of sisters; 4 Favor of great people; 5 Dance, music, fun-loving; 6 Rheumatism; 7 Tranquil marriage and reason; 8 Stroke; 9 Industrial arts; 10 Disfavor at court; 11 Great benevolence by protectors; 12 Great misfortune.

55 ☿ ♉ *Alatus*	1 Intelligent, modest, prudent, faithful friend; 2 Success in business; 3 Proofs of friendship; 4 Gain in the household; 5 Deception in love, employees thieves; 6 Wounds to feet and arms; 7 Thoughts of divorce, discontent of spouses; 8 Another 20 years of life; 9 Hydraulic motors; 10 Loss of court case; 11 Disagreeable reproaches of protectors and friends; 12 Fear, terror, menace, danger.
56 ☉ ♋ *Fortuna minor*	1 Cheerful, generous, good, affectionate; 2 Gain through currency; 3 Gift of silverware from parents; 4 Legacy in capital; 5 Love without disturbance, enjoyment, letters, well-raised children; 6 Languor, dryness, healing when ♈ in ♃ is in opposition; 7 Friendship, victory against enmity; 8 30 more years of life; 9 Agriculture; 10 Advancement by favor of a minister; 11 Aid of protectors; 12 Deliverance form mortal danger.
57 ♂ ♏ *Ruber Nocens Venator*	1 Anger, rancorous, slanderer; 2 Great damage in economy; 3 Trials with relatives; 4 Trials concerning land; 5 Falsehood in love, bad children, bad servants; 6 Podagra, gout; 7 Many enemies, upset household; 8 Short life; 9 Old history of wars; 10 Advancement by hero; 11 Many warlike friends; 12 Prosecution by enemies, theft.
58 ♃ ♈ *Acquisitio*	1 Good bearing, strong, active, inoffensive; 2 Gains assured in all enterprises; 3 Reputation among relatives and acquaintances; 4 Order in the household; 5 Happy in love, recovery of stolen items, new hope; 6 smallpox and other diseases of the skin; 7 Reconciliation; 8 40 more years of life; 9 Mythology; 10 Obtaining employment; 11 Gifts from friends; 12 Saved from danger.
59 ♄ ♓ *Carcer*	1 Inflexible character, deep, irreconcilable; 2 Shrinking fortune; 3 Mischief from an aged relative; 4 Losses in household; 5 Danger of losing one's lover; 6 Bad pimples; 7 Enemies putting up obstacles through abuse of power; 8 Stroke in old age; 9 Negotiation; 10 Failure of petition; 11 False friends; 12 Terrors.

60 61 ♀ ♊ *Pulchritudo* *I*	1 Fine nerves, relaxed, carefree, ungrateful; 2 Losses at gaming and betting; 3 Hate and vengeance of an old woman; 4 Affair succeeding by help of an old woman; 5 Favor and submission of lovers; 6 Diarrhea, loss of strength, decomposition; 7 Love of spouses; 8 Long and painful sickness; 9 Midwife doctor of childbirth; 10 Calumnies towards persons; 11 Princely donations; 12 Evil informant.
62 ☉ ♋ *Fortuna minor*	1 Courageous, fearless, happy in action; 2 Enrichment; 3 Aid of a relative who is an functionary; 4 Legacy of paternal uncles: 5 Enjoyment or love, good news; 6 Loss of strength, fatigue; 7 Hope of conciliation; 8 Triumph of a doctor; 9 Politics; 10 Appreciated in high places; 11 Gifts coming from afar; 12 Misfortune during travel.
63 ♂ ♊ *Puer Fortitudo* *B*	1 Choleric temperament, violent, rowdy; 2 Losses on horses and livestock; 3 Losses by brothers; 4 Disfavor of superiors, loss in household; 5 Falsehood or distancing of lovers, treachery of domestics; 6 Chapping and bad rashes; 7 Evil from enemies or spouse; 8 Death from a fall; 9 Forester; Aborted petition; 11 Embezzlement by friends; 12 Harm by fire.
64 ☿ ♌ *Alatus volatilis*	1 Thoughts revealed, honest, satisfied; 2 Loss in clothing; 3 Obstruction by relatives; 4 Losses on fields and meadows; 5 Hindrances in love, treachery of domestics; 6 Line (sic – PV) and abscess in the neck; 7 Impediments stirred up by enemies in marriage; 8 Danger of death; 9 Mechanics; 10 Loss of employment; 11 Loss of a protector; 12 Anxieties.
65 ☉ ♋ *Fortuna minor*	1 Skillful, cheerful temperament, good counsel; 2 Certain gain; 3 Respect among relatives; 4 Inheritance in money; 5 Fidelity of lovers; 6 Nervous cramps; 7 Peaceful marriage and contentment; 8 Victory of doctor, long life; 9 Metallurgy; 10 Advancement in honorific positions; 11 Gifts of jewelry; 12 Victory over enemies.

66 ☿ ☋ *Alatus* *volatilis*	1 Melancholic temperament, indecisive, incredulous, suspicious; 2 Loss by theft; 3 Division with parents; 4 Lawsuit over land; 5 Falsehood in love, pitfalls; 6 Languor and if ☉ appears in XII a cure; 7 Pursuit by enemies, lies of spouse; 8 Cure of long illness; 9 Agriculture; 10 Under suspicion among superiors; 11 Unpublished among protectors; 12 Sadness and ills.
67 ♄ ♐ *Tristitia* *Tarditas* *Senectus*	Weak temperament, lazy, sad; 2 Profit by usury; 3 Sorrows from parents; 4 Trial for inheritance; 5 Sorrows caused by lovers, new sadness, annoyance against domestics; 6 Stomach cramps, if ☽ is in XII House very ill; 7 Jealous, enduring jealousy; 8 Troublesome age; 9 Astronomy, astrology, magic; 10 The envious intrigue with impediments; 11 Hope restored; 12 Thoughts of death, despair.
68 ♃ ☋ *Lætitia* *Victor* *Gaudium*	1 Well-proportioned body, good soul; 2 Profit from mines; 3 Renowned through travels; 4 Gain by land trial; 5 Agreement by lovers, faithful and active domestics; 6 Hot fever if ♄ is in opposition a cure; 7 Reconciliation with enemies; 8 Another 40 years of life; 9 Theosophy; 10 Advancement in employment; 11 Warm friendship; 12 Danger of death.
69 ♂ ♊ *Puer* *Fortitudo* *B*	1 Coarse nerves, scorner, spying; 2 Loss of clothing by fire; 3 Injuries at relatives' hands; 4 New sorrow; 5 Victory in love, theft at home, notice of losses; 6 Veneral disease if ♀ in XII in opposition, leprosy if ♄ is in VI; 7 Violation; 8 Thoughts of death; 9 Surgery; 10 Rejection of petition; 11 Slander among friends; 12 Danger of injury.
70 71 ☿ ♎ *Albus* *Epistola*	1 Inclined to the spirit, wheedling, self-respect; 2 Loss at trade if opposed – if ☽ in ♊ neither loss nor gain; 3 Agreement with parents; 4 Paternal sadness; 5 Inconstant love; 6 Loss of reason; 7 Female chatter disturbing the household; 8 Dangerous life; 9 Navigation; 10 Reputation; 11 A lot of protection; 12 Misfortune.

72 ♂ ♏ *Ruber* *Nocens* *Venator*	1 Hot temperament, irreconcilable enemy; 2 Loss on travel; 3 Honor despised; 4 Discontentment, mistrust in love; 5 Conception, theft by domestics; 6 Diseases of the skin, natural crises; 7 Violence due to jealousy or discontent in marriage; 8 Will not live more than ten more years; 9 Minerology; 10 Persecution by warriors; 11 Aversion of protectors; 12 Bad reputation.
73 ☉ ☍ *Ruber* *Nocens* *Venator*	1 Harmonious education both internal and external, happy in everything; 2 The greatest gain in the world; 3 Aid of parents and relatives; 4 Hidden treasures; 5 Secure and cheerful lovers, well-raised children; 6 Eye ailments – if ♂ appears ♏ in loss of sight, but if ☽ in opposition loss of one eye; 7 Peace with enemies, respect of husband; 8 Live another 18 years; 9 Financier; 10 Favors in court; 11 Advantageous purchase of diamonds; 12 Triumph over danger.
74 ☽ ☍ *Via*	1 Changeable as the weather, purchasable, uncertain, sulky; 2 Profit from travel and usury; 3 Losses from parents; 4 Paternal abandonment and substitutes; 5 Unfaithful in love, letters from false friends; 6 Fantasies - if ♄♐ in opposition, great illness; 7 Persecution of enemies, spouses agitated; 8 Short and feeble life; 9 Botanist; 10 Happiness with authorities; 11 Happiness among protectors; 12 Deceit.
75 ♂ ♏ *Ruber* *Nocens* *Venator*	1 Anger, ruffian, bold, courageous; 2 Loss of mobile property; 3 Reproaches from parents; 4 Theft by burglary; 5 Seduction of lover, theft at home; 6 Rage; 7 Conjugal war; 8 Death by injury; 9 Metals; 10 Advancement by military; 11 Loss of an important friend; 12 Prison following injury.
76 ♄ ♓ *Carcer* *Impedi-* *mentum*	1 Hypochondriac, cold-blooded, sad, idle; 2 Profit through avarice and usury; 3 Sadness because of embarrassment among relatives; 4 Sadness over household; 5 Love deranged through caprice, bad mood with lover and domestics; 6 Cancer and cankers; 7 Gossip by old men and women disturb marriage; 8 Danger to life but without effect; 9 Agriculture; 10 Jealousy and impediment in advancement; 11 Good counsel of friends; 12 Terror.

77
☿ ☊
Alatus volatilis

1 Evil to the highest degree if ♃ or ♀ aren't in IV; 2 Profit in business or with women; 3 Profit lose because of parents; 4 Increase in number of fields; 5 Many cohabitants, triumph over all, discovery of a theft; 6 Broken arm or leg; 7 Fertile and peaceful marriage, peace with enemies; 8 Inevitable death of invalid in ♐; 9 Subterranean geology; 10 Commission of kings; 11 Gifts from superiors; 12 Full security.

78
☉ ☋
Fortuna major

1 Eccentric, Benevolent, Cheerful donor; 2 Gain without trouble; 3 Honors, respect, reputation; 4 Subterranean treasure in gold; 5 Enormous success in love, rescue from danger by domestic; 6 Illness of the eyes and certain cure; 7 Unexpected good fortune by a woman; 8 Healing and another 18 years of life; 9 Finances and art for enrichment; 10 Profit from a lawsuit; 11 Gifts from superiors; 12 Complete security.

79
♀ ♊
I

1 Dissolute blood, quick tempered, wanton; 2 Small profit; 3 Little respect among relatives; 4 Legacy from an old woman; 5 Enjoyment in love then repentance; 6 Swelling in the stomach and danger of death if ♂ is in ♍ opposed; 7 Disagreement in marriage and with enemies; 8 Life 10 years more; 9 Poet; 10 Advancement in employment by women; 11 Gifts from old women; 12 Persecution.

80
81
☽ ♒
Populus

1 Very irregular complexion, indecisive, hesitant in undertakings; 2 Profit from industry; 3 Joy through a parent; 4 Economic improvement; 5 Love beginning or resumed; 6 For women leucorrhea, for men jaundice; 7 Peaceful but cold marriage; 8 10 more years of life; 9 Hydraulics; 10 Success of petition through female recommendation; 11 Advancement by protectors; 12 Incorrigible losses.

82
♃ ♈
Acquisitio

1 Warm temperament, moist, condescending, honest; 2 Profit by honest ways; 3 Impediments by relatives, but overcome; 4 Gain through economy; 5 Uneasy relations in love, god news from friends; 6 Rash on the chest, natural relief; 7 Triumph over one's enemies; 8 Peacefulness in the house; 9 Diplomacy; 10

Consideration among superiors; 11 Appearance of disfavor; 12 No danger.

83
♀ ♊
Pulchritudo
I

1 Extremely dissolute blood, bad subject; 2 Neither profit nor losses; 3 Swindled by relatives; Coolness of agents; 5 Infidelity in love, and inconstancy in friendship; 6 Venereal or nervous ailments; 7 Strong dispute between couples, enmity of men; 8 Another 22 years of life; 9 Decorative Arts; 10 Success in petition and undertakings; 11 Gifts from women; 12 Trouble from women.

84
☿ ♋
Albus
Epistola
Tabitudo

1 Jealous, contradicter, bad; 2 Without gain by parent; 3 War with relatives; 4 Ill will between fathers or brothers; 5 Slanders towards lover, but reconciled; 6 Loss of reason, bizarre, nervous; 7 Suspicions, violence, silence; 8 Dissolution of the body; 9 Arithmetic; 10 If ♄ in IV in opposition, trouble in court, if ♂ in opposition, success; 11 Feeble help from protectors; 12 Misfortunes in travels on water.

85
♃ ♈
Acquisitio

1 Tender character, endearing, considerate, held in high esteem; 2 Profit from exchange; 3 Aid and assistance of parents; 4 Hopes for an advance age without cares; 5 Victory in love, in danger saved by a domestic; 6 Pernicious fever and if ♂ in ♊ or ☉ in ♈ in opposition, cure; 7 Victory over enemies, openness in marriage; 8 Another 28 years of life; 9 Natural History; 10 Decrees of court; 11 Gifts; 12 Gentle death.

86
♃ ♈
Acquisitio

1 Endowed with all Nature's gifts, reasonable; 2 Profit through commerce; 3 Cheerfulness in good society; 4 Pleasing contract for purchase; 5 Enjoyment, cheerful company; 6 Hydropsy, swellings, colic – ☽, ☿ or ♂ in opposition cures; 7 Good luck in war, love and marriage; 8 Another 22 years of life; 9 Experimental Physics; 10 Hope of advancement; 11 Glory of protectors; 12 Trouble from women.

87
☉ ♋

1 Strained fine nerves, love of order, pocket support; 2 Gain through economy; 3 Enjoyment of a renowned

Fortuna minor	general; 4 Acquisition of capital and fields; 5 Pure and candid love, good servants; 6 Illnesses of the ears and if ♂ is opposed, deafness; Peace in household and with enemies; 8 Age of 80 years; 9 Working mines; 10 Success of business; 11 Goodwill; 12 Security.
88 ☿ *Alatus volatilis*	1 Restless, fickle, mocker, chatterer; 2 Loss at games and commerce; 3 Falsehood from parents; 4 Legacy from an old woman; 5 Love letters; 6 Loss of memory; 7 Marriage with dispute; 8 Another 17 years of life; 9 Navigator; 10 Letters of nobility; 11 Letters from friends and protectors; 12 Disagreeable events.
89 ☿ ♎ *Conjunctio*	1 Bad temperament, ugliness, bad mood; 2 Loss in houses; 3 Vengeance of parents; 4 Loss of a lawsuit; Betrayal by lover or domestics; 6 Scurvy and mouth rot; 7 Demon in household, enmity; 8 Short life; 9 Geography, Topography, Cosmography; 10 Failure in enterprises; 11 Disfavor; 12 Reproaches, bad reputation, shame.
90 91 ☿ ☊ *Alatus volatilis*	Fine nerves but relaxed, noble, conciliatory; 2 Small profit repeated; 3 Indifferent recklessness of parents; 4 Coolness of great people; 5 Lukewarm love, lazy servants, noisy children; 6 Wounds to the head, hair loss; 7 Cold and sterile marriage; 8 Danger of death – and if ♃ is in II, saved; 9 Police; 10 Impediment of a petition; 11 Scandalmongering; 12 Persecution.
92 ♄ ♓ *Carcer Impedimentum*	1 Melancholic temperament, weak body, lazy; 2 Certain loss; 3 Hated by the family; 4 Lawsuit because of legacy; 5 Sorrows in love; 6 Congealed blood; 7 Pursuit by enemies, flight; 8 Stroke; 9 Subterranean treasures; 10 Impediments in cultivation; 11 Trouble with priests; 12 prison, burial.
93 ☿ ♎ *Conjunctio*	1 Harmonious body, orator, lover of order; 2 Profit at games and in commerce; 3 Disputes with brothers and sisters; 4 Rich heritage; Inconstancy in love, unfaithful servants; 6 Disease of chest; 7 Tranquil marriage, order and peace; 8 Another 12 years of life; 9 Politics; 10 Difficulty of advancement; 11 Benefits; 12 Danger from water.

94 ♀ ♐ *Amissio*		1 Sanguine temperament, lightweight, without concern; 2 Poverty, want; 3 Contempt among relatives; 4 Separation from father, mother; 5 Insult to lover, loss of children if ♄ in XI; 6 Consumption; 7 In marriage of convenience; 8 Death of patient due to absence of doctor; 9 Apothecary; 10 Pardon of the court; 11 Gift from women; 12 Injuries.
95 ♄ ♓ *Carcer Impedimentum*		1 Coarse nerves, insensitive; 2 Loss upon loss to ruin; 3 Falsehood of parents; 4 Loss of inheritance trial; 5 Sadness of lovers, conception, a son; 6 Scurvy and rotting senses; 7 Insults and dishonor; 8 Long illness followed by burial; 9 Metallurgy; 10 Disgrace at court; 11 Abandonment by friends; 12 Broken arms and legs.
96 ♂ ♍ *Ruber Nocens Venator*		Anger, violent, murderous; 2 Enjoyment of game, envy of gain; 3 Reproaches of parents; 4 Punishment by superiors; 5 Bold, immoral, apprehension; 6 Contagious diseases; 7 Injured in a dispute, noisy household; 8 Death from injuries; 9 Understanding of horses; 10 Advancement for valor if ♃ is in IV; 11 Favor with women; 12 Banditry.
97 ♀ ♐ *Amissio*		1 Aroused character, jolly, cheerful, musician; 2 Losses of money and clothing; 3 Betrayal by crafty parents; 4 Thieves in the house; 5 Voluptuous, cheerful children; 6 Diarrhea; 7 Another 16 years of life; 8 Doctor; 9 Supported by women; 10 Confidence among women; 11 Loss through theft; 12 Loss of honor.
98 ☿ ♋ *Albus Epistola*		1 Fickle, bad subject, liar, misleading, ungrateful; 2 Inevitable loss; 3 Aversion among relatives; 4 Superiors warned; 5 Love letters, letters of exchange, new friends; 6 Loss of speech, hoarseness; 7 Evil done by enemies, mistrust in marriage; 8 Danger of death; 9 Alchemy; 10 Gossip among superiors; 12 Blackened among protectors; 12 Theft.
99 ☿ V *Alatus*		1 Gentle, benevolent; 2 Moderate gain; 3 Coldness of parents; 4 Profit from a lawsuit; 5 Pleasure in marriage, servants helpful; 6 Nervous paralysis; 7 Indifference in marriage, enemy of same strength; 8 Another 18 years

volatilis of life; 9 Victorious Chemist, improvement of metals, discovery of secrets; 10 Favor of great people; 11 Gifts from protectors, Security.

Chapter 16
Bibliography

In order to complete the posthumous work of Papus, we have grown having to add this bibliography, hoping that this work, which we have made all our care, will be welcomed by all those who are interested in the SCIENCE of numbers.

Paul Chacornac

ANONYMOUS

Ænigma curiosum arithmeticum, genommen auss dem cabalistischen Zahl Vit. Composiert für das Haus von
Oesterreich. S. 1., 1707, feuille in-folio, en vers.
Clavicules (Les) de Rabbi Salomon, traduites exactement du texte hébreu en français. Manuscrit du xviii, siècle (bibl. Arsenal, 2346).
Dictionnaire encyclopédique des amusements de sciences mathématiques et physiques. Paris, 1792, in-4°, et un cah.
de pl.
Explication de l'utilité des chiffres romains. Paris, Jean de Poix, 1652, in-12.
Harmonies comparées des sons et des couleurs. Bordeaux, 1861, broch. in-4o, pl.
Magie naturelle (La) ou mélange divertissant, contenant des secrets merveilleux et des tours plaisans. Paris, 1715, in-12.
Manuel des Sorciers (Le ou l'arithmétique amusante. Paris, 1801, in-12 (carrés magiques); Paris, 1802.
Miscellanea philosophico - mathematica Societatis privatæ Taurinensis. Augustæ Taurinorum, 1759-1773, 5 v. in-4°.
Number (The) six hundred and sixty six and the name of Antechrist. London, 1874, in-8°.
Rara mathematica, or a collection of treatises on the mathematics and subjects connected with them, from ancient inedited manuscripts, edited by JAMES ORCHARD HALLIWELL. London, 1839, in-8°, 1841. Science (La) des Nombres. Paris, Setier, 1827.
Science (La) des Nombres révélée en faveur des actionnaires de la Loterie. Paris, 1793, in-12.
Septenaire (Le), ou louange du nombre sept de George l'apostre à son très vertueux et docile personnage George de Maubuisson, soli mecène. Paris, Lenocier, 1585, in-8°.
Sexte essence (La) diabolique et potentielle, tirée par une nouvelle façon d'alembiquer, suivant les préceptes de la sainte magie et invocation des démons. Paris, 1595, in-8°.
Véritable (Le) oracle du destin, suivi de consultations particulières établies d'après la science des nombres ; par le Comte (CAGLIOSTRO) (sic), Paris.. Guyot, 1896, in-12.

ABARTIAGUE (L. d'). Essai sur les propriétés des puissances des nombres. Biarritz, 1897, broch. in-8°.
ABRAMELIN THE MAGE. The Book of the Sacred Magie, as delivered by Abraham the Jew to his son Lamech A. D. 1458. Translated from the original Hebrew into French and now rendered in to English. Notes and magical squares of letters by L. S. MAc GREGOR MATHERS. London,1 900 in-4°.
ADAMS (Karem). Numerology. Up to date. A key to your fate. London, S. d., in-8°.
AHMAD (M. Là. Sound and Number. The law of Destiny and Design. London, s. d., in-8°.
- Names and their Numbers. Id., id. in-8°.
- Christian Names and their values. Id., id.,in-8°.
ALANDER (Christ) resp. Gust. POLVIANDER. De Magia Numerorum. Thèse, *Abo*, 1703, in-8°. ALBERT (G.). Die Platonische Zalh... Wien, 1896, in-8°.
ALBERTI (G.-A.). J. Giochi Numerici fatti arcani (?). Bologn., 1747, in-8°, planches h.t.
ALEXEJEFF Ueber die Entwickelung des Begriffs der hoehen arithmologischen. Gesetzmæssig Keit in Natur und Geisterwelt, 1904, in-8°.
ALFÉGAS. Introduction aux arcanes de la Mathèse. Quelques secrets du nombre 36. Paris, Le Voile d'Isis, avril, juin à sept. 1913.
- Les Clefs de la Mathèse. Id., id., janv.,mars, juillet 1914. - La Symbolique des chiffres. Paris, Chacornac, 1913, in-8°, grav. ALLENDY (Dr B.). Le Nombre. Paris, Revue de l'Epoque, mai 1921.
- Le Symbolisme des Nombres. Essai d'arithmosophie. Paris, Chacornac, 1921, in-8°.
ALTAIR. Le Nombre. Paris, Mystéria, avril 1913.
AMAND. Nouveaux éléments de géométrie. Paris-La Haye, 1670, in- (carrés magiques).
ARBOIS DE JUBAINVILLE (H. d')., Cours de littérature celtique tome VI. Paris, 1894, in-8° (Les Nombres chez les Celtes.)
ARNOUX. Essais de psychologie et de métaphysique positives. Arithmétique graphique. Paris, 1894-1905, 3 vol. in-8°.
ASHMAD (Sheikh Haheeb). The Mysteries of Sound and Number. London, 1903, in-8°, 2nd edn. London, S. d., in-8°.
AUBER (Chanoine). Histoire et théorie du symbolisme religieux. Paris, 1884, t. 1, p. 97-155.
AZBEL Le Beau et sa loi. Paris, 1899, in-8°.
- Loi des distances et des Harmonies planétaires. Paris, 1903,in-8°.
BAADER (Fr. von). Ueber den Urternar, ans einem schreiben an den Grafen A. von Stourdza. Muenchen, 1816, in-8°.
BAHR. Symbolik der mosaischen cultus. Heidelberg, 1837, t. 1, p. 119-208.
BALDUS (Cam). De ratione cognoscendi mores et qualitates scribentis ex ipsues epistola missiva. Bonaniae, 1664, in-4°.
BALLETT (L. Dow). Success through
Vibration. London, S. d., in-8°.
- The Day of Wisdom according to numbervibration. Id., id., in-8°. - The Philosophy of Number. Their tones and Colours. Id., id., in-8°. - Nature's Symphony, or Lessons in Number Vibration. Id., id., in-8°.
- Number Vibration in question and answers.Id., id., in-8°. BALZAC (H. de). Louis Lambert. Paris, 1832, in-8° ; nombr. édit.
- Seraphita. Paris, 1832, in-8°; nombr. édit.
BARADUC (Dr). Les vibrations de la vitalité humaine. Paris, 1904, gr. in-8°. BARLET (F. Ch.). Les Nombres. Paris, Mystéria, déc. 1913.

BARTHELEMY (J. J.). Voyage du jeune Anarchasis en Grèce. Paris, 1830, 5 vol. in-8° (tome 111).

BASCHET (Cl.-G.). Problèmes plaisants et délectables qui se font par les nombres, etc. Lyon, 1612, in-8°; id., 1624, in-8°; éd. revue et aug. par A. Labosne. Paris, 1874, in-8°.

BELOT (Jean). Les Œuvres contenant... les sciences stéganographiques, Paulines, Armadelles et Lullistes.... etc. Liège, 1649, in-12 (pl.).

BENLOEW (Louis). Recherches sur l'origine des noms de nombre japhétiques et sémitiques. Paris, 1862, in-8°. BERTET (A.). Apocalypse du bienheureux Jean. Paris, 1861, in-8°. BOETIUS (Severians). De institutione Arithmetica. Augsburg, 1488, in41.

- Arithmetica duobus discreta libris adjectocommentario mystica numerorum applicationem, etc. Paris, 1521, in-fol. (fig.).

BONGUS (Petrus). Mysticæ, numerorum significationis liber. Bergomi, Ventura, 1585, 2 parties en 1 vol., in-folio.

- Numerorum mysteria. Opus in quo mirus...Arithmeticœ Pythagorie~~L cum divinœ paginæ numeris consensus probatur. Bergami, 1599, in-8° ; Lutetiæ, 1618, in4°.
- De mvstica Quaternarii numeri significatione. Venetiæ, Hugolinus, 1585, in-8.

BONNEL (J. B.). De l'imagination dans les sciences exactes. Tours, 1890, in-8°, frontisp.

BOSMAN (Léon). Meaning and Philosophy of Numbers. London, s. d. in-8°.

BRETEAU (Mme) Grand jeu de Société. Pratiques secrètes de Mlle Lenormand. Paris, 1845, in-12.

BRITT (Ernest). La Lyre d'Apollon avec prélude de F. Warrain. Paris, 1931, gr. in-8°.

BRUCK (Robert). Manifeste du Magnétisme du Globe et de l'Humanité. Bruxelles, 1866, gr. in-8°.

- Electricité ou Magnétisme du Globeterrestre. Bruxelles, 1851-1858, 3 vol. gr. in-8°.
- L'Humanité, son développement, sa durée.Bruxelles, 1864, 2 vol. gr. in-8°.
- Etude sur la physique du Globe. Bruxelles,1869, gr. in-8°.
- L'origine des Etoiles filantes. Bruxelles,1868, gr. in-8°.

BUKATY (A.). Déduction et démonstration des trois lois primordiales de la congruence des nombres constituant la troisième loi de l'algorithmie donnée par H. Wronski. Paris, 1873, broch. in-8°.

BUTTE (Wilh.). Prolégomènes de l'arithmétique de la vie humaine Paris, 1812, in8°, pl. et tabl.

CAHEN (E.). Théorie des Nombres. T. 1 : le premier binaire : t. II ; le second degré binaire. Paris, 19 1914-1924, 2 vol. gr.

in-8°.

CAMPBELL (Fl.). Your days are numbered. London, s. d., in-8°.

CARAMUEL (JO.). Mathesis vetus et nova. Campaniæ, 1670, 2 vol. in-fol.

CARDAN (Hiérosme). Les livres intitulés de la Subtilité, et subtiles Inventions, ensemble les causes occultes et les raisons d'icelles. Trad. du latin en français par B. Leblanc. Paris, 1642, in-8°.

CARVALLO (Jules). Théorie des nombres parfaits. Paris, 1883, broch. in-8°.

CASLANT (E.). Les nombres rythmiques. Paris, Les Nouveaux Horizons de la Science, juillet 1905- juill. -août- sept. octobre 1908.

- Aperçus sur la théorie des Nombres. Paris, Le Voile d'Isis, juin 1921.

CASTEL (Le Père). Mathématique universelle. Paris, 1728, in-4°.

CAZALAS (Général E.). Carrés magiques au degré n. Séries numérales de G. Tarry. Avec un aperçu historique d'une bibliographie des figures magiques. Paris, 1934, in-8°, portr. et fig.

CHAIGNET. Pythagore et la philosophie pythagoricienne. Paris,1873, 2 v. in-12.
CHAPELLE (F.). Le Nombre 77... article dédié aux curieux de la Cabale. Paris, Revue Spirite, 1895, p. 296.
- Origine géométrique des systèmes de numération décimale et duodécimale. Saint-Elienne, 1895.
CHARDON. Résolution géométrique du célèbre problème de la Quadrature du Cercle, ou sa rectification, tirée d'une équation indertimée du troisième degré, qui n'est elle-même qu'un cas particulier d'une égalité de ce dernier. Paris, 1746, in 81, pl.
CHARENCEY (De). Les Cités Votanides, valeur symbolique des nombres... dans la Nouvelle Espagne. Louvain, 1885, in-8°.
CHEASLEY (CI. W.). Numerology, its practical application to life. London, 1923, in-12.
CHEIRO. Book of Numbers (Fadic System). London, s. d., in-4°.
CHEVKY (Hassan). Révélation astronomique résolvant les difficultés de la création. Paris, Chacornac, 1902, broch. in-8°.
CHRISTESCO (Stefan). Conceptions géométriques de l'espace à trois dimensions. Démonstration des axiomes d'Euclide. Paris, 1923, in-8°.
CHRISTIAN (P.). Histoire de la Magie, du monde surnaturel et de la fatalité à travers le temps et les peuples. Paris, s. d., gr. in-8° (pl.).
CHRISTIAN (P). L'Homme Rouge des
Tuileries. Paris, 1863, in-12.
CLARKE (J. E.). Dissertation on the Dragon, beast and false prophet of this Apocalypse, in which the number 666 is satisfactorily explained. London, 1844, in-8°.
CLICHTOVEUS (Jod.). De mystica numerum significatione opusculum. Parisis, 1513, in-4°.
COLENNE Le système octaval.Paris, 1845. COMBARIEU (Jules). La musique et la Magie. Paris, 1909, in-4°.
CORNAY (Dr J. E.). Mémoire sur la vie des tissus chez les espèces humaines et exposition d'anatomie comparée dans les nombres. Paris, 1861, in-12.
CORNEILLE-AGRIPPA. Opera omnia.
       Lyon, Beringos fratres, 1531, 3 vol.
- La Philosophie Occulte ou la Magie *La Have*, 1727, 2 vol. in-8° ; Paris, Chacornac, 1910-1911, 2 vol. in-8°.
COSTA (L. de). La superstition et les nombres fatidiques. Paris, 1907, in-16.
CROEGAERTS (J. Ed.). Traité complet de la tonalité. Anvers, 1881, gr. in-8°.
CRUSIUS (C. A.). De vera significatione nomini Tetragrammati. Lipziæ, 1758, in-4°.
CUGNIN (E.). Essai de psychologie appliquée aux sciences mathématiques. Nice, 1878, in-8°. DANTZIG (Tobias). Le Nombre, langue de la Science, trad. par le colonel G. Gros. Paris, 1934, in-8°.
DAVID (Thom.). The number and names of the Apocalyptic beasts. London, 1848, in-8°.
DAVIS (J. T.). Colour, Sound, Form and Number. London, s. d. in-8°.
DECRESPE (M.). Du symbolisme des chiffres dits Arabes. Paris, L'Initiation oct. 1895.
DELACROIX. La Science des Arts. Traité d'architectonique. Besançon, 1869, in-8°.
DÉLÉZINIER (Dr). Les Nombres. Paris,
L'Initiation, t. 14, p. 258.
-   Les Nombres. Paris, Le Voile d'Isis, no 4, 23 sept. 1891.
-   Les Nombres plus grands que l'infini et lethéorème de Canter. Paris, L'initiation, mirs 1892.
-   Etudes d'ésotérisme mathématique. Essai dethéorie simple de quelques phénomènes électriques, comme base de mesure des effets de transformation de l'Od. Paris, 1892, broch. in-8°.

DESBARROLLES. Les Mystères de la Main. Paris, 1860, in-12.
DESCHAMPS (J.). Sur la méthode d'Eratosthène. Paris, 1897, broch. in-8°.
DESSOYE (J. 13. J.). Arithmétique de la comptabilité universelle. Paris, 1860, in-4°.
- Algèbre de la comptabilité universelle. Id.,1862, in-4°.
- L'absolu dans un principe et une révolutiondans un seul chiffre ou magie numérale. Id., 1863, in-8°.
- Les preuves directes des quatre règles ougénéralisation absolue. Id., 1864.
- Le positif de la raison humaine. Id., 1866,in12.
- Embryogénie méthodique de l'entendementde l'esprit humain fondée sur la puissance des Nombres. Prospectus spécimen. Paris, 1857, in-12.
DRONIOU (J. H.). Clef de la science ou boussole de l'âme dans le voyage de la vie. Brest, 1840, in-8°, tabl.
DRUMM0ND The Psychology and Teaching of Number. London, s. d., in-8°.
Du CHENTEAU (T ...). Carte philosophique et mathématique dédiée à son altesse royale Mgr le duc Ch. Alex. de Lorraine et de Bar. *Bruxelles et Paris*, 1778, 3 pl., inquarto soleil.
DUPUIS (Jean). Le nombre géométrique de Platon ; interprétation nouvelle. Paris, 1881, in-8°, seconde interprétation. Paris,1882, broch. in-8°.
DUTOIT-MEMBRINI. - La Philosophie
Divine, appliquée aux lumières naturelle, magique, astrale, surnaturelle, céleste et divine. Lausanne, 1793, 3 vol. in-8°.
ECKARTSHAUSEN (von). Aufschlusse zur Magie. Munich, 1792, 4 vol. in-8° (le 41 vol. contient : Magie numérale, trad. française. Paris, L'Initiation, sept. 1903 à avril 1907).
- Eclaircissements sur la Science cachée de laphilosophie et les mystères secrets de la Nature. Trad. française du tome 1er parla veuve du baron d'ORBET, S. 1. (Marseille), 1806, in-8° (frontisp.).
- Zahlenlehre der Natur, oder : die Naturzählt and spricht, was sind ibre Zahlen, was sind ibre Worte ? Ein Schlüssel zu den Hieroglyphen der Natur. Leipzig, 1791, in-8°.
- Probascologie oder praktischer Teil derZahlenlehre der Natur. Leipzig, 1795, in-8°.
Front. et grav, ECKSTEIN (baron d'). Le Catholique. Paris, 1830, 16 vol. in-8°.
ELIPHAS LÉVI. Dogme et Rituel de la Haute Magie. Paris, Germer-Baillière, 1856, 2 vol. in-8° ; 21 édition augm. Id., id., 1861 id. Alcan, 1903 ; id., Chacornac, 1930. - La Clef des Grands Mystères, Paris, Baillière, 1861 : Alcan. 1897.
- Histoire de la Magie - Paris, Baillière, 1860 ; id., Alcan, 1903. - Le Livre des Splendeurs, etc. Paris, Chamuel, 1894 in-8°.
- Les Eléments de la Kabbale. Paris,L'Initiation, t. 9, p 193 t. 10, pp. 303 et 385.
- Cours de Philosophie occulte. Lettres aubaron Spedalieri. T. I et II Paris, Chacornac, 1932-1933, 2 vol. in-8°.
ELLIS (Robert). On numerals as signs of Primeval Unity among mankind. London, 1873, in-8°.
ELY STAR (Dr). Les Mystères de l'Etre. Paris, 1902, gr. in-8°.
- les Mystères du Verbe. Id., 1908, gr. in-8°,pl. en noir et coul.
ETCHEGOYEN. De l'Unité ou aperçus philosophiques sur l'identité de la science mathématique, de la grammaire générale et de la religion chrétienne. Paris, 1836, 1839-1849, 4 vol. in-8°.
EUCLIDE. Les quinze livres des Eléments d'Euclide, tract. du latin en français, par D. HENRION. Rouen, 1649, in-8°.
EULER. De numeris amicalibus, p. 23 et suiv., 2e vol. Opuscula varii argumenti. Berlin, 1746, in-4°.

FABRE (J. H.). Arithmos (Le Nombre). Paris, 1933, broch. gr. in-8°.
FABRE D'OLIVET. Les Vers dorés de
Pythagore. Paris, 1813, in-8°. Id.. 1908 ; id., 1923 ; id., l932.
- La Langue Hébraïque restituée. Paris, 1815, 2 -,-ci. in-4° ; id., 1905; id., 1928.
FAULHABER (Job.). Numerus figuratus, sive arithmetica analytica arte mirabili inaudita nova constans, S. I., 1614, in4°.
FAX (A.M.) Des nombres mystérieux et en particulier du nombre trois. Paris, 1850, in-12.
FILACHOU (J. E.). Aperçus fondamentaux de la philosophie mathématique. Montpellier, 1860, in-8°.
FLEURY (P. H.). Le calcul infinitésimal fondé sur les principes rationnels et précédé. de la théorie mathématique de l'infini. Marseille, 1879, gr. in-8°. FOUCHER. Géométrie métaphysique. Paris, 1758, in-8°.
FOURREY (E.). Récréations arithmétiques. Paris, 1904, in-8°, fig.
FRANLAC. La main (le Fatime. Une clef de la Kabbale orientale. Paris, L'Initiation, juin 1902.
FREVAL (G. de). Essais métaphisicomathématiques sur la solution (le quelques problèmes importans, qui sont encore à résoudre. Amsterdam, 1764, in-8°.
FROLOW (M.). Le problème d'Euler et les carrés magiques. Saint-Petersbourg, 1884. 2 broch. in-8°, dont un atlas.
- Les carrés magiques. Paris, Gauthier- 1886,in-8°.
FULCO (Th.). Ludus geometricus. Londini, 1578, in-4°.
GADOT (Ad.). Les unités de la force décimale déterminées dans la nature de manière expérimentale physique. Paris, s. d., gr. in-8°. GAUSS (C.-Fr.). Disquisitiones arithmetic, Lispsiæ, 1801, in-4°.
- Recherches arithmétiques, tract. (le l'allem.par POULLET-DELISLE. Paris, 1807, in-4° ; id., 1910.
GAY (L.). Les mathématiques du chimiste. Paris, s. ci., gr. in-8°.
GAYVALLET (P.). Unité, Attraction,
Progrès. Paris, 1900, in-12.
GEE. Primitive numbers. Washington, 1900, in-8°.
GENTILE (M.). La dottrina platonique delle idee numeri e Aristotele. Pisa, 1930, in8°.
GHYKA (Matila C.). Le Nombre d'or.]Rites et Rythmes Pythagoriciens dans le développement de la civilisation occidentale. Paris, s. ci., 2 vol., gr. in-8°.
- L'esthétique des proportions dans l'art et dans la nature. Paris, S. ci., in-8°.
GIBSON (W. B.). The Science of Numerology. What Numbers Mean to von, London, s. d., in-8°. GODBOLE (Krishna Shastri). Astres et Nombres. Paris, L'Initiation, juin 1897.
GOSSELIN (Guill.). De Arte Magna seu de Occultà Parte numerorum, quæ -Mgebra et Almacabala dicitur. Porisiis, 1577, in8°.
GOUILLT. Treize et Sept. Nice, Bull. Soc. Et. Psych., 1913. GREEN (H.-S.). The number 777. London, The Theosophist, 1909, n° 9, P. 326.
GREMILHET Application de l'arithmétique à l'algèbre, précédé de l'exPosé analytique d'une nouvelle méthode, dite des facteurs carrespondants. Paris, 1858, in-8°.
GROSSCHEDE (J. 13.). Oratio de disciplinis mathematicis. Copenhague, 1610, in-fol.
GUAITA (St. de). Au seuil du Mystère. paris, 1891, 1:11-8- ; 2e éd. augm., id., 1895.
GUY (P. G.). Théorie toute nouvelle des nombres pairs et impairs dont la connaissance est indispensable à tous. Paris. 1878, in-8°.
GUYOT. Nouvelles récréations physiques et mathématiques. Paris, 17-12, 4 vol. in-8° ; id., 1786, 3 vol.

HAGELGANS (Joh.-Georg.). Sphœra infernalis mystica, das ist höllisches Spinnen-Rad, darinnen das Gcheimnisz der Bosheit, der Fall Lucifers... die dahin zielenden geheimen Zalhen der Heiligen Schrift aufgelœset aus der Zaéhl und Mess Kunst- und in der 666ten, Zahl gezeiget, etc. Francf., 17,10, in-8°. HAPI. Le chiffre de la Bête. Paris, L'Initialion, janv. 1904.

HEILBRONNER (J.-C.). Historia matheseos universæ. Lipsiæ, 1742, in-4°.

HELLENBACH (Baron Laz. Von). Die Magie der Zahlen als Grundlage aller Mannigfaltigkeit und das scheinbare Fatum. Wien, 1882, gr. in-8°; 2, éd., 1898.

HENRY (Charles). Rapporteur esthétique permettant l'analyse et la rectification esthétique de toute forme, avec notice et tables. Paris, 1887.

- Cercle chromatique présentant tous les compléments et toutes les harmonies des couleurs avec une introduction sur la théorie générale du contraste, du rythme et de la mesure. Paris, 1888, in-16. HERBLAY (Noelle). Le Nombre. Paris, L'Initiation, t. 41, p. 264.

HOGENRAAD (Clio). Names and Numbers. Their power and significance. London, s. d., in-8°.

HULISCH (Joh. A.). Zahlenmagie in bezug auf das menschliche leben. Leipzig, 1924, in-8°.

HUTTON (Ch.). Recreation in mathematics and natural philosophy ; containing amusing dissertations and inquiries concerning a variety of subjects. London, 1814, 4 vol..in-8°, fig.

IGURBIDE (JOS. J.). Nature harmonique de l'espace. Barcelone, 1902, in-8°. JACOB (P. L.). Curiosités des Sciences Occultes. Paris, 1862, in-12.

JACOMY-REGNIER, Histoire des nombres et de la numération mécaniqne. Paris, 1855, in-8°.

JACQUET. Mode d'expression symbolique des nombres employés par les Indiens, les Tibétains et les Javanais, s. 1. 11. ci., in-8°, gr. planche.

JOUVIN. Solution et éclaircissement de quelques propositions de mathématiques, en autres de la Duplication du Cube et de la Quadrature du Cercle. Paris, 1658, in-4°, pl.

JOUX (Pierre de). Exposition succincte de la valeur symbolique des Nombres. Paris, L'Initiation, sept. 1905.

KÉPLER. Prodromus dissertationum cosmographicarum. Francf., 1621 (p. 36, de l'origine des nombres nobles). Tubingæ, 1596, in-4°.

K E RVILER. Les mesures de longueur et les nombres sacrés chez les constructeurs de monuments mégalithiques. Paris.

- Bachet de Méziriac. Etude sur sa vie et sesécrits. Paris, 1880, in-8°.

KIRCHER (A.). Ars Magna Lucis et Ombræ. Romæ, 1645, in-fol.

- Œdipus Ægyptiacus, hoc est universalisdoctrinœ hieroglyphicæ instauratio, 1652-1653, 4 vol. infol.

- Arithmologia, sive de abditis numerorummysteriis. Roma, 1663, in-4°.

- De la Cabale Saracénique et ismaélite ou, cequi est la même chose : de la philosophie hiéroglyphique et superstitieuse des Arabes et des Turcs. Trad. du latin pour la première fois en français par Jean TABRIS, Paris, Chacornac, 1895, in-8°.

KOZMINZKY (Dr Is.). Numbers, their magic and mystery. London, s. d., in-8°.

KRAITCHIK. La mathématique des jeux ou récréations mathématiques. Paris, s. d., gr. in-8°.

LACURIA (P.-F.-G.) Les Harmonies de l'Etre exprimées par les Nombres. Paris, 1847, in-8° ; nouv. éd., Paris, Chacornac , 1899, 2 vol. in-8°.

LAFONT (Ant.). Le ver luisant. Le vrai principe du mouvement des invisibles et des visibles. Paris, 1824, in-8°.

LAGRANGE (CIL). Mathématique de l'Histoire (Géométrie et cinéatique). Lois de Brück. Chronologie géodésique de la Bible. Bruxelles, 1900, gr. in-8°, fig. et tabl.
- Sur la concordance qui existe entre la loi historique de Brück, la chronologie de la Bible et celle de la Grande Pyramide de Cheops, avec une interprétation nouvelle du plan prophétique de la Révélation. Bruxelles, 1895, in-8°.

LAGRÉSILLE (11.). Métaphysique mathématique. Essai sur les fonctions métaphysiques, morphologie de l'âme. Paris, 1878, in-12.

LATZ (G.). Philosophie des nombres les nombres comme arcanes (I'utilité, le binaire, le ternaire, le quaternaire, le quinaire, le senaire, - des couleurs des arcanes), s. I., 1903, in-12 (extrait).

LAUGEL (Auguste). Les problèmes de la nature. Paris, 1864, in-12.

LA VILLIROUET (De). Recherches sur les fonctions providentielles des dates et des noms dans les annales de tous les Peuples. paris, 1852, in-8°.
- Le roi Jésus, monarque universel et divinSoleil de l'Humanité, ou l'histoire considérée à un point de vue nouveau.

Rennes, 1873, in-8°.
- vue

LAWSON (W. B.). Numerical Divination. A criticism and demonstration. London, s. d., in-8°.

LEBAILLY-GRAINVILLE VILLE (Fr.). Trinité Principe. - Compendium. Possibilité. Probabilité. Evidence. Vérité. Paris, 1833, in-4° (fig.).

LE BŒUF. De la majorité des nombres impairs. Paris, s. d., in-8°.

LEDOS (E.). Les types physionomiques associés et les phénomènes psychiques (Chap. VI : Les nombres, leur symbolisme avec la nature). Paris, 1903, in-8°. LEGENDRE (A. Théorie des Nombres, 1798 ; 1808 ; Paris, 1830, 2 vol. in-4°.

LE GENDRE (G. Ch.). Traité historique de l'Opinion. Tome IX. De la Cabale et des Nombres, pp. 206-246. Paris, 1732, in12.

LE MARCHAND. Chimie de l'Unité, Etude comparative des mathématiques cosmiques par la science de l'Arithmétique naturelle.Caen, 1885, in-8°.

LEMERLE L.). Note sur les opérations théosophiques. Paris, L'Initiation, janv. 1893. L'OLLIVIER (Emin.). La méthode de Platon. Platon expliqué par lui - même. Première partie : les Atomes. Paris, 1883, in-16. LESETRE. Nombres in Dict. de la Bible de Vigouroux. Paris, 1906.

L'ESPRIT (A.). Histoire (les chiffres et des treize premiers nombres au point de vue historique, scientifique et occulte. Paris, 1893, in-12.

LEURECHON (Jean). Récréations mathématiques, etc. Pont-à-Mousson, 1626, in-8°.

LINDENBERG (Petr.). De Proecipuorum tam in sacris quam in ethicis scriptis numerorum nobilitate mysterium et eminentia, liber unus. Rost., 1591, in-8°.

LOGOTHETA (Is. Char.). Theologia christiana in numeris. Francf. und Leipzig, 1704, in-4°.

LOUVIER (J.-A.). Chiffre und Kabbala in Gœthes Faust nette beitraege zur neuen Faustforschung. Dresden, FI. Henkler, 1897, in-8°.

LUCAS (E.). Récréations mathématiques. Paris, 1882-1883, 2 vol. in-8°.
- Considération nouvelle sur la théorie desnombres premiers et sur la division géométrique de la circonférence en parties égales. Paris, 1877, broch. in-8°.

LUCAS (Louis). La Médecine nouvelle, basée sur des principes de physique et de chimie transcendants. Paris, 1862, 2 vol. in-12.
- La Chimie nouvelle. Paris, 1854, in-12.
- L'Acoustique nouvelle. Paris, 1854, in-12.

LULLE (Raymond). Ars Brevis. Résumé et abrégé du grand art. 'l'rad. pour la première fois du latin en français. Paris, 1901, in16.
MAACK (Dr Ferd.). Das magische Quadrat, ins besondere eine neuendeckte Eigenschaft desselben, die Polarisation als grundgesetz alles daseins. Der Sphinx, t. 17, p. 437.
- Ueber den Wert des magisch-quadratischenPolarisation für die Chemie. Id., t. 18, p. 361.
M. A. E. Tables cabalistiques arithmétiques par le moyen desquelles, quelque demande qu'on puisse faire de l'avenir, ou trouve toujours une réponse suivie et qui a rapport à la question proposée. Paris, 1742, in-4° obl.
MADROLLE (A.). Le Voile levé sur le système du Monde, recherché depuis 600 ans. Révolution dans les sciences, démonstration invincible de tout à tous par la puissance simplifiée des nombres. Paris, s. d., in-8°.
MADROLLE (A.). Histoire universelle inouïe des nombres 13 à 666. Paris, s. d., broch. in-8°.
MAGON DE GRANDSELVE. Les Bois devant le destin. Paris, 1885, broch. in12.
MALFATTI DE MONTEREGGIO (Jean). Etude sur la Mathèse. Paris,1849, in-8°.
MALLEMANT (Jean). Le grand et fameux problème de la Quadrature du Cercle, résolu géométriquement. Paris, 1686, in8°.
MARCHAND (Abbé D.). La Science des Nombres d'après la tradition des siècles. Explication de la Table de Pythagore (première partie seule parue). Paris, 1897, in-12.
MARIAGE (A.). Numération par 8 anciennement en usage par toute la Terre, prouvée par les Koua des Chinois, par la Bible, par les livres d'Hésiode, d'Homère, etc. Paris1857, in-8° gr. pl.
MARQFROY. Loi des Equivalents et théorie nouvelle de la Chimie. Paris, 1897, gr. in-8°.
MARRE (A.). Problèmes numériques, faisant suite et servant d'application au «Triparty en la science des nombres » de Nicolas Chuquet. Paris, 1882, in-4°.
MARTINEZ DE PASQUALLY. Traité de la Réintégration des Etres. Paris, Chacornac, 1899, in-16.
MEERENS (Charles). Instruction élémentaire du calcul musical et philosophie de la musique. Paris, Bruxelles, s. d., in-8°.
MENESTRIER (Ch.-Fr.). La philosophie des images énigmatiques. Lyon, 1694, in-12.
MEURSIUS (J.). Denarius Pythagoricus. Lugduni, 1641, in-4°.
MICHEL (Louis), DE FIGANIERES. Réveil des Peuples. Paris, 1864, in12 (chap. X).
MILLARD (Capitaine). Le Destin de l'Allemagne. Bruxelles, 1904, in-8°. id., 1918.
MOIGNO (Abbé). Impossibilité du nombre actuellement infini. La science dans ses rapports avec la foi. Paris, 1884, in-12.
MOND (L.). Causeries d'Outre-Monde (Indicat. sur la vertu et la superstition des nombres). Draguignan, 1877, broch. in8°.
MOREAU de DAMMARTIN. Origine de la forme des caractères alphabétiques de toutes les nations, des clefs chinoises, des hiéroglyphes égyptiens. Paris, 1839, in-fol. en long (tabl.).
MORIN (Alcide). Ténèbres. Treize nuits suivies d'un demi-jour sur l'hypnotisme. Dentu, 1860, in-12.
Moss (W. W.). The Numbers in detail. London, The International Psychie Gazette, mai 1921, p. 116.
MOUREY (C. V.). La vraie théorie des quantités négatives et des quantités prétendues imaginaires. Paris, 1861, in-12.

MYDORGE (Cl.). Examen du livre des récréations mathématiques (du P. LEURECHON). Paris, 1639, in-8°.
NABOD (Val.). De calculatoria numerorum que Ratura sectiones IV. Colon. Agripp., 1556, in-8°.
NASCIAS (de). Sur quelques particularités fort curieuses du système de l'orbite lunaire. Paris, 1904, gr. in-8°.
NEMZETSEG, (Adam). La puissance des nombres dans ses applications à l'impuissance des bourses. Paris et Alexandrie, 1866, in-12. NISSA (K art). Du zéro à 1'Unité. Paris, L'Initiation, mars 1912.
O'DONNELLY. Les vraies mathématiques aux prises avec la Pierre philosophale. Paris, 1855, in-8°.
- Nouvelle géométrie ou abrégé des mathématiques célestes. Paris, 1856, in12.
OLIVER (Rev. George). The Pythagorean triangle or the Science of Numbers. With diagrams. London, 1875 in-8°.
ONCIACUS (Guill.). Numeralium locorum decas, in omni fere scientiarum genere mysticis referta propositionibus. Lugduni, Car. Pesnot, 1584, in-12.
ORIN (J. M. H.). Le plan astral dévoilé. Etude cosmogonique religieuse et chronologique. Paris, Dinan, 1890, in-8°.
OZANAM. Récréations mathématiques et physiques. Paris, 1778, 4 vol. in-8°.
PALINGENIUS. Remarque sur la notation mathématique. Paris, La Gnose, avril et mai 1910.
- Remarques sur la production des Nombres.id., id., juin et juill.août 1910.
PAPUS. Clef absolue de la Science occulte, le Tarot des Bohémiens, etc. Paris, Carré, 1889, gr. in-8° ; 2e éd., id.,
Durville, s. d. gr. in-8°.
- La Cabbale (Tradition secrète de l'Occident), résumé méthodique. Paris, Carré, 1892, gr. in-8°Paris, Chacornac, 1903 ; Anvers, 1930.
PAPUS. Traité élémentaire de Science occulte, etc. Paris, Carré, 1888, in-16 id., Ollendorff. 1908, in-8°.
- Traité méthodique de Science occulte. Paris,Carré, 1891, gr. in-8° 2 e éd. Paris, S. d., 2 vol. gr. in-8°.
- Traité élémentaire de Magie pratique. Paris,Chamuel, 1893, gr. in-8° ; 2e éd. Paris, Chacornac, 1906.
- Traité méthodique de Magie pratique. Paris,Chacornac, 1924, gr. in-8°. - Le Tarot divinatoire. Paris, Libr. Herm., 1909, in-8°.
- Le Livre de la Chance bonne on mauvaise.Paris, Durville, s. d., in-12. - Almanach de la Chance, pour 1905. Paris, Libr. Française, 1905, in16. - L. Cl. de St. Martin. Paris, Chacornac, 1902, in-12.
- Quelques considérations sur le Septenaire. Paris, L'Initiation, sept. 1895.
- Nombres pairs et nombres impairs. id., nov.1903.
- Anatomie, physiologie et psychologie desnombres. Id., sept. 1903.
- Le conflit russo-japonais et les nombresmagnétiques. Paris, 1904.
PARACELSE (Theo. 13. V. Hoh.). Opera omnia. Genevæ, 1658, 3 vol. infol. (T. II de sigillis planetarum).
- Les sept livres de l'Archidoxe magique,texte et trad. en regard, précédés d'une introd. et d'une préface par Dr MARC HAVEN. Paris 1909, gr. in-8°.
PARAVEY (DE). Essai sur l'origine unique et hiéroglyphique des chiffres et des lettres de tous les peuples. Paris, 1826, in-8°.

PARISOT (Seb.-Ant.). Du calcul coujectural, ou l'art de raisonner sur les choses futures et inconnues. Paris, 1810, in-4, fig.

PAVIOT (A.). L'astral des sons. Paris, S. d., gr. in-8°.

P. D. Les lois cosmiques. Bruxelles, 1867, in12.

PERSON (Dav.) of Loghlands. Varieties of a survey of rare and excellent matters, necessary and delectable for all sorts of persons, etc. (The number 3 and 7, etc.). London, 1635, in-4°.

PIAZZI SMITH (C.). La Grande Pyramide pharaonique du nom, humanitaire de fait, ses merveilles, ses enseignements. Trad. de l'anglais par l'abbé MOIGNO. Paris, 1875, in-12.

Picus Joan. MIRANDULÆ Concordie que comibis Cabalae divino in libro sex. Basilæ, S. il., in-4°.

PÉHAN (A.). Exposé des signes de numération usités chez tous les peuples orientaux, anciens et modernes. Paris, Impr. Impér., 1860, in-8°.

POIGNARD. Traité des neuf carrés sublimes contenant des méthodes générales... pour faire les sept quarrés planétaires et tous autres à l'infini, par les nombres, en toutes sortes de progression. Bruxelles, 1704, in-4°.

POTIER DESLAURIERES (L.). Nouvelle découverte qui embrasse toute la géométrie, qui donne la solution de ses plus grands problèmes et qui va reculer les bornes de l'esprit humain ou identité géométrique du cercle et du carré. Paris, 1804, in-4°.

POTTER (Francis). An interpretation of the Number 666. Oxford, 1642, in-4°.

PORTIER (B.). Le carré diabolique de 9 et son dérivé ; le carré satanique de 9 (carré de base magique aux deux premiers degrés) : tirés du carré magique de 3. Alger, Jourdan, 1895, broch. in-8° ; Paris, 1902.

- Le carré cabalistique de 8, diabolique aupremier ordre, magique aux deux premiers degrés (satanique) ; solution donnant en plus huit compartiments sataniques : exposition pratique. Paris et Alger, 1902, broch. in-8°.

- Le carré panmagique à grille du module 8 ;exposition pratique. Toulouse et Paris, 1904, broch. in-8°.

PRÉMONTVAL (de). Discours sur l'utilité des mathématiques. Paris, 1743, in-12.

- Discours sur la nature du nombre. Id., 1743,in-12.

PRÉVOST (Jean). La première partie des subtiles et plaisantes inventions, contenant plusieurs jeux de récréations et traits de souplesse. Lyon, 1584, in-8°.

PREYER (W.). Ursprung des Zahlbergriffs ans der Tonsinn und Wesen der Primzahlen. Berlin, 1891, in-8°.

PTOLÉMÉE (Claude). Almageste.
Composition mathématique. Texte grec et traduction française de l'abbé HALMA. Paris, 1813, 2 vol. in-4° ; id., 1930.

PUJALS DE LA BASTIDA (Dr Vie.). Filosofia de la numeracion o Descubrimiento de un nuevo mundo scientifico. Barcelone, 1844, in-12.

RABETT (Beginard). Lateinos, or the only proper and appelation name of the man. London, 1835, in-8°.

RAGON (J. M.). Orthodoxie Maçonnique suivie de la Maçonnerie occulte et de l'Initiation Hermétique. Paris, 1853, in-8°.

RAGUSEI (G.), Veneti. Epistolarum mathematicarum, seu de divinatione libri duo. Paris, 1623, in-8°.

RAYNAUD (G.). Les nombres sacrés et les signes cruciformes dans la moyenne Amérique précolombienne. Paris, Revue Histoire des Religions, t. 44, p. 235 ; Paris, 1901, in-8°.

RICHARD (P. G.). La Gamme. Introduction à l'étude de la musique. Préface de M. Casadesus. Paris, S. d. in-16.
RIEDERER (J. F.). Die bedenkliche und geheimnusrciche zalil Drey, in Theologicis, historicis et politicis. Francf., 1732, in-8°.
RIOLLOT. Les carrés magiques. Contribution à leur étude. Paris, G. Villars, 1907, in-8°, fig.
RIST (Dr A.). La philosophie naturelle intégrale et les rudiments des sciences exactes. Paris, 1904, in-8°.
BITT (A. P.). De la réduction théosophique. Paris, L'Iniliation, août 1898.
ROBIA (L.). La théorie platonicienne des idées et des nombres. Paris, Alcan, 1908, in-8°.
ROHLF (Nie.). Künstliche Zahlenspiel oder Anweisung, wie die magischen Quadrate zu verfertigen. Hambourg, 1742, in-8°.
ROLLOF (Armide). La Science de Pythagore ou l'art de découvrir les nombres et les dates qu'il faut connaître et étudier pour arriver a être heureux dans la vie et les numéros qu'il faut choisir dans les combinaisons du hasard pour faire rapidement fortune, etc. Toulouse, 1888, in-8°.
ROSCHER (W. H.). Enneadische studien... Leipzig, 1909, in-4°.
ROUSE BALL (W.). Récréations mathématiques et problèmes des temps anciens et modernes. 2e éd. française... par J. Fitz Patrick. Paris, 1907-1909, 3 vol, pet. in8°; Id., 1926-1927.
ROY MELTON (Dr). Metaphysics of numerology. Vol. 1. Number ontology. Boston, 1934, in-8°.
ROZIER (Dr F.). Calculs. Paris, L'Initiation, août 1898.
RUBIN (S.). Die Symbolik der Zahlen in der Philosophie und dem Mysticismus aller Voelker (En hébreu). La symbolique des nombres dans la philosophie et la mystique de tous les peuples. Wien, 1896, in-8°.
SABATHIER (R. P. Esprit). L'Ombre idéale de la Sagesse Universelle. Paris, 1679, in-16 ; id., 1897.
SAGITTARIUS (Paul-Mart.). Oratio de numero septenario. Allenburg, 1672, in4°.
SAINT-MARTIN (L. Cl. de). Des Nombres. Œuvre posthume. Edition autographiée. Paris, 1843, 2e éd., 1861, gr. in-8°; 3e éd. Paris, Chacornac, 1914, in-8°.
SAINT-YVES D'ALVEYDRE. Brevet d'invention du 26 juin 1903. Instruments de précision. Poids et mesures. Instruments de mathématiques, n° 333-393. - Moyen d'appliquer la règle musicale à l'architecture, aux beaux-arts, métiers et industries, d'arts graphiques et plastiques, moyen dit: étalon - archéométrique. Paris, nov. 1903, br. gr. in-8°.
- L'Archéomètre. Clef de toutes les religions et de toutes les Sciences dans l'Antiquité. Réforme synthétique de tous les arts contemporains. Paris, 1911, in-4°.
SALOMON. Questions inédites de magie arithmétique polygonale. Etoiles magiques à 8, 16 et 20 branches et rosaces hypermagiques. Paris, 1913, broch. in-8°
SANDER (C. G.). Practical Numerology and Character Analysis. London, S. d., in-8°.
SCHMIDT (J.-J.). Biblischer Mathematiens. Zullichau, 1749, in-8°.
SCHOTTUS (Gasp.). Magie universalis naturæ et arte. Bembergæ, 1677, 4 vol. in4°.
SCHWALLER (R.). Etude sur les Nombres. Paris, 1914, in-8°.
SÉDIR. Note sur les noms de nombres hébraïques. Paris, L'Initiation, t. 22, p. 11, janv. 1894.
SEPHARIAL. Fortune Telling by Numbers. London, S. d., in-8°.
- Your fortune in your name, of Kabalistic Astrology, being the Hebraic method of divination by the Power of sound, number and planetary influences. London, 1892, in-8°.

SEPHARIAL. A manual of Occultism, etc. London, W. Rider, 1910, in-12 (Part 1, numerology). - The Kabala of Numbers. London, 1911, in8°; London, 1920, 2 v. in-8°.
SERRE (Joseph). Un penseur Lyonnais, un grand mystique, un Pythagore français. Lacuria, 1806-1890. Portr. Paris, 1910, in-8°.
SEVANE (Marquis de). Elliptische Philosophie des verbogen Wirkenden. Pantanamische Pantanomie, oder das fünffache Universal gesetz. Publié avec le texte français en regard; Philosophie elliptique du latent opérant. Pentanomie Pentanomique ou loi quintuple universelle. Francf. S.-M., Rommel, 1880, in-8°.
SEXTIUS, philosophe pythagoricien. Sentences, trad. en français avec des notes et des variantes, précédées de la doctrine de Pythagore et de celle de Sextius, par le comte P. de Lasteyrie. Paris, 1843, in-12.
SHIRVOOD, anglicus. De ludo arithmomachiæ. Romæ, 1482, in-4°.
STIFEL (Mich.). Ein sehr Wunderbarl wortrechnung saint chi merckl. erklerung etlich. zalen Danielis und der Offenbarung St. Johannis, S. 1. Christ. Ottendorffer,1553, in-4°, 55 ff.
STOURDZA (Prince G.). Les lois fondamentales de l'Univers. Paris, 1891, in-8°.
STUART (S.). Mystic Numbers and Occult Chronology. Benarès, The Pilgrim, février 1914.
TABRIS (Jean). La Qabbalah Initiatique. Paris, L'Initiation, no 10, juillet 1897, p. 46.
TATY. Franklin et les Nombres. Paris, L'Initialion, mars 1908. TAYLOR (John). Wealth the number of the Best, 666, in the Book of Revelation. London, 1844, in-8°.
THEONIS smyrnæi, eorum quæ in mathematicis ad Platonis lectionem utilia sunt, expositio, Parisiis, 1644, in-4°.
- Epilogue, le nombre de Platon. Texte grecet trad. de J. Dupuis. Paris, Hachette, 1892, gr. in-8°.
THOMAS (Edme). Histoire de l'Antique cité, d'Autun. Illustrée et annotée par l'abbé Devoucoux. Autun. Paris, 1846, in-4°.
TRANSON (A.). Réflexions sur l'événement scientifique d'une formule publiée par Wronski en 1812, et démontrée par M. Cayley en 1873. Paris, 1874, broch. in-8°.
- Two SERVANTS OF CHRIST. The computation of 666. London, 1891, in-8°.
TYCHO-BRAHÉ. Calendarium naturale perpetuum magicum. S. 1. (Uranienborg), 1582, in-8°.
UBRICHT (C.). Anleitung zur leichten und doch richtigen Niifertigung der so wonderbaren Zauber-Quadrate. Mit erlænternden Beispilen und Kurzen
Berechnungen Nebst 6 Zaubertafeln mit Spruch und 7 Kleinen Zahlentabellen. Quedlinburg, 1854, in-8°.
ULIC (J.-C.). Y.-King, Tao-sec, Taote-King et la numération. Paris, L'Initiation, t. 37, p. 266, dée. 1897.
UNCIACUS (G.). Numeralium locorum decas... Lugduni, 1584, in-12.
UPJOHN (J. A.). The number counted 666. Neenah, Wisconsin, 1882, in-8°.
USENER. Dreiheit, ein versuch mythologischer Zahlenlehre. Bonn, RheinMuseum, 1903.
VAGETIUS (Augustinus) et ALB. ZUM Felde. Dissertatio de pari aliisque quadrati magici generibus. Witlembergiœ, 1695, in-4°.
- Dissertatio de quadrato magico impari. Id., 1695, in-4°.
VIGENERE (Blaise de). Traité des Chiffres, ou secrètes manières d'écrire. Paris, 1587, in-4°.
VILLOT (F.). Origine astronomique du jeu des échecs, expliquée par le calendrier égyptien, ou mémoire relatif à la méthode de formation d'une table qui présente d'une

manière distincte, et dans le plus petit nombre possible, toutes les combinaisons d'un nombre de signes donnés, etc. Paris, 1825, in-8°. Avec un gr. tabl.
VINCENT (H). Passage du traité de la musique d'Aristide Quintillien, relatif au nombre nuptial de Platon, etc. Rome, 1865, in-4°.
VIOLLE (B.). Traité complet des carrés magiques pairs et impairs, etc., suivi d'un traité des cubes magiques. Paris, 1837, 2 vol. in-8° et Atlas, in-fol. de 54 Pl.
VIVIANI (V.). De maximis et minimis geometrica divinatio in quintum conicorum Apollonii pergæi nunc desideratum. Florentiæ, 1659, in-fol.
VULLIAUD (Paul). La Tradition pythagoricienne. Paris, Les Entretiens Idéalistes, 1914; Id., Le Voile d'Isis, 1934. VURGEY. La quadrature du cercle. Paris, L'Initiation, t. 8, p. 425.
- Contribution à la philosophie des Nombres.Paris, L'Initiation, t. X, p. 331, janv. 1891.
WALTON (R. P.). Names, Dates, and Numbers. A system of Numerology. London, S. d., in-8°.
WARRAIN (P.). La Synthèse concrète. Etude métaphysique de la vie. Paris, 1906, in-8°; id., Chacornac, 1910.
- Les modalités universelles. L'Espace. Paris,1908, in-8°.
- Réflexions sur le système décimal. Paris, LeVoile d'Isis, mai 1913.
WEBSTER (Doris) and HOPKINS (M. A.). I've got your Number. London, s. d., in-8°.
WELLING (G. de). Opus mago-cabbalisticum et theosophicum darinnem der Ursprung, Natur, Eigenschafften und Gebrauch des Salzes Schwefels und Mercury... Francf. und Leipzig, 1760, in-4° (Pl.).
WEST. Exposé des méthodes générales en mathématiques d'après Wronski. Paris, 1886, in-4°.
WESTCOTT (Dr Wynn). Numbers, their Occult power and mystic virtues. London, 1890, in-4° ; 21 édition, London, 1902, in8°; id., 1911.
WILKINS (S.). Mathematical magie of the wonders that may be performed by mechanical geometry. In two books. London, 1648, in-8°.
WOEPCKE. Notice sur une théorie ajoutée par Thabit ben Korrah à l'arithmétique spéculative des Grecs. Paris, L'Initiation, mai 1903.
WOLFII (Ch.). Elements matheseos universæ. Genevæ, 1694, 4 vol. in-fol.
WRONSKI (Hoëné). Œuvres mathématiques. Paris, 1811, 4 vol. gr. in-8°. ; réimpression 1930, avec portr. en photot.
- Messianisme ou réforme absolue du savoirhumain. Paris, 1847, 3 vol. in-4°. - Nomothétique messianique. Paris, 1861, in4°.
- Apodictique messianique fondant péremptoirement la vérité sur la terre. Paris, 1876, in-4°.
X (Colonel). Des nombres dans l'Univers manifesté. Paris, Annales Théos., ler trim., 1908.
X. Note sur un point de la théorie des nombres. Paris, L'Initiation, no 9, juin 1898.
YVON-VILLARCEAU (M.). Application de la théorie des sinus des ordres supérieurs à l'intégration des équations linéaires. Paris, 1886, broch. in-8°.
ZAHN (J.). Specula phisico-mathematica. Norimbergœ,, 1696, 3 vol. in-fol.
ZITSCHER (H.). Philosophische Unterzushungen. Leipzig, 1910, in-8°.

On Numbers

by Louis-Claude de Saint-Martin

1861
(posthumous)

Figure 19: Portrait of Saint-Martin provided to the publisher by Matter.

Foreword

A few words are needed to explain both the reason for this publication and the origin of these documents: the *Book of Numbers* and *Shedding Light on Human Association*[216].

Fifteen years ago, and we admit this with complete candor, *Saint-Martin* and his Works were completely unknown to us.

We acquired a large number of books and manuscripts at an estate sale, among which was one entitled: *The Book of Numbers*.

In our profound ignorance we initially believed that it was a translation of the *Liber Numerorum* from the Bible, and a quick read confirmed that our understanding was incorrect. But then, from whom did this singularly apocalyptic work come? Consulting our sources, we learned that it was a posthumous work by Saint-Martin.

Who was Saint-Martin? Who had he been? We learned about him at The Imperial Library.

This is what we read in Michaud's *Biography*, from which we give here only a short excerpt, leaving it to a more skillful writer to publish shortly a biography of Saint-Martin, whose clear merit means it will be both an act of justice and one of literary rehabilitation.

"Louis-Claude de Saint-Martin, called the *Unknown Philosopher*, was born in Amboise to a noble family on the 18th of January, 1743. He owed the first elements of his tender and pious education to his mother-in-law which, he said, made him love God and men throughout his life. At the college at Pont-Levoy, to which he had been sent at an early age, the book he liked most of all was Abadie's, entitled: *The Art of Knowing Yourself*. It was to the reading of this book that he attributed his detachment from the things of this world."

"Intended by his parents to follow a career in the judiciary, in his legal studies he focused on the foundations of justice rather than on

---

[216] In French *l'Éclair sur l'Association humaine*. **Note**: as explained in the Foreword at the beginning of this book, *Shedding Light on Human Assocation* is not included in this publication as it has no bearing on the subject of Numbers – PV.

the rules of jurisprudence, whose study he found repugnant. However, he preferred a military profession to his duties as a magistrate, since he felt he would have to give all his time to the latter. As it was peacetime, this left him with plenty of spare time to spend his hours in meditation. At the age of twenty-two, he entered the Regiment of Foix, then garrisoned in Bordeaux. Initiated through formulas, rituals and practices into *theurgic* operations managed by Martinez de Pasqually, the head of the Martinist sect, he often asked: *Master, but is all this necessary to know God?* This path, which was one of physical manifestations, never seduced our philosopher. However, it was through this means that he entered into the path of Spiritualism."

We will pass over his studies, his works, his travels and his relationships, to add only these few lines taken from the same biography:

"In 1803 he said that, now being in his sixties, he was moving towards the great pleasures that had long since been told to him. In the summer of that year, he travelled to Amboise, Orléans, etc., to revisit a few friends. On his return, a meeting he had wanted to have with a profound mathematician concerning the science of numbers, whose hidden meaning still occupied him, took place with Mr. de Rossel. At the end of the meeting, he said, finishing, *"I feel that I am leaving. Providence can call me, for I am ready. The seeds I have striven to sow will grow. I give thanks to heaven for giving me the last favor I asked of it."* The next day, one of his zealous followers saw him get into the carriage which took him to the home of Senator Lenoir La Roche in the village of Aunay. After a light meal, having retired to his room, he had an attack of apoplexy. Although his tongue was obstructed, he was nevertheless able to be heard by his friends, who had come running and were gathered around him. Sensing that all human help had become useless, he urged those around him to put their trust in Providence and to live together as brothers in evangelical affection. Then he prayed to God in silence and expired without pain on the 13th of October, 1803."

The works of Saint-Martin have aroused a pleasant yet ardent curiosity in us. We have often wondered how this man, of such rare merit, endowed with all the qualities of heart and mind, and with such exemplary manners could become so forgotten in such a short space of time...

The idea then came to us to search for all his literary works, and our efforts have been crowned with complete success. These works, of a mysticism purified by a burning faith can, to our mind, occupy the human mind in a useful and pious way.

To this end, we will successively publish all the works of Saint-Martin, of which we have the rarest editions, all reviewed and corrected by the only too modest *Unknown Philosopher*.

It will be a most curious collection, because these books are profound in knowledge of all kinds and can spread a fortifying and comforting balm through the mind. Any ideas which respect Christian belief, and which have God as their object are worthy subjects for meditation, even if one found therein but ten lines capable of silencing us in order to better love the Creator of the Universe.

And if we are asked by what right we may publish these works, we will reply with these lines of Saint-Martin, a true *literary testament*, which we have taken from one of his letters addressed to Baron von Kirchberger, drawn from the unpublished correspondence between those two remarkable men, from the 22nd of May, 1792 to the 7th of November, 1797, which manuscript we also possess.

Paris, 8th June, 1792. . .

"You desire, Sir, to know what other works have come out of the pen that wrote *Of Errors and Truth*; they are, hitherto, *Le Tableau Naturel*, printed in 1782, and *L'Homme de Désirs*, printed two years ago. The edition was few in number, and there are none left; but I learn that a publisher of the name of *Grabit*, on Rue Mercière in Lyon, had just issued a reprint on his own account. Besides these there are now in the press two works from the same pen; one called *Ecce Homo*, the object of which is to forewarn people against the wonders and the prophecies of the time; it is a small volume in12mo: the title of the other is *Le Nouvel Homme*, a much larger work, the aim of which is to describe what we should expect in regeneration; it is one volume 8vo. This last has large and direct relation to the object in which you are interested, and on which I have briefly given you my ideas above. Both works are being printed in Paris (Cercle Social, rue du Théâtre-Français). *I have nothing whatever to do with the costs of this undertaking; I will have no part in any profit, should there be any; I leave all to the publisher, who by his advances had made himself the legitimate owner.*"[217]...

The experience which we have had of the moral effect produced through studying the works of the *Unknown Philosopher* over the past fifteen years has inspired us to undertake a reprint of the works of this admirable man, who sought good and not noise and reputation, and whose fame is so below what he will one day attain among discerning minds.

Those who follow us in this a study will, we believe we can affirm in advance, discover treasures of consolation and appeasement for the soul, things which are always most desirable, especially in our days of turmoil and unrest, when there is sometimes no refuge other than solitude, or at least silence.

And how many times did Saint-Martin say to his friends, who almost always ended up becoming his disciples: "During the days of disorder, the best advice to give to those we love is contained in these three words which were so often the rule of my life: *Fuge, Late, Tace*.[218]"

L. SCHAUER
Paris, the 20th of October, 1861

---

[217] Translation taken from Edward Burton Penny, *Theosophic Correspondence*, first published 1863 – PV.
[218] Run away, hide, keep silent – PV.

Preface by Matter

Invited by a flattering confidence to express my thoughts on the interest this publication might offer in our environment of critical studies and negativity, I accepted without ignoring the difficulty of such a task, however small it may appear. If I didn't hesitate, it's because, in my opinion, there is something important to be said about the most obscure of the writings by the greatest French mystic of the end of the last century.

Mysticism is one of the most rarified and least appreciated forms in our philosophy. Yet it is an element which, while it shouldn't dominate, certainly shouldn't be absent from religious thought; and if there are times when it must be opposed, there are others when we should return to some extent to its speculative audacity and its powers of belief. It is, in matters of faith, the highest poetry.

In general, every mystical thinker is welcomed by philosophy with the esteem his thoughts deserve. But, with regard to Claude de Saint-Martin, there is a specific criticism: it is that in many of his writings, and notably in *Numbers*, his language has damaged his own cause.

It has been said that, by explaining his thoughts in terms more obscure than was necessary, he brought French mysticism away from the path which Fénelon had introduced with such taste and brilliance; that as an imitator of a Portuguese and a German[219], he threw thick veils over what, on the contrary, demanded the brightest rays of light; and as a curious patron of those novelties which seduced so many other enthusiasts of his century, using mysticism and Theosophy on the one hand and secret or occult knowledge on the other, he created that blend which debased his doctrine and compromised it in the eyes of wholesome philosophy.

It is very true that Saint-Martin singularly broadened the paths of mysticism by embracing in his studies everything which his times could offer him. But that is the great merit of his aspirations: they are universal, even if his ideas were communicated less than

---

[219] Referring to Martines de Pasqually and to Jakob Böhme – PV.

perfectly when compared to those of Fénelon. While never intending to put his writings within everyone's reach, in most of them his thoughts are very lucid, if not wherever they address the great mysteries – and even there they are sufficiently transparent for readers who have some familiarity with these kinds of studies – at least everywhere else.

But we shouldn't ask any more of him than we would of anyone else.

The *Treatise on Numbers* is, moreover, an exception in several respects. It is an essay on the most mysterious of problems, a gauge of science which, if not secret, is at least apocalyptic[220].

For those who wish to decipher the mysteries hidden by Saint-Martin beneath the veil of *Numbers*, the special study strongly recommended by the new editor of *Baader's Commentaries* on Saint-Martin, Baron von Osten-Sacken, while he states that he doesn't claim to judge the value of the treatise, will find some guidance in those *Commentaries*. The best ones, the only good ones – that is to say the only ones which give the key to the figures of the Unknown Philosopher – are found in an unpublished Treatise[221] by his master: a Treatise which, by a singular coincidence, came into my hands as I was writing these lines. Perhaps those who one day will manage to fathom the enigma by means of such assistance, will do well to push the art of deciphering a little further, and embrace in their research an as yet unpublished notebook of hieroglyphics, to which Saint-Martin seems to have attached the greatest price[222].

Normally, any speculative treatise on Numbers is a little frightening at first glance. But in my opinion this is wrong. A study which occupied Pythagoras' great intelligence should not alarm our

---

[220] In the sense of being revelatory – PV.

[221] This is clearly referring to Martinez de Pasqually's Treatise on the Reintegration of Beings, in which Pasqually's special treatment of the numbers 1 to 10 are clearly set out, and whose interpretation is reflected by Saint-Martin in his writings – PV.

[222] This is almost certainly the *Registre des 2400 noms d'anges et d'archanges*, or *Registry of 2,400 names of Angels and Archangels*. This book contains a large number of tables linking the names to sigils which the Elu Cohen would use to identify the name of the angel whose sigil he had seen while performing one of the theurgical operations prescribed by Pasqually – PV.

reason so easily. Basically, we're less afraid of the loftiness of such a study than we are of public opinion, of the misfortune of being taken for a seeker of mysteries. Searching for mysteries? What an aberration in the eyes of the masses! Yet what a common thing to do: for that's what reason is concerned with. And reason would certainly complain if there were no more mysteries.

And wanting to know the value of mysticism doesn't make you a mystic, moreover: it only makes you a philosopher.

After all, to speculate about numbers is only to consider the relationships between things in nature, whether material or spiritual.

To the first point, the relationships between principals and consequences, or causes and effects, are poorly expressed in numbers. However, don't we express the proportions which exist between them in numbers?

It is also true that the question of relationships implies other issues, such as that of origins, and that the question of proportions implies that of the end of all things. But here again the science of numbers finds a place: aren't time and space two necessary factors in these issues, and aren't they both expressed in numbers?

And indeed, these questions are precisely the greatest ones in all of philosophy!

So perhaps we should be encouraging the trust of those who are still tested by these questions, even in their most abstract forms, instead of doing the opposite. This would be just as well, since it is the eternal mission of those very questions to test the human mind.

What Saint-Martin, who had a good knowledge of physics, put forward in his treatise *On Numbers* in a style which is peculiar to him and cherished by mystics, even at the risk of not always understanding it, others have also suggested from their point of view, some from the angle of mythology interpreted by pantheism, others from the angle of cosmology explained by both positive science and free speculation. The mystical science of numbers has grown, and without dwelling on the considerable work of the pious Eckartshausen, a learned pupil of the Martinist school, Mr. de Herbert has, in manuscripts that I have before me, left striking comparisons, even though the mind might distrust or reject them, as mine does.

So, Saint-Martin's treatise has its own intrinsic value to friends of philosophy. I thought, however, that I owed the generous eagerness that Mr. Schauer has put towards publishing *Numbers*, and to his zeal to glorify the first mystic of our century, the counsel of adding to such an apocalyptic writing by a thinker who is so little read by us after a period of sixty years, a publication which is by its very nature accessible to all, and which has become very rare. By this I mean *Shedding Light on Human Society,* which even the most avaricious bibliophiles have not always been able to find.

Besides, this piece of writing is appropriate in order to provide at the same time the principal features of Saint-Martin's morality, politics and philosophical speculation.

Following the *Letter on the French Revolution*, which its author, who singularly esteemed everything he wrote, thought of so highly, I know nothing by him which would make him better known and be more in his style.

Indeed, in his works on religious morality and theosophy, it is usually his masters, Martinez de Pasqually and Jakob Boehme who we believe we hear; while in his pages on morality and politics, it is him who speaks. However, however inferior he may be to the genius of the one of two guides he follows the most – Boehme – he is nevertheless more lucid and eloquent when he is himself than when he is translating. When he interprets or imitates the Teutonic philosopher, he is more profound, that is true; but when independent he is more original. He is then free to the point of going everywhere, as far as an extreme limit of disdain for the opinions of everybody else.

This is the reason that the following two things happened to him: firstly, he was listed among the thinkers who were abandoned, and secondly, he was condemned as a retrograde spirit.

Above all, he was misunderstood and seen as a political writer through his *Letter* and through his *Shedding Light.* He was arrested in 1793 and 1797 as a defender of the old ways, and as the misguided apostle of a theocracy outlawed as an experiment or swallowed up by the torrent of that century. This was despite the unique theocracy which was his, in which there was no serious place for the priesthood! Claude de Saint-Martin wanted the reign of God, this is true, but what a difference between his politics and those of Bossuet!

I would like to expand on this point of view elsewhere, in a special work on Saint-Martin, his master and his disciples.[223]

What is needed in his very mystical concept is the restoration of the original relationship between God and man, the pure and complete submission of human thought to Divine Thought, from human law to Divine Law. Undoubtedly his politics, which were straightforward, was religion; but his religion was not pure theocracy, it was the most abstract theosophy to which it is possible for the human mind to go. To speak in his terms, so to speak, it is the highest speculation which is possible for the Divine Mind to bring to the human mind; because that was his theory.

As we can see, this stance, which is completely theosophical, has nothing in common with the system withered by history under the name of theocracy. A system in which God's ministers call themselves His natural delegates in the government of this world, didn't work at all for the mystic who found it unwelcome that "so many people believe themselves to be priests, because that prevented them learning to become priests."

For my part, I put a low price on pages on politics attempting the impossible: rehabilitating a doctrine that no longer had any life. I believe, on the contrary, that an element of high social speculation might to mix usefully with our all-positivist systems, and that a politics of pure discussion, beginning with Helvetius and Rousseau, would today be offered to us as a novel attraction. And that is the character and merit of *Shedding Light*. This is the writing of one of the most enthusiastic admirers of the author of the *Social Contract*. Indeed, despite their differences, it is not a contemporary

---

[223] Indeed, Jacques Matter published *Saint-Martin le Philosophe Inconnu* in1862, the year after this book, and which remained the definitive work until those of Papus, A. E. Waite, Robert Amadou were written based on updated facts, and which continue up to the preset day as more information comes to light – PV.

writer that the Unknown Philosopher puts above the Citizen of Geneva.

It is not, therefore, only the rarity of the piece that my advice relates to: I considered its usefulness, its speculative utility, that is. Let's not claim to make Saint-Martin what he wasn't and cannot become: a critical metaphysicist and practical guide. The role delineated for him is different. He despised all human science. In this regard he never hesitated. His mind knew no doubt: it is God himself who governs everything. His life was almost not of this world. He only came here by dispensation. What he loved was to isolate himself from men, to detach himself from the earthly to contemplate the divine. He turned away from all the things we love so much. To all those things we care little about, he attached himself with a burst of enthusiasm. He often explained this. It was his favorite master, Jacques Boehme who made of him a sort of inspired enthusiast. I was going to say the German metaphysicist. Perhaps that is what makes it easier to understand the sympathies he held for Germany, and the singular affinities he felt for Schelling, that other admirer of Boehme. That also explains the admiration which Francis Baader and his large school professed for him, where the idea of giving the works of Saint-Martin an edition as accurate and complete as those of the Works of Schelling by the son of the great thinker, and those of Baader's Works by his eminent disciple Hoffmann of Wurzburg, publications that have not yet received the attention they deserve among us.

Nothing will serve these pious purposes better than Mr. Schauer's publication and the generous research he continues which are so worthy of gratitude.

Two facts are certain: the first is that the works of Saint-Martin are very poorly published, and that there are a number which remain unpublished; the second is that all of them demand to be published carefully, and if not with rich clarifications, at least with clear annotations.[224]

For me, having been in possession of the most beautiful of the portraits I know of him for a long time, I did not hesitate to entrust

---

[224] And it is Jacques Matter's advice which I have tried to follow in all my translations of Saint-Martin and Papus – PV.

it to the editors of this volume in exchange for a number of copies. Having this portrait from a person whom Saint-Martin honored with devoted friendship, I must assert my ownership of it by making a public declaration.

The editors have done me too much credit by asking me for permission to reprint two articles about a few people who were connected with Saint-Martin, and who are not well known; especially Mrs. de Boecklin, who was believed to be the Duchess of Bourbon, since Saint-Martin usually referred to her only by her initials, which was confusing.

MATTER.
Paris, the 20th of October, 1861

Having read the learned and valuable work with which Mr. Matter, Honorary Inspector-General of Public Education, has kindly seen fit to honor the publication of these two works by Saint-Martin, the reader will be grateful, we hope, for the reproduction here of two articles written with such erudite knowledge and perfect elegance, so suave and so clear, published by Mr. Matter in the Journal d'Alsace in November 1860 and April 1861.

S-M, Mme de Bœcklin, Two Salzmanns, Goethe

FIRST ARTICLE

Dear Sir,

I am writing to appeal to the *Revue d'Alsace* and its readership to obtain, if possible, information of general interest that I haven't been able to find elsewhere and, in this instance, to rectify a biographical error which is becoming too common everywhere, and which is particularly extraordinary in Alsace[225]. The purpose of my letter is therefore twofold, but I will be as brief as the nature of things will permit.

One of the most distinguished men of the end of the last century, and who described himself as the *Unknown Philosopher* in his early writings, but who did not remain unknown – or a philosopher – for long, Saint-Martin, went to Strasbourg around 1790 to spend what became the most decisive years of his life. Applying his fine abilities and noble tendencies to the study of the mystical sciences, but dissatisfied with the practices and pretensions of some of the secret associations with which he was affiliated, and even less satisfied with the spirit of other societies which courted him, he suddenly began to study German to allow him to read the greatest mystical philosopher of the seventeenth century, Jakob Bœhme. The ex-officer fell in love with that philosopher, who is now also advocated by Schelling, Baader and Feuerbach, but who was then little praised, with such enthusiasm that he worked to publish a French translation of some of his works, setting aside the writings of Swedenborg and interviews with the nephew of that great visionary, Mr. Silfverhielm, whom he had met in Strasbourg.

---

[225] Strasbourg is in the Départment of Alsace in France, on the border of the Rhine, and Matter is saying that it is all the more extraordinary that historians of the very region of Strasbourg should make a major error in their writings concerning Mr. Salzmann – PV.

Two people from Strasbourg, Madame de Bœcklin and Mr. Salzmann, were the initiators[226] of Saint-Martin into the study of mysticism – or rather – of the theosophy of Bœhme. It is regarding these two people that I need to seek information and also make a correction.

Who was Madame de Bœcklin? That is the information sought.

Twenty years ago, all I had to do was ask Mrs. Salzmann this question to get all the information I needed. Mrs. Salzmann, to whom Saint-Martin liked to read his early writings, and from whom I possess a beautiful portrait of the noble thinker, had known him and his friends in Strasbourg just as Mr. Salzmann himself had. She had known better than him Saint-Martin's female connections, just like those who connected her to the Duchess of Bourbon, all of whom were focused on the sanctification of life and the progress of mystical studies. We know how devoted Saint-Martin was to the Duchess: it was something more absolute, and above all more mystical, than Abbé Barthélemy's devotion to the Duchess of Choiseul: yet his relationship with Madame Bœcklin was even more precious to him. He had difficulty raising Madame de Bourbon up to his level. The somewhat gullible mind of the princess inclined her to the aberrations of the day; in addition to Mesmer and the Puységurs[227], she listened to rather vulgar oracles and somnambulists, and his conversations with her did not exceed a certain level. Madame de Bœcklin, on the other hand, understood Saint-Martin completely, and he helped her to raise herself higher. She tore him away from those theurgical operations of Martinez de Pasqually and the secret societies of Bordeaux, Marseille and Lyon for which he had developed a taste. She made him understand that theurgy didn't lead to true theosophy, and she showed him the purest source of that study, which rarely remains pure, which strays so easily and wanders so far off. Saint-Martin – and his *Memoirs* attest to this – followed these signs, for they were simply that, with docile ardor. He made Jacques Bœhme his true master, the judge

---

[226] In the sense of introducing him to the writings of – PV..

[227] The Marquis of Puységur and his wife were ardent followers of animal magnetism, or mesmerism. Being from one of the most illustrious French noble families, his opinions carried some weight at that time – PV.

of all his doctrines, the guide of his highest aspirations. He preferred him to Swedenborg himself. He states quite clearly that he had only two masters, Martinez de Pasqually, whose name he wrote as incorrectly as that of Madame de Bœcklin, and Jacques Bœhme.

Mr. Salzmann, as enthusiastic about the Teutonic philosopher as Madame de Bœcklin, recommended him – as she did – to their mutual friend. He understood the texts of the famous mystic as well as she, his writings tell us, and it is difficult, even impossible today to distinguish the share of influence of each of these two initiators. Saint-Martin, who said that he found many people who wanted to be masters barely capable of being disciples, speaks too much of Madame de Bœcklin, and too little of Salzmann. Madame de Bœcklin's authority was predominant over his mind, as her friendship was with his heart, which leaks out once or twice either in his memoirs or in his correspondence: Saint-Martin calls her a little colloquially, if I can be forgiven the word, *My Dear Bœcklin*, or *My Darling B*. But this familiarity is more than redeemed by these lines: "I have a friend in this world like no other. I know it is she alone to whom I can pour out my soul with ease, and discuss the great subjects that concern me, because I know it is she alone who has placed herself in that position to the extent that I desire someone to be useful to me. Despite the benefits I obtain when I am with her, we are separated by circumstances. My God, Who knows the need I have of her, send her my thoughts and send me hers; and, if possible, shorten the time of our separation."

Now, how can it be that, in a city as literary as Strasbourg, such a distinguished woman could have gone unnoticed? Or indeed, should I ask the question in a different way, and ask *myself* how it happened, and to *myself* alone perhaps, how I had not even heard her name spoken in my youth? And how is it that I find no trace of it today? Undoubtedly, if I had read the *Historical and Philosophical Portrait* of Saint-Martin written by himself earlier, that is the memoires of Saint-Martin, and if I had known how to pose the question earlier, I would have more easily obtained an answer. That educated women who shone thirty and forty years ago in Strasbourg society, Baroness Frank, whose hospitable home received and attracted the most distinguished in the country and also those from foreign lands; Madame de Montbrison, the spiritual daughter of the spiritual Baroness of Oberkirch, who united all the advantages of birth with those of a singular education; the Baroness of Faviers, whose mind was so vast and heart so high: those women so eminent in the former society of Strasbourg, the last two having ended their days in Paris, but who in their youth had met in the salons with the noble friend Saint-Martin, had not only known her, but had certainly listened to and appreciated her. Today there are still a few people around who enjoyed the charm or instruction of her words, but is there one who received confidences from her during their studies? This is the information that in desperation I seek through the channels of publicity, having knocked fruitlessly on the door of the only man of my acquaintance who still bears the name that was so dear to Saint-Martin, and then at the door of the eldest daughter of the illustrious Schweighæuser; and finally, at the door of the dean of the men of letters by whom Alsace is honored, Mr. Lamey.

I now come to the second initiator of Saint-Martin and the *rectification* which concerns him: Mr. Salzmann. In this case it is not a matter of a mere oversight, but a complete expunging.

This theosophist writer, born in 1749, shares with an educated woman the merit of having snatched the noble abilities of the "Unknown Philosopher" from the study of occult sciences by engaging him in the mystical sciences; sciences of lesser worth in the eyes of some, but immense in the eyes of others. Mr. Salzmann had other and even greater merits; but today he has the misfortune to risk even his person, threatened not only by having himself merged with another person, but even being completely annihilated thereby. In fact, there were in Strasbourg during the last thirty years of the eighteenth century and at the beginning of ours, two men of letters with the same name, belonging to the same family, and quite close relatives. One was the Secretary of a Municipal Commission (*Actuarius*) and a regular guest of Goethe, Jung-Stilling and Herder during these three characters' stay in Strasbourg in 1771, when they were young and unknown, before later becoming so famous. The other, an adviser to the legation of the Duchy of Saxony, was closely linked with Saint-Martin during the philosopher's stay in Strasbourg in 1790. Out of that connection, not really continued through correspondence, came another with Jung-Stilling, continued from 1791 to 1810, and embellished with a correspondence of the greatest interest for the history of mysticism during this period (it is in my possession), and which seems to have singularly eclipsed the relationship between of Salzmann and Saint-Martin, who was somewhat harassed, like Salzmann, during the Terror, and who died in 1803.

One cannot conceive of two men more different than the two cousins Salzmann, the one, Goethe's friend, who died in 1812; the other, Saint-Martin's friend, who died in 1821.

Nor can one conceive a more restless life than that of the one, the legation adviser who was a journalist under Louis XVI, the Republic, the Terror, the Directory, the Consulate and the Empire; nor a quieter life than that of the other, who was an *Actuarius* and Goethe's friend.

And yet it is precisely the latter, the one who was nothing except a man of taste and a good man who has become a famous figure who, as a friend of Goethe, is assured of living forever in the history of letters: for he will appear in perpetuity in all the biographies of the incomparable poet; while the other, the author of fifteen printed volumes and as many manuscript volumes, is known only in the very small circle of the most pious and mystical theosophists.

That's not all: since his cousin never put his name on any of his books, the fortunate *Actuarius*, a true skinny cow[228], threatens to swallow the fat cow, the legation advisor and author of so many volumes, to the point of leaving no trace of him. Indeed, not only are these two men who are so different confused with one another, making the two one and the same individual; but we have seen the one absorbed by the other. And this isn't just vague tradition nor ignorant carelessness: it is history and biography which makes this mistake. At least it is not foreigners, for example the English or the

---

[228] Matter is making reference to the story of the Pharaoh's dream in Genesis 41, where the seven skinny cows ate up the seven fat cows, signifying seven years of plenty followed by seven years of famine. Here Matter is equating the Actuarius with the skinny cows as a metaphor for the untalented cousin swallowing the reputation of his far more talented relative – PV.

Americans, who did this: in fact, it is scholars, it is even their compatriots who propagate this. They are, in a word, people who you might have jostled in the small streets of the erudite city on the Rhine. You yourself, my dear Sir, are a little complicit in the fact, whereas you may think yourself completely innocent. Dietrich's elegant biographer, one of the most brilliant members of the phalanx of Alsace historians indeed does this in the Review, when he confuses the advisor and the *Actuarius*, in saying that Goethe's spiritual friend supported the worthy mayor of Strasbourg in his diary.

There's more. Among the councilor's own friends, the very learned Schubert, who had just finished his glorious career so honorably, provides an example of absorption. It is not possible to speak of Mr. Frédéric-Rodolphe Salzmann in a more touching and admirable way than Mr. de Schubert, who had visited him in 1820, did two times; and yet Mr. de Schubert, who knows so well the writings of his friend the colleague of Saint-Martin, believed that he was speaking with the *Actuarius*, Goethe's friend, the man who had died in 1812, a man he had never read and from whom he had never received a letter – but whose name illuminated by a reflection which came from Goethe dominated his thoughts, and misplaced his imagination to the point of making him commit the most striking nonsense and anachronisms.

If this happens with friends, is it any wonder that this happens with others, and since the purpose of the *Alsace Review* is to illustrate former illustrious men of Alsace, and as it is, besides, a little complicit in this confusion, is it not right that it would be the main organ to *rectify* this error?

It is not unusual to confuse two relatives with the same names living in the same period and far away with the passing of time: but that this confusion should take place in the midst of compatriots and contemporaries, is frankly astonishing.

To forget within a single generation the person who guided an illustrious philosopher distresses me deeply, for it shows us only too well what humanity is worth, what our abilities are worth, our attention, our memory, and what our traditions and our history – even contemporary and local – are worth to us.

Think about that.

When I dealt with the final years of the School of Alexandria, the fall of polytheism, the proscription of its last priests, the silence imposed on its last philosophers, the supreme covenant between them in the sanctuaries, concluded in the days of persecution after their long quarrels entertained during the days of prosperity, I found in the families of each of them certain women of idolatrous piety, educated, eloquent, who took on the task of initiating some of the most distinguished thinkers and the most loyal characters in their cult into science, religion and philosophy. In Eunapius and other historians, Ædesia, the two Asclepigenias, Sosipatra and others, I have found more precise information than I can obtain today concerning the person who exerted the happiest influence on Saint-Martin, my grandfather's friend by marriage. From Madame de Bœcklin, all I have left is the name.

We print a lot. Do we write enough? Do we notice enough?

Do we distinguish enough between what should not even enter our thoughts and what deserves to be noted and passed on to posterity?

Do we like to ask our fathers enough what they would most like to teach us?

Do we value great and beautiful family memories enough?

Do we honor, as we should, the fine examples and the great teachings which, wherever they come from, must not be given over to abandonment and indifference?

The answers to these questions are too easy. I do not ask these questions to have them answered, and it is not the basis of the questions which I ask: but rather these are lessons that I would like to suggest in this manner.

So, let us finally renounce this bizarre indifference to everything which isn't a scandal or a head-turning event; to this gross prejudice which only shows interest in the dramatic events that are related to big names. All beautiful things create beautiful names and establish beautiful traditions; and time, which is poetry, aids the memory. But we need these two powers. Let us note the beautiful things and pass them all on to posterity, they will be great examples for it.

SECOND ARTICLE

Dear Sir,

There is a real pleasure in appealing to the taste of literary investigation and the feelings of fraternal devotion in the field of historical exploration in this excellent country of Alsace: there we are understood by men of all ages, as one would be by the belligerent youth when telling him to mount a horse.[229] You kindly aided my call by asking for help and assistance concerning a person not then well known to me. Now we find she is known by everyone. Receive my deepest thanks. And above all, let me add here to the public the expression of my personal gratitude for all those who have so generously responded to my wishes.

At their head I have to name a friend, a former mayor of Strasbourg, who kindly sent me a volume, nowadays quite forgotten – the *Voyage à Paris* by Storck (of St. Petersburg) – a volume in which we read the most invaluable information concerning the Salzmann who was Goethe's friend. It seems that "this friend of a great man" was simply a charming man, and I am pleased to have the opportunity to give his memory all the tributes due to him. Rest assured that, regarding my obsession over the fact that his name threatened a sacred name for me, I now only have feelings of the most earnest justice for this involuntary usurper.

My friend's kindness has been more active and happier still. His family's relationship with the late Baroness of Ratzenried, Madame de Bœcklin's close friend, allowed him to send me interesting letters from this initiator of Saint-Martin, and precious excerpts taken from the manuscripts she admired the most.

Thanks to these documents and the correspondence of Saint-Martin with Baron von Kirchberger of Liebisdorf, which has just been made available to me by its current owner, the Earl of O.; thanks to unpublished fragments of a biography, which I owe to the

---

[229] This is an abstruse comment indeed, unless it was an epithet common in mid 19th century France! One can only assume the responses, though helpful, were not always in the most cordial of tones! Indeed, it may have been that some were none too happy with his tone when writing about Goethe's friend, a belief borne out by the following paragraph – PV.

kindness of Mr. Taschereau, Chief Administrator of the Imperial Library; and finally, thanks to a notable series of oral traditions, collected with the necessary critical review, concerning the role Madame de Bœcklin played in the studious life of a very distinguished man is now perfectly known to me, and I am able to credit Madame de Bœcklin with an appreciation that, to be less contemporary, may be more accurate.

The article which Mr. Muller published in the *Courrier du Bas-Rhine* on 28th February 1861 adds, with regard to her person and her family, indications of a richness and precision for which we most eagerly and sincerely thank the author.

Now that the truth has come to light from all sides, let us stick to history without fable or poetry. Let us no longer confuse Madame Charlotte de Bœcklin with any of her relatives. Let us not make her a 'personality'. Let us not exaggerate her role with regard to the "Unknown Philosopher" or others. She played no part in his writings. Together with Rodolphe de Salzmann, she introduced him to J. Boehme, and proved a less ecstatic guide to an excessive admirer of Swedenborg. She translated some texts of the "Teutonic philosopher" for Baron Liebisdorf. A spiritual, pious and simple woman, she ended in a somewhat modest situation a career whose beginning had promised to shine brightly, and after introducing her overly enthusiastic friend into the sanctuaries of German mysticism, she soon stopped guiding him. That is her entire role. She had the good sense not to even try rise to the level of expert. She wrote only clear letters of the highest interest.

As for Saint-Martin himself, let's not exaggerate either. He was never a "brilliant officer", and he was no longer in the service at all in 1790 when he came to Alsace. He is the greatest mystic of France in modern times; but he is neither an eminent philosopher nor an original thinker: a pale disciple of J. Boehme, he is an excessively religious soul, but pure and serene, normally a little dreamy, often more epigrammatic than was necessary.

Did his stay, which was longer than we believed, leave any physical traces in Strasbourg?

This is not the place to consider the role that mysticism and theosophy played on the banks of the Rhine at the beginning of this century, and the intent I may have suggested by drawing attention to a distinguished woman who appears in the memoirs of an enthusiastic writer from Strasbourg, who called Strasbourg his earthly paradise: that goal being fully accomplished, I reserve for other times and other pages what the papers of Mr. Salzmann, Jung-Stilling, Madame de Bœcklin, Saint-Martin and Liebisdorf teach us on this subject. As for the relationship between the great mystic and Madame Charlotte de Bœcklin, I think we should be content to know that it was above reproach. Perhaps at first glance not everyone will see, as we do, that it was always with regard to theosophy and mysticism that Saint-Martin so often speaks of her in his memoirs. And yet everyone must be clearly convinced, even in reading the lines I transcribe below, if only for the instruction of those who do not yet know enough how much one should understand her writing when she speaks about their affections and their friendship, as holy as they were.

"One of the thunderbolts of the *One who has constantly contended with me* is what happened to me in Strasbourg in 1791."

"I had been seeing my close friend every day for three years."

I'm quoting these lines to show that Saint-Martin arrived in Strasbourg as early as 1788. Until now only a one-year stay had been reported.

"For a long time we had a plan to stay together, without being able to carry it out. Finally we achieved it. But after two months, I had to leave my paradise to go and take care of my father."

"The uproar over the king's escape caused me to return from Lunéville to Strasbourg, where I spent another two weeks with my friend. But the time had come for our separation. I commended myself to the beautiful God of my life to be excused from drinking this cup; but I read clearly that, though this sacrifice was terrible, it had to be done, and I did so while shedding a torrent of tears."

Werther's century is certainly recognized in this style and over-excitement.[230]

---

[230] This is a reference to Goethe's first successful book *Die Leiden des jungen Werthers* [*The Sorrows of Young Werther*], written in 1774 in the 'Sturm und Drang' (Storm and Stress) style which preceded the Romantic novel. Full of misery, it is about a young man

"The following year, at Eastertide, when everything was arranged to return to my friend, a new illness came over my father again, at the exact time to stop all my plans..."

Who would realize that it was a fifty-year-old theosophist who was writing to a mystic born in the same year as his correspondent?

And what glory it must have been for two people to experience such friendship which was at once so alive, so enthusiastic and so holy!

It was not exclusive, however, and another page of these *Memoirs* – a page which I shall make a point of publishing one day – will reminds us that there were a number of local and foreign families which Saint-Martin saw in Strasbourg, whose society was so full of attractions for him that he made this city "his earthly paradise."

Many of these noble families are unknown to me, and I would like to risk a few more questions.

But today I would rather end these lines with an expression of the feelings with which they began: my most eager and sincere gratitude for such a courteous and generous audience.

Accept, Dear Sir, the expression, etc.

MATTER

---

who falls in love with a women, Charlotte, engaged to another man eleven years her senior. She marries the older man and Werther is forced to live next to her, knowing their love can never be requited. Eventually, from pity and duty, she tells him he can no longer see her. He visits her one last time and the emotional farewell eventually leads him to suicide. A worthy quotation indeed for Madasme de Brœcklin's predicament – PV.

Preface by Sédir

Presenting a book like this would bear witness to a somewhat risible boldness, if I did not immediately tell the benevolent reader that I am not pretentious enough to claim I can give an explanation of these precious notes, which we owe to the pious care of one of the Unknown Philosopher's posthumous disciples, Mr. L. Schauer.

Complete Knowledge is nothing more than an incarnation in our mental body of the essence of biological phenomena; its first phase is conception, its second understanding. We can conceive any phenomenon that finds in us a nerve cell capable of perceiving it: and we can only understand those phenomena whose laws are perceivable by our mind. It follows that, in our current state of advancement we can only know an infinitesimal part of the Universe, and even now our knowledge is only a proportional intermediary between the receptive capacity of the recording brain, the current appearance of the phenomenon perceived, and the state of the medium of transmission, whether fluid or mental.

There are therefore an infinite number of subjects which, by their nature, their sublimity or their complexity, remain unknown to us; those whose radiation does not reach us, whose metaphysical place is too distant, whose form is too developed.

Among all these mysterious subjects, the theosophical science of numbers occupies the first rank. It was in vain that Moses, Fuxi, the Chaldeans, Pythagoras, the Kabbalists, Trithemeus, Agrippa, Kircher, Bungius, Welling and so many others buried themselves in sublime meditations; and if they reached the goal of their abstract research, they could not or did not wish to communicate the result to us.

Among the moderns, Ragon, Abbé Lacuria, Baron Hellenbach and some others have only managecd to reproduce the general ideas of the Ancient Mysteries. J.-B. Dessoye (1863) performed original studies on the duodenary method of counting. Father Marchand (1877) presented a very suggestive arithmetic theory. But the two authors who seem to have best sensed the mysterious march of arithmosophy, are Eckartshausen and Louis-Claude de

Saint-Martin, who, although living in at the same time, seem to have known each other only by name.[231]

I do not claim to explain the systems of the two mystics here, but simply to define qualitative arithmology through negation, and to help make the whole unknown concept visible.

Take any creature: plant, animal or star. The physical, chemical and natural sciences analyze its physical form, and its homology reveals the relationships and differences of that creature with others of the same race, species or kingdom. Art can try to depict the color, shape and aesthetic movement of that creature; the philosopher ultimately discovers a series of general laws in all those observations which he extricates, and which, characterizing the essence of this creature, places it within the frameworks of a general intellectual synthesis.

But this huge agglomeration of knowledge is a building where there are no inhabitants: the walls, the windows, the doors, the sculptures, the woodwork are there: but there is no-one to vivify that slumbering palace. In other words, physical and mental knowledge constructs its structures by working from the bottom up, from the outside to the inside, from the material to the immaterial: neither scalpel, nor microscope, nor reagents, nor analysis, nor meditation, nor memory can force the object of study to show us unveiled its essential form, its type, its soul. In a word, for that it would be necessary for the thinking self to enter into that central place of Nature where Cosmic Life, the Word, works openly.

This plane, the pivot of the World, is the boundary of the junction between the Relative and the Absolute. There, creatures see themselves as God produced them at the dawn of time and at the initial point in Space. There, for every being the primitive spark by means of which he exists transitions from birth to death, from planet to sun, from sun to nebula, from physical form to fluid form, from manifest form to occult essence, from matter to spirit. Thus, every physical individual is connected in this central place to all individuals of the same spiritual root, like the leaves which make a

---

[231] However, even if they didn't meet, it seems inconceivable that Eckartshausen did not read Saint-Martin, since so much of his material reflects that of the Unknown Philosopher – PV.

tiny cosmos in the air are connected, through successive condensations from twigs to stems, from stems to branches, from branches to the main trunk.

Thus, just as all the results of experimental observation and philosophical meditation find in the mathematical sciences a precise means of expression; all possible investigations of science, both physical and intellectual, lead to the idea of time and that of space. These two cosmogonic principles Pythagoras represented respectively by the '1' and the '0' which, by splitting themselves produce number and form. The reciprocal action of these two ultimate elements is dynamism or the Word as the factor of vital manifestations. And so, we can state:

- The study of the Word[232], that is to say words, that is, the essential names of creatures.
- The study of Space, that is to say forms, or qualitative geometry.
- The study of Time, that is to say ontological number, or qualitative mathematics.

One may, if one wishes, equate these three sciences with the Son, the Spirit, and the Father. In exoteric knowledge, the above remarks find their application in the sciences of language, geometry in all its branches, and ordinary or higher mathematics.

Finally, in esoteric knowledge these remarks gave rise to the knowledge of both intellectual and magical hierograms in each case.

To the science of diagrams, seals, pentacles, etc.

And to the science of numbers.

But exotericism and esotericism are, in their current state of development or present transmission, only two aspects – manifest or hidden – of an essential pole which is integral knowledge.

Exotericism characterizes the phenomena as studied by three formulae, which are human speech, the technician's working draft and the algebraist's equation.

---

[232] This is difficult to translate: *verbe* (f.) means 'verb' in French, but *la Verbe* also refers to the Christological concept of the Word, as described in the opening verses of the Gospel of St. John. Equally, however, Sédir is referring to the idea of naming things, which gives power over them, according to the ancient Grimoires – PV.

Esotericism refers to the results of its investigations through its hieroglyphic alphabets, by its pentacles, and by its theosophical arithmetic. It should be noted, however, that the adept only penetrates the secret of creatures to a certain point; so that the verbal formula, the pattern or the magic number express only a slightly deeper aspect of the creature studied. As if the official scientist, for example, discovered the mystery of a being on Earth and the occultist discovered its connection to the Sun; but if we want to continue this analogy which should not be taken literally, know nonetheless that, beyond the Zodiac and higher than the Empyrean, beyond all physical substances and all fluid oceans is that central region of which we spoke earlier, in the annals of which all creatures without exception are indexed by their true name, their spiritual talisman and their eternal number.

But only those who have earned the title of Friends of God can leaf through that Great Book. Needless to say, there is no man on Earth who possesses the true knowledge of numbers.

Everything has a number: a nebula, a single-celled organism, a flood, a visitation, a blade of grass, a thought, a feeling, an object.

Names, shapes and numbers are not inventions of the intellect, they are like all things of which we are aware; indeed, they are objective, intelligent and free beings. Just as knowledge of the true name of a being can make that being appear, even on the other side of the world, as the *Magic of Arbatel* declares and the Evangelical traditions affirm, so its pentacular signature gives power over the form of the individual, and knowledge of its true number confers an absolute authority. However, no current human intelligence has successfully realized these ideas.

Like all branches of knowledge, numbers will only be available to us when a connection in the brain is ready to receive it. The sense of numbers, which is in fact located where the phrenologists locate it, can develop in two ways. The first, which is mnemonic, recording, quantitative, is pursued in the study of ordinary mathematics; the second, the only one which interests us, relates closely to the power of attention, to the ability of being aware of two or more intellectual objects at the same time. It develops mainly through exercising the sense of hearing, which allows the musician the analytical sensation of each individual orchestral part and at the same time of the ensemble. This is especially possible for individuals who have a particular wrinkle between the eyebrows and whose upper eyelid extends over the lower, beyond the outer corner of the eye.

If one could isolate oneself from acoustic phenomena through monodeism[233], it would be possible to obtain, by means of this, some intuition as to the ontological development of the numeral series. In any event, if one studies the precious notes which follow without analyzing them, having momentarily set aside all previous notions and mental prejudices, indulging more in contemplation than meditation, there is no doubt that in a few months the numerical theories of Unknown Philosophy will become understandable.

Of course, it is appropriate to ask for the help of the One to Whom our author devotes all his efforts and who is our Master over all.

SÉDIR – the 22nd of December, 1909

---

[233] It seems that Sédir is suggesting a disinterested approach, just as the concept of monodeism refers to a disinterested Creator who doesn't intervene in human affairs but observes us rather like an impartial scientist. In other words, here one must set aside any feelings or emotions arising from listening to music, focusing on the notes only as a series of numerical progressions – PV.

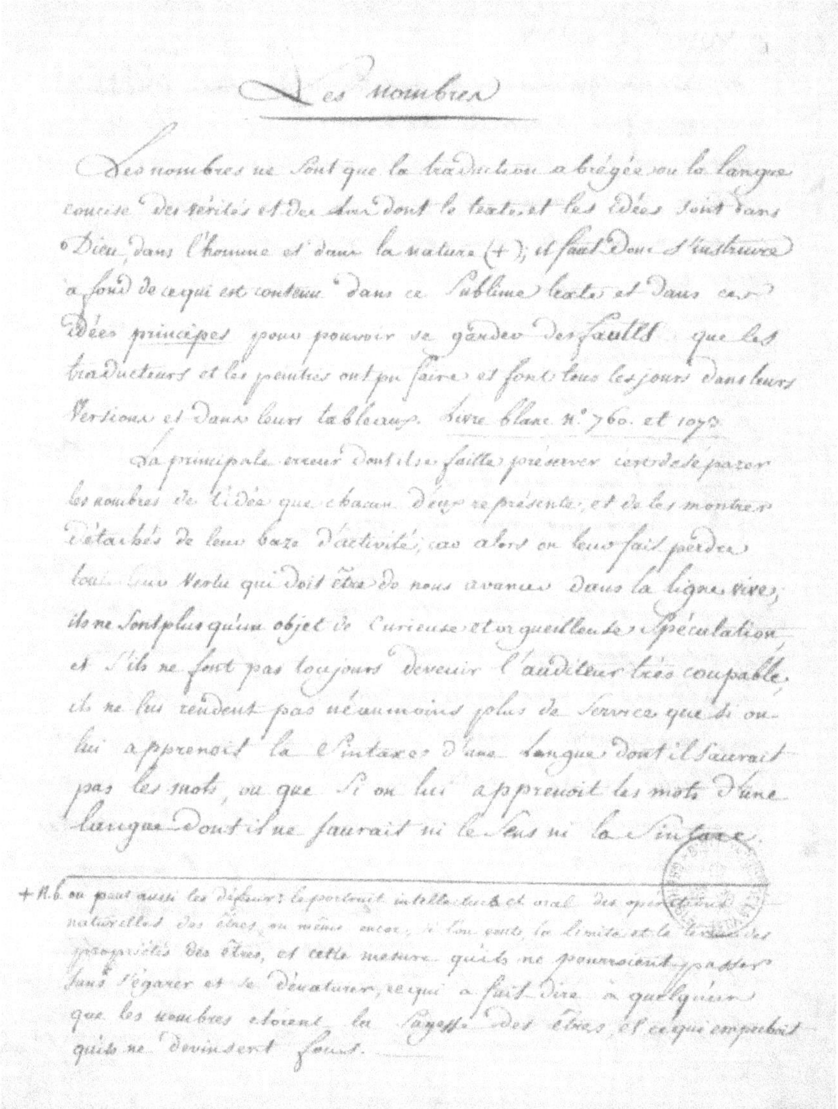

Les nombres

Les nombres ne sont que la traduction abrégée ou la langue concise des vérités et des lois dont le texte, et les idées sont dans Dieu, dans l'homme et dans la nature (+); il faut donc s'instruire à fond de ce qui est contenu dans ce sublime texte et dans ces idées principes pour pouvoir se garder des fautes que les traducteurs et les peintres ont pu faire et font tous les jours dans leurs versions et dans leurs tableaux. Livre blanc n.° 760. et 1077.

La principale erreur dont il se faille préserver c'est de séparer les nombres de l'idée que chacun d'eux représente, et de les montrer détachés de leur base d'activité; car alors on leur fait perdre toute leur vertu qui doit être de nous avancer dans la ligne vive; ils ne sont plus qu'un objet de curieuse et orgueilleuse spéculation, et s'ils ne font pas toujours devenir l'auditeur très coupable, ils ne lui rendent pas néanmoins plus de service que si on lui apprenoit la sintaxe d'une langue dont il sçaurait pas les mots, ou que si on lui apprenoit les mots d'une langue dont il ne sçaurait ni le sens ni la sintaxe.

+ N.b. on peut aussi les définir: le portrait intellectuel et oral des opérations naturelles des êtres, ou même encore, je l'ai écrit, la limite et le terme des propriétés des êtres, et cette mesure qu'ils ne pourroient passer sans s'égarer et se dénaturer, ce qui a fait dire à quelqu'un que les nombres étoient la sagesse des êtres, et ce qui empêchoit qu'ils ne devinssent fous.

Figure 20: Front Page of Des Nombres.

From the Fonds Léonard-Joseph Prunelle de Lière, T.4188.14 *Les Nombres* Louis-Claude de Saint-Martin in the *Bibliothèque Municipale de Grenoble*. While the handwriting is not proven to be that of Saint-Martin, it closely resembles his handwriting photocopied in Robert Amadou *Traité Sur La Réintégration des Êtres*, pub. Diffusion Rosicrucienne 1993, ISBN 2-908534-44-4 – PV.

ON NUMBERS

I. *General Considerations*

Numbers are simply the abbreviated translation or concise language of the truths and laws whose text and ideas are in God, in Man and in Nature. They can also be defined as the intellectual and oral portrait of the natural operations of beings or even, if one wishes, the limit and the term of the properties of beings, that boundary which they couldn't cross without straying and denaturing themselves; which prompted someone to say that numbers were the wisdom of beings, and what prevented them from going mad.

It is therefore necessary to thoroughly learn what is contained in that sublime text and in those *source* ideas, in order to guard against those errors which translators and painters have made and continue to make every day in their translations and their images.

The principal error one must guard against is to separate numbers from the idea which each of them represents and to show them separated from their base of activity; for then one makes them lose their purpose, which should be to advance us along the living path, and they become nothing more than an object of curious and prideful speculation; and if they do not always make the listener more guilty, they do him no more service than if he were taught the syntax of a language whose words he didn't know, or if he were taught the words of a language whose sense or syntax were unknown to him.

Now, to demonstrate how they are related to their base of activity, let's start by observing the conduct of *Unity* and the number *Two*. When we are contemplating an important truth, such as the universal power of the Creator, His majesty, His love, His profound wisdom or any other of His attributes, we are totally drawn towards this Supreme model of all things; all our faculties go silent to enable us to fill ourselves with Him, and we are truly one with Him. This is the real image of Unity, and in our languages the number *One* is the expression of that Unity or Indivisible Union which, existing intimately amongst all the attributes of that Unity, should also exist between Him and all His creatures and creations. But if, having focused all our powers of contemplation towards this Universal Source, we focus our eyes back upon ourselves and fill ourselves with our own contemplation, so that we see *ourselves* as the author of some of the splendor or internal satisfaction which this Source has provided us, at that moment we establish two centers of contemplation, two separate and rival principles, two bases that are no longer linked. Thus, we establish two *Unities*, but with this difference: one is real and the other apparent.

But let's go back to the earliest time of this irregular number. We cannot make *One* produce anything nor take anything away from it, as we know and as we shall see in several articles in this collection. Therefore, it is impossible for *One* to give birth to *Two*, and if something comes out of it through violence, it can only be illegitimate and as a diminution of itself. Now, what is the first diminution which must appear? It is the one connected with the Center, because those connected with the two extremes would only be apparent diminutions, since they could always be restored through generation from the center without the center having to move. However, the diminution made by the center is like that which is made by the middle and is the only one possible. If I walk up to a tree wishing to harm it, because of my height I can neither strike at its branches which are too high, nor at its roots which I cannot see; and so, I can only hit its trunk, that is, its middle. But dividing a being by the middle is to divide it into two parts: it reduces the whole to the quality of a half[234], and this is indeed the true origin of the illegitimate binary, whose results and properties can be seen in Chapter 3. However, that diminution by means of the center doesn't stop the Unity from remaining whole, since change cannot affect it, but only the being who wishes to attack it and who receives nothing more than a broken measure, rather than receiving all and in full measure. So evil is foreign to Unity. Nevertheless, as there is something of it in the diminished being, this diminution has induced the center to move in order to rectify this *two* and this *half*, and this without the center leaving its class

---

[234] In the original text: "…à la qualité de moitié ou de demi…". Both 'moitié' and 'demi' mean 'half'. Saint-Martin was merely emphasizing this point by repeating it – PV.

since Unity is indivisible: and this is the most sublime of the mysteries and the inexhaustible source of wonders from which the mind and soul of man can eternally slake their thirst.

This example is enough to show us the birth of the number *Two*, to show us the origin of evil, assuming that one is well-versed in the question of freedom (see the *Traité de l'origine et de L'Esprit des Formes*[235]), and at the same time to teach us that this number *Two* is not just the result of mere speculation, since we all visualize it in almost every moment of our existence.

Moreover, there can be no doubt that it operates actively in the *Senary*[236] of forms which, by themselves, are only a passive addition of the two *Ternaries*, while the *Two* itself is not only the root of these two *Ternaries*, but is also the driver of their movements and sensations by means of the multiplication of its own elements. Also, the senses become unfeeling when it ceases to inhabit them, and as soon as they are restored again, one can be sure that ¼ or the square of the corrupted number is also there. For it is a certain truth, albeit distressing, that *Five* and *Six* are and shall be until the end of the world in a measure of activity which is both reciprocal and proportional. Here the curious man might care to consider why the square of the corrupted number thus provides the *Senary* with so many of its rights, and can conceal the active death of its power under the flame of illusion of this *Senary* and if he discovers it, as I have no doubt he will, he will have acquired a great insight; and if he wishes to observe how the product of this false root gives in its sum an apparent being, *Five*, which can only be falsehood itself and a lie, but that this product shows in Nature and according to the simple arithmetic figure, the true emanation of man and his very certain destination, which is to make the 5

---

[235] Saint-Martin is referencing his own paper, *Treatise on the Origin and Spirit of Forms*, also known as the *Traité des Formes*. Two-thirds of the document, a part of the Archives of Prunelle de Lière at Grenoble Library, was published in a series by Robert Amadou in an esoteric magazine, but the magazine closed before the final parts were published – PV.

[236] Saint-Martin, like Pasqually, uses archaic terms to describe the numbers, in almost a hieratic or hieroglyphic way, including 'ternary' for 3, 'quaternary' for 4, 'quinary' for 5, 'senary' for 6, 'septenary' for 7, 'nonary' for 9 and so forth. His use of the term 'root' must also be taken in the context of Theosophical Addition, so that a root is a source rather than a base. Hence $3 + 3 = 6$ or $3 \times 2 = 6$, both meaning that 2 is the 'root' by which the two ternaries (3) become a senary (6) – PV.

disappear by his presence 4, he will have no less important an insight. For man can really be only a quarter Unity; but that is enough for him to be bound by its essence, and by its work, to the whole *One*.[237]

There are no numbers in the decade[238] whose character we cannot discover in this manner, by not separating them from the particular task to which they are joined or from the object upon which they are based, a living teaching which can only be

---

[237] The complexity of Saint-Martin's numerology is far too broad to go into detail, and indeed the entire Treatise has been labeled a difficult read by all who have published it. The reader is referred to Saint-Martin's first two books, *Of Errors & Truth*, and *Natural Table* to gain further insights, as well as Martinez de Pasqually's book *Treatise on the Reintegration of Beings*. Each of the numbers from 1 to 10 represented a concept, and sometimes several. Generally even numbers represented balance and therefore good or positive influences; while odd numbers (apart from '1', which represented God, and in a way was beyond numbers) were considered imperfect and therefore evil or negative. Since '2' was considered an evil number (in part because that represented man's attempt to perform an act of creation when he attempted to create Heva – or Eve – out of red clay, which resulted in his losing his original rights as the closest being to God). '3' represented man and Nature, and the Elements (Saint-Martin only recognized three physical Elements: Earth, Water and Fire). '4' the Quaternary, represented the line, the square and also man's primitive abode. Before being condemned to earth. '5' was the number of Evil, death, and one aspect of Man. But '5' also represented the Repairer, who had been set in man's original place at the center until such time as man would return to his glorious body and resume his original station. '6' represents the days of creation. So, one interpretation of the first part of this paragraph might say that creation is represented by the intersection of two triangles, like the Seal of Solomon which, in many esoteric traditions represents the eternal motion, or evolution and involution of the forces which maintain life. The '6' is formed by two triangles, or '3's, and the introduction of the number '2' immediately implies that creation as it now exists is flawed, since duality has been introduced, exposing its beings to both good and evil. But the Senary '6' can also be composed of 1 + 5, or man and God, showing the direct link which there originally was between them. Then if $3 \times 2 = 6$, so $3 + 2 = 5$, reflecting man containing duality or evil.

In this instance Saint-Martin is playing with several concepts at once. For example, the 'essential root' is calculated through theosophical addition. For example, as will be seen many times in this book (as it was in Papus'), $1+2+3+4 = 10$, and the essential root of 4 is therefore 10, which would seem counterintuitive to a mathematician! However, some figures will also give 'false roots', and here the root of 2 is $2+1 = 3$. As mentioned above, 5 and 6 are eternally with us, but they will be a constant source of confusion, since 5 is made up of $2 + 3$, where the '3' can be good (the trinity) or bad (the root of 2); and 5 expressed geometrically as a pentagram can represent man (head and four limbs) or fallen man (inverted pentagram); or even, as we saw above the 'Repairer' or 'Christ'.

This lengthy sidebar is really to encourage the reader to see numbers through the eyes of Theosophical Mathematics and their values through the eyes of Saint-Martin: this will make *On Numbers* rather easier to follow – PV.

[238] The numbers 1 to 10, as mentioned in the previous footnote – PV.

appropriate for those who are on the path, and who have come to an inner understanding. It would be lost on everyone else. But this simple explanation is enough to teach us that the virtue of a being doesn't exist in the number; but rather, it is the number which exists in the virtue of beings and derives from it. (Someday I may not be able to stop myself from going through all the numbers in the decade to show how *Two* becomes *Three* through its mirrors, how *3* becomes *4* by its center, how *4* is false by its double center which makes *5*, as *5* is imprisoned by the measure of *6, 7, 8, 9, 10*, which bring about the correction and rectification of the evil *Quinary*.)

One cannot deny the immense advantages that man's mind and intelligence can derive from the use of numbers, as soon as one has managed to sense the individual task to which each of them is joined and the purpose upon which they are based. For since the progress of the characteristics of beings is an active one, and since these characteristics have a thousand expanding and diminishing relationships between them, the combination of these numbers taken according to the regular meaning they bear along with those from sound observation, should be able to guide us in our unreliable speculations, and even correct us in false speculation; seeing that it's from such true and spiritual calculation or this algebra of reality – like conventional calculation or algebra – where once all the values are known they will lead us to precise and sure results without error. The essential difference which must be noted is that in conventional calculation values are arbitrary and their combinations, though based on fixed rules, only lead us to very secondary truths, which are entirely foreign to the true light that we all need and seek, even when it would seem to be counterintuitive; whereas in true and spiritual calculation the numbers receive their value from the nature of things and not from the will of our minds, and regardless of the fact that they are also brought together through fixed rules like conventional values, they lead us to the highest truths, truths which are positive and invariable and fundamentally related to our being. – The reason should be obvious enough: it is because then numbers simply accompany us, and direct us to those same positive, invariable and eternal realms in which they continually take birth, in which they make their home, and from which they can never leave. Now, these truths being infinite, we can judge that the numbers that soar above can show us wonders and treasures.

There is a division of the universal tableau which is recognized by all observers in the order of true philosophy: it is the distinction between the divine realm, the spiritual realm and the natural realm. It is also recognized that there is a relationship between the divine realm and the spiritual and natural realms; and as a result the numbers of the divine order must also have their representations and images in those two realms. But those who do not have the key to numbers expose themselves to serious misunderstanding when they wish to understand or contemplate these relationships.

The main cause of their mistake is that they approach such speculations through their knowledge of regular arithmetic, where numbers are recognized by their multiples or by their analogous or similar parts and not by their properties, since arithmetic doesn't recognizes any properties of numbers other than those that are generally accepted and depend on man's will.

The second mistake is to want to contain the three divisions mentioned above in three consecutive decades, so that after *Thirty* we would no longer need any more numbers.

Finally, the third mistake is to want to find in the second and third decade the same series of principles as in the first, because indeed one finds the same order in the numbers and the same arithmetic alignment.

To combat the first mistake, we must recall the two different laws of multiplication and addition, which, although they are both used as the basis of calculations, have far from the same effect. The first one begets. The second makes known the nature of what is produced and the true spirit of the result, both in relation to itself and in relation to its root source.

In arithmetic, on the contrary, since these two laws of multiplication and addition aren't used in the same manner, they cannot give rise to the same insights. Indeed, since arithmetic retains the products of its operations in their gross nature, and doesn't know how to separate the Spirit from the *Caput Mortuum*, it seeks nothing beyond similar multiples.[239] Also for arithmetic, products, roots, powers, everything is of the same nature: that is to say nothing is distinct, and everything is confused except in terms of quantity. Nevertheless, this isn't a disadvantage for the objects one is focused on and for the class of things on which it operates, since, dealing only with things which are apparent and dead, it has only *parts* to consider and no *Spirit* to seek; and since these dead parts which they consider only have to relate to our dead needs, the dead calculations which can be applied to them are appropriate to their inert or relative scope.

To combat the second error, that of three contiguous decades, not only can we repeat what we already said above, namely that after *Thirty* we would no longer have a need for any more numbers; but we must take note of a much greater problem, in that there would be no interaction between all these decades, and God would have no interaction with the spirit, nor would the spirit have any interaction with Nature. For there cannot be any interaction except one based on similar numbers, on relative multiples, and on products which have relationships with their roots only through form and not through the laws of their generation, that is to say, through their principle. Now, these disadvantages and therefore these errors are impossible to avoid if the three divisions – divine, spiritual and natural – are each contained in one of the three contiguous decades, because one is then reduced to the need to confine the number instead of allowing it to expand in as it grows, with the result having only the very false figure of that same number instead of having its true output, which should really be another like it which is able to travel through the various realms open to it, albeit in varied appearances.

---

[239] Saint-Martin interestingly uses an alchemical phrase, *caput mortuum* or *death's head*, to describe this process. In Chapter 2 of his *Course on Martinism* (pub. Institut Eléazar, 1990-2007), Serge Caillet describes this as follows: "This alchemical term refers to the by-products of an operation. When one extracts the spirit of a number, we always "obtain 9 for the *caput mortuum* and for the corpse". If we use the example of 25 reduced theosophically to 2+5=7, we obtain 7 for the spirit of 25. Let us subtract 7 from 25, that is, the number from the spirit, and we get 18, which is 1+8=9, the *caput mortuum*. There is nothing surprising here, as we shall see that 9 is, in fact, the number of matter." We also saw this covered in Papus' book earlier – PV.

This is where one can find the means to fight the third error, or that of wishing to find the same series and the same arithmetical alignment in the three divisions, so that the same series is identical in form and in the arrangement of the numbers in the three contiguous decades. If the law of compound roots, standard in arithmetic, cannot be accepted in the order of things we are observing, then the multiplication of simple roots gives us as a reward a generation of numbers that, in one stroke, will reverse the whole edifice of the three contiguous decades and change all the similar alignments of their respective numbers.

Indeed, except for the first three numbers whose squares don't exceed the divine decade, all the rest exceed it the moment they are raised to their first power or to their square. And where do they go through this exercise? Only one goes into the spiritually named decade. Five more go in the following and later decades, and there are still three decades in which none of these five numbers, such as the sixth, eighth and tenth, ends; all observations which are likely to be subject to significant review and which can shed great light.[240] It should be noted, however, that it is only to conform to customary language that we call the first power or square the action in question; for among the first numbers that remain in the divine decade by this action, there is one to which this operation cannot be appropriate (and this number is *Two*), and all that can be said

---

[240] If the error is made by wishing to identify 1 – 9 with the Divine realm, 10 – 19 with the Spiritual realm and 20 – 29 with the Natural realm, only 1, 2 and 3 can be squared and still remain in their own decade (producing 1, 4 and 9 respectively). The number 4 squares to 16, ending in the second decade, 5 ends up as 25 in the third decade, and 6 through 9 end up in still higher decades, which according to this argument, are in neither the Divine, nor the Spiritual or Natural realms. Worse, although 1 squared remains Unity, 2, as we saw earlier, is the number of evil or Adam's aberrant attempt at creation: this number squared remains within the Divine decade, and indeed its cube, 8 also remains there. However, since it was by the number 4 that the evil powers tempted man to perform his act of creation and deceived him, so its cube the number 8 is associated by Saint-Martin with the Christ, or by Pasqually with the doubly-powerful Spirit, since by arriving at it through the cube of 2 instead of creating the Christ we create the perverse Christ, the false Christ, the anti-Christ (as we see a couple of paragraphs later). This example goes to show the complexity of this numerical theory, and the importance of understanding not just the dead numbers but what they represent, and thereby how theosophical mathematical operations can be used with numbers to tell a myth or a story. Indeed, the fact that early alphabets also represented numbers show the source behind this approach, when we consider *Gematria* and *Notarikon* in Hebrew, for example – PV.

here is that it is through this false operation that the perverse mind deceived man.[241]

If, by this elevation to their first power, we already find in the numbers a progression so very different from that presented to us by the three contiguous decades, surely this progression will experience much greater changes when we will raise these numbers to their cube, which is the perfect term for any number? This difference will be easily felt; for by this cubic operation or elevation to the second power there will be only two numbers which remain in the divine decade (yet one of them will remain there only by the abusive laws of arithmetic[242]), and just as it is by the square of that number that the perverted beings deceived man, it is by the cube of that same number that the falsehood populated, populates and will continue to populate the world with false Christs. As for the other numbers submitted to the same operation, none remain in the contiguous spiritual decade; another immediately passes from the divine decade into the natural decade; another in the seventh decade; the next one even leaves the tenth or centenary decade, and all the others move further away from the three contiguous decades and leave between them spaces so large, so varied, that their rank no longer retains any relation to that which they have, by the laws of arithmetic, in those same contiguous decades. And even when one is struck by the relationship between the order of numbers in the three contiguous decades, one hasn't noticed that this order is always diminished by one degree as a direct result of the number of decades that one must pass through: a profound truth that visibly teaches us why all spiritual and

---

[241] The theosophical operation of raising 2 by its power to 4 (which Saint-Martin calls an inappropriate operation) creates the quaternary or 4, but not through the emanations of of Unity or the Father, the Son (2) and the Holy Spirit (3) to create the fourth term, which is the correct way. However, it was this very number 4 behind which the prevaricating evil forces hid when they persuaded man that he was equal to God and could perform an act of creation on his own. However, by adding their own will (1) to this falsely created number (4) they changed it into a number of perversity, falseness and bounded by the material, 5, which is why man failed in the operation and as a result was thrown down from his primitive position of felicity into a place bounded by time and space – PV.

[242] Those numbers being 1 and 3, since 1^3 gives 1 and 3^3 gives 9, a number of matter, Incidentally, for eloquent images of how quickly the square and cubes of numbers in the first decade go far beyond the third decade, refer to diagrams 4 – 13 in Papus' book earlier – PV.

temporal movements are circular, and why everything that exists is composed of so many wheels that constantly rotate around their center and ever strive to draw closer to it.

Those who have pierced the course of numbers will be able to admire with what luminous wisdom Providence spreads her treasures before us and shows us how she brings her powers to the various realms. They will recognize that numbers themselves are fixed and complete in their root abilities, though they are infinite in the play of their power and in the innumerable emanations that can arise and will arise forever from these root abilities. They will recognize that Unity is the only number that not only doesn't move out of the divine decade by its square or cube, but also that it never departs from its own secret or its own center, and which concentrates all its operations within itself. They will recognize that when this being *One* is transported to the Divine realm, to the Spiritual realm, or to the Natural realm, it is transported there by its own root abilities and by the emanations which correspond to them; but that the planes and the properties which it manifests there are superior to the material concepts of arithmetic, and do not contain its coarse and monotonous meaning. They will recognize that through these root abilities and their corresponding emanations, this being *One* carries its life and spirit into all three realms, and that, therefore, they can spiritually regard those three realms as a great tree whose root is always hidden in the Divine realm as if in its mother's land; whose trunk or body is manifested in the Spiritual realm by the square; and whose branches, flowers and fruit are manifested in the Natural realm through the operations of the cube. From this they will recognize the interaction and the active union which must reign between these three realms or three worlds, because they have a common root, and because there are Spiritual squares which extend into the Natural realm, and Natural cubes which are completed in the Spiritual region, while the Divine Unity, like the sap that produces everything and fills everything, operates at the same time and in concert with the Spiritual and Natural realms, in that it constantly influences it invisibly by its own root, by its own square and by its own cube, to vivify the cubes, squares and roots of all the other numbers and to make them operate in turn, each according to their properties and their *virtues*. They will recognize that although the being *One* doesn't itself transport into all those realms, nevertheless it is through the influence of its root, its square and its cube that all its works and all its spiritual and natural creations appear completed and clothed in that expressive character of Unity, which everywhere shows us our God, and everywhere the harmonic cooperation of all His abilities and powers.

Amidst these wonders which the course of numbers can offer to those who tread there with care and, so to speak, in silence, not only do we learn to admire the rich magnificence of our God, but we also learn to discern what is permitted for us to know and what will be forever forbidden to us to penetrate and remains hidden from our understanding.

What will forever be forbidden to our ability to penetrate and hidden from our understanding is the knowledge of the manner of our emanation or our generation in the Divine Unity. This veil is placed over our eyes because the work of our emanation being reserved only to this Supreme Principle that we have the happiness to be able to call *Our Father*, knowledge of the manner of that work must be reserved to Him too; otherwise, if like Him we had that knowledge we would not have needed Him to exist, we could have done the same work, or performed the same emanation as Him, and then we would be God like Him. (The order of material generation shouldn't be taken into account here, since it is circular like everything which is created and which comes out of the Universal center; for being circular, it is natural that its fruits rise up when its seeds descend, and that, coming together at the same point on the wheel, all knowledge of their order necessarily becomes common to them). Moreover, it is because of this veil placed over our eyes that the Sovereign Principle of our being becomes an eternal object of our tributes, and has a true right to our veneration; for, regardless of this insignificant favor which He has given us through our existence to sense His own Divine life, we are compelled to recognize His superiority over us by this very existence which He has given us, and by the evident impossibility for us to be able to enter into His secret on this important point. Let us join to that the hope or rather the certainty of eternally increasing the bliss which He has made us capable of feeling by giving us being, if we know how to stand before Him in the humble submission which is due to the Holy and Universal Dominator of all things. In the sense of our noble origin, in our profound ignorance of the manner of our emanation, and in our true spiritual interest we have all the motives necessary for us to honor our Divine Principle, to tremble before His redoubtable power and to ardently love the inexhaustible goodness which He asks no more than to pour abundantly into our souls: for these are the fundamental conditions that truly constitute the religious man and the faithful servant to his Master.

But if the law of numbers absolutely forbids us knowledge of the manner of our emanation, they must be able to offer us proof that this emanation is Divine, and they must offer us an obvious and demonstrative testimony that we come directly from God; for without this demonstrative witness, when we call God *Our Father* we would be uttering words that would not have a complete meaning for the intellect, though the pure and pious soul could experience in itself all the sweetness of this beautiful Name. Also, this evidence exists in numbers and adds to all that which can be found in metaphysics. God, as infinite in His wisdom as in His love, did not want to let the human soul come out of Him without giving him as consort a salutary clarity, in whose name He might demand from us the respectful tribute He is entitled to expect from His creature. It is only right to expect us to pay this tribute, seeing that at the same time He has provided us with the means to examine and recognize its convincing legitimacy; and we ourselves would no longer inexcusable before Him in refusing to offer this same tribute, if He had given us the slightest opportunity to conceal our debt to him.

This evidence, however, is entirely separate from the arithmetic process that is commonly followed by numbers, and it is because this evidence is clear that arithmetic pathways do not suit Him. For the same reason, the raising of powers in arithmetic is only repeated addition, and the extracting of roots is also only repeated subtraction; and in this type of calculation we go from the roots to the powers and return from the powers to the roots, without *numbering* the objects and without doing anything except counting them. So, there are only sums and never numbers. The evidence in question follows an opposite course. This is why there is a greater difference between the two kinds of products which result from the one and the other than there are between the smallest of plants, which is a child of nature, and the most beautiful of buildings erected by the hands of men.

To give a small idea of this difference, it suffices to say that in true calculation there are essential roots and roots which are not, and that the same is true of some powers, whereas in arithmetic calculation all roots are contingent, and all powers are as variable as their roots. It should be added, however, that in true calculation, the name *essential power* belongs specifically to man, but that the name *essential root* does not belong to him; and it is in considering those two titles that we find both proof that we come from God, and the impossibility of knowing how we come from Him: truths described more fully elsewhere, and which we mention here only in passing, as a simple summary.

A third gift that Divine Justice couldn't refuse men was a demonstration of the falseness of the second number when considered as a root, yet without prejudice to any metaphysical convictions concerning this subject. That demonstration was as important as the one which clearly proves our emanation from the Divine, for otherwise we would inevitably have become the victims of evil: we wouldn't have been able to discern it, fight it or repel it, and then Adam should never have been punished since he would never have known that he was guilty of anything. But since it is through the false application of arithmetic processes that mistakes about the second number have entered into the world, it is by means of the law of those same arithmetic processes that the irrational manner by which those errors were accepted is proven; and all that one should remember here, is that we must resort to fractions in order to demonstrate this. And here true calculation works with arithmetic calculation only to bind it and contain it within bounds by showing it that the more it operates, the more it diminishes; while the more true numbers operate, the more they grow and become more vibrant. For it is the second number which forces us to use fractions for, since fractions are not part of the true measure of beings, it effectively excludes itself from that true order by showing itself, and by being able to reveal itself only as a fraction.[243]

This is an abbreviated summary of the treasures that can be found in numbers, treasures which show us the power, love, wisdom and justice of our God, and make us see how everything is filled with His spirit.

As for the popular opinion that the second number, like any other number, can have a dual use and be applied both for and against, the laws of numbers also show us to what extent such an opinion should prevail, and at what point it should cease. True numbers always produce life, order and harmony. Thus, they always act for and never against, even when they act as the scourges of justice and vengeance. When numbers degenerate in free beings, they change their character so much that another number comes to take their place, although in their essence their radical title endures and remains the same; otherwise the eternal conventions of God would be perishable, and confusion could overtake everything. False numbers, on the other hand, produce nothing. They do have the power to mimic true numbers, but they don't have the power to imitate them; they show themselves as dividers and never as generators, since it is through separating that they have become false and lost the ability to generate. The example of the five foolish virgins is proof of this. They were without oil because they separated from their five companions and because of their behavior, and they also ended up without husbands. As for the five

---

[243] To repeat part of a footnote in *Of Errors & Truth* (trans. Piers A. Vaughan, pub. Rose Circle Publications, 2017): "Saint-Martin uses Theosophical Mathematics to make a point about the powerlessness of the number '2', which it should be remembered is the number of confusion, representing both the separation of the Evil Principle from the Good Principle, and man's attempted act of creation independent from the First Cause's cooperation. He points out that 1 divided by 2 makes ½, which "is spiritually the true root of 2." Yet this number ½ cannot be multiplied by itself to return to '1'. Instead it makes ¼. In other words, having created confusion, the number '2' cannot simply return to Unity, or 1 by the act of squaring itself, but now, without an act of grace, it's doomed to continually subdivide itself into null." Further, since Unity can only exist alone, you cannot add 1 to 1 in Saint-Martin's system without compromising the Divinity and Unity itself: thus, 2 cannot come from 1 + 1 but rather from 1 torn violently from 1 against its will, as we saw earlier – PV.

wise virgins, they will not become pregnant without their husbands, and when they have husbands there will be no longer be five but ten, since each of them will have a husband; or there will be six if you count the spouse only as one. And so, these five wise virgins are so few in their true number that, being unable to renew their own oil, they are forced to restrict themselves to prudence and leave undisturbed that charity which can only be found in vivifying numbers, whose power flows only from the center of love.[244]

Sometimes false numbers still show themselves as instruments of renewal, and this is one of the most profound splendors of the Immense Wisdom and Eternal Love. In these circumstances it requires a fastidious glance to be able to follow the revelation of these types of numbers, for example in the fifty days which elapsed following the resurrection of the Savior to the first Pentecost. What must be grasped and understood is the difference between these false numbers when they are used to work a renewal, and when they operate their own iniquities. When they are given over completely to themselves, they are totally separated from the true path with which they have lost all communication. When they are used in a renewal, it is the True Being who takes on their form and character in order to be able to descend into their infected region. But in taking on their form, He rectifies it, bringing it closer to the true number, and through this union opposing the true against the false, He becomes the death of death.[245]

---

[244] Matthew 24: 1-13. In the story the 5 foolish virgins forget to charge their lamps with oil while waiting for the bridegrooms, and when the bridegrooms are delayed their oil runs out. Then they beg the 5 wise virgins to share their oil. But the 5 wise virgins refuse, saying there is not enough oil for all of them and that the foolish virgins will have to go out into the streets to buy more. So, they meet their grooms while the foolish virgins have departed to find oil; and when they return to the house the door is locked against them. Saint-Martin argues that the addition of the husband or husbands moves the false number 5 to a true number – 6 or 10: a 'restoration' he mentions in the following paragraph – PV.

[245] This may be a reference to the book *The Death of Death in the Death of Christ*, by John Owen (1647), a still controversial Calvinist polemic in support of limited atonement versus universal atonement, in that Christ's death upon the cross granted redemption for only the Elect or Chosen, and not for all mankind. However, his thesis suggests that those who work for redemption (in Saint-Martin's eyes, not the 'Men of the Stream' but rather 'Men of Desire') are indeed the Elect, or 'Elu'. It is interesting to note that, although not directly from Saint-Martin, in one of the Grades of Martinism, a lecture explains how the

This mystery, which cannot sufficiently fill us with admiration, becomes simple to understand when we go back to the elements of the true numbers and false numbers which combine in this operation, but which do not merge for it. We see both kinds of numbers coming to the same term, each by different paths, and this is why we must maintain our guard so strongly against those well-known additions resulting in numbers which are identical in appearance, while their constituent elements are completely different. I will give only one example here, which may perhaps seem strange to those who are not well-versed in this language, but which is nevertheless a truth. It is that in that operation of the fifty days mentioned above, that 8 and 5 walk side by side and end up meeting at the same point, one to the truth to triumph, and the other to be annihilated; but having an apparent union which could easily be misunderstood if one were to adhere to the additional sum indicated by the number fifty. Finally, in this great work, 8 becomes 5 and 5, and 5 becomes 8^{246} and in this we find written in

---

number 5 was transformed from being the number of fallen man, symbolic of decay, corruption and death, to a true number when the profaned name of God (the Tetragrammaton) was reenewed by the Repairer (or the Christ) by inserting the Holy Spirit or the three tongues of fire of the Hebrew letter Shin to form the Pentagrammaton, Yeheshuah, or Christ, the emblem of man's redemption. Thus 5 transforms from being a number of evil to a power for good when commandeered for renewal, instead of being left to its own – evil – devices. Alternatively, one can read that the evil number of man, 5, the microcosm, is restored by the Divine influx, 1 or Unity, to become the number 5+1=6, the number of the macrocosm and of creation before the fall, which is another way to see the parable of the 5 wise virgins restored to the number 6 through addition. However, again this implies this path may only be open to those who follow it, and that redemption is not automatically universal in his view; whereas later Saint-Martin uses the phrase of the Repairer: "He came to save all." – PV.

[246] To show how this kind of argument works, a possible explanation is offered here. We cannot be certain of everything that was in Saint-Martin's mind, but this is one interpretation. Note that not every passage will be interpreted for the reader: this is simply to put him or her in a suitable frame of mind when approaching such passages. Saint-Martin is giving us an example of where a number might be arrived at by two completely different paths. We have already seen that 5 can be the addition of 4 + 1 or 1 + 4 (as well as 3 + 2 or 2 + 3). If we focus on 4 + 1 we can see the introduction of the prevaricating spirits inserting themselves as a false unity into man in his original perfection (who bore the number 4). Then in 1 + 4 we can see the positive side of Christ himself entering a human body to become one with it. Also, remembering that in theosophical arithmetic 40 has the same value as 4 (4 + 0 = 4), 10 as 1 and 50 as 5, we are drawn to the period between the Resurrection and Pentecost, being 50 days. This period is divided into two:

numbers, and in the most significant way, the explanation of the 24th verse of the 89th Psalm: *et veritas mea and misericordia cum ipso: and in nomine meo exaltabitur cornus ejus*[247], a verse which alone contains so many truths that the mind of man is not adequate to contemplate them, any more than his language could be adequate to express them.

I am not afraid of assuring you that, of all the wonders that the Sacred Sciences have afforded me since the pure mercy of God was willing to allow me to be admitted to them, this is one of the most considerable, containing both the admirable course of Divine Love for our wretched humanity, and the industrious Wisdom with which that Love has used His powers to separate our enemy from us in order to relegate him to his abyss, and to open to us the only holy door through which we may return to the Divine Kingdom which is our true homeland.

Don't judge me of committing a crime by not elaborating further on this. To begin with, one must have a common language; and for all the truth that the Holy Fathers may have written concerning such subjects, I am quite convinced that if the ones in question were known to them, they did not write about them.

Nor should I be accused of contradiction when I claim it is possible to know how man is to be restored, when I previously argued that it is impossible to know the manner of our emanation. These two operations are different in that emanation is concerned with our essence, whereas our restoration is concerned with our abilities. The first took place at the Divine Center; the latter,

---

40 days from the Resurrection to Ascension, when the Man-God walked the Earth ("do not touch me, for I am not yet ascended unto the Father"), and 10 days from Ascension till Pentecost and the descent of the Holy Spirit upon the Disciples. Theosophically it is represented again by $4 + 1 = 5$. Finally, remembering that 5 is the number of fallen man and 8 is the doubly powerful spirit or 4×2, indicating the Christ or Saint-Martin, we see a hint of gnostic thought in that he appears to separate the human and the divine in Jesus. So '8 and 5 walk side by side' can mean that Jesus contained both human and divine elements following the Resurrection, and hence His injunction to His followers not to touch Him; then at the Ascension His human part was shed and the divine alone ascended ('the one to truth and triumph, the other to be annihilated'). Finally, 'in this Great Work' (an interesting alchemical phrase for the transmutation) 8 becomes 5 and 5 becomes 8, or God becomes Man, and then Man becomes God – PV.

[247] My truth and my mercy shall be with him: and in my Name shall his horn be exalted – PV.

although also occurring in the same Center, will be accomplished in the realm of time, and it is one of our very rights to know this so that we can apply its spirit and *virtue*, which is the only way to let it bring forth its efficacity in us by means of the proper use of our freedom; whereas the secret of our emanation can remain hidden from us since it was carried out independently of us, and must forever remain so, even if we become as criminal as the Perverse Being. This does not stop that restoration from being such a wonderful work that nothing can be compared to it, as is stated in the *Man of Desire*[248], Section 33, seeing that, considered as love it is above our own emanation; while, considered as strength it is beneath it, since it operates only on our faculties, and because our emanation has given being to our very essence.

Let us return to that truth outlined above about the second number and false numbers, namely: that, by themselves they can only ever work their own iniquities, seeing that when they are employed in an act of renewal the true real insinuates itself and takes on their form in order to divide them, just as medicine penetrates the remotest parts of a sick body which illness has filled and infected. One senses that, when they are employed by the hand of Justice, they are still far from being a generative power, for then Justice will gather them in His powerful hand like so many painful canes which are thrown into the fire, after they have been used to punish and trouble the wrongdoer. What will it be like when we see them reduced to themselves? It is then that we will recognize them for what they can do, and we will no longer be able to deny that the Author of all justice, love and wisdom has given us the opportunity to learn the properties of these false numbers, and by that has prevented us from indifferently harvesting both the fruits which come from them, and those which come from true numbers.

To achieve this goal, let us take as an example what happened in the most important period of the mission of the Repairer. I am referring to when the time was approaching to consummate His sacrifice. When was it, in fact, that the hour of darkness came? When was the Savior delivered to the officials and people armed with staves? When did his disciples abandon him? When did St.

---

[248] Saint-Martin is referencing his book of that name – PV.

Peter deny him? This was when the number of Apostles was reduced to eleven by the apostasy of Judas. This was when the number 2 which Judas represented was repeated by the separation that took place between the Master and the disciples. It was then that the Prince of Darkness put all his powers into play. It was then that he blinded the Jewish people and urged them to demand the death of the Righteous One and the deliverance of the criminal Barabbas, who was guilty of sedition and murder. It was then that the executioners seized Him and deicide was committed. There is no need to look longer at the dreadful fruits of this number. After those examples we have just given we cannot find any which are as terrible as them, and we leave it to the mind of the intelligent man to consider what is to be expected of such a number when it is delivered over to its own iniquitous powers. (We also see why all these things happened is because 7 x 7 = 13 the sum of 49 through multiplication, and the sum of 7 and 6 by way of addition. When 49 went up to 50, it let 13 go back to 12; but 12 could not support itself alone, for then it was too overworked by the active root ½. So it went down to 11; and it was only then that Judas, being set upon by *evil*, who was obliged to deviate and who sought to take his revenge, was able to give scope to all its evil designs).[249]

On the contrary, what happened when the number of Apostles was restored by the election of Matthias? It came to pass that the Comforter was sent to them; it came pass that the gift of tongues was granted to them; it came to pass that being gathered there for their Master, Who is the Word, with respect to them they abolished the number 2 as now they were but *One* with their Divine Master,

---

[249] It is important to remember that theosophical multiplication in Saint-Martin's eyes was to return to the root number. Therefore, 7 x 7 = 49, and 4 + 9 = 13, which here represented the 12 disciples and the Repairer. But by arresting the Repairer and subtracting Him from the number, this left 12 which, Saint-Martin argues, was unstable due to the fact that the root of 2, or ½ – in a way the numerical representation of the power of the Prince of Darkness mentioned in the previous paragraph – was working upon the mind of Judas, operating on his disappointment that Jesus was not the new king come to overthrow the Romans, and so by Judas' prevarication and revenge, brought the number of disciples down to 11 (a dangerous number as it represents 1+1 = 2, and whose stability needed to be restored, as we see in the following paragraph). Indeed, to take the analogy further, almost all the bad decisions during the trial of the Repairer were also binary in nature, such as the crowd choosing Barabbas over Jesus, and Pilate's decision to wash his hands of Jesus instead of asserting Roman Law – PV.

and they opened to all the Nations the means to be *One* with them in turn, and therefore with the One Who came to us save all.

The immense and powerful property of that regular number which was restored among the Apostles is marked enough to show us, by its contrasts with the properties of the previous number, how indeed Supreme Truth and Wisdom have provided man with every means to distinguish the vivifying seeds from the darkness, and poison from the most beneficial plants. For the warning that has been given to men in this immense manifestation of the Savior must spread a universal clarity, since it comes directly from the Eternal Sun and the Universal Author of all illumination. Thus this act of His love is enough to enlighten us about the true numbers which we have carried since our origin, and about those we shall bear at the time of our regeneration; and it fully justifies everything we've said about the harmonic and generative virtues of regular numbers, and especially what we've said about the impossibility of composing those regular numbers with false numbers, which would truly be an offense to truth.

But let's state it once more: what makes this discernment difficult is the power of the false number to exhibit the same results as true numbers; what I called above: *to mimic the truth*. The example we have just seen provides the proof. It was through the apostasy of Judas that the regular number had broken into a double binary, and the measure of iniquity overflowed; it was through the election of Mathias that the regular number was reestablished, and the double binary disappeared. However, if one did not keep up one's guard, one would be exposed to a great error and a very embarrassing uncertainty by considering only the fruits, and not the elements and the roots. For if one wanted to manipulate the false number, one would clearly see come out of it the same number 13 of which Jesus Christ alone could be the principle and complement. But by monitoring this manipulation, we see at every step the corrosive venom of its poisoned elements. We see them, I tell you, at every step, because the love of our Eternal Principle for us doesn't want us to become lost, and He watches ceaselessly over the holy ark; He had it move continually in the camp of Israel to show us at all times the difference and superiority of the one God over the idols and gods of the other Nations.

He even gives us an important teaching about the limits of the power of evil, in relation to the saving work that Divine Mercy wished to operate in favor of Adam's posterity. It is that if, by the laws of calculation, the meeting of the two binaries produces the same number as the election of Mathias, it is proof that the division of that regular number had taken place only in its fruits and not in its roots.[250] For if it had taken place in those roots, it would have been forever impossible to have any new fruits, as one would expect from a tree whose roots had died. It is proof, indeed, that the powers of this evil only extend to its appearance and that as the vivifying principles are beyond its reach, they can resume their full activity as soon as its disastrous time has passed and it is relegated to its abyss; a new truth and immense light which numbers offer us in order to fill us with consolation in our spiritual miseries, and with hope in the ineffable and inexhaustible life of our God.

Finally, regardless of the divine spiritual formation of this number 13 through the operation and union of Jesus Christ with His Apostles, regardless of the temporal and false formation of that same number 13 by the two binaries, there is a simple spiritual one which has only the world and man as its elements; and that is why in the book *Of Errors and Truth* that number was presented as the number of Nature[251]. It is for the intelligent mind to follow the characters of these various teachings, and we would be prudent to warn ourselves not to follow the science of numbers without the greatest precautions.

One of the keys this caution can provide us is to make us see why there are so many relationships between such different numbers.

---

[250] It is worth remembering that the number 13 was the result of Jesus joining with the 12 Apostles, and similarly here the number 13 is achieved by the Holy Spirit joining with the 11 + 1 Apostles (including the newly-elected Matthias) – PV.

[251] In Chapter 6 in *Of Errors & Truth*, Saint-Martin says: "I was speaking rather of the true East of which the rising of the Sun is only an indicative sign, and which manifests visibly and more appropriately in the plumb and the perpendicular. This East, which by its number *four* can alone embrace all of space, since in joining itself with the number *nine* or that of expanse, that is, uniting the active and the passive, forms the number *thirteen*, which is the number of Nature." 4, being the *four* directions, embraces all of space, and 9 represents the circle, with God as the point – PV.

And here we will show one of the principal causes: it is because the Eternal, Sovereign Author of all Wisdom directs His plans for renewal in proportion to the evils we have done to ourselves; and that not only does He steer His plans for renewal in accordance with them, but He uses them to determine the kind of remedy He will employ for our healing; so that in the great scheme of things the attentive man can recognize our illness, our remedy and our Doctor, and with careful eyes he will distinguish these three things perfectly, though he sees that they are connected to one another, and present the same measurements and the same numbers. For when we consider our physical ailments and wounds, doesn't the type of wound determine the equipment to be employed, and isn't it in order to treat that wound that the skilled doctor will combine the equipment and everything else which should go into its treatment? Yet, despite all the connections between the actions going into that healing work, nobody would confuse the equipment with the wound or the doctor with the equipment, because all have their particular character or number.

II. Concerning the Natural Quantity of Numbers

Scholars claim that they can perform all their numerical operations with more or less than 10 numbers, which is the quantity of numbers recognized throughout all times and in all countries.

To protect ourselves from their false opinion on this point, we simply have to remember the principle and observe how many numbers there are for evil, how many there are for the true spirit since the separation, and how many there are for matter.

However, since nothing exists that doesn't belong to these three realms, we will soon see that for evil there are only two numbers; that for the true spirit since the separation, there are only five, and for matter there are only three. It will be easy to get to clarity on this point: because the two evil numbers are 2 and 5; the five numbers of the true spirit are 1, 10, 8, 7 and 4; and the three numbers of matter are 3, 6 and 9.

Thus, putting together of all these numbers only gives us 10, and being unable to find anything that exists outside of these numbers, that suffices to show us how scientists have gone astray with their hasty conjectures.

III. On the Root of Two

According to the rules of arithmetic, the fraction closest to 1 is ½. Nothing more is required to see where we can go with this ½ which is spiritually the true root of 2, and it is possible to never see it go back to its source, since the more you multiply a fraction, the closer it comes to sterility and nothingness. And quite to the contrary, the more you multiply whole numbers, the more you bring them towards fertility and abundance.[252]

IV. The Essence of Numbers 1, 2 and 3

One has the principle within it and possesses it.
Two has it within it and doesn't possess it.
Three doesn't have it within it nor does it possess it.

These truths are evident both in the spiritual order and in the material order; but they are more physical for us in the material class, since we are imprisoned here. They are also written clearly in the action and laws of the three Kingdoms of Nature, although in its essence this Nature has nothing in it which it has not received. Let's consider this analogically.

The animal carries its strength within it and draws everything from it.

---

[252] ½ x ½ = ¼, and fractions will continue to shrink the more they are multiplied; whereas 2 x 2 = 4, and whole numbers will continue to increase at an ever-greater rate. And to reiterate, for 'true' numbers the square of the root equals the original value, but not for 'false' numbers. Thus, the root of 4 ($\sqrt{4}$) is 2 and the square of 4 (2^2) goes back to 4. But the root of 2 ($\sqrt{2}$) is ½, and the square of ½ ($½^2$) is ¼ – PV.

The plant has strength within it, but it can only use it by means of the earth.

The mineral has no strength within it, and for that very reason derives nothing from it.

This leads us to observe the three main Classes of the material order. Each is quaternary (4) under the name of superior, major, lower and minor.

	1	10	8	7		
FIRST CLASS Divine	God.	Thought.	Will.	Action.	= 17	= 8
	10	8	7	4		
SECOND CLASS Spiritual-temporal which is double	Divine Thought.	Divine Will.	Divine Action.	Man.	= 29	= 11
	8	7	4	3		
THIRD CLASS For corporeal and material creations	Divine Will.	Divine Action.	Man's cooperation.	Elemental creations.	= 22	= 4

The First Class has everything in it and possesses everything in it;

The Second Class, or the man it has produced, has everything in him, but possesses nothing in him;

The Third Class or elemental creations have nothing in them and possess nothing of it, because they received their form through the cooperation of man, who has everything in him but who possesses nothing in him.

One must always be perceptive regarding the difference the essence of things and their laws and actions, so as not to disturb the content of this Table, because there is a progressive chain which binds each Class to its neighbor through a common property, although in the two adjoining Classes there is always a property which is missing from the second which establishes the difference and superiority of the first. It is through this regular progression of similarities and differences that the Unity or the Divine Life is linked, and extends Himself to the most distant branches of beings.

It is because of this law that God is everywhere, that God is everything, though nothing is Him except Him.[253]

---

[253] This section is difficult to follow without some idea of Pasqually's notion of the creation. God exists in the Divine Immensity, and conceived the act of Creation through the process of Though, Will and Action, corresponding to some extent to the Platonic process of Creation of the Kabbalistic notion of the four worlds, in which the Divine thought (Atziluth) becomes a blueprint (in the Supra-heavenly Realm (Briah), which becomes a plan in the Heavenly Realm (Yetzirah), before being created as a material object in the Earthly Realm (Assiah). In His act of Creation, He emanated four types of spiritual being: the Superior Spiritual Beings, the Major Spiritual Beings, the Inferior Spiritual Beings and the Minor Spritual Beings. (Note that *emanation* was, for Pasqually, an act of individuation of an eternal spiritual being; whereas *creation* was reserved to bodies of matter which must die and decay). While the higher Orders functioned only in the Beyond, the lower two Orders functioned both in the infinite and also in the temporal (where the law of time functioned), although there was a barrier between the two; the Inferior Spirits creating the heavenly bodies and the Inferior Spirits creating the Earth. So in the Table we see the First Class of the Divine in which God works in himself, then passes his concepts on to the Spirits who translate His divine Thought, Will and Action into the creation of Man, who in his turn and cooperating or operating with God exercises God's Divine Will and brings it into Action in the material plane by bringing about the creation of all physical living beings (in Genesis 2:19-20: "And out of the ground the Lord God formed every beast of the field, and every fowl of the air; and brought them unto Adam to see what he would call them: and whatsoever Adam called every living creature, that was the name thereof. And Adam gave names to all cattle, and to the fowl of the air, and to every beast of the field." In old tradition, naming something gave one power of it.)

The Superior Spirits are denary spirits (10), which reflect and transmit the thought of God. The Major Spiritual Beings are octenary (8), joining the quaternary power of God with their own quaternary power giving them a double quaternary (i.e. octenary) power of transmitting the Divine Will through the barrier which separates the eternal from the temporal. The inferior Spirits are septenary (7) and the direct agents of Divine operating action, the third creative power of the process. These finally extend to man, the reflection of God and the quaternary power (4), who cooperates with God to bring about material Creation. Thus, we can see the diminution of power as we proceed down the chain and down the Classes.

V. The Historical Order of the Elemental Course of Nature

$23 = 5$ $\begin{cases} 1. \\ 2.\ \text{Creation of essences or immaterial principles} \dots \dots 3 \\ 3.\ \text{Creation of elements} \dots \dots \dots \dots \dots \dots \dots \dots 6 \\ 4.\ \text{Creation of bodies} \dots \dots \dots \dots \dots \dots \dots \dots \dots 9 \\ 5.\ \text{Putrefaction} \dots \dots \dots \dots \dots \dots \dots \dots \dots \dots 14 \\ 4.\ \text{Defacement of forms} \dots \dots \dots \dots \dots \dots \dots \dots 9 \\ 3.\ \text{Disappearance of elements} \dots \dots \dots \dots \dots \dots 6 \\ 2.\ \text{Disappearance of essences} \dots \dots \dots \dots \dots \dots 3 \\ 1. \end{cases}$

$\overline{25 = 7}$[254] $\qquad\qquad\qquad\qquad\qquad\qquad \overline{50 = 5}$

There should be no question in this Table about the causal creation of the Universe, nor of the directing numbers which oversaw and created its existence, because all those numbers are spiritual, and here we are only talking about elemental things in their principle, their life and their term. It shows that the same numbers are used to reintegrate the products which they created. It is a fundamental law that we see everywhere.

As for the course of things in the spiritual order, they must also have progressive numbers for their ages and their reintegration; but we have to look at them in a different series, and we will not consider them here.

---

[254] Remember that this is all theosophical addition, where $1 + 2 + 3 + 4 + 5 + 4 + 3 + 2 + 1 = 25 = 2 + 5 = 7$, and $3 + 6 + 9 + 14 + 9 + 6 + 3 = 50 = 5 + 0 = 5$. As an aside, the correlation of elements to the number 3 arises partly because Saint-Martin believed there were only 3 elements – Fire, Water and Earth – as he explained in his book *Of Errors & Truth* – PV.

VI. The Course of Elemental Things Considered In Light of the Generative Power of Women

In the process of the generative power of women we see the physical and progressive representation of everything which embraces the heart of beings.

It is from $\frac{13}{4}$ to $\frac{14}{5}$ years of age[255] that she acquires the power of generation, and her form transitions from a state of innocence to that of puberty and impurity: an image of the primitive alliance of 4 to 5.

It is from $\frac{44}{8}$ to $\frac{45}{9}$ years that she loses that same generative power, or at least begins to experience its degradation: an image of the new dissolution which destroys all bodies and all the body's powers.

She retains this power from around 14 years of age up till the age of 44 or 45 years of age, that is, for the space of about 30 to 31 years: an image of the Elemental number to which the human species is subject.[256]

After this expired and completed period, women who survive it commonly have more robust and more constant health: an image of what awaits us when we are delivered from the law of blood.

Her menstrual flow appears to me to be a result of the fact that, in the beginning, she had not fulfilled her purpose, and that she did not use her generative power for the true reproduction which was ordained for her. I presume this since the flow stops during pregnancies, a condition that results from the natural and regular use she has made of this same generative power.[257]

This flow usually follows a lunar period in duration, although it is not always subject to phases. – Let us remember that there is

---

[255] Note these are not fractions! The top figure is the age and the bottom figure the sum through theosophical reduction. Thus, $\frac{13}{4}$ means 13 years of age and $3 + 1 = 4$ – PV.

[256] See footnote 254 above, or the section on Air in Chapter 3 in *Of Errors & Truth* – PV.

[257] True from a biological standpoint; but the paternalistic and judgmental tone of 'should be constantly pregnant' do not reflect well in present times! – PV.

something that formerly weighed upon the waters and still weighs upon them today: I say *weigh* so as not to say fall.

Man is not subject to this flow. Could it be because he didn't make the same use as woman of his generative power?

He acquires that power at about the same age as women: one can easily see the reason. He retains that power much longer than she does, and even without having such a generally determined period of potency. That's also easy to see why.

Beneath all the laws of generation there are a multitude of other hidden connections and relationships which rightly apply to the order of things: but it is better to be refined than to be well informed. And that's why I'm not writing them down here.

VII. Concerning Creation

> *In the eyes of the Lord a day is like a thousand years, and a thousand years as a day.*
> (II. St. Peter, 3: 8)

Every action by the Eternal One constitutes a center with three angles. The emanated center is the image of the being created; the three angles, the image of its abilities or powers. In all beings nothing is fixed except the centers. All their powers are changeable. The Supreme Being is the only One Whose powers are as fixed as their center.

The stability of the centers is represented by 1, since it is this Unity which governs everything in each being. The mobility of the powers is represented by 0 (zero), since among numbers this zero only expresses the powers of beings, and does not change their root value.

When the Creator formed the world through six acts of thought, or in six days, each of those days was the creation of a center with three angles, that is, a Unity with three *zeros*, or again, the number *one thousand*. Each zero indicates a power which has travelled around its circle in a complete revolution (and that is how creations appear to the mind of the Eternal One. – For Him they are complete from the moment of their existence; time being resolved for Him as soon as it began). This is what we have called 'year', from the word *annus, anneau*[258]. And so, these three zeros or circles of years, preceded by Unity or 1, present a thousand years to man's mind, and all the more so to the mind of the Eternal One.

Each action – called a day – showed Him in one point the unfolding of the one thousand years which were to follow; and conversely, that unfolding of one thousand years is for Him but a single day, since He sees everything both in the deed, and in its accomplishment.

VIII. Elements of the Messiah, Without the Binary

Christ was ternary in his operating elements as he is in his essential elements. His 8^{ary} (octenary) number can only be drawn from the four simple and primitive roots 1, 2, 3 and 4, by adding together 1, 3 and 4, whose development of 4 produces 149 by the joining of 1 to the multiplication of 7. This kind of extraction, which should not be confused with that which shows 10 in 8, teaches us that, during His temporal work Christ was both divine, sensate[259] and physical; while considered in the eternal order of things, He is divine in all His three elements. – (He was the way, the truth and the life. *John, 14:6*).

He was conceived on the 14th of the moon in March: that was to represent Him temporally, it was to show the denary power attached to the quaternary of simple power; join to the incarnation the fact that He was resurrected at the identical time of the 14th of the moon in March. The inverse laws correspond to the direct laws, where they are intended to return everything back to its original state.

---

[258] The Latin for 'ring', and the French for 'ring', showing the close connection between the two words – PV.

[259] That is, reacting by means of the senses. The French use the word 'sensuel', but today it means the same as its English homonym 'sensual', so is best avoided – PV.

$$10 \ldots\ldots 8 \ldots\ldots 3.3 \; {}^{\circ}_{\circ}4{}^{\circ}_{\circ} \quad \Big| \quad {}^{\circ}_{\circ}4{}^{\circ}_{\circ} \; 3.3 \ldots\ldots 8 \ldots\ldots 10$$

Since the remedy is proportionate to the disease, it only takes a rule of *three* to be convinced of the Master's age: but it should be reentrant and not direct. Indeed, how can we doubt the coming of Christ? One only has to count the years of the world, and see if the 4th action has passed.

$$\frac{010}{0} \quad \frac{0}{010} \quad \frac{010}{0} \quad \frac{0}{010}$$

It was necessary for there to be in Him the divine, a sensate soul and the corporeal body to operate here on earth upon the physical order and upon all Creation, because just as our thinking soul could not join with our gross personal envelope without the intermediary of an individual sensate bond, so the Divine Repairer could not have joined with His bodily form, albeit pure, without the help and medium of a sensate soul.

This sensate soul bore within in it the 4th number. His divine being carried ONE, and His body carried 3. In us the divine soul bears 4; the body 9. I do not know the number of our sensate soul (some think it bears the number 15) but I presume that in us it does not carry the same number as in the Savior, since I see that in all the other elements in which He is similar to us, He always bears superior[260] numbers.

---

[260] That is, lower numbers; closer to 1. Just as, following the Table below, when Saint-Martin says 'we must also be lower than Him in the element whose number we don't know', this means the number must be *higher* than 4, since that is the number of the sensate soul of the Repairer, and ours is inferior to His, or further away from Unity or 1 – PV.

IN THE MESSIAH		IN MAN	
The Divine Soul.......	1	The Divine Soul.............	4
The Sensate Soul......	4	The Sensate Soul............	
The Body................	3	The Body....................	9

If, in those of our elements where we know the number we are lower than the elements of the Repairer, we must also be lower than Him in the element whose number we don't know: that is, in the number of our sensate soul. It is in that sensate soul that the true key of man is found. It is by it that he is joined to the sensitive or to the animal body. But since, unlike Christ, he is not placed voluntarily within this prison, it is not natural for him to know the key which keeps him locked here. That is why we do not know the number of our sensate souls. (Though I have reason to believe that the sensate soul bears the number 6[261]).

IX. *The Spiritual and Circular Progression of the Quaternary in the Universal Circle*

1 - Divine.
   1. 3. 3. 4. 10
2 - State and destiny of man in his primitive election 4
3 - Prevaricating state of man, in a state of suffering, in resipiscence and regenerated.
   5. 6. 7. 8. 8
4 - Destruction of forms and reduction of material appearance to its three constituent principles.
   6. 7. 8. 9. 3
5 - Reintegration of beings into their spiritual virtues.
   7. 8. 9. 10. 7

---

[261] Note that Saint-Martin isn't disagreeing with those who suggest its number is 15, because $1 + 5 = 6$ – PV.

6 - Reintegration of beings into the divine virtues of unity through the operations of the quaternary.
   8. 9. 10. 1. 1

X. From Whence Numbers Draw their Quality

Everything is true in Unity. Everything which is co-eternal with Him is perfect. Everything that is separate from Him is altered or false.

Nothing is false in the decade when taken collectively. Taken separately, nothing is true in it except when it has a mediate or direct connection with Unity. In *Zechariah* 4:14, *the two olive trees* or *the two anointed ones* are good because they *attend the Lord of the whole earth*. That is why both the animals called *unclean* and others called *clean* or *pure* were brought into the ark. That is why the beast of Revelation has a number which isn't real. That is why Swedenborg (*Heaven and its Wonders and Hell* vol. II, pp. 78 and 79) says in N°. 512, that those who rush into hell don't pass through the third state of man after death and suffer only the two states which follow our corporeal dissolution; that is to say, condemnation and pain. That is why the two laws of physical Nature are pure, because they are linked to the third law which governs them, and the latter to the fourth which gives rise to them all. That is why all our efforts, all our virtues and all our knowledge are worthless if we confine them to the conception of thought in the mind and the whim of our feeble desire in the will, and do not then realize them in deeds through action. And that is why the number 2 was not included in the elements which served as the basis for the Master's appearance and His temporal operations, because the Sovereign Master had come to combat this number which had become iniquitous in having separated itself from the decade, and because the Divine Repairer *was made manifest to take away our sins; and in Him there is no sin. 1st Epistle of John*, 3:5.

And He was in all points tempted like us, yet was without sin (*Heb.* 4:15), because this sin or this number 2 didn't enter into the elements of His temporal operations. He was announced as *ex Deo natus ante omnia secula*[262] *(see the Nicene Creed). (Ex utero ante Luciferum genui te.* Ps. 110:3[263]). These are His Divine elements in which all numbers are contained, because none of these numbers, taken in the Divine Order, can be separated from the decade.

God once said to Him: *Hodie genui te* (Ps. 2:7[264]) That was His mission in time.

XI. Numerical Formulae

1st formula

Square a number.
Perform theosophical addition on that number.
Perform theosophical addition on the number which precedes it.
Add the two numbers arithmetically.
You will have the square of your first number.
Example: 6 x 6 = 36.
Theosophical addition of 6 (the sum of the numbers $1 + 2 + 3 + 4 + 5 + 6$) = 21
Theosophical addition of 5 (the sum of the numbers $1 + 2 + 3 + 4 + 5$)   = 15

$$\text{Total}.....36$$

2nd formula

Multiply a theosophical product of a number by 8.
Add 1 to the result.
Find its square root.
Take the lesser half of this root.
You will have the root number of the original theosophical product.
Example: 21 is the theosophical product of 6 (see example above).
21 x 8 = 168 + 1 = 169.

---

[262] Begotten of his Father before all worlds – PV.
[263] From the womb before the Daystar I have begotten you – PV.
[264] This day have I begotten you – PV.

$\sqrt{169} = 13$. $\dfrac{13}{2} = 6 \ldots$ [265]

6, the smaller half = the number creating the theosophical product.

3rd *formula*

Add a square number theosophically. Square the sum.

You have a product which will contain the sum of the cubes of all the elemental numbers of the square you initially added theosophically.

Example: The square of 3 = 9.

Theosophically add 45 (the sum of the numbers 1+2+3+4+5+6+7+8+9) x 45^2[266] = 2,025.

1^3	1
2^3	8
3^3	27
4^3	64
5^3	125
6^3	216
7^3	343
8^3	512
9^3	729[267]
Total	2,025

One can find an infinite number of these types of formulas in the numbers; but they are of little use in that we don't know how to apply them. Besides, there is a problem with this approach, since it restricts all the numbers to the same operation when there are some which must refuse to do so, as in the last example: we had to regard 8 as the cube of 2, which repugnant to the arithmetic spirit.[268]

---

[265] Saint-Martin appears to be telling us to divide the number by 2 but only use whole numbers as the result (remember he has an abhorrence of fractions). Then take the smaller of the two results. In this example, 13/2 is 6.5, but he avoids fractions by saying 13 is the product of 7 + 6, then takes the smaller of the two figures: 6 - PV

[266] That is to say, 45^2 – PV.

[267] That is to say, 9 cubed, or 9 x 9 x 9 = 729 – PV.

[268] This is an odd statement, since $2^3 = 8$ is a standard formula in arithmetic. One possible conclusion is that Saint-Martin was actually trying to point out that, while this works in

Finally, it seems to me that bringing numbers down to the level of vulgar calculation, where geometricians and mathematicians have made great strides in calculating the performance and movement of beings, adds nothing to our knowledge of the motivation and the spirit of those beings. Thus, we are very knowledgeable in this century about the revolutions of the stars, their distances, the law of the refraction of light, the proportions of time and speed, etc.; but we have not yet taken the first step towards learning the reason for the least of these wonders; and I repeat, this is because we are only concerned with calculating the laws, and not calculating the reasons.

However, let us acknowledge the person who discovered the formulas mentioned above. It is a testimony to intelligence and a focused mind.

4th and 5th formulas

Nevertheless, I do know of two very useful formulas:

The first is that of manipulating the number 9, which, whatever one does to it, always gives the answer 9, and never even changes the value of other numbers which we might try to join to this 9 (nonary), and which theosophically always remain the same.

Example: $9 \times 9 + 81$; $8 + 1 = 9$.
$9 \times 1,255 = 11,295 = 18 = 9$.
$4 + 9 = 13 = 4$.

---

standard arithmetic, in his theosophical system it did not sit well since the cube of 2 (the number of evil or duality raised to the power of 3, or divinity, resulted in the double quaternary, the number 8, which he often used to represent Christ. This would appear to be borne out by Serge Caillet's quotation of this passage as translating to: "repugnant to the spirit of numbers, although it is true to the spirit of arithmetic." Which he cites as being from Section 13 (paragraph 49 from Chapter 2. Numbers in *A Course on Martinism* pub. Institut Eleazar, 1990). However, since the version of *Des Nombres* used in this current translation is the 1861 edition by L. Shauer, one has either to assume that Mr. Caillet has access to a different version (indeed, in the Schauer version this passage is in Section 11, not 13); or that, French being his native language, he is more attuned to subtlety and nuance than a foreign translator! The passage in French in the Schauer version (and copied in two other more modern French copies, is: "où il a fallu regarder 8 comme le cube de 2, ce qui répugne à l'esprit arithmétique" – PV.

The second formula is the one by which one extracts the spirit of any number and which always gives you 9 for the *caput mortuum* and for the corpse.[269]

Example: 13 = 4. Take 4 from 13, which leaves 9.

1,255 = 13. Take 13 from 1,255, which leaves 1,242 = 9.

The first of these formulas tells us that matter does not mix with spirit.

The second formula, which derives from the first, is that one can always detach this matter from the spirit it envelops.

These are truths whose employment and use are given to man in relation to himself as being free; when compared to other beings, when he is powerful and has received the key of St. Peter *(Matt. 16:9*[270]*).*

It is only through fermentation, by stirring and making the different essences react that one may extract the spirit from them.

XII. Multiplication and Addition

One of the great keys to numbers is not to confuse these two operations. It is by being careful to distinguish between them that, when considering two numbers in the spiritual sense, one can know which is the root and which is the product. The one obtained

---

[269] Although mentioned in an earlier footnote, this point bears reiterating. In the spiritual alchemy of Pasqually and Saint-Martin, the overall number contains both the spirit and the material envelope of the being. Through theosophical addition we can identify the spiritual element, and then remove this from the composite being to obtain the number of the material part. As an example, using the number 42, theosophical addition gives us 4 + 2 = 6, which represents the spirit of that number. By subtracting the spirit from the total number we get 42 − 6 = 36, which is the material part, which he calls the *caput mortuum* (using a familiar alchemical phrase) as well as the more prosaic 'corpse', indicating the lifeless matter remaining. This is the number 36, and we can verify this by adding the 3 to the 6, making 3 + 6 = 9, the number of *matter* – PV.

[270] This should read Matt, 16:19, and reads (including part of verse 18): "...Thou art Peter, and upon this rock I will build my church; and the gates of hell shall not prevail against it. And I will give unto thee the keys of the kingdom of heaven: and whatsoever thou shalt bind on earth shall be bound in heaven: and whatsoever thou shalt loose on earth shall be loosed in heaven." Note that these words are also used in the ceremony of Ordination, which passes to the priest the power to hear confession and to forgive sins – PV.

through addition is the root; the one obtained through multiplication is the product or power. That is why 10 is the root of 4, because you go from 4 to 10 by addition; but 16 is the power of 4, because you can only obtain that through multiplication.[271]

We see here that the powers of numbers are not limited to those set by scientists. For, although 10 is most certainly the square root of 100 and the cube root of 1,000, it is still the root of 4. Now, this root can be called an essential or integral root. These three roots are sufficient to complete all beings, because through the essential root it has life or existence, through the square root it has progression, and through the cube root it has its term or purpose. The other powers which calculators assume are beyond these are simply multiples of these three original roots. They are only repetitions carried out by extending these original roots; but they are not given by the root germ of Nature; they are only secondary saps and superfluities.

10 is also the essential root of 7, because 7, through its addition to 28, sums to 10.

Whereas 4 is simply the square root of that same 7 by 16, and the cube root of 64.[272]

To summarize:

4 is not an essential root, since it produces only squares, and we know no number that belongs to it by simple addition.

10 is a doubly essential root, namely: for 4 and for 7. These are its two radii, its two powers; one divine, the other spiritual.[273]

4 and 7 are not essential roots; but they are essential powers. However, I am only talking about 7 when it comes from 16. There

---

[271] Again, this now familiar formula uses theosophical addition and multiplication. Here the root is the source of the number, so $4 + 3 + 2 + 1 = 10$, making the number 10 the root of 4; while the power or product of 4 is 4^2 or $4 \times 4 = 16$ – PV.

[272] Again, for clarity: $7 + 6 + 5 + 4 + 3 + 2 + 1 = 28$, and $2 + 8 = 10$. This means 10 is the root of both 10 and 4 (as we saw earlier). And 4 is the square root of 7 since 4^2 or $4 \times 4 = 16$, and $1 + 6 = 7$; while 4^3 or $4 \times 4 \times 4 = 64$ – PV.

[273] According to Pasqually, the number 4, being the number which contains the decade, is referred to divine creation; while the number 7 is referred to the Holy Spirit. In his *Treatise*, Pasqually stated: "…the septenary number, which proceeds from the absolute denary number, is the more than perfect number that the Creator used for the emancipation of every spirit out of His divine immensity…" – PV.

is a primitive 7 that does not come from it and which will be discussed below.

I will also say nothing more about the 8 (octenary), which depends on 1 for the operation of its distinctive abilities, but which must here be equated with Unity[274]; for in the real, fundamental, divine order there are no numbers. 1 is everything, and there is only 1 and 10: 1 for the essence, and 10 for operations and products.

1 is thrice the essential root, namely: of 10, of 4 and of 7. But 10 isn't separate from 1. Thus, it is He who acts in 10, and in a coeternal union, when 10 operates 4 and 7. The 10 and the 1 are the principle; the 4 and 7 are the products. So, these numbers are only square roots, not essential roots, because only the Principle Unity and His denary, which is His own power, can create beings, that is to say to bear the name of 'essential root'.

But why can this essential root be known only through addition, and are the square and cubic root to be found in the extraction of the roots, that is by the opposite of multiplication?

The essential root can only be known by addition because it is enough for beings to know that they receive everything from that essential root, or Universal generative principle, and that they shouldn't know how they come from it. The *fact* is all that is necessary to prove to the beings produced in this way: the *means*, the generative principle, is reserved to Him alone. Now, this fact is proven by this law of addition: $1, 2, 3, 4 = 10$.

Multiplication, on the other hand, is the route used to get from square and cubic roots to their powers, and *vice versa*, because this second product is only due to the abilities of beings: they must have the ability to produce them and to withdraw them into themselves, which becomes a new argument for freedom which, independent of our natural sense, is proven here by the laws of numbers.

If the generative linking of the essential root to His powers is not recognizable, it is because that essential root principle only belongs to the act of Creation, and because, if His powers could be set in motion in this secret linkage, they would want to create like Him and could do without Him.

---

[274] And this is because 1 stands for God and 8 for Christ – PV.

But the link between square and cubic roots and their powers is known to us, that we might have proof that we can exercise and develop our abilities, and that it is inexcusable for us not to do so.

Another wonder to note here is that, in the extraction of the square and cubic root, or to put it another way, in the *retiring* of our abilities, the square or cubic powers or abilities they represent fade until not the least trace remains; whereas in the law of addition that brings the essential powers back to the essential root, they remain intact and they are still permanent. This is strong proof that our abilities are not being; whereas our essential power, that is, our constituent *self*, is an immortal and inextinguishable being.

Here I will add two very instructive formulas:

$4 \times 4 = 10 + 16 = 7$, the essential power entrusted to primitive and perfect man over the divine and the temporal, represented by the spirit or the septenary. This is why the number 4 is the father and mother of man who indeed, according to Genesis; was created male and female by this septenary power containing 4 and 3. Pythagoras and his disciples were wrong when they said that 7 was fatherless and motherless, unless they meant to speak of the primitive septenary, which is the root and universal wheel from which everything derives.

$7 \times 7 + 40 + 9$, the power of the spirit or the divine and the temporal over man imprisoned in matter, and within the temporal: "*Minuisti eum paulo minus ab angelis.*" *Ps.* 8:5[275]. Indeed, if man had not prevaricated, the septenary would have remained in its state of integrity and in its natural rank, which was to be inferior to man, since 4 goes straight back to 10 by addition, whereas 7 returns to it only by means of two steps and by means of an intermediary, being forced to go there via 28. But because of his prevarication, since man became materially corporealized, he bears the number 40 instead of 4. It was then that the septenary became superior to him, because 40 can only return to the essential root or to 10 via 160, whilst 7, despite its extension of 49 that it is obliged to take in

---

[275] For thou hast made him a little lower than the angels. Note the original text cites verse 6, whereas it is actually verse 5. Here 40 – or 4 – is the number of creation or man in his primitive glory, and 9 the number of matter (though in this case 40 refers to 4 x 10 or glorious man enmired in matter, the dual being of matter and spirit comingled) – PV.

relation to us and as an effect of mercy, remains no less intact in its essential power of 7 and because of that is closer to a degree of the essential root that we have in common with it.

Nevertheless, it is important to note the relationship which exists between the temporal operations of these two numbers 4 and 7 taken to their conclusion, namely: 160 and 49. They are so linked to one another by consanguinity, their rights are so well coordinated together, that 40 passing via 160 can go back to 7, to 28 and to 10. Its colleague 49 is obliged to go back to 13 and 4 to return to the same denary root. Here we see two things: firstly, that we can't do anything without the spirit; and secondly, how dear we are to it.

The numbers of matter, 3, 6 and 9 are also powers; but are not essential powers like 4 and 7, because unlike those two numbers, they do not derive their origin from the essential root 10. However, though not essential powers, one cannot refrain from looking at them as roots, since indeed all numbers are, each according to its class. Then we perform the same operations as we did on 4 and 7 upon these numbers. They are raised to their square and cubed powers; they are reintegrated through extraction; they even repeat in their order an image of the three great laws previously considered: that it takes three degrees of action to complete the circle. However, these three degrees are found in the number 3, which in this case, is the being or the principle; secondly in 6, which is the progress and finally in 9, which is the term. But this repetition is only apparent because in the material order the number 3 is itself only apparent and transient, and expecting from it only what is given to it, neither the unfolding nor the reintegration of its powers or abilities are as free as 4 and 7. Also, its works are not counted like ours.

As for number 8, we have lost so much knowledge of it that only the temporal can convey it to us; that is, now we only possess it in forms or combinations, which will be more clearly set out in the paragraph on the properties of the 8^{ry} (octenary). Indeed, the pure and divine octenary cannot manifest itself in its pure nature, given the lower state in which we are. *Eight* is not a number of matter. It is even greater than 7 and 4; it is the Divine summary, but a complete summary where everything is as strong in God Himself as in 10. The difference is that in 10 the whole Deity acts through extension and expansion, and in 8 it acts by pure concentration; but the harmony of these two numbers is complete. That is why Jesus Christ said: *"I am not alone, because the Father is with me." "All things that the Father hath are mine."* (*John* 16:32 and 15). Again, that is why it is said: *"Minuisti eum paulo minus ab angelis."*

One can also see the reason for *"hodie genui te"* (*Ps.* 12:7).[276]

But we should avoid the danger of confusing the rank of 8 and 4 by having them go back to 10. 4 goes back by 1, 2, 3 and 4. *Eight* goes back by 3 and 4 as the musical scale proves. So, 4 appears to be only the extract of 10, while 8 is the *operator* since it is calculated with its own actions delineated within the scale. Thus, it is even less possible for us to find the root link from 10 to 8 than from 10 to 4, since 10 is not the root of 8, but an essential and co-eternal number with it, and only distinguished by another operating character.

We also have to be careful not to add 8 theosophically, since that would denature it. It gives 36, which is far from its relative number. Only 4 and power 7 can be reduced to 10 in this way because they have descended from it, whereas 8 is not produced by 10, but it has a right to it and the Holy Spirit is its left side. *"Ego rogabo Patrem, et alium paracletum dabit vobis ut maneat vobiscum in æternum"* (*John* 14:16).[277] This Holy Spirit is also septenary as it is the direct agent of the octenary. *"Ille me clarificabit, quia de meo accipiet et annuntiabit vobis"* (*John* 16:14).[278] But this septenary is not of the order of those who were subject to man in the beginning. It is the essential root of both 8 and 10, since it acts together with them and without any interruption in the Divine order. As for the temporal-spiritual order, their action is alternative. Music tells us: the octave is silent when the seventh speaks, and vice versa when the octave speaks the seventh is silent. What music indicates, the Gospel proves *(John,* 16:17) *"Expedit vobis ut vadam; si enim non abiero,*

---

[276] This day have I begotten thee – PV.

[277] And I will pray the Father, and he shall give you another Comforter (Paraclete), that he may abide with you forever – PV.

[278] He shall glorify me: for he shall receive of mine and shall shew it unto you – PV.

Paracletus non veniet ad vos; si autem abiero, mittam eum ad vos".[279] – 1, 10, 8, 7: here is the Divine, or all the essential roots. Man, or 4, is its extract and the first essential power.

It was to regenerate this quaternary, man, that the Repairer came into the world and left His virtues and gifts there, when He left it. It is not without reason that there were only four soldiers at his crucifixion, and that they tore his clothes into four parts *(John 19:23)*. It is also not without reason that His seamless robe was not shared.

If Divinity is an essential *root*, one must hear what Jesus Christ said in *Matthew 26:53*: *"Thinkest thou that I cannot now pray to my Father, and he shall presently give me more than twelve legions of angels?"* Every Divine action is the product of a real being. A poet said:

"*God cannot think without creating His image.*"

Also, Isaiah said of God, (57:16): "I will not contend for ever, neither will I be always wroth: for *the spirits have come out of me, and it is I who have created all souls.*"[280]

As for the numbers 2 and 5, although in ordinary arithmetic they can be elevated to powers, we must be careful not to consider them as pure and true roots in spiritual arithmetic. As a result, they should never be squared or cubed as one does from other roots, because indeed they lead to seductive results, but which are only good in appearance. Such is the privilege of iniquity. The angel of darkness has the power to transform himself into an angel of light, but see what elements make up his results: $2 \times 2 = 4 \times 2 = 8$. $5 \times 5 = 25 = 7 \times 5 = 35 = 8$, and you will recognize that this deceitful and captivating being, while appearing to hide only hands under his coat, actually hides claws. Therefore, let us never allow his corrupt roots to grow, let us refuse them and on the contrary, cultivate them in a manner which will make them as sterile as possible.

---

[279] It is expedient for you that I go away: for if I go not away, the Comforter will not come unto you, but if I depart, I will send him unto you – PV.

[280] The King James Version does not read like this, so to preserve Saint-Martin's intent the passage has been translated directly from the French – PV.

There is nothing more delicate than the manipulation of numbers; there are very few rules; and all attention should be focused on the art of applying them.

Addition and multiplication: these are the sum techniques of this sublime science. But it would be completely distorted if these two means were used equally on all numbers. Numbers of the same nature can be multiplied; those who are heterogeneous may only be added. All this is to prevent monstrosities.

XIII. Number of Elements, their Connections with the Perverse Beings and Those of Divine and Spiritual Powers with the Universal Circle

Paris, 1775, in Luxembourg with Abbé Rosier.

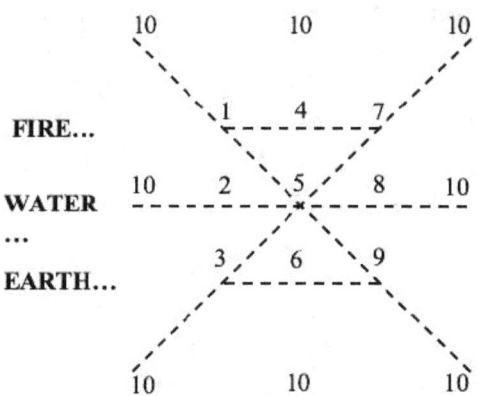

In each of these Elements one should consider the principle or beginning, the progress and the term.

Fire is 1 in its principle, because it is the physical image of the Spirit. And it always rises up to its source. It is 4 in its progress as occupying the center of bodies which are all represented by a triangle. It is 7 in its term, because it ends by reuniting with the Spirit from which it emanated. (This is nothing to do with material fire).

In the Elemental order, the number and actions of physical agents are identical: Water – 2, Earth – 3, Fire – 4, Air – 1.

Water is 2 in its principle, being the opposite of fire. The horizontal line it makes cuts the line of fire at right angles. It is 5 in its progress because, in the image of the impure quinary, it tends to break down all barriers and to extinguish the action of generative and productive fire. It is 8 in its term because, its action being moderated by measure, it reflects the action of the Repairer which is to temper everything and lead everything to produce.

Earth having being already discussed well enough, I will say nothing more about it.

The sum of the numbers of fire gives.....3	New image where the
That of the numbers of water gives......6	general law of physical
That of the numbers of earth gives.......9	beings is found again.

In the spiritual order, the 5 in the middle is taken to be the perverse being. The other eight numbers surrounding him are taken to be the spiritual, temporal, divine powers that create a barrier around him and hold him in his prison, such that, by forming a continuous and unbroken enclosure about him, it is impossible for him to avoid the torments and troubles which these powers cause him.

It should be noted that these powers are *eight* in number, to remind us that they are the weapons of the Divine Agent charged with manifesting the justice of the Creator.

It should be noted that by adding these powers that are opposite one another two by two, we always obtain 10 as a result.[281] It is here that the image expands and proves the great property of the octenary, which is the expression of the denary and its own substance, as will be shown elsewhere. But at the same time we should see that we cannot add the two corresponding numbers without extending their power and having them pass over the quinary which, by this means, is continually crossed and wounded by the violent action of the eight denaries. Such is the predicament of all the prevaricators who have become his followers; they will

---

[281] That is, 1+ 9, 2 + 8, 3 +7, 4 + 6 – PV.

go with him to that place *"ubi nullus ordo sed sempiternus horror inhabitat."*[282] *Job,* 10:22.

XIV. Properties of the Octenary (8^{ry})

It was only after the addition of the square of the spirit that the operation of the 8^{ry} was able to be accomplished. The forty-nine gates opened by Solomon had to have received their Sabbath before the fiftieth opened.[283] The work of the octenary can therefore be clearly known only in the spirit of the number 50, because then the number of iniquity and the number of matter are dispelled by the

---

[282] Where no order but everlasting horror dwelleth. (A direct translation, since the King James Bible gives an altogether feebler translation! – PV.

[283] This is based on the Talmudic teaching that 'The world was created with Fifty Gates of Understanding' (Note: the Hebrew of 'Understanding' is *Binah*, and they are sometimes therefore referred to as the 'Fifty Gates of Binah', or the 3rd Sephira on the Tree of Life), and the Prologue to the Sepher Zohar: "In that Temple there are 50 Gates." The Tree of Life which bear the 'fruits' of God's graces has been used by Jewish and Western mystics to create the diagram of the Kabbalistic Tree of Life, in which the 'fruits' of the Tree are the Sephiroth. Leviticus 23:15-16 requires that, during the 50 days between Passover (the sparing of the first-born of the Jews in Egypt, and the beginning of harvest; and *Shavu'ot*, marking the arrival at Mount Sinai and transmission of the Ten Commandments, as well as the end of the harvest season and the first fruits (note the lunar connection), the faithful must perform the 50-day practice of the 'Counting of the Omer'. Moses was said to have mastered the first 49 Gates, but not the final one. Nor did Solomon, since the 50th Gate represents full knowledge of God; and it was not until the Messiah came – or comes – to open the 50th Gate that we shall behold God (the difference in tenses depends on whether this is viewed as having already happened through His sacrifice, or that it will happen at the Second Coming of Revelation). This Jewish mystical notion was continued in the Renaissance as the "Hermetic Gates of Intelligence", founded on alchemical, astrological and mathematical practices. It was from these that William Wynn Westcott derived the modified version of the Gates of Intelligence for the use of members of the Hermetic Order of the Golden Dawn in late Victorian times. In a way this reflected the Medieval concept of the Chain of Being, in which all of creation from the lowliest plant to the Archangels had their assigned and immutable place in this great chain. However, in this latter version, which grouped the 50 Gates into six Orders – 1. Elementary, 2. Evolutionary, 3. Humanity, 4. The World of Spheres, 5. The Angelic World, and 6. The Archetype or Ain Soph – the basis of magic allowed the mortal to communicate with any Order in this hierarchy (largely summarized from part of *Chapter One: The Gates of Heaven and the Enochian Tradition*, found at kheph777.tripod.com and accessed on Nov. 26, 2019. Sadly, no more information can be given since this Chapter appears to stand on its own, with no other attributions or even the title of the book or paper from which it is extracted) – PV.

strong and generative influence of Unity, which comes to take their place.

Now, how many eyes it takes to read the numbers! Who could ever believe that 50 is equal to 8?[284] And that with the distinctive signs of all the marvelous and Divine actions which have been used towards the regeneration of human posterity. We must also be careful to look at this Unity which only joins 49 through an octenary connection. (Basil of Caesarea, *"De Spiritu Sancto"* Ch. 27, speaks of the square of 7, but he does not appear to have the key to the rest). Nothing is separated in the order and operation of this Divine metaphysics. Unity unites and blends with this septenary, and that is all we can know here on earth. The Son and the Spirit are all that are granted to us. As for the Absolute Unity or the Father, no one has been able to see or will see Him in this world, other than in this octenary which is, indeed, the only way by which we can reach Him. And thus the Savior said: *"(No man) knoweth the Father save the Son, and he to whomsoever the Son will reveal him"* (*Matthew*, 11:27). *"My Father is greater than I"* (*John*, 14:28). *"I and my Father are one"* (*John*, 10:30). The contradictions of the last two quotes soon disappear before the illumination provided by numbers. 50 is for the first passage, 1 is for the second.

Whoever knows the relationship between names and numbers after that, will judge what he can expect from his faith in the name of the Repairer. The number lets us understand through intelligence that this Being is the Universal Depository of all the treasures of the Divine and Triune essence; the name makes it understood by the fact that it is the active and operating principle of every work and action, and the name by which the Father grants to all those

---

[284] Since the Holy Spirit bears the number 7, the square of the Spirit is 7 x 7 = 49. Now, we saw earlier that the Spirit was in part emanated from the Repairer (8), being the essential root of both 8 (Christ) and 10 (or 1, God the Father). Adding God to the 49 Gates makes 50 and the final 1 means we will see God face to face. Therefore, here Saint-Martin says that 50 is equal to 8 since, by opening the final Gate and seeing God, we are also seeing Him through the connection of the Octenary, His Son the Repairer – PV.

who ask him by this means and with confidence. *John*, 15:16.[285] (*"Without me ye can do nothing"*) *John*, 15:5).

The number 50 also tells us why the Savior said in *St. John*, 16:7: *"It is useful for you that I leave, for if I do not leave, the Comforter will not come to you; but if I leave, I will send it to you."*

As long as He was busy preparing His work, Unity and the septenary concentrated together within the bounds of our lower realm could not deploy their full effectiveness, and the fruits of their virtues grew secretly until they had reached their realization.

When that time came, when Unity now loosed from His shackles could reach His Divine Center, and the septenary could embrace the entire circumference of the circle He had come to regenerate, it was then that it was beneficial for the apostles – and for the world – that when Unity returned to His source, He left to the septenary the free power to put into action all the virtues which had blossomed within Him, and charged it in consequence to teach all things and all truths to His elect; while upon returning to His Father He took up once more all His splendor and majesty, to return at the end of time, surrounded by glory to operate fully before both man and the Universe what the septenary or the Holy Spirit would have operated partially and gradually in this base world. *"He that believeth on me, the works that I do shall he do also; and greater works than these shall he do, because I go unto my Father"(John,*14:12). *"And whatsoever ye shall ask in my name, that will I do, that the Father may be glorified in the Son." (John,* 14:13). This superiority of works that is promised is conceived when the octenary, then reunited with the Father, will be able to provide those who call upon Him with the powers and strength of the root denary, whereas the Repairer could only operate in this low world as a representative of the same denary. *"I say not unto you that I will pray my Father for you" (John,* 16:26); *"For my Father Himself loveth you, because ye have loved me, and have believed that I have come out from God*" *(John,* 16:27).[286] What a superb

---

[285] "Whatsoever ye shall ask of the Father in my name, he my give it you." In other words, the number 8 (or octenary) is the number and the Repairer (or Jesus) is the name

[286] It is worth remarking in these two passages from St. John that Saint-Martin uses the term '*my* Father' twice, whereas the King James Version only states '*the* Father' – PV.

confirmation! The Word is united with the Father: by praying to one, we get the aid of both: our prayer necessarily connects us with the Father! Let us prostrate ourselves, to pray and to tremble with joy!

The number 50 disappeared when this holy 8^{ary} drew near because they couldn't exist together. Iniquity and appearance could not survive before Unity and its power. This was that divine Church outside of which no one can be saved, and against which the gates of Hell shall never prevail, according to the promise made to St. Peter *(Matthew,* 16:18). This is the key which opens and no one closes, that closes and no one opens. *(Revelation,* 3:7).

XV. Intrinsic Value of Geometric Measurements

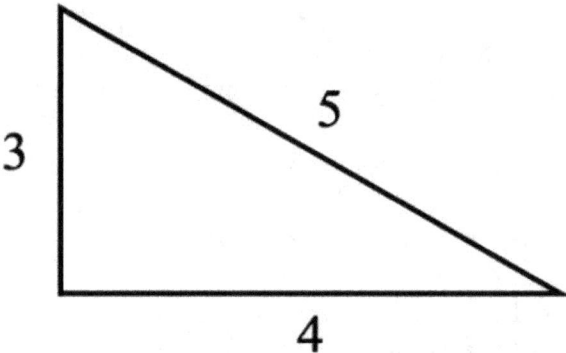

The hypotenuse has a value of 5. The other two sides of the rectangular triangle have values of 3 and 4. The square of 5 equals the sum of the squares of 3 and 4.

This is the image of the original crime, when the perverse one wished to control the third and fourth innate causes concealed within the Supreme Principle. This hypotenuse is an alteration, a decomposition, a dismemberment of the circle. For when the circle is intact, it has diameters in all directions, that is, from 4 and from 10. But at the same time, it is clear that this hypotenuse is spiritual, since it is confused with the diameter and it is attached to the center; and that is why its triangle is false, because in the true order of things, triangles should be attached to the center by only one of their angles and not by their bases or sides.

Multiples of 3, 4 and 5 give the same results, and with the same accuracy and intelligence.

You can see the march of the Elements according to their numbers 6, 8 and 10; where Fire shows itself operating everything and filling everything, since its square 100 equals the sum of 64 and 36, squares of 8 and 6.

For now, let's look at *Lettres édifiantes*, Volume 26, page 146, pub. Mérigot, Paris 1783.

There we find texts or fragments of the Chinese book called: *Chou Pei*. This book is recognized as authentic by the Chinese, and predates the book burning that occurred in 213 BC, under Emperor Qin Shi Huang.

3rd text: The foundations of numbers have their source in the *Yuan* (the round) and the *Fang* (the square).

4th text: The round (*Yuan*) comes from the square (*Fang*) 4 = 10.

5th text: The *Fang* (square) comes from the *Ku*.

6th text: the *Ku* comes from 9 x 9 = 81.

7th text: If we separate the *Ku* in two we make the *Hou* wide of 3 and a long *Ku* of 4. The *Ching* line joins the two sides. *Ku* makes angles. The *Ching* is 5.

Missionary's Note: "These texts refer to the rectangular triangle where one side is 4, the other 3 and the base 5. This figure is called *Hou-Ku*; and those in China who are considered to know the *Hou-Ku* well have a reputation for possessing a sublime and profound knowledge."

10th text: The two *Ku* make a long *Chang* of 25; this is the *Chi Chü*, the sum of the *Ku*.

11th text: It was by means of a fundamental knowledge of these calculations that Yu (the first Emperor of the Hia dynasty) brought the empire into a good condition.[287]

I cannot deny having experienced the most vivid satisfaction in encountering ancient traces of a profound truth which, thanks to

---

[287] These terms are more clearly explained on page 569 in the book *5000 Years of Geometry*, by Christoph J. Scriba, Peter Schreiber et al., pub. Birkhäuser (English translation of the 3rd German edition, 2015) – PV.

God, had been made clear in my meditations more than a year before I read the Chinese volume which transmits them to us. The Author of All Certainty knows what it means; that is enough for my heart and mind, and I respectfully adore the One who has allowed the making of such parallel discoveries from times more than 4,000 years ago and at a distance of 4,000 leagues.

If the material philosopher dares to say that these laws and calculations are arbitrary, enlightened intelligence will tell him that they are as fixed as the nature of beings. It will show him in the three lines that make up the rectangle in question: 1st the number of iniquity; 2nd the number of matter; 3rd the number of man. It will show him the separation of light and darkness by the *sine*. It will show him the primitive and glorious reign of man over matter and over iniquity by his connection with the center. It will show him with what inexhaustible power the Supreme Wisdom always sets against iniquity a sum of force equal to its perverse number, in order to balance and contain it.

It is essential that the rectangular triangle be *scalene*[288] to perform all these wonders, for if it were *isosceles*, the two equal sides would each give an equal square, the sum of which would no longer form a square, and would therefore oppose balance, harmony and reunion. But everything being related, this reunion, this harmony would no longer be wished for, since then there would be no more disorder, there would be no more hypotenuse, and the *Ching* would no longer have a value of 5, since it has this value only when the sine is not total and when it has a base next to the center.

It is the same central point of the circle that constitutes the value of 4 on the long side of the rectangle, otherwise it would be worth 3 like the short side.

It is not too much to note that this hypotenuse or base of the triangle is called *Ching* among the Chinese, and that the same word means 'king' in several European dialects derived from Celtic. כון in Hebrew means base, disposition and preparations for idol

---

[288] A scalene triangle is one whose sides are of different lengths – PV.

worship. Why shouldn't the *quinque*[289] of the Latins trace back in some way to this source, either in meaning or in letter?

There would be volumes to write on this figure, and I'm not surprised that there has been the greatest veneration in China for Fo-Hi, who is said to have developed knowledge of it, as well as for the other scholars who meditated on it, understood it and used it with success.

For me Pythagoras is also a person worthy of the greatest respect for having discovered some of the properties of the rectangular triangle, although the complement to this knowledge had existed in ancient China. The Chinese also knew the 19-year cycle, which made Methon[290] so famous among the Greeks. Such insights are communicated everywhere and to all those who do not reject them, since it is natural to man for he was born in the very midst of light.

18th text: The *Fang* (square) represents the earth. The *Yuan* (round) represents the sky. The heaven is *Yuan*; The earth is *Fang*.

The missionary explains everything by ordinary trigonometry.

The 20th text gives the sky the colors brown and black, and the earth the color yellow and flesh pink.

21st text: He who knows the earth is called wise and skillful. The one who knows the sky is called *Ching* (very wise) Knowledge of *Chi Chü* gives wisdom. By this we know the earth. By this knowledge of the earth one comes to knowledge of the sky, and one is very wise and without passions: one is *Ching*. The sides of *Chi Chü* have their numbers. *Knowledge of these numbers procures all things* (these last words show how much the point in question was venerated among the Chinese). The Chinese have both celestial and earthly numbers. The first are: 1, 3, 5, 7, 9. The second are: 2, 4, 6, 8, 10. In olden times they designated the sky by 1 and 3. The first terrestrial number is 2, its square 4. This is why the *Chou Pei* took for the sides of the triangle the numbers 3 and 4, whose base necessarily becomes 5. This is from the missionary and shows his ignorance about the true root of 4, which is not 2, and on

---

[289] *Five* in Latin – PV.
[290] The so-called Metonic Cycle, a period of 19 years, is named after Methon, whose astronomical observations of the sun and moon led to the realization that the year was not made up of 365 days, but rather 365¼, requiring the addition of a day every four years – PV.

the source of the hypotenuse which, far from coming from sides 3 and 4, is on the contrary the occasional cause.

The same missionary tells us that the Chinese circle is divided into 360¼ degrees. That of Europe in almost all the Nations is only divided into 360. To solve the problem, one must know the ratio of the circumference to the radius.

The Chinese year was 365¼. As for the division of Chinese numbers into celestial and terrestrial numbers, all were based on two arithmetical progressions, and that division could only be demonstrated after the science of numbers was already altered by the Chinese. Nothing is more false, nothing more risky than that division. It is not the order of numbers which creates their intrinsic quality, it is on the contrary, their intrinsic quality that creates their order, and when we know the intrinsic values of these numbers, we are still a long way from classifying them according to the two progressions above.

XVI. Number Six

This number seems to be at the heart of all operations. It isn't an individual agent, but its character seems to have a necessary affinity with everything which operates, and no agent can see its action through to completion without going through that number.

This *senary* is the co-eternal relationship of the Divine circumference with God. That is why God, Who begets everything, embraces everything and sees everything.

Even algebra itself, which has retained some laws of true calculation, but which has by no means preserved its spirit since it is solely focused on data, even algebra, I say, passes through this number in the elevation to cubic powers. It takes six actions to produce a cube whose root has two terms:

1st The cube of tens;
2nd Twice the product of the square of tens by unities;
3rd The product of tens by the square of unities;
4th The product of the square of tens by unities;
5th Twice the product of tens by the square of unities;

6th The cube of unities.[291]

Lettres édifiantes, 9th anthology, former edition. The theosophical doctrine of the Indians gives us five kings who are brothers and have the same wife, who are each condemned to confess their faults in order that a fruit knocked down by one of them from the top of a sacred tree, six cubits high, can return to its place.[292]

The circumference is composed of six equilateral triangles and is the product of two triangles that operate on each other[293]; it is the expression of six acts of Divine Thought which were manifested during the six days of creation, and which must be reintegrated.[294] Thus this number six is the mode of creation, although it was neither the principle nor even the agent of it.

It is in the theosophical addition of the number 3 that evidence of a senary influence in incarnation is found.

By bringing this information to bear on Nature, we must not overlook the hexagons of volcanic materials overrun by water. The Vivarais offers a thousand examples.[295] *Six* is shown in the known

---

[291] This passage eludes explanation. The word *dizaine* can mean '10' but usually means 'around 10', which is a shaky start for any calculation. The extensive use of the word *unités* which properly means '1s' or 'unities' similarly renders any attempt at calculation void. No do the steps appears to be linked or sequential. Other than the fact that there are 6 steps to whatever Saint-Martin is attempting to demonstrate, the translator can shed no further light on these steps – PV.

[292] This is the fable of Draupade, a beautiful woman married to five Brothers who ruled Madura. One of the Princes shot an arrow at a miraculous tree belonging to a famous penitent, which produced a fruit every month which was so nutritious that one bite could satisfy a person's hunger for a month. Fearing the penitent's wrath they consulted Vishnu, who told them to confess their sins in public. Since the tree was six cubits tall, each confession would raise the fruit one cubit, and finally with Draupade's reluctant confession, the fruit was reattached to the tree – PV.

[293] This refers to the Star of Solomon or six-pointed star, formed from two equilateral triangle intersecting - PV

[294] This reflects Pasqually's and Saint-Martin's theosophical view that God appointed six major spirits to perform the act of creation, reviewing and blessing their work on the seventh day: in their view God was not involved in the actual act of creation Himself, since the operations created a temporal space, and God is infinite – PV.

[295] For English speakers, this is probably most clearly seen in the hexagonal basalt column of the Giant's Causeway in Northern Ireland. Saint-Martin is referring to a similar French equivalent called the Pathway of the Giants of Vals in the region of Vivarais in Ardêche. However, Saint-Martin's comment about the involvement of water in fact points to a

properties of the magnet, where we can so far distinguish between attraction, repulsion, communication, direction, declination and inclination.

This *six* is even more active and notable in music. The so-called fifth or dominant has a value of *six* according to the calculation of Nature:

(1) Because it is composed of two thirds, since the median is both the third of the tonic and the lowest note of the dominant taken as a third;

(2) Because this median completes the major or minor tone, and it is capable of being either;

(3) Because the division of the vibrating string gives 1 for the tonic, 2 for the octave and 3 for the fifth, and the addition of these 3 numbers makes 6.

Now, it is impossible to make any progression in music without going through that dominant which, as we have just seen, bears the number 6. And so, all musical progression is senary.[296]

Music also teaches us that each tonic has its analogue, then two relatives each of which have their analogy, which still makes the number 6.

---

major geological controversy raging in Europe at the time: whether basalt was as sedimentary or volcanic rock. The two camps were referred to as 'Neptunism' and 'Vulcanism' respectively. Incidentally, a book written in 1809 describes the basalt columns in the Vivarais region as having between 3 and 10 sides... – PV.

[296] While this is covered in detail in the Translator's footnotes to Chapter 7 in *Of Errors & Truth* (pub. Rose Circle Publications, 2017), remember that a musical scale covering an octave, or eight notes is in fact 7 notes followed by a repetition of the first note an octave higher. The dominant note is the fifth, but considered as being the cumulation of two triads, this can give it a value of six. In the scale C, D, E, F, G, A, B where C is the root, G is the dominant. C-D-E forms the lower triad and E-F-G the higher triad, making six notes in all. From point (2) this holds whether the key is a major one (as above) or a minor one, in which case the two triads become C-D-E$^\flat$, E$^\flat$-F-G. To point (3), a vibrating string halves in length (for example, but applying a finger to hold the string to the fretboard) will double its pitch to an octave above the base note; and another half (making 3 dominant segments in all) will raise the pitch another fifth. Finally, all music requires a tune which results in a resolution. Unless atonal or twelve-tone music is being written, the ear is most satisfied by hearing a cadence which brings that melody to a close, before embarking on the next section. This is most often accomplished by what is called a perfect cadence, in which the music closes on a chord based on the fifth, dominant (or in Saint-Martins terminology *senary*) note in the scale, which produces a satisfying conclusion for the listener – PV.

Scripture shows us the senary from the beginning of things to after their end, since, after telling us about the six days' work, in Revelation it depicts this scene: before the throne of the Eternal are four animals with six wings, and twenty-four Ancients who prostrate themselves before Him[297], which suggests to us that the same senary number is the universal mode of things because it has the same character in the Universal Order; and therefore, our triune faculties are obliged to follow it in order to achieve their full action: Thought 1, Will 2, Action 3 = 6.

The twenty-four Ancients of the Apocalypse equal six who are 1, 3, 4, 7, 8 and 10. These numbers added together give 33, including the 0, the image and proof of corporeal appearance.[298]

But excluding the 0 they give 24. So, it is only those six numbers which have acted, which are real and which will act forever; that is, there have eternally been two powers, that of God and that of the Spirit.

This senary suffered in the various prevarications which made the Repairer descend here below. He had to repair its potency. That's why He turned the water in the six urns into wine at the wedding of Cana. (*John*, 2:6.)

We should also remember the twelve shewbread arranged six by six, the forty-two encampments, the six days of work, the six steps of Solomon's throne, the six hundred and sixty-six talents that his fleet of ships brought him every year, etc.

It is no less true that the senary, being the only manner by which all the agents operate, cannot consider itself exactly as a real and active number, but rather as a co-eternal law forming a basis for all the other numbers. This number 6 is the one by which man should have ruled in former times, and by which he should rule after his restoration. Butterflies, which are resurrected beings, have four wings and six legs. Man, see your law, for it is written everywhere.

---

[297] 4 creatures each with 6 wings, 4 x 6 = 24, the number of the Ancients; and 24 by reduction is 2 + 4 = 6 – PV.

[298] We know that 2 and 5 are evil numbers, and that 9 is the number of matter, so these numbers cannot be represented in the court of the Almighty. Therefore the 6 numbers of the Ancients are , 3, 4, 7, 8 and 10. Note that they add to 33, the age of the Repairer when He sacrificed Himself. and 3 + 3 = 6 – PV.

XVII. Difference Between the Mind and the Body

Regardless of the numerical evidence we find in the theosophical addition of 3 and 4, in order to be assured that 4 is a number of the center and 3 a number of circumference, the laws of geometry provide us with very convincing evidence to allow us to distinguish our origin from that of matter, to show us our superiority over all physical nature, our direct relationship with our principle and the immortal duration of our soul which has drawn life from immortality itself.

All these truths are written in the circle divided naturally into six parts.

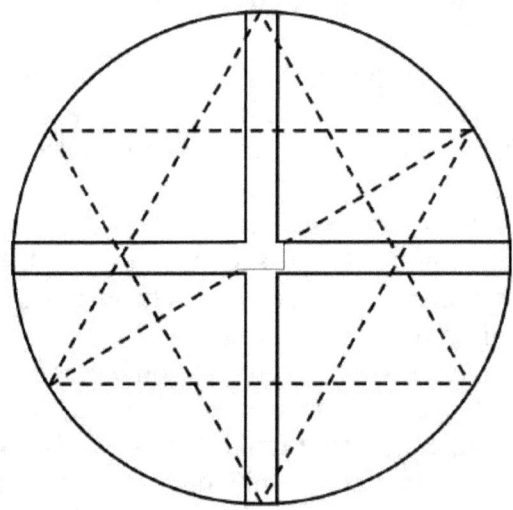

This natural circle is formed differently from the artificial circle of the geometricians. The center has called forth the upper and lower triangles, which, through mutual reaction, have brought about life. That is when quaternary man appeared. It would be impossible to find this quaternary in the circle without using obsolete and superfluous lines, if we were limited to the method used by geometricians. Nature loses nothing: it coordinates all parts of its works, each for the other. Also, in the circle it draws with precision we see that the two triangles, in uniting, determine man's emancipation in the Universe and his place relative to the Divine Center; we see that matter receives life only through the flashing reflections of opposition by which truth is proven by means of falsehood, light by means of darkness, and that the life of that matter always depends upon two actions; we see that man's quaternary embraces the six realms of the Universe, and that as those realms are linked two by two, man's power exercises a triple quaternary in this abode of his glory.[299]

This is where the laws of this superb knowledge, of which the Chinese have left traces – I mean the knowledge of *Chi Chü* – are made manifest.

Man, let to prevaricate at the incitement of the original guilty ones, strayed from that divine center in which he had been placed; but though he is now distant from it, the center has remained in place, for no force can shake that formidable throne. (*Sedes tua in seculum seculi. Ps.* 14:7).[300] So, when man had abandoned that glorious post, it was the very Deity Who was prepared to replace him and Who operates on his behalf that same power, of which he was stripped as a result of his crime, in the Universe. But as soon as He came to take the place of man, He clothed Himself in the same appearance attached to the material regions where man had originally been established[301], since one cannot appear in the center of that circle without being placed in the midst of all those realms.

This is what studying the natural circle can teach to the intelligent gaze. The figure, once drawn – even imperfectly – is more than enough to put one on the right track.

Let us add two more observations about the number 6:

One observation is taken from a grain of gunpowder. It is claimed that if other grains of gunpowder are arranged in a circle around it, it would set them on fire up to a distance equal to 60 times its size.

---

[299] Many will recognize in this diagram an early prototype of the Martinist pantacle – PV.
[300] Thy throne, O God, is forever and ever. Incidentally the 1861 edition incorrectly cites Psalm 14:7, whereas in the Vulgate it is 44:7 (King James Version Psalm 45:7) – PV.
[301] The height of man's body is equal to eight times his head. (*Footnote from the original 1861 edition*).

The other is taken from the age that man needs to reach to be capable of committing a crime. That age is set at 15. At 7 years old he is only capable of tarnishing himself. Up to the age of seven he's incapable.

XVIII. Progression of the Active Ages of the Repairer

8	>>	1	Representation of Divine Unity in the universal, celestial and earthly circle.
16	7	2	Power of Divine Unity hidden in the 8^{ary} and acting through the 7^{ary} on disorder.
24	6	3	Power of the Divine Unity 8^{ary} and 7^{ary}, acting through 6 for the formation of bodies.
32	5	4	Divine Unity 8^{ary} and 7^{ary}, emanating the quadruple power and placing it on the senary to rule there.
40	4	5	Man incarnated in the Universe and fighting the prince of disorder.
48	3	6	Spiritual man uniting with the Divine power 8^{ary} and 7^{ary} to free himself from his material fetters.
56	2	7	The perverted being struggling with the principles of Nature and given over to his own justice. The spirit of the Universe going back to its source.
64	1	8	Complement of the circle 8^{ary} where the powerful number, having traversed all the depths of the regions and the of existence of beings, restores Divine Unity in its simple number, where it had been divided, and the action where nothingness and death reigned.

In this progression : 8 1
                                        7 2
                                        6 3
                                        5 4
                                        4 5
                                        3 6

```
           2   7
           1   8
```

It is important not to add together the two numbers placed next to one another, because, far from having a number which is vibrant and acting through a principle of life, we would only obtain the number of death. It should be noted that the octenary is the depository of 8 actions which He was to spread abroad in the corrupted circle from creation through progressive ages. Therefore, as each of these actions is emanated by Him, it should be deducted from the generating number instead of being added to it. By this means we will have positive proof of the universal action of the octenary, since each epoch will be marked by that number *(Revelation,* 1:8).[302] Therefore, he is supported by the power of His word. *(Heb.,* 1:3).[303]

XIX. Complement of the Quaternary

Metals vegetate[304], but horizontally, since they do not leave the earth except when they are absorbed by plants. Plants vegetate vertically but adhere to the earth. Animals vegetate without adhering to the earth but are nevertheless fixed to its surface. For the quaternary to be complete, there must be beings who are not subject to any such obligations.

There are beings who are the object of God's wrath and who live in reprobation. There are some beings who live under His justice. There are some who live under His mercy. The quaternary wouldn't be complete if there were none who lived under His mercy.

---

[302] I am the Alpha and Omega, the beginning and the ending." – PV.

[303] Who…upholding all things by the power of his word…sat down on the right hand of the Majesty on high. (This is incorrectly cited in the 1861 version as *Hebrews*, 1:13) – PV.

[304] In the sense of growing and developing; not in the modern negative sense – PV.

If a second law had not been given to man, we would not know God in his most beautiful virtue which is free love, and manifesting Himself among men without caring whether or not they are guilty.

XX. Operation of the Number 3 in the Three Worlds

The ternary operates only as a director of forms in the earthly and in the celestial planes, that is to say that in all bodies the number of spiritual principles being the ternary, any name or any sign which falls under that number will belong to forms, or must have some effect on forms.

This number is noticeable in levers where we can distinguish strength, support and resistance, and since these three classes can each have three different dispositions, that gives 9.

Some also give this number to rain.

It is also noticeable in the decomposition of light. Stare at one fixedly, then move your sight away from that light, and you will see a red dot in the center, then a black circle, then a blue circle. This image illustrates the three principles of bodies.

In the super-celestial, it is only the thought of the Deity which conceives the design to produce this world, and Who conceived it as a ternary because this is the law of forms which it innately has within it. Then, God's thoughts are beings.

The Divine ternary always acts in concert and unanimously; this is what the three Officiants at the Mass represent when they move together.

The three circuits around the cadavers at funeral ceremonies are to ward off the *evil* elementals.

XXI. Unity of the Decade

So long as numbers are united and linked to the decade, there are none which present the image of corruption or deformity. It is only when they are separated that these characteristics appear. Among these particular numbers, some are completely bad, such as 2 and 5. They are the only ones which divide the denary. The rest only operate actively in suffering and in curative operations, as do 7, 4 and 8. Others are only given to appearance, such as 3, 6 and 9. Nothing like it is seen in the entire decade, because in this supreme order there is no deformity, nor illusion, nor suffering.

XXII. Phases of the Moon

$3 \times 9 = 27$, terrestrial factors and results. This is the visible period of the moon on our surface.

$4 \times 7 = 28$, celestial factors and results. Indeed, the four phases depend on the angle of the sun. But here we no longer see the twenty-eighth day of the moon, because the quaternary and the denary no longer belong to the material Earth. They have been returned spiritually, and matter cannot see them. The sun has its noon, and the moon must also have its own; but what comparison is there between these two noons?

The Chinese only counted up to $25 = 7$; they left the last three days while the moon is absent. They also agreed that the first two phases were the most favorable and used the other two only in the most pressing needs.

XXIII. The Content Larger Than the Container

In the universe, the content is larger than the container, since the content is 4, 7, 8 and 10, whereas the container is only 3, 6, 9. Also, without that all beings wouldn't suffer as they do; without that bodies wouldn't be destroyed; without that temporal man would be eternal; without that ultimately the Universe would be God. The systems of the philosophers lean towards that abominable idea. But with an understanding of numbers can we fear their efforts and their chimerical undertakings?

XXIV. Progression of Numbers and the Resulting Figure

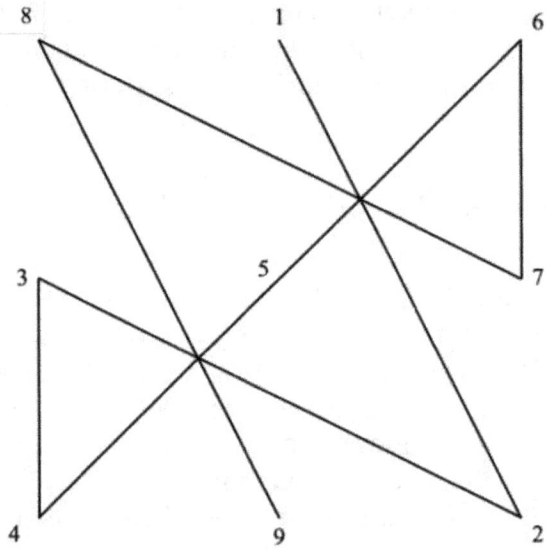

XXV. The Septenary

The septenary is known only by the temporal 4 x 4 = 16 = 7. But at the same time, it is clearly the number of the spirit since it comes from the Divine and gives 28, because of its double power as opposed to lunar power.

Let us also observe what this 28 indicates, namely: that the operation of the Word only took place at the second prevarication.

Let us not forget, however, that all this is only in images, because 7 coming from 16[305], is not a root, and it is also not the essential power of 4, since it does not return by means of addition to its root. All the more so because the same is true of its product 28, because in all the operations I have detailed in the article on Addition and

---

[305] The 1861 version says '*parce que 7 venant du 76…*' – PV.

Multiplication (No. XII), everything must take place within the decade.

There is a great truth to be inferred from this passage: it is that in making a form, everything is twofold, namely, the temporal principle and operation. The number 9 especially can serve as proof, 3 x 3 = 9, for there's the form in principle, because it does not come out of the decade (and this links perfectly with the origin of things according to the R.[306]). All the nonaries which arise from it can only be temporal operations.

XXVI. Number 9

Why does the nonary, whatever the powers to which one raises it, always make nine? It is because it is only a third power, along with 3 and 6; whereas 4, 7, 8 and 10 are second powers, and Unity is the only first power. Thus, Unity always makes 1 despite all the possible multiplications by itself, because it cannot come out of itself, nor produce another like itself. It is not able to be added, since there would have to be several Unities: and there is only one. It is able to manifest outside of itself through its second or third powers, by means of which we sense the co-eternal connection with it, and whose laws we see written when we open the eyes of our mind; but we cannot know the active way and the means by which it operates that manifestation, that expansion of its powers, because then we would be equal to it. However, one thing we are sure of is: that it only operates these expansions within its decade.

On the contrary, these expansions operate outside of the decade. But because there are spiritual expansions and expansions of form, the laws by which they operate are different, as well as the results that come from them.

This is why the powers 4, 7, 8 and 10 show us, each in its personal multiplication, a variety of results subordinate, however,

---

[306] This reference to 'R' is very cryptic. The only suggestion might be that it refers to the *Réaux Croix*, or R+, since the members of Pasqually's *Order of Elect Cohen* were the only ones permitted to hand copy and read his *Treatise on the Reintegration of Beings*, which contains his view of the origin of all things and the numerical system being discussed here – PV.

to a circular number in which these results can only turn. These powers which I have named second powers have a region to travel through because they are directly connected to the center. The third powers are connected only indirectly and have no other purpose to fulill than that of producing forms. They are therefore more closely bound than the second powers. They do not have the creative law that belongs only to Unity. They do not have the administrative law that is entrusted to the second powers. They have only the executing and operating power which, being always the same (since the object of their work does not change) only transmits itself from one being to another through necessary generation. So, all their actions are equal.

XXVII. Concerning the Number One

Unity multiplied by itself only ever makes *one*, because, according to what was said in the preceding chapter, it cannot come out of itself. But in this idea there is a deeper, hidden one, which becomes clearer and more gratifying when examined, which is: if this Unity could produce in this manner and thus raise itself to its own power it would destroy itself, just as the action which operates in each particular root is ended by its very operation (though there is no being, nor any part of a being, that doesn't become a unity at some point when it is divided). Let us not be afraid of this proposal; it can be verified by a thousand examples.

The seed of a plant which has produced its annual fruit in accordance with the number of actions which are included in its powers, no longer produces and returns to its principle.

Our ability to think is truly inextinguishable, since it can draw upon infinity; but it is no less certain that every thought that comes out of us is the product of an action of power which is relative, and which, by being like the seed, ends with the particular thought it produced when it has completed its purpose. So even though we are made to forever think, we never have the same thought twice, because although the number of our seeds of thought is infinite, each of those seeds is finite and limited to a single action, after which it is no longer of use to us.

The creative, operating and thinking abilities of Deity must most certainly be governed by the same law, since we are His image. Also, although Deity is the Infinite, Unique and Eternal Source of all who have received being, every action of His operating and productive abilities is used for a single work and is retained by Him without being repeated, because that action is completed and accomplished. That is why we see that with each emanation of the classes of spirit which He has operated, He manifests a new ability which makes us see that each of those operations has, so to speak, a individual motive power, an individual seed which, having fulfilled its work, yields to another seed, from which another operation must result. We also see that none of those operations are repeated. We see only a circle of the first prevaricators, only a circle of two's, only a circle of denaries, only a circle of men, only one Sophia, only one Jesus Christ, only one Holy Spirit. Thus, since each operation is one, and each root of that operation is new, it is probable that that the root which acted in its creative function, acts only in its conservative function as soon as it has produced its work, even though the resulting works are permanent and immortal (as we saw in the paragraph about addition and multiplication) because roots are only like the organs and channels by which Unity manifests and achieves the expression of His abilities outside of Himself. However, in all possible philosophies, only the means are transient, and the end is stable.

Now let us go to the center and see what would happen if we applied the law which we've just outlined to it. For Unity to produce an essential and central truth, there would have to be a difference between the seed and the product, between the root and the power. Then, according to the law of seeds and roots, once they had produced their power, they would become useless, since they could no longer produce similar ones. God could not reproduce Himself without perishing and destroying Himself. From being the principle, He would become the means, and annihilate himself at His appointed time. But as these three things are not distinct in Him; as He is both His principle, His means and His term; and as there is no more successiveness in their action than any difference in their qualities this Unity may multiply by itself, it can never happen; and thereby this proves that He has never been created. For those who think there is a great demonstration of God's existence in this.

(Since the multiplication of Unity by Unity only ever produces Unity and never rises to new powers since He is eternity, we can see whether it is possible for the Unity of Elemental matter to ever be accepted as a creator of bodies, since Unity does not raise itself to powers; and whether there is then a strong need to regard the principles of matter as roots which have already been produced out of Unity, and therefore already bearing a composite number. It is this secret, misunderstood law that has taken the form of aggregates in doctors' minds in order to explain the principles of bodies as roots; but now there is no further difficulty in seeing all these roots rising to their power and forming the various bodies).

The continual succession of physical generations forms a temporal unity, a symbol and disfigured image of the simple Unity which is Eternal and Divine. Nevertheless, these images are not to be ignored, since they can always lead us to perceive their model from afar. (In spiritual generation the means passes into the term, and that is what makes life. But the principle does not pass into it, and that is why they are inferior to it even though they are immortal. See below, Chapter XLIII, on *Time*). Extremes touch one another without looking alike. Also, pure beings live a simple life; beings in atonement live in a life consisting of life and death, that is in mixed death; sovereignly criminal beings and those like them live and shall live in simple death or in the unity of evil. – Now, what can be their hope and their return?

XXVIII. Double Numbers

All temporal beings have two numbers, one for their existence and the other for their action. It is through the second number that they work that universal reaction which we observe everywhere, and which is inferior to existence, which can be demonstrated from the individual to the universal. It is for that reason that beings connect with one another only though their powers or though their faculties. It is through this point of contact that they can communicate. Without it the impassive soul could not be subject to the passive soul.

XXIX. The Manner in Which the Mind Should Be Examined

The mind is considered only by its operations and the colors that serve as a sign to it. White is denary, blue is septenary, green is quaternary, red is ternary, black is nonary, bronze is 5^{ary} (quinary). Unity is colorless.

The root number of mind is 7 because it operates on 4 and 3, or on the soul and body.

When the soul is united with its intellect and spirit, it has its power, which makes it quaternary. Therefore, it should listen only to wisdom and the spirit if it wants to retain its power, its knowledge and its virtue; because the vivifying spirits of the soul and body join with it and support it with their power and number. This is the purpose and effect of ordinations. By their means it establishes a constant and effective activity in the ordained person, which makes them an organ of all numbers, that is to say of life itself, for numbers are but the signs of life. But if we were to have the good fortune to unite with the spirit of Jesus Christ, we would have all the activities and effectiveness we could desire, since it is in Him that all numbers exist.

XXX. Why is the Circumference[307] Physically Three times its Diameter – About 13

It is a physical proof of the ternary relationship of all creations with its principle. The straight line or diameter is seen as the principle of the circle. It has the number 4 which is the number of all generation and the number of the elevation of powers, since it's from 4 that all visible and physical powers arise. However, one cannot elevate the ternary powers of the bodies to their first term or square 4 without having 9 as a result, because 3 x 3 = 9.

At the same time, if every principle manifests itself only through *three*, this law must be observed in the most physical creations and the same relationship must be written there. So just as 3 is triple 1, although it is nevertheless a square 4, since it comes from 1 or 10, which is the ability of 1, so the circumference is triple its diameter, which is a unity for it. And by joining 9 to 4, we obtain 13, or 4 which plays the same role with regard to 9 as 1 to 3.

However we don't know the positive and active relationship of 3 to 1, nor of the circumference to its diameter, because it is hidden in the mystery of generation, and having only one Creator, and therefore only one Generator, He is the only one Who knows the laws of life and the secret connections by which He propagates Himself and creates all beings.

But we only need to know that 3 characterizes all creations of any kind; that such is the number of all the abilities of beings and of our principle, the one on which the balance of all our virtues depends. Now, we cannot doubt the supreme necessity of this number, since a being can only produce by his own means, and that if that number is printed on his works, he surely acted through that number in order to create them.

An inspection of the circle compared to its diameter; of the triangle compared to its center; of the dimensions of the body

---

[307] Saint-Martin's – and Pasqually's – concept of the relationship of the square to the circle, or point to the circumference, is fundamental to an understanding of how he makes theosophical use of numbers. The reader is referred to Chapter 6 on Mathematics and Geometry in *Of Errors & Truth* (pub. Rose Circle Publications, 2017), and specifically to footnote 67 – PV.

compared to the solid; of the subdivision of the principles of those same bodies; of our three sensory, vegetative and passive faculties; and of our three spiritual faculties: all that truly shows man the path he has to take to fulfill his law. He must work to put into effective action, force and value the three faculties which compose his triangle.

Finally, 4 plays in 13 the same role towards 9 as 1 towards 3, because 1 is added to 3 simply to bring together the divided faculties and return them to unity. In like manner, 4 is added to 9 only to bring it back to the harmony of this quaternary number, and hence to the harmony of unity.

Now, if 9 is the spiritual outcome of the union of 4 and 5, it was necessary, in order to erase that imperfection, for another 4 to come and join to 9, for it to cross 5, for it to divide it to obtain the other 4 which was linked to it, and through this is make it the 8^{ary} or the double power in which is contained the fundamental source of all justice, balance and the law of order.[308] Here we see the necessary, positive and infinite action of the great Repairer of Nature. At the same time, we see how impenetrable the paths of that regeneration are to man, since he can only know this higher number 4 when it has come upon him.

XXXI. *The Universality of Quaternary Points*

If our spiritual soul is quaternary, everything that comes from us must have the same number. Now, as everything that comes from us must fill the Universe (*crescite and multiplicamini, and replete terram*[309]), we see how truth and Divine Unity could fill the whole atmosphere of the earth and the heavens if we all developed the quaternaries which comprise our essence. The Supreme Wisdom

---

[308] The reader should take this segment in the context of man's fall and the incarnation of Jesus, the celestial power 4 joining with original man's 4 (which had become 5 due to the insinuation of the false 1 by the prevaricating spirits, when they told man to perform an act of creation without the cooperation of God) to create 8, the number of the Repairer – PV.

[309] "Be fruitful and multiply, fill the earth..." (*Gen.*, 1:28). God's instruction to Adam and Eve – PV.

has made us responsible for that sublime work. Prayer reminds us of this: but what regrets are in its consequences, since they remind us of what we have lost!

It is a truth which is both constant and terrible that we are perpetually operating, that all our spiritual movements come to fruition through imitating our model from which, as we saw earlier, all our creations are from essential powers. But the frightening difference which sets us apart from Him is the realization that, in our place of abode, any action can be for evil as well as for good, and that every action of our existence can surround us with real and living poison, as well as beneficial and indestructible balms.

This quaternary ability is marked by the four operating times of each day which are every six hours. The most favorable time is the first and the last hour of the day, because then temporal action ceases, and the mind, having no time, needs an interval between one and the next senary, and that interval is not understood in the time of temporal action.

That quaternary was reflected in Adam and his three children; Noah and his three children; Abraham, Isaac, Israel and Jacob; Moses, Aaron, Ur and Joshua. Just as 4 was emanated to contain 5, so every corporeal being is opposed to an evil ternary, because all bodies in Nature are persecuted as is everything which is emancipated, and they must have *evil ones* of many kinds, since it is consistent to believe that the 7^{ary} and 8^{ary} were counted as soon as we knew two evils, the physical and the moral.[310]

I have been told that there are five parts innate in all forms. The form of man bears this number, and especially that of woman in the division of the circle. The reason for this is well known. The form of animals must also serve as a receptacle for the persecutions of

---

[310] This paragraph and the preceding one reflects Saint-Martin's membership in the Order of Elus Cohen. Without going into detail, there was set times for prayer each day, two being at sunrise and sunset (considered the most efficacious for both prayer and theurgic operations). Pasqually described the elders of the Old Testament as working operations for the purpose of reestablishing the direct link with God. Indeed, much of Pasqually's Treatise on the Reintegration of Beings describes the key people in the Old Testament as working theurgical operations in order to accomplish this, including all the Leaders and Prophets mentioned in this list – PV.

the quinaries, persecutions which we ourselves exercise against them in imitation of those very quinaries.

The number five is full of difficulties: time cannot be divided into 5 equal parts; and music has no 5 beat measure.

XXXII. Septenary Power of the Soul

Apart from the numeric root 16, which expresses the septenary (7^{ary}) power of the soul, we find it exercising its power over the ternary of the Elements, and over the ternary of the principles of the Central Axis. For the soul is the center of these two triangles. If, instead of this center, one wishes to include the power of the soul over the celestial, by which it actually caused a minor to descend, one will understand far better, and in a more active way, the septenary power of the soul over both the physical and the spiritual.

XXXIII. Quaternary of Speech

Man's speech is the extract of his three faculties, as man himself is the extract of the three eternal virtues; which proves that man is a quaternary in his essence as he is in his action. Thus, it can be shown that by his quaternary he measures the square perfectly, by attacking his enemies, commanding his subjects, mingling with his equals and worshipping God; but in geographical actions, this is accomplished by purifying himself in the West, reviving himself in the North, successfully fighting in the South and receiving the laurel of victory in the East. This is the correct manner of ascent.

The manner of descent is to be ordained in the East, to be recognized in the West, to take the army to the North and to lead it to the South, or rather to enlist in this Northern army and to march courageously under the banner of the Great General.

To operate this quaternary, however, we have only three words, that of suffering or supplication, that of justice or command, and that of praise or recompense. This latter, being above the other two, is also the one which, if withheld, is terrible. However, here on earth we can remember its glimmers, and it is by all of these means that we can prove God's law and that He is spirit, that is to say He operates everything in ways that are not material and composite; and therefore He can find neither equal nor master. O God, nourish me with the hope of regaining my likeness, and there You will find your glory and I will find my happiness!

The word of justice is given in the temporal; that of perfect praise will come only at the end of time.

There is a symbol of this quaternary in the accuracy with which the revolutions of the sun are marked. The ecliptic contains 360 degrees. The equator serves as its diameter, the tropics tangents parallel to the equator, so that the ecliptic is divided into four equal parts of 90 degrees each.

The Equinox is considered to be most favorable among the wise. No doubt it is because then the sun occupies the central point of the Elemental world, and communicates in a more equitable and proportionate degree the influences it receives from above. It is known that it is about eight days longer in the North than in the South.

One should also note a difference in the two Equinoxes. It is at the March or Spring Equinox that fermentation takes place in all bodies. Production takes place at the September or Autumn Equinox.[311] We should not even object to the identity of the progress of Nature in the two Poles. The North Pole is clearly the seat of earth. The South Pole is the seat of water, because of the inclination which has brought it in greater abundance to this part.

XXXIV. *Work of the Triple Octenary*

The first three days could be devoted to the Spirit; the 4th to the double spirit up to the septenary (7^{ary}); and the 7^{ary} to the divine.

By this means one would have:

---

[311] In other words, procreation leads to germination in Spring, and the result is the harvest in Fall. In alchemy, the stage of Fermentation has always been closely associated with procreation – PV.

for the first day[312]	1 and 7 =	8
for the center	4 and 4 =	8
for the last day	7 and 1 =	8
		24

I have always had confidence in this plan of action; I don't know when I'll execute it.

Let us always remember that some object is required to be the focus of one's request. Then the operation [*thing/'la chose'*] becomes simple, and that only surprises men of vague intentions who think the operation [*thing/'la chose'*] should work without one. But they are usually disappointed. It is in this very privilege that we recognize man's greatness, for then he has proof that he has influence, and that the Divine Goodness has truly established this operation for him alone.

The bodies themselves must conceive the operation in order to perform it. It is therefore natural that the spirit of man should command it.[313]

---

[312] Given the passage above it, this Table should probably read: for the first 3 days (i.e. days 1 – 3), for the next three days (4 – 6), for the last day (7) – PV.

[313] Continuing the theme of Chapter XXXI, in Chapters XXXIII and XXXIV, Saint-Martin continues to make obtuse references to his practices in the Order of Elus Cohen. Again, while not going into too much detail, three examples will suffice. Firstly, his description of the movement between the quarters follows the distinctive East – West – North – South pattern which describes what looks like a reverse '4' (if looking upwards and not to the floor) – both an imaging of the quaternary and the common signature among members of the Order. Also, the second journey begins with the person being Ordained in the East, then moving West, North and South, which perfectly reflects the ritual of Ordination in the Order of Elus Cohen (indeed, since it is believed that 'Jesus, or the Repairer, will come from the North, it is entirely appropriate that he 'enlist in this northern army and to march courageously under the banner of the Great General' to the South). Secondly, his mention of the Equinoxes being "considered to be more favorable among the wise" and receiving the greatest influx from above: indeed, the Elus Cohen considered this the most important theurgical operation of the year, and a time when they believed they were most likely to achieve communication with the higher powers. Thirdly, the operation he describes in Chapter XXXIV is a seven-day working which requires rituals to be done on each of the seven days, with the appropriate names of tutelary angels and spirits being substituted in each working with the intention of receiving a communication from a higher power. Now, these visible signs were known as 'passes', but more importantly, the power permitting this was known as 'la chose', prosaically translated in English as 'the thing'. That is why, although this translation has substituted the word 'operation' to make the intention clearer at two crucial points, Saint-Martin actually used the word 'la chose' or 'the thing' (indicated in the square brackets) – PV.

XXXV. Receptacle

The receptacle is a universal figure for the temporal, and this figure has two numbers, in that it goes from the center to the circumference. It depicts the advantage of the sign of Christians who cannot trace it without writing upon themselves and upon objects on which it is placed the marks of the double power of our Divine Repairer.[314]

Then, when we then think about the infinite number to which this receptacle is multiplied, we see the immensity of the active powers and mercies of the Deity. Each of those individual receptacles is an image of the total receptacle, as partial eternities are – through their intensity – the image of universal eternity, which is shown by this figure.

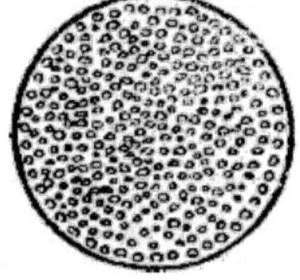

The general body is the receptacle of the superior, the inferior major and the minor spirits.

The *Virgin* is a receptacle.

Her heart is the friend of man.

Her spirit is that of man.

XXXVI. Descending Progression of Powers

$1 + 4$ □. This explains how the powers weaken as they move away from their original source, since having only one line, which is the perpendicular, the more you divide that line, the more parts

---

[314] This, of course, refers to the Sign of the Cross, more clearly imaged in Section XVII. This also refers to the figure '4' of the Elus Cohen referred to above, in that one cannot draw a cross without tracing the figure 4– PV.

of the division become shortened. This also proves the impotence and nothingness of the nonary number or circumference, since in that circumference the line is so subdivided that it is no longer so much a line as curved.[315]

Ezekiel's ת (Tau), 9:4[316], was only a preparation for the receptacle +.[317] It was a sympathetic seal of reconciliation granted to hearts which were contrite and groaned over the iniquities of Jerusalem, and it was to those whom Christ was to address, according to *Isaiah,* 61:1: *Spiritus Domini super me ... ut mederere contritis corde.*[318] This was repeated by Him in the presence of the doctors in the Temple. (*Luke,* 4:18)[319].

XXXVII. Increasing Law of the Repairer

All Divine, spiritual and human powers had been concentrated and focused in Jesus Christ at His incarnation in the womb of the Virgin. By His circumcision, and by His mother's offering of Him at the Temple where the Song of Simeon was sung, He was the chosen man. In His presentation to the Temple in His twelfth year, when He taught the scholars, He was septenary (7^{ary}) man. Through the operation of St. John the Baptist, He was man-God or octenary (8^{ary}), because the number 10 or 1 came out of Him and joined His

---

[315] We should recall the earlier reference to the circumference being created with an infinite number of radii of the same length extending from the center, thereby creating the curvature of the circumference or circle – PV.

[316] "And the Lord said unto him, Go through the midst of the city, through the midst of Jerusalem, and set a mark upon the foreheads of the men that sigh and that cry for all the abominations that be done in the midst thereof." (*Ezek.,* 9:4). Tradition has it that Ezekiel marked the foreheads with the last letter in the Hebrew alphabet, though many scholars dispute this. Saint-Martin mention the receptacle, since Christian exegesis has it that, since this mark was a primitive form of the cross, it foreshadowed redemption by the cross of Christ, making the person a receptacle for the Holy Spirit – PV.

[317] The reference to receptacles in this and the preceding Chapter – especially the image of the receptacle being a cross – relates closely to the Ordained Elus Cohen member's sash. The reader is referred to the many sites displaying an image of the 4=7 sash, which may be found using a search engine (in some examples the receptable are shown as small bowls, but they should be crosses) – PV.

[318] "The Spirit of the Lord God is upon me … to bind up the brokenhearted" – PV.

[319] "The Spirit of the Lord is upon me …he hath sent me to heal the brokenhearted" – PV.

septenary. This progression was indispensable since Christ had subjugated Himself to the temporal stream, and so He had to follow all its laws.

Without that denary coming to join with the septenary, He would have operated only spiritually and not divinely. At the end of time He will manifest himself in simple Unity, and it is then that He will appear in His glory, and the ungodly will no longer be able to hold His gaze as they held it when He appeared to them only under His temporal numbers and envelopes.

XXXVIII. Correspondence Between 4 and 1, and the Inverse of Those from 1 to 4[320]

Unity manifests itself through 4, and 4 manifests itself through 7. The solar action which is *one* is proof of this. It manifests itself by 4 upon the moon, and the moon manifests itself by 7, seeing the 7 days it takes to take on its different quarters.

It will therefore be necessary for 7 to reenter 4 and 4 to reenter Unity, because everything reenters its source, and this in an order inverse to that of its emanation. These truths are no more than corollaries of the principles laid down in the various parts of this series of observations.

Moreover, it is necessary to prove geometrically that 4 is worth 10, and as such, that it has correspondences with 1.

We can prove it:
(1) by tracing the circumference;
(2) dividing it into six by the radius;
(3) forming the double triangle.

This presents the three creative actions.

---

[320] "*The Word is surely quaternary since its sound is.*" This footnote was in the original 1861 edition. Perhaps the sense of this is that in French, *la parole*, or the word, has four syllables when pronounced in earlier times (*La Pa-ró-le*). Oddly, although most French bibles will give the passage at the beginning of St. John as using the other word for Word – *Le Verbe* – most exegeses and commentaries immediately qualify this as being '*la parole de Dieu*' (The Word of God) – PV.

However, it is only as a result of these three actions or the double triangle (six) that the number 4 can appear, since it is impossible to find it previously without using superfluous lines of intersection, expedients not found in Nature. Thus, joining this number 4 to the senary which precedes it, we will have proof that it is denary, or that it has within it an originating correspondence with 10. For if one looks at the quaternary itself and simply as an action, it is only 4, because it does indeed follow the 3^{ary} action; but if one looks at it in the outcome of its action or in its universal subdivision, we will see clearly that it has intimate relationships with 10 and therefore with 1.[321]

XXXIX. Concerning the Number 21

Number 21 is the number of destruction or rather universal termination, because as 2 is separated from 1, there must be a means for it to reunite if it so desires. This number, I tell you, shows both the order of the creation of things and their end, both in the spiritual and the physical, as well as the order of their duration in the number 17 = 8. For from the number that follows 2 to the number which precedes it, there are 17 for the interval, as follows: 1. 2 + 17 + 21.[322] However, in this formula it must be observed that the two extremes are each a ternary, which shows at a glance all the laws, all the numbers and all the actions of beings.

If we consider this number 21 in relation to 3 times 7, it will indicate the ternary action of the seven spiritual beings attached to the direction of temporal things[323]; it also tells us that as it was this

---

[321] As noted earlier, but here seen manifestly, this is the method of drawing the Martinist pantacle. The circle contains the hexagon, which generates the hexagram. Extending to the circle are the four lines of the quaternary forming a cross, which go through the center or Unity. This is the physical manner in which to draw the pantacle: the meaning of this diagram is reserved to initiates of the system – PV.

[322] This formula is difficult to understand. However, going by the words alone, the number that follows 2 is 3, and there are 17 intervals between 3 and 21 (being 4, 5, 6, 7, 8, 9, 10, 11, 12, 13, 14, 15, 16, 17, 18, 19 and 20). Since he goes on to say that at each end there is a ternary (3 and 21, or 2 + 1 = 3), this appears to be the point he is making – PV.

[323] Traditionally North, South, East, West, Up, Down and the still Center – PV.

number by which those agents constituted temporal things, it is for them to dissolve them and reintegrate them.

XL. Complement of the Great Name

The law and the election of the Jews were directed by the Great Divine Name consisting of 4 letters, and those letters are all vowels.[324] However, vowels are only the expression of feelings. That is why the law of the Hebrews was very physical, and why the people were so often unintelligent and hard-headed. However, the Great Name was composed of four letters because it was completely Divine and Spiritual, and because it exercised influence over the sensory, metaphysical and moral planes, and not the sensual material plane which has its own particular agents.

But when the time of intelligence came, then a powerful letter descended to incorporate itself into the Great Name to complete its worth and value. This letter is the 21st in the Hebrew alphabet. It is triple in its form ש. One could even find a sort of resemblance to a tongue, and sense why the Holy Spirit descended as if in the form of tongues of fire upon the Apostles. It is sibilant. Thus, there was then a great sound as of a violent and impetuous wind coming from the heavens. There are many characteristics which make it important.

The number 21 divisible by 3, offers the three universal spiritual actions. The ternary form of the letter ש presents the three eternal Unities. It is sibilant like *Ruach* or Spirit. Thus, it came to join the Superior Intelligence to the physical law practiced by the Hebrews, and by that it complemented all things and spiritualized everything, because, whether considered to be 21 or considered to be 3, it fully manifested the power of the septenary (7^{ary}) by uniting itself doubly with the quaternary (4^{ary}).[325]

---

[324] A strange comment since the four letters are all consonants! Further, Saint-Martin appears to be familiar with Hebrew, which makes the comment even more strange – PV.
[325] There can be no doubt that Saint-Martin subscribed to the generally-held Christian view of his times, that the Jewish faith had been superseded by the Christian religion, and

XLI. On the Septenary Power of Man

7 x 7 = 49 x 7 = 343. Man was not established in his post, or, to put it better, emancipated, until his power had reached its cube 343. And it is in the elements of this cube that we can clearly see the destiny of primitive man, since he is placed there between the upper triangle of which he held everything and the lower triangle over which he dominated. To know the true properties of a being, one must always consider the cube of its power. It is only there that the picture of his abilities develops.[326]

XLII. Proportions

How does the number 4 contain double, triple and quadruple proportions?

The double proportion is the surface, the triple proportion is the solid body, the quadruple proportion is the point and its three results which, considered first as in their ternary and then in their reunion with their source, demonstrate the septenary in all bodies.

There is no simple proportion, since a proportion or a relationship assumes two objects are being compared. Thus, God is in proportion to nothing, since He is One and He is Sole.

Mathematicians have noted that:

---

this description of the People of Israel being somewhat brutish, until Divine Understanding in the person of Christ came to enlighten the people of the world was a common – if misguided – notion. However, what is interesting is ho close Saint-Martin comes to expressing a somewhat gnostic belief that the God of the Old Testament was somehow transformed, by the introduction of the Shin, from a brutish deity into a compassionate one. Occasionally, both Pasqually and Saint-Martin appear to want the best of both worlds, to talk about a Trinity in the traditional sense, and at other times to express ideas which bear closer resemblance with some of the beliefs of the early gnostic leaders – PV.

[326] This image has been wonderfully captured in the Martinist pantacle, which shows the circle by which the creator bound the universe in temporal space, and reflecting the evolution and involution of creation by the two triangles (3 and 3), with man before his fall originally placed at the center (man being the minor creator who operated in cooperation with God, so represented by the quaternary, or 4. Thus, in his original position, at the center of the intersecting triangles, we see 4 between the two 3s, or 343 – PV.

(1) in an arithmetic progression the sum of the extremes is equal to the sum of the two terms equidistant from the extremes.

(2) when the number of the values in the progression is odd, the sum of the extremes is equal to double the middle value or the one which occupies the center.

These laws are beautiful, but they are of little value in the use the mathematicians make of them!

XLIII. Time

It is a constant truth that perfection is based on the unity of time as well as the unity of *virtues*, and that the faster creations are generated, the more wonders they offer. It takes years, or at least entire months for plants to produce their own seed, while the agents of the animal kingdom project it in an instant. The time taken to form an animal is nothing compared to that for a forest tree. And that is much faster than the time needed for minerals. Thus, in each of these classes one may note that perfection follows an inverse progression of time.

From this, let us judge the short time that must have accompanied the creation of the Universe by the greatness and all the wonders that compose it and constitute it. But as it was formed by means of time, in comparison with our being it is still but an imperfect creation, and it doesn't offer us a complete picture of true perfection. It is therefore in simple beings[327] that we can find traces of this perfection of creation, since they are created outside of time, without succession and by the sole power of the Indivisible Unity of Supreme Virtues.

What idea should we not, therefore, form of the existence of this Supreme Unity Who not only has not known time in order to have being, but Who has only experienced Himself, and therefore has never experienced time and has never had to know an interval of time between any of His affections, between any of His felicities,

---

[327] By simple (i.e. not composite) beings Saint-Martin means spiritual and angelic beings – PV.

between any manifestations of His virtues (see above, Chapter 27, on the number *one*).[328]

XLIV. *On the Nature of Number*

Nothing can exist without number, and God himself has His own. But the number of God is not God, a distinction that is applicable to all beings. None of them can survive without their number, since the number is their guide, their pivot and the first character of their existence. But the number can never pass for a being. Thus, in any spiritual being we can recognize:

---

[328] It is interesting to note that, in Pasqually's creation story, God did not create the Universe, since that would require him to interact with Time. Rather, he commissioned six major spirits (or archangels) to perform the act of Creation, and inspected and blessed it on the seventh day, or seventh epoch. In a way it reflects the Kabbalistic concept of *tzimtzum*, or withdrawal, where God withdraws from a part of the infinite space in order to create a region where time (and therefore mortality) can exist. However, this does create an interesting theological dilemma. Can God be omnipresent, omniscient and omnipotent in this creation? If he has withdrawn from a part of infinity and cannot breach the temporal 'gap', instead sending agents (major and minor spirits and agents) to govern this part, can He be truly omnipresent? If he gives man free-will, does he know what man will do before he does it, or does He prefer not to know since He cannot do anything about it without denying His own decree: in a word, can He truly be omniscient? Finally, if he can only act indirectly through agents, can He truly be omnipotent? Another issue with this approach is that, since it appears both Pasqually and Saint-Martin were well-versed in Kabbalistic thought, how did they reconcile some of the differing values they attributed to the notion of 'good' and 'evil'? For example, if God created consciousness in Kether, the first Sephira, the next emanation was Binah, or Wisdom, which carries a value of '2'. Yet it has never been suggested that this was not a conscious and positive action on the part of God: whereas in Pasqually's system '2' is an evil number (for that matter the letter Beth – ב – carries the value of 2, and Beth means 'house', as in Beth-El, or House of God). Another 'evil' number is 5, which in Hebrew is the value of two of the four letters in God's Name (Heh ה); though it should be added that the numerical sum of the Tetragrammaton, YHVH adds to 26, and 2+ 6 = 8, the number of Christ or the Repairer. Also, the 10 Sephiroth (equating to God and the Universe in Pasqually's system, a positive number) and 22 Paths (equating to the 22 letters of the Hebrew alphabet, and adding theosophically to $2 + 2 = 4$, the quaternary) is another good number in Pasqually's system. However, when added theosophically, they amount to $10 + 22 = 32$, $3 + 2 = 5$, which is the number of evil. So, there are clearly some issues with using the Kabbalistic and Pasqually's systems together. Indeed, in Chapter XLIV, Saint-Martin intimates this – PV.

(1) the being;
(2) its number;
(3) its action;
(4) its operation.

Kabbalistic numbers cannot evaluate the relationships and properties of bodies whose results are false according to this calculation. It is only by their principle or essential number that they should be measured. Mathematics operates even more falsely through its numerical conventions. Men profane the science of numbers by only applying it to matter. Indeed, what do they know? A double square of another square is possible geometrically, but not arithmetically. However, that double square must exist in numbers since it exists as a shape. And then, what do they know about anything which has no common standard of measurement? The false measurements and false calculations of men prove that there is a true measurement and a true calculation. And where can we go without that guiding compass?

I was once told that, in order to obtain the root of a number, you must take the first. This comment has never been explained properly to me, and I am waiting for it to be. I also don't know what this proposition means: that a third of a number is its principle, and that *three* is its circular. The *vulture*[329] is circular.

XLV. Synoptic Table of Numbers

DIVINE	TEMPORAL	DISSOLUTION	REINTEGRATION	
1 2 3 4	5 6 7 8	9	10	in 12, how many times 10, etc.
1 2 3	5 6 7	8	9	1 – 10 – 1
4				
GOOD	EVIL			

If from 5, 6, 7, 8 or the temporal you take Unity from the quinary, to return it to its simple quaternary power and then you add the rest,

---

[329] *Vautour* literally means vulture, which seems to make no sense here. However, it is possibly a misprint for *vautoir*, which means to ravel, as in a fishing net or complicated knot. Calling a recondite problem a knot would appear to make more sense – PV.

you will have 25 = 7, the time of terrible atonement, and after this atonement, Unity will be reunited with the septenary (7^{ary}) for the perfect restoration.

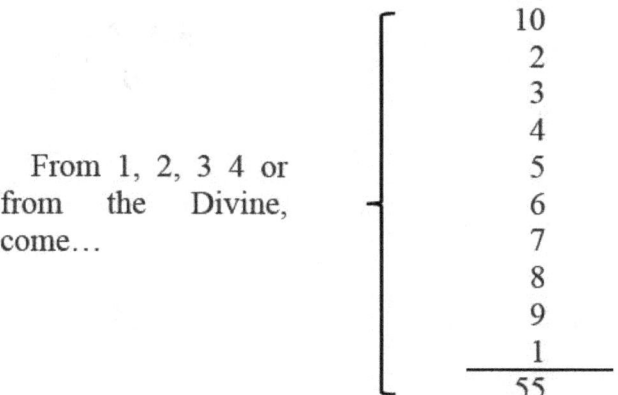

The total addition falsely gives the number of 10, because the original 10 is a number of accumulation. A sum of numbers cannot be equal in essence at its root. It can only have the appearance of similarity in its results.

XLVI. Plan of Things by the Number and Order of Their Principles

I

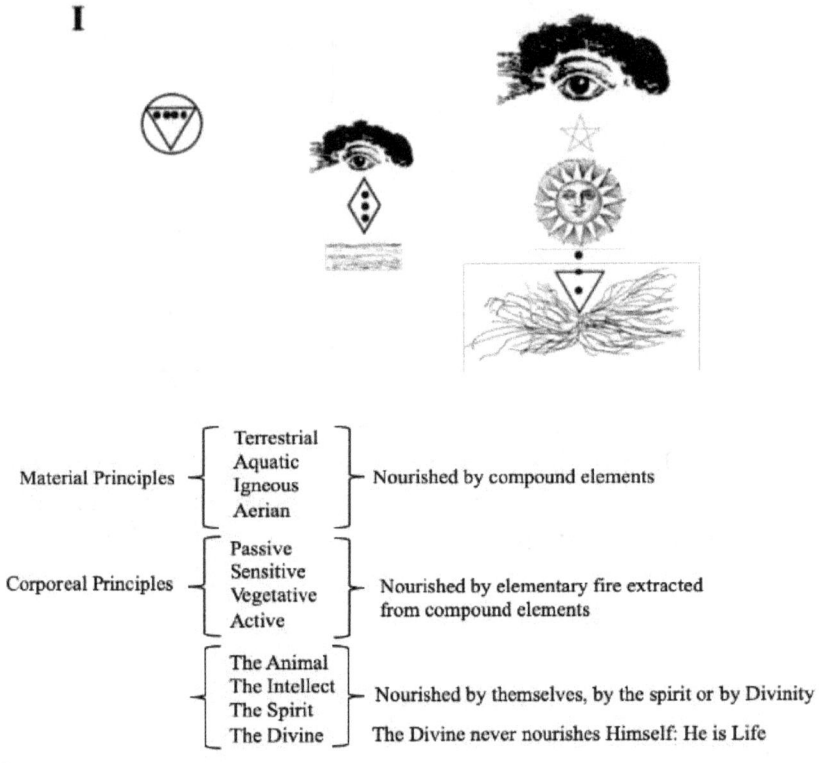

Material Principles	Terrestrial Aquatic Igneous Aerian	Nourished by compound elements
Corporeal Principles	Passive Sensitive Vegetative Active	Nourished by elementary fire extracted from compound elements
	The Animal The Intellect The Spirit The Divine	Nourished by themselves, by the spirit or by Divinity The Divine never nourishes Himself: He is Life

The 18 cubits of the column equaled 9, square of the terrestrial 3. Its circumference = 3 x 4, triple the Divine Power. Its thickness, 4 fingers, represents human temporal power.[330]

Man has 243 bones;
3 doors in the Porch;
4 in the Temple;
3 in the Sanctuary;
1 in the Holy of Holies.

---

[330] These are the dimensions of Boaz and Jachin, the two columns at the entrance to King Solomon's Temple, which the Old Testament tells us were 18 cubits tall, 12 cubits in circumference (3 x 4), and 4 fingers thick, since they were created hollow to contain the archives and records of the Temple – PV.

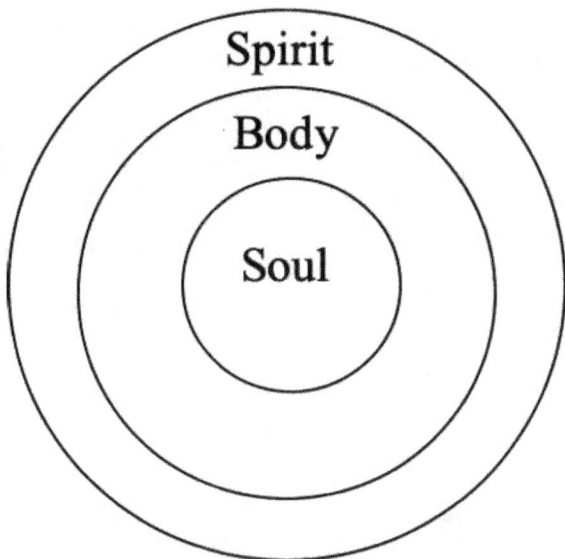

Man has in him and around him a hundred thousand proofs of his trinity, the image and likeness of the uncreated Trinity.

God has given a terrestrial power which He placed in the center of the earth. At each quarter He placed a power which is also quaternary and corresponding to the power of the center 4 x 4 = 16. – If we add 16 to 9^{331}, we will obtain 25 = 7, the junction of the spiritual or Divine with the terrestrial. If we consider the quaternary power as the Unity, we will have 4 + 9 = 13 = 4.

It is from this relationship between the center and the four quarters that all corporeal beings have the same number as their constituent principles. Nature is *one*. The length, breadth, and variations of bodies cannot obstruct its progress, nor contradict its correctness. Bodies are but the veil. Nature multiplies them as long as she is responsible for doing so. It is up to them to take shape through the principle they contain, and not for the principles to give them shape in matter, which doesn't give rise to forms. If the mind is above matter, is there anything that comes from it which should surprise us?

---

[331] The original text says "…If we add 16 to 19, we will obtain 25…" – PV.

There are 9 spheres which each have their own spirit. Others have only 7 with their creations.

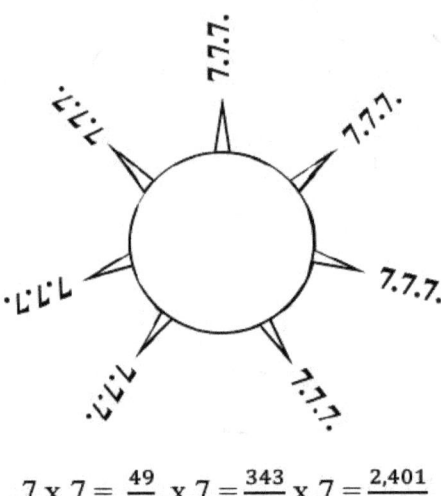

$$7 \times 7 = \frac{49}{4} \times 7 = \frac{343}{10} \times 7 = \frac{2{,}401}{7}$$

The planets change every hour: Saturn corresponds to the head of man. But for all that it isn't superior to Mercury, which is the principle of life. However, Saturn may contain more than physical laws.

God always uses intermediary powers to reunite the superior with the inferior. The vegetative is joined to matter by the passive, the sensory by the vegetative, man's soul by the sensory, the intellect by the soul, the spirit by the intellect, and God by the spirit. There are undoubtedly several hidden nuances between these various powers by which everything is linked, and nothing appears alien to each other.

Man's body was situated in the central element which, not being mixed, could not be subject to corruption. Today, given its Elemental nature, it is composed of solids, fluids, signs, weights numbers, measures, proportions, obtuse angles, rectangular triangles, simply triangles, double, triple, perfect and long squares, names, words, actions, thoughts, intentions, circumferences up to the number of 3, 5, 6, 7, 9, 10 – 64. The sum of the numbers = 6, the sum of their value = 4, so the two sums are 64. The simplest explanation is that man is formed from earth and water: *de limo terræ*.[332]

3. The active, the passive, the vegetative Δ, the simple triangle.
5. Incarnation.
6. The soul, ☿ double triangle composed of the simple animal triangle and the simple spiritual triangle

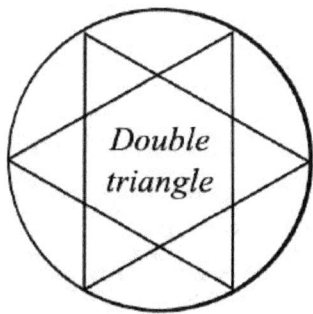

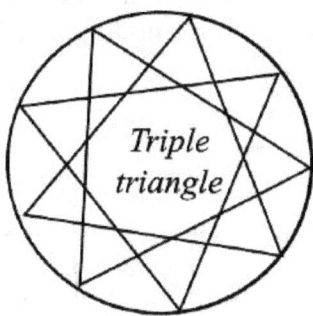

7. The spirit.
9. Ternary division of each principle.
10. Resemblance of the Deity by 6 and 4.
40. Animal power; perfect square.
64. The six operations by which God drew the human soul out of Egypt and placed it in corporeal matter.

Nothing is stronger than the square in the corporeal as in the spiritual.

When you work in the Air, you trace on the Earth. This is where our military entrenchments come from. We also work in the Water, but as much possible these waters should be stagnant. In either case, nothing can be done without Fire and New Fire. In every case, first the scapegoat must be hunted, or to fix the serpent. The desert is the place where the results of the operation take place.[333]

---

[332] *From the mud of the earth* – therefore literally from a mixture of earth and water – PV.
[333] This paragraph is referring very cryptically to two operations known to the Réaux Croix, the members of the highest Grade in the Order of Elus Cohen. Indeed, it is rather surprising that Saint-Martin makes these allusions, since they add little to the narrative for most people. However, one may guess that either Saint-Martin was showing off (a trait we have seen in his previous books, along the lines of "I've got a secret…"); or

So it is that 2, which has been the path of corruptible things, also becomes the 2 which leads them back to their purity. For it is the rectification which brings substances back to the color of white; such that good must follow the reverse order of evil. *Two* is clearly a number of confusion: its source (which should not be confused with its square root, since it has none) is 1 + 1, that is to say, two numbers that are each their square, their root and all their powers; which are in the final analysis the first of all numbers. There cannot be two of this kind together.[334]

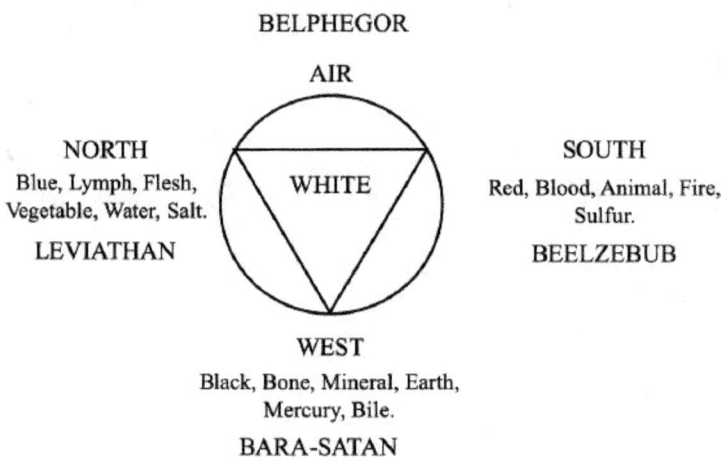

---

because his intention was for at least some of these writings to educate his fellow Réaux Croix. New Fire refers to fire which had not been kindled by mechanical or sulfurous means. It is also used to light the brazier outside churches at the start of the Paschal Vigil on Holy Saturday, when the flame should preferably be produced by focusing the light of the sun, making the fire 'new', or not taken from another flame or from sulfurous materials – PV.

[334] The extraordinary diagram is nothing less than a theurgical operation in summary, showing both the names of power to be used as well as the corresponding substances taken from colors, humors, kingdoms, element and alchemical elements. If the use of Qlippotic names is alarming, one must remember that a large part of the Elus Cohen work was to cleanse the aura of the Earth and bring the negative forces into submission. Therefore, several rituals actually involve invoking the evil powers in order to fix them and bring them towards reintegration. The demonic names invoked are odd: the usual list of the four princes of Hell are Lucifer, Leviathan, Beelzebub and Satan. Here Lucifer has been replaced by Belphegor (sometimes identified with Belial). Curiously, he is sometimes referred to as the 'Disputer', and in Kabbalah he rules the inverse or Qlippotic sephira which opposes Tiphereth, the Sephira of Christ in Christian Kabbalah, or the Repairer in Saint-Martin's parlance – PV.

XLVII. Progression of Divine Laws Concerning the Various Prevaricators

In the evil which preceded man (according to the rabbis), Deity acted by means of emanated powers. In man's prevarication, He acted Himself and without intermediary. This is where the Quaternary shows us His wonderful power. It's here that we see our immense relationship with the Divinity, since because of our number, His own virtue has descended upon us and must remain with us until the end of time in heavenly Jerusalem, as He dwelt in early Jerusalem. For this very reason, since the circle of Divine powers has run its course, I do not believe that there could be any new great prevarications, because there are no more new great powers left to sacrifice in order to heal them. The first emanated powers were in pure and perfect peace. They had neither intelligence, nor did they have any combative abilities, nor even the great authority which was successively granted to those who came after them. But they didn't need it, since that evil did not yet exist, and since all those things were given only as means towards restoration. Those are a burden rather than a pleasure. All employment and the work of the various civil offices of the State are under the peaceful and happy estate of the beloved people of a good king, who pass their time with him where they are in the presence of the source of all that is in the process of emanation within the State.

When all shall be completed, those gifts spread through mercy over the various orders of these restorative powers will disappear, and we will enjoy the presence and feeling of pure life without them being mixed with deprivation, suffering or disorder.

XLVIII. The Cube

The cube is the last power to which one can raise a root, since it is the last dimension of matter. Therefore, the number 27, the cube of 3, is the seed of universal nature. (The lunar course tells us this because ends with this number. The moon then undergoes a 3-day period when it is hidden from us, during which it works towards its rebirth or renewal). It is there that matter associated with evil will restore spirit 7 to its primitive freedom, by separating itself from the number *two* upon which it will first raise itself up. (There is an even more instructive side in which one can consider the cube of matter. That is 729, the cube of 9. The reason is physical, because all laws are imaged in Nature). One can observe the same progression in the cube of man which is 64[335]. On coming to this term, he is once more assimilated into the denary; and the number 4 is freed from the temporal senary to which it had been subjected during his period of atonement, and which then detaches itself from him to leave him free and return to his principle of material action.

When mathematicians invent so many different degrees of power to which they raise their artificial numbers, they do not realize that they alter their entire essence, and that they produce works which Nature disavows.

XLIX. Proportional Mean

According to physical calculation, the further away numbers are from the original root or from unity, the weaker their powers become; and we know this law is easy to observe, since there is no number that is not a proportional mean between unity and the square or cube of each number. But the number closest to unity, according to the intellectual order, is the furthest away in the physical order.

Let's take 10 as an example. It is the first number after unity according to the intellectual order. So, its square 100 and its cube 1,000 make the complement all things in their action, their division and their duration. But if we look at this number in the physical order, it will appear, in fact, to be the furthest away from unity and the weakest in these powers:

---

[335] That is, 4 (the quaternary number of man) x 4 x 4 = 64 – PV.

(1) because it is the last in the decade which ends everything according to our physical eyes, yet begins everything according to our intellectual eyes;

(2) because the powers of this number, considered physically and in their division, present us with a considerable weakening compared to the powers of the other numbers closer to physical unity.

L. Concerning the Number Eleven in Two Respects

As things stand, eleven is formed from 2 and 9, both of which are the power of 5 and 6 respectively. In the future eleven will exist by 6 and 5, which are the agents of the two powers above. That's why the suffering will be so rough and why there will be grinding of teeth.

However, perhaps the following proportion should be established: 2, the agent or principle, is to 9, the power or product, what 5, the power or product, is to 6, the agent or principle.

In this proportion, the terms are balanced, and they must be to ensure duration. However, in the end 2 and 5 will be more violently harried than now because they will be pressed by the agent 6; instead of being attacked by 9 alone, which is easier for them to break through, and which happens continually.

LI. The Calculation of Probabilities

You don't need to have the first idea about the principles of things to avoid focusing your attention on the calculation of probabilities.

(1) There can't be any for the physical order, where everything is fixed;

(2) Those probabilities which we might consider establishing for the moral order would be uncertain since, in that order the agents are free.

In mixed examples, and where the moral and physical orders are combined, the difficulty increases further because the particular characteristics of both of these two orders are altered or obscured by each other.

The calculation of probabilities is therefore reduced to a series of experiments, based on the assumption that the same data will produce the same results. If you wish to look more deeply, you will see that by acquiring knowledge of each particular principle of action, you can predict its effect without fear of error; and therefore there is no more probability. It is a word that ignorance has invented to refer to what it does not know, as it has invented *imagination* to depict the receptacle of all our ideas.

What errors haven't resulted, therefore, from men's systems which wanted to introduce numbers into probabilities? If they don't really understand the *number* of the cause, how could they understand the number of the effect? Even in regular geometry they cannot use their conventional numbers without making mistakes, since it is impossible to apply proofs of arithmetical calculations to geometry. Let the mathematicians become masons, carpenters, surveyors if they want, but they shouldn't call themselves geometricians; for the knowledge of true geometricians is sure, and all their evidence is positive.[336]

---

[336] Saint-Martin's apparent contempt for 'mere mathematicians' arises for three key reasons. Firstly, as we have seen throughout this treatise, he, like Pasqually before him, focuses on the theosophical mathematics of addition, powers and roots, and has little time for prosaic calculations which merely use 'physical numbers' to arrive at other, equally dead and meaningless numbers to his eyes. Secondly, he would have been educated in the traditional manner of all colleges and universities, in the Seven Liberal Arts and Sciences. The first year would have provided a grounding in the *trivium* (three ways) of Grammar, Logic and Rhetoric (that is, the structure of language, how to put together a convincing argument, and then how to deliver this to one's professors and peers in a convincing manner); all of which provided a solid foundation for the *quadrivium* (four ways) of the second and third years, which successively covered Arithmetic – or number, Geometry – or number in space, Music – or number in time, and Astronomy – or number in space and time. In this classical training, following which a person was considered ready to embark on the study of philosophy and theology, arithmetic – or mathematics – was seen

LII. Demonstration of Our Ignorance of the Principles and Essence of Beings

The true root of 4 is 1, since it's the center that gives birth to the triangle. But it is forever impossible for us to know how this center produces the triangle, or how Unity produces 4. However, all subsequent roots are connected to 4 and derive from 4. So how can we know how they operate, since we do not know how this 4 is created by 1? Thus the multiplications used by mathematicians to raise the roots to their powers are only false figures which lead them to regard all beings as being composite; whereas they could draw from this same image, albeit false, the most enlightened conclusions about the formation of things which is allowed to man's limited mind to form ideas about this important subject.

LIII. Difference Between Quantity and Quality in Numbers

It is the qualities, and not the quantities, in numbers which make beings, because qualities bear a character, and the quantities have none. 2 times 2 horses does indeed result in 4 horses, but 4 horses are not one being; whereas in the true order number 4 proclaims an existing being having properties which constitute its existence. The

---

as the basic building block for the more sublime studies of numbers as applied to the higher realms of space and time. For Saint-Martin, therefore, since God caused the Universe to be created, in one of his favorite Bible verses: "in number, weight and measure" (Wisdom 11:21), the only true use of numbers was as a tool by Divinity in the act of creation, and as a means of identifying the divine spark within all creations through their thought, will and action. Therefore, any other use of numbers was vain and superfluous to him. But their application to the manner in which God had made use of them in circles, squares and other dimensional objects, in order to create the harmony of the spheres and set the planets upon their courses, all showed a far higher level of application. So, to him numbers were the building blocks of Creation, and to manipulate them without understanding that they were the inputs to more sublime processes was little more than meaningless tinkering. Thirdly, Saint-Martin was a Mason for a significant period of his life, and the term Grand Geometrician to indicate Deity would have been very familiar to him – PV.

same is true of any numbers. And simple, ordinary calculation can shed some light on this. 2 can exist only as a diminution of 1, and can never appear as an integral number because there is only one Unity. In place of 2, we should really only count half of one or ½. Now, according to the laws of calculation ½ x ½ does not result in 4, but ¼, because as soon as you use fractions or debased numbers for roots, the more you multiply them, the more the results grow smaller. We can also see in this example what the original 2 has produced. Let's put its elements together: from ½ we have 3. Let's put the elements of the second ½ figure together, and we have another 3. These are the two original ternaries. 2 is their occasional cause, 9 will be the product or material result; and for the spiritual result we will have 5 by gathering the elements of the first product ¼.[337]

LIV. Miscellanea

I. Progression of Knowledge

It would be a beautiful picture to make: that of the progression of knowledge from the Divine down to purely mechanical matter, to show numerically the different combinations of wisdom, gifts, intelligences and powers, or the innumerable and progressive relationships between the divine, the spiritual, the temporal, the elemental, the material, and even the demonic. That's where everything would be complete and in motion.

The R.[338] have provided all this in principle, in the table below:

---

[337] The mechanics of this can be explained as: if 2 is the 'occasional cause', since 2 is not a true integral number according to Saint-Martin's theosophical approach – one not shared by regular or 'physical' mathematics, of course), it must be represented as a fraction, being ½. But if we multiply ½ x ½ the result is ¼, showing that fractions, on being multiplied by themselves, result in something even smaller. He then adds the elements of the fraction together, that is, he takes the 1 and the 2 in ½ and adds them to get 3. The formula of ½ x ½ then yield 1+2 and 1+2 or two 3s which, if multiplied, result in 3 x 3 = 9. Meanwhile, the product of ½ x ½ gives ¼ which, using the same method, results in 1 + 4 = 5. So, the physical result of the ternaries is 9, and the spiritual result is 5 from the first product ¼ – PV.

[338] Although the table is taken from the Book of Numbers, the letter 'R.' suggests this is also part of the operations of the Réaux Croix– PV.

II. Feast of the 15th Day of the 7th Months
(Numbers, Ch. 29:12 - 38)

On the 1st day	13 calves	2 rams	14 lambs
On the 2nd day	12 ---	2 ---	14 ---
On the 3rd day	11 ---	2 ---	14 ---
On the 4th day	10 ---	2 ---	14 ---
On the 5th day	9 ---	2 ---	14 ---
On the 6th day	8 ---	8 ---	14 ---
On the 7th day	7 ---	7 ---	14 ---
On the 8th day	1 ---	1 ---	7 ---

I leave the reader to meditate upon this progressive order up to the 7th day, always moving as 14, and that difference of the 8th day, which moves by 9 and 8 = 17.

III. On the Names of the Elements

Knowing the numbers of the Elements, we can live in the hope of one day knowing their true names, which must surely be connected with the numbers already assigned to them, and which will be theirs again once more; because they change numbers according to the different actions to which their law subjects them.

There are already some indicated in the Square Table of Numbers (Section 13).

IV. Epochs Across the Ages

The great scourge by water, in 1656. The renaissance of Virtues, 2448. From then to Christ, 1552. From Christ to the 15th century, when the New World was discovered, and where the schisms blew up, 1500.[339]

---

[339] These dates are clearly based on Bishop Ussher's famous calculation which set the creation of the world to October 23, 4004 BCE. For example, subtracting 1,656 from

V. Universal Triangle

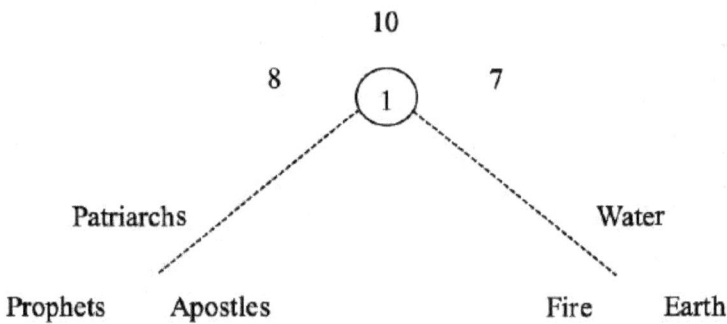

However, a subject is needed to receive the action; the body to receive the secondary ones, formerly the intellect; the soul to receive love; the mind to receive intelligence; the general spirit to receive the Holy Spirit; everything to receive God.

VI. Operation of Restoration

It was when 2 had separated from 3 that 4 appeared. It was when 4 was delivered from 5 that 8 took on the role of mercy, because 4 could not tear itself away from 5 without making the nonary (9^{ary}) veil disappear by that very action.

VII. The Line of Two Wheels

When a wheel moves on a plane, in a full revolution it will draw a straight line equal to its circumference. If there is assumed to be

---

4,004 gives 2,348 BCE, which was the accepted date for the Great Flood using calculations based on the ages of the descendants of Seth when they 'begat' their successors. Curiously, adding 2,448 and 1,552 gives 4,000 not 4,004. This may be an error; or equally reflect the fact that Freemasons – as Saint-Martin was – have traditionally given their dates from 4,000 rather than 4,004 (assumedly so as not to tax their minds too much!) – PV.

a smaller concentric circle in that wheel, like a hub in a carriage wheel, that hub, during the same revolution, will trace a straight line which is equal to the circumference of the entire wheel, rather than to its own circumference.

This problem has confounded the greatest geometricians, from Aristotle to M. de Mairan. At first, he put forward some fairly clear ideas, but ultimately, he didn't account for the proposed problem.

Here's my idea on the problem:

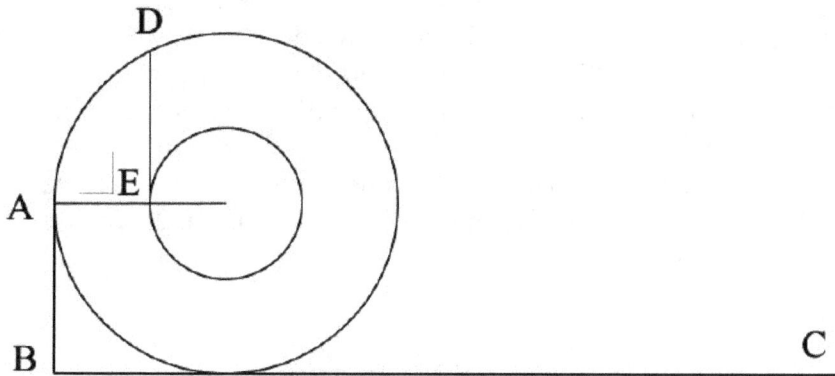

Point D on the wheel corresponds to point E on the hub, since the line DE is both the sine and the tangent. This Point D precedes point A by the length of the AE line. During the revolution, however, D must draw a line equal to the circumference, as will point A. Once the revolution is made, D will be in front of point A the same distance that it preceded A before the revolution.

Point E, which is in correspondence with point D, can only follow the same law, and it must travel the same space, therefore drawing a line equal to BC.

The difference in speeds (although the speed of the wheel is greater than that of the hub since the circumference of the wheel is greater) should not be considered in this phenomenon, for all their movements are made in equal time. But what makes it even more important to ignore this difference in speed is the fact that it is not a question of considering the rotation of the two circles, which certainly produces an unequal result, but only the lines drawn by the corresponding points, given the relative proportions of these two wheels. Thus, the error comes about because of a confusion between the lines of rotation, which are different, with the straight lines drawn by all these points, which will all have the same length.

VIII. Age of the Origin of the World

I could say that this was the year that Saladin took Jerusalem and two popes, Urban II[340] and Gregory VIII, died under Philip Augustus; but, since by searching in history we would soon discover the year was 1187, I prefer to shorten the research. In this number, leaving apart the archetype, we will see in principle the nature and faculty of evil expelled by the power of truth, which pursued them in their domain.[341] By uniting it with the archetype, we will find the principle of temporal things, because it is but Him who is the Principle of all.

IX. First Image of God

There can be no doubt that it is *ten*. For it is a truth that is demonstrated by the primitive laws of eternal extension which are first imaged by emanation, and then by creation.

---

[340] In fact, it was Urban III who died in 1187, succeeded by Gregory VIII who died two months after his enthronement – PV.

[341] These comments appear to be at odds with Saint-Martin's gentle adherence to the established Church. Given that 1187 was the year that the Western Crusaders *lost* Jerusalem and ultimately Outremer, and that two popes who were generally favorably regarded should have died, identifying the year as one that 'evil' was 'expelled' seems strange indeed. The reference to King Philippe-Auguste is more understandable, since it was under his kingship that England lost much of his territory in what is now France, and Philippe-Auguste consolidated the realm of France as a major European power and establish the French monarchy as a major player in European politics – PV.

X. Double Sign of the Cross

He leaves the East; he goes to become incarnate in the West; he goes to assume his temporal power in the North; he goes to fight evil in the South. Man also leaves the East, but it is out of mercy that he is allowed to go; whereas the *first Orient* came out of love. Man is also incarnated in the West, but in addition he has to purify himself there. That's why our realm is mixed and double. He also goes to assume his power in the North, or rather he goes to receive it there; he goes to fight in the South with the power of his Master, and then he will go to give thanks in the East. Yet people would deny that the octenary was the number of salvation![342]

XI. Venomous Serpents; Innocuous Serpents

A tail a *fifth* of the length of the body is, in general, one of the venomous characteristics, although there are exceptions.

Several such observations of this kind can be found in Gray's book entitled: *Observations on the Natural History of Reptiles*. (See the *National Gazette*, N°. 32, Monday, February 1st, 1790, London article).

END

---

[342] This reflects the description in Section XXXIII, which refers to man. Now we see it reflected in the Repairer – PV.

www.ingramcontent.com/pod-product-compliance
Lightning Source LLC
Chambersburg PA
CBHW071951110526
44592CB00012B/1053